GW00750167

Divided Affections

MARIA COSWAY

Publish'd as the Act directs 29 Jan.! 1785 by G. Bartolozzi & to be had at M.! Torres Hay Market 27.

DIVIDED AFFECTIONS

The Extraordinary Life of Maria Cosway:
Celebrity Artist and
Thomas Jefferson's Impossible Love

Carol Burnell

Column House

Copyright © Carol Burnell 2007
First published in 2007 in the UK by Column House
Case Postale 5463, 1002 Lausanne, Switzerland

Distributed by Gardners Books, 1 Whittle Drive, Eastbourne,
East Sussex, BN23 6QH
Tel: +44(0)1323 521555 | Fax: +44(0)1323 521666

The right of Carol Burnell to be identified as the author of the work has
been asserted herein in accordance with the Copyright, Designs
and Patents Act 1988.

All rights reserved. This book is sold subject to the condition that it shall
not, by way of trade or otherwise, be lent, resold, hired out or otherwise
circulated without the publisher's prior consent in any form of binding
or cover other than that in which it is published and without a similar
condition including this condition being imposed on
the subsequent purchaser.

British Library Cataloguing in Publication Data
A catalogue record for this book is available from the British Library.

ISBN 978-2-8399-0153-6

Typeset by Amolibros, Milverton, Somerset
This book production has been managed by Amolibros
Printed and bound by T J International Ltd, Padstow, Cornwall, UK

Contents

List of Illustrations

JACKET ILLUSTRATION: Maria Cosway, *Self-Portrait*, 1787, Print, Private collection.
FRONTISPIECE: F. Bartolozzi after Richard Cosway, *Maria Cosway*, engraving, 1785, Private collection.
ENDPAPERS: *Cahier des Modes, Cahier 14*, 1786.

Section One (after page 72)

1. Thomas Patch, *A Punch Party*, 1760, The Stamford Collection, Dunham Massey (The National Trust), © N.T.P.L./Derrick E. Witty.
2. Johann Zoffany, *Leopold I, Grand-duke of Tuscany (1747-92) and his Family*, Kunsthistorisches Museum, Vienna, Austria/ The Bridgeman Art Library.
3. Thomas Patch, *A View of the Arno in Florence by Day*, The Royal Collection © 2006, Her Majesty Queen Elizabeth II.
4. Johann Zoffany, *The Tribuna of the Uffizi*, 1772-1778, The Royal Collection © 2006, Her Majesty Queen Elizabeth II.
5. Thomas Patch, *A Distant View of Florence*, c. 1764, The Royal Collection © 2006, Her Majesty Queen Elizabeth II.
6. Johann Zoffany, *George, 3rd Earl Cowper, with the Family of Charles Gore*, c. 1775 (oil on canvas), © Yale Center for British Art, Paul Mellon Collection, USA / The Bridgeman Art Library.
7. Johann Zoffany, *Charles Townley and friends in the Townley Gallery, 33 Park Street*, © Towneley Hall Art Gallery and Museum, Burnley, Lancashire/The Bridgeman Art Library.
8. William Chambers, *Townley Dining Room, 7 Park Street*, © Copyright the Trustees of The British Museum.

26. John Condé after Richard Cosway, *Mrs. Fitzherbert*, engraving, Private collection.

27. *Vue du jardin du Palais Royal*, engraving, cliché Bibliothèque nationale de France.

28. Elisabeth Vigée Lebrun, *Self-portrait*, 1791, The Bristol Collection, Ickworth. (The National Trust) © N.T.P.L./Angelo Hornak.

29. Jacques-Louis David, *Portrait de l'artiste*, Paris, musée du Louvre, Photo R.M.N./© Droits réservés.

30. Richard Cosway, *La leçon de dessin et de musique*, 1786-87, Chantilly, musée Condé, Photo R.M.N. / ©René-Gabriel Ojéda.

31. *Promenade du jardin du Palais Royal*, engraving, cliché Bibliothèque nationale de France.

32. John Trumbull, *Thomas Jefferson*, Portrait miniature, 1788, White House Historical Association (White House Collection).

33. Pierre Denis Martin, *Vue générale du château de Marly*, Versailles, châteaux de Versailles et de Trianon, © Photo R.M.N./Gérard Blot.

Section Three (after page 360)

34. Maria Cosway, *Galerie du Louvre*, engraving, 1802, cliché Bibliothèque Nationale de France.

35. F. Bartolozzi after Maria Cosway, *The Hours*, engraving, 1788, Private collection.

36. Maria Cosway, *Young Bacchus*, 1787, Private collection, Photo courtesy of Julian Simon.

37. F. Bartolozzi after Maria Cosway, *Lodona*, engraving, 1792, Private collection.

38. Maria Cosway, *The Death of Miss Gardner*, 1789, Vizille, musée de la Révolution française, Photo R.M.N./© Michèle Bellot.

39. Richard Cosway, *Anne, Marchioness Townshend*, Portrait miniature, Private collection.

40. Richard Cosway, *William Combe*, Portrait miniature, Private collection.

41. John Condé after Richard Cosway, *Mary 'Perdita' Robinson*, engraving, Private collection.

42. Maria Cosway and Richard Cosway, *Portrait of Maria Cosway, No. 1, The Winter Day*, 1800, Private collection, © Copyright Photo Bonham's.

Illustrations in the text

WITH CAPTIONS

33. P. Dupont after J. B. Suvée, *André Chenier le 29 messidor l'an 2*, engraving, 1838, Cliché Bibliothèque Nationale de France.

34. H. Ramberg after Vivant Denon, *Self-portrait*, engraving, 1792, Cliché Bibliothèque Nationale de France.

35. Maréchal, *Extérieur de la Halle au Blé*, 1786, Cliché Bibliothèque Nationale de France.

36. Née after Meunier, *Vue du Château de St. Cloud*, engraving, Private collection.

37. Née after Meunier, *Vue du Château de Madrid*, engraving, Private colleciton.

38. *Vue de l'Hermitage de Bagatelle*, Cliché Bibliothèque Nationale de France.

39. B. Hilaire, *Le Labirinthe du Jardin des Plantes*, Cliché Bibliothèque National de France.

40. *La Machine de Marly*, engraving, Private colleciton.

41-43. Le Rouge, *XIII Cahier des Jardins Anglo-Chinois*, engravings, 1785, Private collection.

44. Richard Cosway, *Princess Lubomirska*, Frick Art Reference Library.

45. F. Bartolozzi after Richard Cosway, *Henry Lubomirski*, engraving, Private collection.

46.-48. Pietro Martini after Johann Heinrich Ramberg, *The Exhibition of the Royal Academy, 1787*, engraving and etching, Private collection.

49. Janninet after Dutertre, *Madame Dugaʒon*, engraving, Cliché Bibliothèque National de France.

50. Pietro Martini, *Lauda-conatum, Exposition au Salon du Louvre en 1787*, engraving, Private collection.

51. *Hotel de Langeac, élévation sur le jardin*, Cliché Bibliothèque Nationale de France.

52. Philip James de Loutherbourg, *Self-portrait*, c. 1805-1810, National Portrait Gallery, London.

53. Richard Cosway, *Maria Cosway*, c. 1790, Beinecke Rare Book and Manuscript Library, Yale University.

54. François Xavier Fabre, *La contessa d'Albany*, 1793, Galleria degli Uffizi.

55. F. D. Soiron after Edward Dayes, *The Promenade in St. James Park*, engraving, 1793, © Copyright the Trustees of The British Museum.

56. P. W. Tomkins after Maria Cosway, *The Birth of the Thames*, engraving, 1803, Private collection.

57. Maria Cosway, *Queen Caroline and Princess Charlotte*, 1800, Private collection, Photo courtesy of Witt Library, Courtauld Institute of Art, London.

58. George Romney, *Mary Moser*, c. 1770-71, National Portrait Gallery, London.

59. Anthony Cardon after Richard Cosway, *Mrs. Udney*, engraving, Private collection.

60. Becquet frères after Fischer, *Cardinal Fesch*, Cliché Bibliothèque Nationale de France.

61. *Almanach historique et politique de la ville de Lyon*, 1805, Detail, Private collection.

62. G. Manfredini, *Monumento a Maria Cosway*, detail of bust, 1839, Fondazione Cosway, Lodi.

63. After Sir George Hayter, *The Queen's Trial in the House of Lords*, engraving, Private collection.

64. Charles Picart after Richard Westmacott, *Memorial plaque to Richard Cosway, St. Marylebone Church*, 1821.

65. Paolo Lasinio after Richard Cosway, *Woman and child*, engraving, 1823, Private collection.

66. *Memorial to Baroness Maria Hadfield Cosway*, 1838, Santa Maria delle Grazie, Lodi. Photo courtesy of Fondazione Cosway, Lodi.

WITHOUT CAPTIONS

Page 1, Unknown medalist, *Maria Cosway*, Medal in gilded bronze, 1797, Bargello.

Page 27, David Allan, *The Arrival of a Young Traveller & His suite*, c. 1775, The Royal Collection © Her Majesty Queen Elizabeth II.

Page 51, George Keate, *A Manner of Passing Mt. Cenis*, 1755, © Copyright the Trustees of the British Museum.

Page 67, Matthew Darly, *The Miniature Macaroni*, 1772, © Copyright the Trustees of the British Museum.

Page 85, L. Schiavonetti after Richard Cosway, *Mrs. Cosway*, engraving, 1791, Private collection.

Page 311, Angus after Demachy, *South View of the Old and New Louvre*, engraving, 1803, Private collection.

Page 340, Delpech after L. Dupré, *Laetitia Bonaparte*, Cliché Bibliothèque Nationale de France.

Page 343, Philibert-Louis Debucourt after Wery, *Vue de la ville de Lyon prise du quai de Saône*, Paris, musée Eugène Delacroix, Photo R.M.N. / © Gérard Blot.

Acknowledgements

In looking back over the genesis and development of this book, I sometimes feel it is less of an individual effort than a collective one, for which I served as a conductor and then recorder. Originally planned as a four-year project, as often happens, the research and writing stretched out over three times that span. It would never have begun without the gracious welcome of those dedicated to the conservation of Maria Cosway's archives and her memory in Lodi. First I must thank Dott. Valerio Manfrini, Presidente, and Dott. Tino Gipponi, *conservatore storico artistico*, of the *Fondazione Cosway*, for their kindness in permitting me to consult the Cosway papers. I feel special gratitude to their fellow citizen, Ercole Ongaro, who so generously gave of his time and advice during my visits to Lodi. I also benefited from the assistance of another expert on Cosway's life, Angelo Stroppa, and the help of the efficient staff of the Biblioteca Comunale Laudense and the Archivio Storico del Comune, Lodi. Other institutions and individuals in Italy who were especially helpful were Dott. Riccardo Spinelli, who did invaluable research for me in Florence, Dott. Giovanna Giusti of the Uffizi Gallery, who facilitated my access to the Gallery's archives, Dott. Giovanna Balzanetti Steiner, of the Faculty of Architecture in Florence, Amanda George of the Biblioteca Berenson , and my long-time friend, Giovanna Legnani, who was ready with help and advice. Dotts. Vicenzo Intelligente and Magda Noseda of the Archivio di Stato in Como did a very thorough investigation of the history of Maria Cosway's property in Blevio, for which I am most grateful.

The research actually began in France, where I had the good fortune to know Hélène Baltrusaitus, a fountain of information on the Parisian art scene, past and present. We soon discovered our mutual interest in Thomas

Jefferson's years in Paris. Hélène introduced me to the work of the pre-eminent authority on the subject, Howard Rice, and then to Olivier Choppin de Janvry, who has dedicated many years to his passion for the restoration of the Désert de Retz. He showed me this historic garden before its recent restoration and, even overtaken by dense forest, it had lost none of its evocative power.

When work on Maria Cosway's life began in earnest, Charles Morazé helped me launch the project with the support of his colleagues of the *Fondation Maison des Sciences de l'Homme* and, most particularly, the foundation's Director, Maurice Aymard, who so graciously put his network of contacts in Italy to work on my behalf. I shall always be grateful to them and for the attentive interest and friendship of Monique Morazé. In Lyon I wish to thank the archivists of the Archbishop of Lyon, Messieurs Henri Hours and Henri Peyrelongue, for sharing their knowledge of Lyon's history. The late Ambassador Pamela Harriman kindly gave me access to the U.S. Embassy in Paris's substantial collection of works on U.S.-French history and diplomatic relations. Monsieur Daniel Wildenstein accorded his permission to examine his interesting documentation on Jacques-Louis David in the *Fondation Wildenstein*. In France I would also like to thank Madame André Laurencin for her welcome and assistance during my visit to the *Musée Denon*.

Much time was spent in the United Kingdom researching Maria Cosway's role in British artistic life. Dr. Stephen Lloyd of the Scottish National Portrait Gallery has most generously shared his enthusiasm and his knowledge of the Cosways' careers, often calling new source material to my attention. During many trips to the U.K., I was always welcomed and assisted by the staffs of the British Library, the Bodleian Library, the London Library, the National Art Library at the Victoria & Albert Museum, and the Public Record Office. I owe special thanks to Nicholas Savage and his helpful staff in the library of the Royal Academy of Arts, to Carol Blackett-Ord of the Paul Mellon Centre for Studies in British Art, and to Angela Roche and Alison Wright of the Department of Prints and Drawings in the British Museum. Margaret Richardson, Curator of Sir John Soane's Museum, was most helpful. One of the most enriching aspects of researching an eighteenth-century artist is the tracing of portraits and family history. In this endeavour I enjoyed the hospitality and interesting family stories of Viscount Cobham at Hagley Hall, Lord and Lady Fitzwalter at Goodnestone Park and Mr. and Mrs. Matthew Dugdale at Merevale Hall. Charles Noble, Curator of the Chatsworth collections, was an amiable host and – with the Duchess of Devonshire's kind permission – showed me Maria Cosway's most successful picture, her portrait of Georgiana, the fifth Duchess. I would also like to thank Joyce Purnell for her help in arranging my visit to Hagley Hall and to Mrs. Robin Bailey for our useful discussions there.

Although she never visited the United States, there is much information about Maria Cosway to be gleaned from collections there. My most pleasant memories are the days spent at the Lewis Walpole Library in Farmington, Connecticut, where Anna Malicka and Joan Sussler opened the door to this fascinating repository of Walpoliana with a friendly approach, which made working there easy and joyous. Jay and Merrill Toole tolerated with good humour a long stay with them while consulting the archives of the Huntington Museum in California.

The fuel which revives one's flagging perseverance in any long-term project is the continual support and spontaneous service rendered by friends. Many helped with the daunting task of translating numerous Italian documents. The most faithful and efficient were Isabella Comba and Francis Ley, whose continual interest in my slow progress was truly appreciated. In this regard a *tour de force* of historical translation was performed by Monsieur Ansgar Wildermann, a palaeographer, who was able to decipher the private shorthand of Franz I, the Austrian emperor. In addition to translation, those who performed favours or offered encouragement were Axelle Costerousse, Stephen Lesher, Chris Freeman, Walther Richter, Chantal Burns, Françoise Reynaud, Hélène Pillet-Will, Marcus Staff, and Angela John. I am grateful for their disinterested contribution.

The beautiful photography of Pascal Hinous enhances the visual aspect of the book. I am deeply indebted to him.

Outside of my family my greatest debt is owed to Julia Marr Robinson, not only a friend but an able editor. She has picked the manuscript apart, offering many helpful suggestions and criticisms, which certainly improved the final result. Her unflagging belief in the book was a precious encouragement.

Finally, there are a few who bore the brunt of this effort along with me and learned far more about Mrs. Cosway than they cared to know. My step-son Matthieu had to put up with absences and long periods of being excluded from my office. His generous and forgiving nature has enabled him to be of great help in the later stages of the work. There is one, however, without whom there might never have been a successful conclusion to this endeavour for I would have given it up without his support. No words can describe the ministrations of my husband, Thierry Pillet-Will — his tolerance, patience, steady encouragement, helpful suggestions, diplomatic skills — these are a very few aspects of his contribution. For all of them I dedicate this book to him.

To the Reader

The intention of the author to write a biography, presenting all the long-known and newly discovered facts of Maria Cosway's life, has never wavered. The entire story of her life is found in the following pages in a conventional chronological order. Paradoxically, in a quest to bring these events to life, certain scenes have been dramatised with conversations. For the historian, the author has flagged these scenes by placing them in italics. By referring to the notes the reader can gain a precise understanding of the documented facts and what is presumed or imagined to have happened. In Chapters Fifteen, Sixteen and Seventeen, however, the italicised scenes have been taken directly from Maria Cosway's diaries and letters and, in one case, Joseph Farington's *Diary*. The reader can be assured that there are no invented characters in this account. All the persons cited are historical figures who played their parts in Maria Cosway's life as described.

The original spelling, grammar and syntax have been retained in the Cosway letters.

Prologue

1786

On a rainy October evening in Paris Thomas Jefferson sat near the fire to write a letter.

With his left hand he scratched quill on paper awkwardly. The right wrist, broken in a fall two weeks earlier, was painfully stiff. Emotion propelled the pen, enabling him to surmount the effort. Over the course of a week he continued writing until he had filled twelve pages. The result was a 4,000-word declaration of love. The normally reserved Mr. Jefferson, slightly embarrassed by the unveiling of his feelings, enclosed a brief note to his correspondent, advising her lightheartedly how to read the letter: 'Divide it into six doses of half a sheet each, and every day, when the toilette begins, take a dose.... . By this means its length and dullness can aspire to that of assisting your coiffeuse to procure you six good naps of sleep.'

The lady in London who received the letter – conceived by its author as a Dialogue of the Head and the Heart – could hardly have been put to sleep. She was supremely flattered, but was she pleased? What sort of woman had penetrated the carefully preserved public façade protecting the wounded feelings of a private man? What sort of woman could inspire the affection of a man whose discriminating tastes were a barrier in themselves? Certainly a woman as extraordinary as the letter writer. Who was she? Which of her many gifts impressed the talented American? Her name was Maria Cosway, and her story will make clear how she came to fascinate the American Envoy to France.

1

'Daughter of the Arno'

The Seine and the Thames, sisters united forever,
Admire the daughter of the Arno, endowed with a golden lyre,
André Chénier to Maria Cosway

'I must snatch another heretic from hell! … Drink, my child…join your brothers…the angels in paradise,' an old woman muttered and bent low over a baby's crib. The atmosphere of the darkened room was close, sultry, still. In the afternoon heat Florentines were drowsing in silence. The rushing Arno, just beside the house, could be heard through the shutters. The woman held a small vial up to the rose infant mouth. Surprised by a creaking door, she flung the vial to the floor. Porous tiles soaked up the mortal liquid. A young woman entered. Sensing the danger, she swept the babe into her arms.

The intended victim of this bizarre crime was spared the horror. She only knew what her parents had often repeated – that she was the first of her siblings not to be murdered. Saved by the alertness of a nurse, she often pondered the wonder – Providence chose to save her, thereby revealing a hidden evil in her family's midst.

This evil took the benign appearance of an old servant. Brigida, a laundress, had given no cause for the Hadfield family's concern until she was surprised with a vial of poison. Why would an apparently harmless old lady commit such an act? The distraught parents soon discovered, upon questioning the crone, that 'plural' was the accurate qualifier for her deeds. The series of crimes began in 1755. Their firstborn, John, then Horace Arthur, two years later, and perhaps one or two unchristened children – each one had been sent to the Tuscan countryside with a wet nurse. Mrs. Hadfield visited each child often, always finding her offspring in robust health until the day the wet nurse came to announce a mysterious death. After Maria arrived on a hot July 11th in 1760 she and her nurse were kept at home under close watch. The motive for several infanticides was explained by the religious fanaticism of the servant. She had it worked out theologically that if the children were dispatched immediately as innocents, before they had the opportunity to become practising Protestants like their parents, then they might get to heaven straight on.

Maria Hadfield's story was just one in a series of cultural and religious conflicts which arose in Tuscany between the considerable number of English families living in Florence and Leghorn and some of the more devout Italians. Great passions could be aroused on both sides of the religious divide. Half the population of Florence were in religious orders. Rather than resist hostile influences, the Hadfields chose to shield their surviving children from bigoted attacks by allowing them to become Catholics although they had baptised them as infants in the Church of England

For an Englishwoman a Catholic education was an unlikely choice in the days when a Roman Catholic was barely tolerated in England. No

Catholic marriages were recognized there. No Catholic could hold public office. But the Hadfields spent the first two decades of Maria's life in Italy, where her faith seemed natural. The way she escaped death from bigotry gave Maria a feeling that God had preserved her for a special destiny, that she was different from her brothers and sisters. From an early age it became evident that her talents exceeded theirs, that she might be destined for something greater than her father's circumstances could procure for her.

Charles Hadfield, her father, said that he came from a family of rich merchants in Manchester. He seemed to be moderately prosperous, but derived his means from keeping an inn in the little Palazzo Medici – not exactly the occupation of a gentleman. Travellers called their house, whose rear windows overlooked the dun-coloured Arno, the *Locanda di Carlo*. 'Carlo' was somewhat of a fixture in Florence, having settled there in the 1740s. It was in Tuscany that he met and married Elizabeth Pocock. They were wed in Siena in 1753 by a Mr. Lepeatt, a clergyman who was serving as a 'bear-leader' or tutor to Lord Bruce on his Grand Tour. The young lord had been detained at Siena by his duties as a *cavalière servente* to an Italian lady.

1. Caricature of Charles Hadfield *by Thomas Patch*.

Maria later defended her social origins proudly to an Italian friend, suggesting obliquely that her mother may have come to Italy in service:

> My father was a brave and honest Englishman of Manchester, came to Italy, settled in Florence, saw with pain that his

compatriots were badly housed, took a fine palazzo, opened an inn with English taste, met my mother who was travelling with an English family, married her, and this was useful for his aims… to take away the truth of my birth would be injurious. I am not then offended in England because little attention is paid to this, but if the Father is grand, the children participate with impunity in this honour without thinking of the poor mother.

It is clear that Maria never held her mother in the same esteem as her beloved father. Elizabeth Hadfield, or Isabella as she was called in Italy, seems to have been a strong, capable woman. The one possible portrait of Isabella shows a woman with a rather sharp nose. Her voice and manner could be affectionate, but keeping three houses scrubbed and clean, supervising the servants, teaching them English cookery and caring for her five children must have taxed her good humour. She and her eldest daughter never seemed to understand each other. They had different convictions, different ambitions. Mrs. Hadfield wished to see Maria well-married, whilst Maria was sceptical of the institution of marriage.

Maria was most likely her father's favourite, his spoiled one, and she returned his affection. He was round, full-faced and jolly. One of his guests called him a 'saucy, imposing man'. Full of good humour, generous, he was somewhat of a *bon vivant*, the hospitable, accommodating innkeeper. Much of the success of his enterprises was due to the warmth of his personality. Maria's earliest memories of her father's voice must have been his shouting for the servant to take the travellers' cloaks, to bring them cups of wine, help with their boots, carry their valises, all the while chuckling for no reason but his own bonhomie.

Later, she would have heard riotous laughter downstairs, echoing up to her room through the staircase. Her curiosity must have been piqued. What were these gentlemen finding so hilarious during their punch parties? One object of their amusement was the work of Thomas Patch, an English artist who sketched guests in caricature. Their exaggerated features were sometimes hilarious. Lord Cowper's chin touched his nose. Sir Horace Mann, Envoi Extraordinaire of His Majesty George III to the Great Duke of Tuscany, managed to save some of his dignity. Mr. Patch turned his wit on himself. He variously depicted himself with the body of a lion, or a bull or sitting on a donkey. The artist was in and out of the Hadfields' house almost every day, selling his caricatures or his views of Florence to English tourists. His popular paintings of the bridges spanning the Arno were frequently done right from their windows. He was a peculiar fellow, who had a smoky reputation because of his expulsion from Rome for reasons which were left unspoken.

Charles Hadfield was portrayed twice in Patch's large paintings – once as a tiny portrait on the wall in one of the caricatures. The lady in the companion portrait next to Hadfield is most probably his wife. In 1760, the year of Maria's birth, Patch painted a large picture in which Charles is the central personage, raising a large punch bowl ceremoniously before placing

2. Gathering at Sir Horace Mann's *by Thomas Patch.*
By comparing the portrait on the far left wall with Patch's caricature of
Carlo, it seems certain that the two are likenesses of Charles Hadfield,
leading to the assumption that the lady in the portrait on the right of the left
wall is that of Isabella Hadfield.

it before his guests. One of the revellers in the picture was Sir Brooke Bridges, Maria's godfather. (About this time, Sir Brooke began to avoid English society, who disapproved of his liaison with an Italian dancer.)

3. Detail of Gathering at Sir Horace Mann's *showing the presumed portrait of Isabella Hadfield.*

Maria's other English godparents were Lady Lucy Boyle and a Miss Thulis. She was not christened in the Church of England until 22nd November 1760 when the Hadfields took the baby to see Mr. Everard Hutcheson, Chaplain to the British Factory in Leghorn. The only Protestant Chapel and Burying Ground permitted by the Grand Duke was down the river at Leghorn so either the English clergy came up to Florence as often as they could or the English were obliged to travel to Leghorn to be married, buried, or baptised. The little girl was christened Lucy – probably after Lady Lucy Boyle, daughter of the Earl of Corke, who with the Countess and Lady Lucy had stayed at Carlo's during their tour of Italy. Her full name was Maria Louisa Catherine Cecilia Hadfield. Maria was the name used by the family. It was no doubt pronounced the Italian way even though her mother persisted in calling her Mary. Maria, a child of Italian culture, seems to have felt more Italian than English, although her hard-headedness and perseverance, her obsession with order, must have been from her English character.

Maria always lived in two worlds, spending her childhood in Italy, but very much a part of the English colony in Tuscany. The Hadfields' house was a few steps away from the Palazzo Manetti, the home of Sir Horace Mann, where all important persons of rank called. Sir Horace received the Duke of York, the King's brother, on the Duke's tour of 1764. Carlo's lodgings were much appreciated by young gentlemen and their 'bear-leaders' (travelling tutors) on the Grand Tour because he did everything 'in the English way' as Mrs. Piozzi ironically phrased it. She scorned the tourists who wanted to see Italy without leaving London. The English *were* demanding, but who could blame them for not wishing a filthy mattress full of maggot-like creatures or scorpions under the bed, to say nothing of rats and mice whose nocturnal scurrying caused sleepless nights in many Italian inns. Carlo's guests were indeed relieved to find low small beds with soft sheets and down pillows in clean rooms cleared of vermin. They especially appreciated joints of beef, which the Italians refused to eat, mincemeat tarts, apple pies, and puddings.

While it was true that many English were insular, limiting their artistic touring to one morning in the Grand Duke's Gallery and one afternoon in the Pitti Palace, the Grand Duke's residence, others were serious about their visits to one of Europe's greatest assemblages of art, rivalled only by those of the Duke of Orleans or the Pope. This attraction brought aristocrats, artists, and scholars to the Hadfields where they lived congenially together in the same way, without great fussing or ceremony. Curiously the little *locanda* was a cultural gathering place where young men stopped before going on to creative success, even fame.

Before Edward Gibbon published the first volume of his great work on the Roman Empire, he spent the entire summer of 1764 with the Hadfields. He was one of the serious tourists, studying Italian in the evening and visiting the Grand Duke's Gallery fourteen times with great method. Mr. Gibbon then proceeded to Rome where he conceived a plan to describe the decay of the city. Later he expanded his idea to explain the Empire's decadence. Another of these young talents was James Boswell. After Maria had grown up and gone to London, she must have heard acquaintances occasionally remark that they had sojourned at Carlo's in Florence. Was it a provocation to put her in her place? Possibly, but her friend, Mr. Boswell, was surely not guilty of such oblique snobbery. During his brief stay in Florence, did he remember seeing a small girl with blond curls silently observing everyone from her post at the top of the stairs like a vigilant cat? After leaving the Hadfields' inn, he sailed for Corsica and an interview which made his reputation. Youthful audacity enabled him to win the friendship and confidence of the Corsican leader, General Pasquale Paoli.

Mr. Boswell's account of this voyage was the basis of his first celebrity, causing a sensation back in England. A few years later the Grand Duke ordered a life-size portrait of General Paoli, commissioned by Boswell, to be transported from Leghorn to Florence. With childish curiosity Maria must have gazed at the picture of a portly man, who seemed very old. She could never have divined that this heroic figure, already in his middle years, would one day become a member of her circle of intimates, perhaps her truest friend.

Charles Hadfield's talent for hospitality gave him an indispensable role in the small expatriate community. When Sir Watkin Williams-Wynn, a rich Welsh aristocrat on his Grand Tour, decided to fete Sir Horace Mann after the envoy's investiture in the Order of the Bath, it was Carlo who orchestrated a grand feast, concert, and ball in the Palazzo Bruciato, the Hadfields' country house in the hills north of Florence. His usefulness to English travellers included negotiation and dispatching of their numerous acquisitions of art and antiquities and perhaps some picture-dealing.

Maria was too young to remember many of her father's distinguished visitors, but she always considered her childhood city to have been set in a sun-blessed Eden. Its natural setting in a valley of luscious kitchen gardens and fruit orchards, the woods of umbrella pines filled with pheasants and nightingales, the clean, fresh streets washed by the river and a system of modern drains – all united to make Florence physically comfortable as well as culturally rich. The childish Maria's favourite corner of Florence was tucked into an angle of the city's walls. Her parents' desire to protect her from further religious persecution led them to confide her at a very young four years of age to a place that ever after retained its place in her heart – Il Conventino.

Her concept of home was profoundly influenced by this convent. One can imagine that she felt the warmth radiating from the stones of the Via del Orto as she and her mother, hand in hand, walked past the scarlet hollyhocks and pinks thrusting up from the dust against ochre walls. As the porter opened the massive dark doors she must have had a moment of fright. But then she saw a cloistered garden looking warm and safe with its spiky palm trees. The charm of the place certainly took hold. Peaks of dark cypresses stood guard outside the cloister wall. All was silent but for the song of blackbirds in the pines and the swish of swallows high against luminous blue. Deep within, Maria always nurtured this image of monastic life as sunny serenity.

Everything the adult Mrs. Cosway later accomplished and the discovery of her talents began at Il Conventino. The Italian sisters were gentle and kind, not severe and unbending like some of their Northern counterparts. They gave her lessons in Italian, French, geography and history, embroidery and music. The musical instruction was not as fine as that in Venice in the hospitals for orphan girls such as the Mendicanti and the Pieta where Vivaldi was master. Dr. Charles Burney said the music of Florence was not of a high standard compared with other Italian cities. Yet the Master of the Grand Duke's Chapel was the composer Signore Campioni. Signore Nardini, the violinist who played with such ravishing tone, was a member of his ensemble. While still a child Maria was once honoured to play with them before the Court of the Grand Duke. She had learned to play the harp, the harpsichord, and the organ. The precocious child sang with a lovely voice and began composing her own airs. She loved making music; it was like play to her. At six years she could play astonishingly well. Soon she was playing the organ for the masses at Il Conventino.

Maria's childhood impressions were not totally circumscribed by the white walls of the convent. Part of the week she must have spent at home playing with William, or 'Melmo' – as he was called after his Italian name Guglielmo – and George. Her sisters were much younger. Although she loved them, they were never playmates or confidantes as girls. The children's nursery was probably under the roof. They may well have grown up with the tempting odours of meat braising or sugary tarts baking in the kitchen next to their room. Florentines often had the kitchen at the top of the houses to isolate the smells of charcoal and cooking and mainly to prevent the servants from walking off with the stores.

In summer, if there were not too many guests, they may have been permitted to sleep downstairs to be cooler. One had to open the windows, and sleep under gauze curtains. Despite this protection the children were covered with red welts in hot weather from mosquitoes. Although they suffered from these insects, there were others to enjoy – the cicadas clicking in the Boboli Gardens, so loudly that conversation was almost impossible on summer evenings and the glowing amber beads of the *lucciola* – or fireflies – which they chased along the river terrace, capturing them in closed fists and then freeing them to light up the nightly walks of the Florentines. For it was the summer nights that brought out the young and old, fashionable and lower orders, awakened from the lethargy of a close, airless siesta. They revived with fruit ices, cold orangeade or lemonade. Ice had been carefully harvested from the mountains to cool the city. Florentines could not survive without their ice. They adored these perfect nights under a moon set in clear, dry air. They walked, sang, and talked long past midnight. The city came to life after long, sleepy days.

Florentines' favourite night of the year was the eve of the Feast of San Giovanni, the patron saint of Florence, on the 24th June. The fete began on the 23rd with processions and a chariot race in the antique Roman style in the Piazza Santa Maria Novella. The children may not have been allowed to see these events, but they could surely stay up to see the fireworks from their windows. The showers of brilliant sparks exploded above the

4. Self-portrait *by Violante Siries Cerruoti, Maria Hadfield's teacher and confidante.*

Piazza del Gran Duca across the river, illuminating the silhouette of the Duomo, scattering light-ripples over the water as if the fire had become molten, kindling gasps of delight in their throats.

In the midst of this little Italian paradise Maria's education took a turn which would lead to great events in her life. When eight years old she saw another girl drawing; she took the pencil and discovered a passion which soon surpassed even that for music.

Soon after Maria discovered the magic of

colours and pencils, the nuns were unable to guide her with sufficient knowledge. They asked a famous lady, whose portrait hung in the Grand Duke's Gallery, to instruct her. That is how Signora Violante Siries Cerruoti became Maria's second mother. Violante Siries had seen the court of Louis XV when only sixteen. She accompanied her father, who was goldsmith to the king. Having already mastered watercolour and crayon techniques in Florence, Violante studied oil painting for five years in Paris with Flemish masters and was asked to do portraits of the Royal Family. For about four years she patiently and kindly demonstrated painting and drawing to the young Maria until the child mastered the first elements. They talked of art, but also of religion, since they shared the same faith. Art vied with religious faith for first place in Maria's affections. Her mind became divided between a girlish desire to remain cloistered in a convent and an equally ardent wish to pursue her studies in art. This tension provoked an emotional state. The child had a vivid dream at this time.

She was in the Grand Hall of the convent playing with some of her friends. The ceiling opened and among the clouds appeared the Madonna with her babe. She came down to earth and took Maria up with her. Halfway to heaven, she must have had a change of heart, because she abruptly set the child back on earth. Maria awoke in tears, but fell back into slumber. She dreamt that the same Madonna lifted her up forever. Whatever did this mean? She asked the nuns. Later, she had long intimate talks with her beloved painting mistress, Signora Violante Cerruoti. The painter predicted that until the middle of Maria's life she would be raised toward heaven, then return to the world, and finally her hopes would be happily fulfilled. This explanation was simple enough for the child to understand then, but the inner conflict in her character was never completely resolved. Retirement to a convent always had an irresistible pull for Maria Hadfield. Yet each time she faced the gates – in Florence, in Genoa, in Lyon, in Lodi – there was always a reason not to take the step: her mother, her husband, or the Emperor Napoleon who temporarily forbade it.

Since Maria could speak to Signora Cerruoti of matters that her mother did not want to hear, Mrs. Hadfield may have become jealous of the Italian artist's influence and was certainly satisfied when the painting mistress admitted that she could do no more for Maria, that the child needed teaching from a greater artist than her. Maria was then twelve years old. That very summer a greater artist appeared and Florence was abuzz with the news. Johann Zoffany, the favourite painter of Her Majesty Queen Charlotte, had been sent to Florence for the express purpose of painting a detailed picture of La Tribuna, the most famous room of the Grand Duke's Gallery, indeed the most famous room in all of Europe!

The Medici Grand Dukes collected on a grand scale. Not content with one or two cabinets of antiquities, engraved gems, objects of *virtu* and a few choice pictures like many *amateurs,* the Medicis had housed their collections in an immense Gallery with treasures piled up over the centuries in no particular order. Among the disparate mass one octagonal room had acquired an international reputation as the *schatzkammer* or treasure room of the Grand Duke, the Tribuna. This was largely due to the presence of six statues which the Medicis had brought from Rome: *The Grinder* or *Scythian Slave, The Wrestlers, The Satyr with Cymbals, Venus de Medici,* a peerless example of feminine beauty that outshone the two other statues in the Tribuna portraying the same goddess: *Venus Victrix* and *The Celestial Venus.*

5. Self-portrait *by Zoffany*

Queen Charlotte had heard about these wonders from her brother-in-law, the Duke of York, after his tour of Italy. Her curiosity was Maria Hadfield's good fortune. Since Charles Hadfield sooner or later crossed paths with all the English in Florence, he was introduced to Zoffany, who moved in English society despite being German. They entered into an arrangement, whose monetary terms were not revealed, which permitted Maria to have instruction. The great thing was that through Zoffany's influence – his Royal introduction had persuaded the Grand Duke to let him rearrange the pictures in the Tribuna, bringing over seven pictures from the Pitti Palace to be included in his painting – Maria was given permission by the Grand Duke to enter the Gallery and copy his pictures for her studies. Since Zoffany was spending most days working in the Tribuna, it was very easy to supervise the young girl's work.

On the day the young Maria hastened down the long U-shaped corridor of the Gallery, she discovered the antique world, stretching out in 400 feet of marble busts rhythmically punctuated with statues. She hurried past the heads of every Roman emperor from Augustus to Caracalla: Julius Caesar, strained and old for his age; Cicero's long neck and thin face; Seneca, another old man, only muscles, bones and veins; Vetellius, a handsome and heavy glutton; Vespasian, a beautiful head of an ugly man; Trajan with a mocking smile and the Empress Domitia with her forehead curls in the form of a sponge.

By entering the treasure house of the Medicis and the Habsburgs, Maria began to absorb the taste of centuries of culture and connoisseurship. From these mute and noble witnesses she began to understand the classical history that infused the art of her time. This was also a test of discrimination as no order had been imposed on the Grand Duke collections. From exquisitely carved ivories to wax figures of decaying bodies, from Florentine hardstone tables to antique kitchen utensils, from Etruscan vases to a lion in the form of a priapus – covered with a cloth to prevent ladies from seeing it – there were ample distractions to keep a child from her work. In a chamber called the Arsenal where Maria copied a painting, she could also be amused by elephant tusks, the horn of a unicorn (vulgarly called a rhinoceros horn), a model of the Palazzo Pitti, 120 bound volumes of drawings and prints, and an entire stuffed hippopotamus.

Such exotic objects could have distracted a young girl, but the always dutiful Maria realised her incredible good fortune to know Zoffany. When she entered the Tribuna, she would find her teacher in a paint-smeared smock hunched before his easel and occasionally peering at her over two small round wire circles perched on a bulb of a nose. His heavy German accent must have been difficult for Maria to understand for her English was still poor. Yet his total dedication to art was transmitted to his pupil. Maria was in awe of his skill while she watched him succeed in rendering the most delicate details of picture frames or small bronzes in the Tribuna. Zoffany had to place the tiny paintings within his painting in perspective and to distinguish between the heads of his living models and those in the pictures, and even try to show the different textures of canvas. This *tour de force* he achieved.

The Anglo-German was a wonderful teacher, able to draw on his vast knowledge of the history of art and the various styles and genres. He had established a good rapport with his fellow countryman and mentor, Anton Raphael Mengs, the leading classical painter established in Rome. Zoffany had studied with him in Rome as a young man. When Anton Raphael Mengs came to personally place his self-portrait in the Gallery, a few months after Maria began working there, she was presented to him. He spent several months in Florence. These two established painters were daily in the Gallery, and from them she surely learned of the influential theories of their compatriot, Johann Joachim Winckelmann. This historian, assassinated five years before in Trieste, had – according to Zoffany and Mengs – written the definitive works on art and the canons of beauty and taste, explaining that the ideal beauty attained by the Greeks was far superior to the Roman and

6. Self-portrait *by Anton Raphael Mengs in the Uffizi Gallery.*

Etruscan, that the artist must imitate the Greeks, must imitate nature, then choose the best of nature and attain the ideal, the perfect. Therefore artists could do nothing better than study classical elegance, containment, and sometimes abstraction, to perfect their talents. Now Maria understood more fully why the Grand Dukes had so many statues and busts, so many bronzes and copies of the antique.

Zoffany guided her choice of pictures to copy. She began with the Grand Duke's collection of portraits of painters. Since the time of Cardinal Leopold de Medici, the Grand Duke had written to many of the best artists, asking for their portraits. With over two hundred from which to choose, she began with the founder of the Bologna school, Annibale Carracci, and one of his disciples, Domenichino. Continuing with two artists of the last century, she followed the taste of the times: choosing a portrait of Carlo Dolci, whose neat and finished style, pleasing colour, rich costumes, and rigorous detail were much admired and skilfully emulated by Zoffany and then Karl de Moor, an excellent Dutch painter, whose highly-finished portraits imitated the taste, dignity, force and delicacy of Van Dyck. His flowing draperies and soft flesh tints were universally praised.

These portraits were all rather dark and sombre in the seventeenth century tradition, serious, pensive men in black with white collars. After these badly-needed exercises in masculine portraiture, Maria returned to feminine subjects. Young girls had little experience with men as sitters and were never permitted to draw unclothed men from life. This considerably slowed her grasp of the necessary anatomy. She was allowed to copy the statues in the corridors, however; these studies became the basis of her grasp of the male figure.

During Maria's first months in the Gallery, many changes were afoot, partly due to Zoffany's rearranging of many pictures, but also because of the Grand Duke's desire to put some order in his collections. During 1773 many paintings were moved from the Imperial villa at Poggio a Caiano, enabling her to study pictures that had not been much seen. So in the spring of 1774 she turned from dark and formal portraits of men to ladies. Her natural bent toward the grace, finish, and elegance of the Bolognese painters such as Carlo Cignani or the religious fervour of Guido Reni drew her to their madonnas, sibyls, and angels. A portrait of a lady by Rubens introduced her to the glowing, natural colours of the Low Country painters, their force, and their freedom.

With more maturity at fifteen, Maria was permitted to carry her easel into the inner sanctum of the Tribuna to begin a picture after the great 'Il Correggio', a Virgin and Child of infinite grace and masterful handling of light and shade. That same year, when a portrait of Sir Joshua Reynolds, President of the English Royal Academy, was hung in the Chamber of

Painters, she was one of the first to render him homage. Her impressions are recorded in one of the earliest letters from her hand. Writing to Ozias Humphry, another young English artist studying in Italy, she is dazzled by the modern technique of Reynolds:

> The colouring is so beautiful that it throws to the ground all the other portraits, especially that of Sir Mengs, which is just above it. This new portrait seems to have beaten him because his face is full of bruises. Some people don't hesitate to disapprove of its quality of drawing, but I don't know enough to give an opinion about this; I like it and have already started to copy it. If Cimabue was the first to deserve that his works should be accomplished by the sound of trumpets and celebrations, if Leonardo deserved the honour of dying in the arms of a king, and if…Correggio could have said, 'I am also a painter' what will the man who can throw an entire gallery of portraits to the ground say?

7. Self-portrait *by Reynolds in the Uffizi Gallery.*

It was then that she began to see that Mengs' classical restraint was nothing compared to the life and energy that an inspired painter could express.

By the summer of 1775 Maria had been working diligently for two years. It was the summer of her coming of age. An artist came to Florence who impressed her more than the others and changed her attitude toward her studies. Joseph Wright, or Wright of Derby, only spent two weeks there, but Maria always remembered their talks. Wright stressed to her that endless copying of pictures, even of great painters, was not the way to become an artist. She reminisced much later:

> He seeing perhaps my natural disposition told me that I was not on the right road. In only three days he opened the world to me and gave me a taste for greater things.... I needed to go away to other places to make a name for myself.

At fifteen Maria Hadfield already had the ambition – unseemly for a young lady – to succeed as an artist. Her father wished to send her to London, but this did not seem possible now. He was not always in good health and had too much work to leave Italy. He said that perhaps she could go to Rome, but proper arrangements would have to be found. Maria began to wish much to go to Rome, but as she wrote to Humphry:

> As I cannot come to Rome I content myself with staying in Florence; often one's reward is according to one's merit and this is what is happening to me.... But patience, when the merit will blossom, the rewards will appear.

Probably shaped by her convent education, she meditated the verses of Leonardo da Vinci, who wisely counselled that one who cannot do what he wishes can become mad with wanting, so a man is wise to keep his desire away from something he cannot do. How much more should a young girl without connections heed that counsel, for Maria soon realised that she was socially handicapped.

This was brought home to her one day in the Gallery when she was the subject of a conversation between Zoffany and Charles Townley, a sophisticated collector of antiquities. Townley teased both Zoffany and his pupil saying:

> I like Miss Hadfield very much. She is a charming girl. I wish she had a better master to teach her painting, she would paint much better. Oh! I wish she had a good fortune. I would marry her directly.

Although Maria recounted this anecdote in a letter to Ozias Humphry and did not seem displeased at the time, Townley's casual remark revealed Maria's precarious situation. For all her talents and accomplishments, for all her fairness – as by this time, gentlemen had begun to notice her silvery grey eyes framed in an aura of blondeness – she had one impossible defect. She had no fortune. The best convents would not accept her as a novice, and a good marriage was highly unlikely for a young girl without connections and no dowry. Her prospects were not encouraging. There was nothing to do but keep painting and hope that one day she might attain a level of skill to permit her – like Angelica Kauffmann, one of two women elected to the Royal Academy in London – to make her way in life by her own efforts. It was not thought proper for ladies to have ambition so she kept this desire buried deeper than her desire to go to Rome. She decided that she did not want to marry. Either she would pursue her childhood inclination to pursue a religious vocation or she would be a paintress. After all, at that time art was considered a search after the ideal, the good, and the beautiful, and a source of moral instruction.

The realisation of her unfortunate situation did not prevent the advantages of youth and friendship from cheering Maria's first steps into the world. During the summer of 1775 she became friends with several young English artists who had come to Italy to enlarge their artistic horizons, just as Joseph Wright suggested she must do. Every morning they would walk to the Gallery about nine o'clock, where they worked until about one in the afternoon. One of Charles Hadfield's servants would then bring the artists a good dinner of a joint, fruit, cheese, and wine, which they enjoyed together in a sort of indoor picnic, sometimes among the Flemish, sometimes among the Bolognese, sometimes among the Venetian pictures. The circle of young painters, who surely teased the youngest and prettiest of the group, included Henry Tresham, an Irishman, about twenty-four years old. Already his reddish hair receded from a high forehead. He and the other Irishman, Hugh Primrose Deane, made them laugh until they ached, especially Deane, full of outrageous mirth. There was also poor Edward Edwardes, a deformed little man, whose appearance caused him much misfortune. Yet, he persevered and later became Professor of Perspective at the Royal Academy. The best of her friends was Ozias Humphry, already an accomplished miniature painter, who wished to study oil painting in large scale. Mr. Humphry was a romantic and slightly melancholy young man. He had been cruelly disappointed by his lack of success in winning the hand of the daughter of James Paine, the architect. Now he was assiduous in his flirtations with Maria. In the first full flush of excitement of being noticed and flattered by young gentlemen, of sharing her interests in art, in opera, and theatre with charming companions, Maria tasted a different sort of happiness. It was a good time, probably one of her happiest.

8. Ozias Humphry *after George Romney, 1772.*

She profited from these years to the fullest. As the Florentine summer of 1775 drew to a close, most of her new friends – Tresham, Humphry, and Edwardes – moved on to Rome, leaving her to follow her daily routine alone. In a letter to Humphry she describes her day:

> I go every morning at nine [to copy pictures] until one. After lunch I study as usual architecture until half past four. My singing teacher comes at five. At six I go drawing until nine. The evenings of the opera I go to listen to the talent of the *prima donna* and to see the beautiful person Milico and to make a sacrifice to Apollo and Daphne because, for me, it is a sacrifice to have to stay and watch such ugly dancing.

She continued to play her harp and harpsichord in the evenings. About that time Maria enjoyed singing with another Englishman, William Parsons, who was in Italy to study singing. They enjoyed music together, but little did she realise at the time what an impression she was making on Parsons. She was to find out after he had returned to London.

Humphry wrote Maria a number of letters from Rome, which she answered in Italian. They exchanged packets of books on architecture and opera. She even sent him mince pies for Christmas, which were heartily appreciated by all the English artists who met in the English cafe in Rome. In one of her letters to Humphry she described Florence in an unusual winter garb.

> I had started to do the portrait of Sir Reynolds, but, because of the cold I had to stop going to the Gallery and hoping to finish it when this great cold is over; this cold weather is this year, I can assure you, excessive. Even the beautiful Arno has…become an entire piece of ice; in the streets the water immediately freezes…. I suffer a lot from chilblains on my hands and feet, to such an extent that sometimes I cannot play, draw or write.

Maria's letters written during the winter of 1775-1776 reveal a young girl discovering the world and its pleasures with delight. She adores music, the opera, painting, dancing, and sharing her passions with her friends, interestingly enough all young men. She does not mention other young girls nor does she seem bent on a religious vocation as she professed in later life. For a girl of fifteen she already displays critical judgment in her appreciation of different musical artists and painters, comparing the *castrato* Rubinelli with Milico or judging Sir Joshua Reynolds far superior to Mengs.

That winter Maria went to the Opera for the first time dressed in a simple frock as was the custom. Operas were performed in the Teatro de la via Pergola, a very large, handsome theatre where she heard the most thrilling performances of the great male sopranos and contraltos like Milico and Rubinelli. These *castrati*, who enhanced the popularity of the Italian opera at that time, were 'first men' of extreme attractiveness despite their difference. Sometimes they had high speaking voices, but when singing they had such astonishing range from tenor to soprano, such power from their masculine chests to project ravishing feminine sounds, and such agility from vocal cords of childish flexibility that the effect overpowered the senses. Even if the music and the dancing were mediocre, one could always count on several moments of intense pleasure from these *virtuosi*. She went to the Opera often, sending her opinion of the performances to Humphry.

The first singer's name is Rubinelli and he is a contralto. He cannot be praised enough for he has a very handsome appearance and if the 'prima donna' is beautiful, the main male singer is even more so; his voice is the most beautiful I have heard; it doesn't have that harshness that Milico had, but such a soft unity that it's a pleasure to listen to; …I cannot favour him over Milico because of the latter's *cantabile*, nor can I favour him over Aprile for variations; but Rubinelli displays elements from both of the above with his handsome appearance and beautiful voice.

Maria found the world enchanting that winter because she was able to enter into all that the Grand Duchy had to offer. She was not part of the world of rank or fashion, but the customs of the Grand Duke and Grand Duchess and the smallness of the English community were such that without actually being a part of society she was able, nonetheless, to participate in most of their rituals, with the exception of the Casino. This was a sort of public assembly hall and gaming room for the Florentine nobility. No one was ever admitted to the Casino balls and routs without a proof of pedigree. Even the ladies had to prove they were wellborn and could not rely on their husbands' titles. This was of no consequence. The young nobles who went said the Casino was horribly stiff and boring. Furthermore, when the Grand Duke gave balls, sometimes out of doors, anyone could attend, provided he or she was properly dressed. It was quite easy to be properly dressed, even for a young lady of modest means, for everyone, even the Grand Duchess and the ladies of the court, went to the theatre and to the balls in the Venetian *bautta*. This was an ample black silk veil, which fastened over the lower face and chin, covering the shoulders and upper body. During the weeks of Carnival, fine ladies could go in mask alone and on foot to the Casino, to the theatres, to balls, in fact anywhere with the perfect liberty of a man.

Even the court of Peter Leopold, the Grand Duke, was a curious mixture of protocol and informality. There were very few formal galas at the palace other than January 1st, and one or two other days. For these occasions, strict Imperial etiquette was followed according to instructions received from Vienna, where Peter Leopold's mother the Empress Maria Theresa and his brother the Emperor Joseph ruled together. Even the servants' livery had been copied from designs sent from Vienna. Most of the time the young Imperial couple, only eighteen when they arrived in Florence, observed little formality at dinner or in public appearances. At balls in the theatres they mingled with persons of rank and no rank, where some were masked and some in ordinary dress. The Grand Duke danced with chambermaids and even in the same set with Lord Tylney's footman. One evening one of Lord Tylney's servants took a lady that an English lord had asked to dance and danced away with her. Many English were shocked by these strange ways.

Maria Hadfield must certainly have enjoyed this loosening of social conventions, freeing her to enjoy the company of all ranks. She may well have shared the dance floor with a future Holy Roman Emperor, as Peter Leopold later became. She was certainly present at most of the English colony's social occasions. During the Carnival of 1776 she was out most nights, probably discreetly covered in a flowing black silk *bautta* and mask. As she breathlessly recounted to her correspondent in Rome:

> The first ball I attended this Carnival was at Mr. Ebdon's who gave a small dance party, but Mr. Townley gave another in our home on Thursday night followed by a dinner for 50 people. I danced so much that I caught a small cold…
>
> Please tell Mr. Tresham that I am expecting him for the last days of the Carnival…to dance with him at the celebrations of the 'Pergola'… . Next Saturday Mr. Zoffany will give a great ball and Mr. Houlston will give one the Saturday following, to which if you wish to come, you will be welcome with great pleasure.

It seems that Maria's invitations, extended to friends in Rome, were not accepted. She was often escorted by Hugh Primrose Dean, the landscape painter, who had been in Italy eight years without seeing his wife and child. Maria was apparently unaware of Dean's marital situation and found him highly amusing. In one anecdote sent to Humphry, which illustrates the social fluidity of Florentine society, she seems quite pleased with her escort:

> There have been…balls at the two theatres where I found myself for most of them in the pleasant company of Mr. Dean,

who…tormented Mr. M…in such a manner as to amuse the entire company…the gentleman cited above wore on his breast a lovely dried rose and Mr. Dean removed it, offering it to the Countess Albany; this was enough to make everyone laugh and the Grand Duke and Grand Duchess were amused by this…

The Countess Albany was Louise de Stolberg, a fair-haired beauty, who had recently married Prince Charles Edward Stuart, the Last Pretender to the English throne.

After Ozias Humphry painted her portrait in miniature, he wrote to a friend that he had considered her exceedingly beautiful when he saw her in the theatre, but when he saw her at home found her rather ordinary and haggard. Her hair was loose and thin, her complexion rather sallow and covered with spots. Despite Humphry's disillusion Louise became known as a great lady of character and intelligence, who apparently befriended the young Maria from their first meeting in Florence.

The Stuarts, known as the Count and Countess of Albany, were a sad couple, ignored by the Grand Duke and Duchess, the Florentine nobility, and certainly the English, who were watched like a hawk by Sir Horace to see that they had nothing to do with the Stuart rebel. The Prince's life had been a tragedy. He wandered Europe, sometimes living off French subsidies and then a pension from the Vatican, but having no country, no home, no real rank, only his increasingly hopeless pretensions. He had taken to drink years before. The English expatriates were no doubt disgusted to observe him in the theatre so drunk that he fell over on his couch in a stupor. He was red in the face, much older than his years, dissipated and rheumy-eyed. There was little sympathy left for him, especially after it became known that he abused his wife terribly.

Maria's sister Charlotte spread it about many years later that their father was a follower of this prince. This is not certain. It is true that Charles Hadfield offered to receive Charles Edward Stuart in his house on two occasions. When Maria was about ten years of age, the Count of Albany visited Florence and wished accommodation with Carlo. All was arranged. Then Hadfield was summoned to see Sir Horace, who told him with vehemence that he must not receive such a visitor, that such a visit would be quite prejudicial to his family and to the English colony. At first Hadfield resisted, but eventually gave in to these arguments and sent word that he could not provide lodgings to Charles Edward and his suite. Several years later the princely couple wished to settle in Florence. They were offered one of Hadfield's three houses after the Countess of Albany had discreetly sounded out Sir Horace through the French ambassador. This time the English envoy agreed, provided no English lived under the same roof. The Stuarts decided later that the house did not suit them. Although Hadfield was not known to support the Stuart claim to the throne openly, it is possible that he had some long-forgotten connection to this forlorn and forsaken prince.

Besides consorting with royalty, real or pretended, Maria's talents brought her to the notice of the highest ranking member of the English colony, George, the 3rd Earl Cowper, who had become a permanent resident of Florence as a very young man. He liked to spend part of his comfortable fortune on glittering concerts and theatricals, given in his large house between Florence and Fiesole, the Villa Palmieri. Most of the time the English did not see Milord because he stayed mostly with Italians. He had recently married Miss Hannah Gore, the youngest daughter of a respectable English family in residence. Lord Cowper was a fine patron of the arts and music. His treasure was a Madonna and Child by Raphael, which – to Maria's delight – he asked her to copy. She was also flattered, as she wrote to Humphry, 'I had the honour of singing "*No sparse tante lacrime*" for Mr. Parsons and Milord.'

The young Maria's head must have been turned by the attention she was receiving and by the temptations of the Carnival. She wrote to Humphry:

> I hope you realize that it's only because of the Carnival that I haven't written. It also stopped me from working, I am ashamed to say; engaging in such silly amusements, I now regret having wasted this time which to me should be so precious but I couldn't do otherwise. I don't know how to tell you how I have been spending my time over the last few days…you can imagine, and while I think about this, I can see that time has passed in front of my very eyes at a fast pace and that the figure of VIRTUE is reprimanding me…

She soon went back to her painting and faithfully returned to the Gallery, turning her mind to religious subjects like Saint Elizabeth and a Madonna and Child of Carracci. But now she had less powers of concentration as she mused over her palette, hearing young gentlemen laughing in the Gallery's empty halls, the spellbinding arias of Rubinelli in the magic glow of hundreds of candle flames, or the rhythmic shuffling of sixty pairs of slippers executing an intricate figure on the boards of the magnificent Pergola theatre. If she was not dreaming of the past year, she was dreaming of Rome, of the future. In spite of all difficulties, surely she was to have a future. Yet she would never have believed that one day she would be mistress of a collection of the same quality as the one she so assiduously copied. She would soon be living with Rubens, Raphaels and Rembrandts – and countless other masters – of her very own.

THE ARRIVAL OF A YOUNG TRAVELLER AND HIS SUITE
DURING THE CARNIVAL.
in Piazza De' Spagna Rome

2

Grand Tour

'Fear God and preserve your religion, my child,' Charles Hadfield advised the sixteen-year-old Maria before she set out for Rome. As they embraced, she did not suspect that these would be the last words she would hear from his lips. As a young person, eager to embark on a journey full of promise, she half-listened to his parting counsel. She had left her desire to see Rome in the hands of Divine Providence. As often happens when one has mastered desire, the desire is easily fulfilled.

It came about through the good offices of the Gore family. Mr. and Mrs. Charles Gore, accompanied by their three young daughters, were in Italy for Mrs. Gore's health.

Mrs. Mary Gore had inherited a nice fortune from her family's shipbuilding enterprise in Scarborough. The Gores were a cultivated and charming family, very musical and assiduous in their drawing lessons. They first visited Florence in 1773, but then spent most of their time in Rome. After meeting Hannah Gore, the youngest daughter, Lord Cowper was bewitched. A year after their marriage, Lady Cowper produced an heir, Lord Fordwich. This important event in the little English colony of Florence gathered lustre when the Cowpers received news that King George had agreed to be the child's godfather. The King's Envoy, Sir Horace Mann, stood for him.

The christening of George Augustus, held on 23rd August 1776, was another event on the path of Maria's destiny, as Mrs. Gore, his grandmother, must have come from Rome for the ceremony. All the English gentlemen and ladies were there. The Grand Duchess sent Lady Cowper a toy set of small tea cups of Viennese china for little Lord Fordwich. When Mrs. Gore prepared to return to Rome, Maria's father decided that his daughter could accompany the Gores. Rome would be the next step in Maria's artistic education. Hasty preparations were made, and the party set out on the road for Siena one September morning.

This, the young girl's first voyage, absorbed every sense. The countryside before Siena was similar to scenes she had known – cornfields, olives, oak groves, and vineyards. Still, the thoughts of Rome vested all in a glow of anticipation. Even the savage, wild, and barren landscapes on the south side of the Apennines could not dampen her enthusiasm. The post-houses and inns were primitive, lacking the English comforts of Carlo's. At Bolsena the inn's dining room had no glass in the windows, permitting a half dozen cats and chickens to join diners under the table. At the same time relics of the ancient past lent cachet to the rusticity. Pieces of antique sculpture were placed here and there; the horses and mules drank from an ancient sarcophagus in the courtyard. Travellers made about five posts a day, each post house providing a change of horses. On the fifth day they approached Rome. Strangely, the country was completely empty just before the city without inhabitants or farms, just a dry, rock-strewn space. At the distance of a full post from the city, voyagers could see an astonishing sight rising from a wasteland – the dome of St. Peter's. It was tiny, but only the largest church in the world could have been seen. When the rooftops of the city became visible, the many church belfries appeared to be miniatures, completely dominated by the extraordinary, almost inhuman dimensions of the great basilica of St. Peter's.

As Maria's party passed through the gates of the Porta del Popolo in the ancient walls, they could see an imposing entrance gate on their left, which led to one of the princely villas surrounding Rome on all sides. These villas and their fabulous pleasure gardens were both inside and outside the city walls. Rome had twice as many people as Florence, but had greatly shrunk from the million inhabitants of imperial times. Vast tracts of vineyards and gardens now lay within the city walls. Temples and palaces were buried beneath, partially emerging as vine-covered ruins and still yielding sculptures to adorn the villas of the princes of the Church. Throughout Europe the upper classes imitated these gardens with false grottoes, false temples of Eros, false ruins, copies of Roman statues. Here the follies were authentic antiquities. The city was living on top of the ancient empire as on a royal tomb from which antiquarian grave-robbers were continuing to exhume bits of treasure. Peasants still unearthed engraved gem stones with their ploughs; builders found fallen columns of marble when digging foundations. The princely families of Rome furnished popes and cardinals to the Church. The Church's livings and sales of indulgences all over Europe gave these churchmen fortunes to be spent on their collections of classical antiquities, cameos, medals, and pictures of all periods, Renaissance and modern. Their town houses and country villas were treasure houses, attracting artists and gentlemen armed with letters of introduction to study and admire the best art of all periods.

Now Maria was to discover the Grand Tour like all the gentlemen, scholars, and artists who passed through Florence on the way to their ultimate destination – Roma. Little did she suspect that she was also passing through the gates of British society, that she would now belong to that elite coterie of British travellers, largely composed of the ruling classes, who knew Italy: its music, the most popular in Europe; its art – ancient and modern – the supreme reference for the best in taste; its architecture, the inspiration for the neoclassical building so evident in British country houses;

its rural prospects, dreamily idealised in the paintings of Claude and Poussin. By knowing Rome, as well as Florence, she would have made her 'Grand Tour', a unique advantage for social ascension, enabling her to enter a small circle who shared a community of interests, experiences, friends, and language.

Although important for her future, these matters were probably of little concern to her as they passed through the ancient walls to the Piazza del Popolo. They were in Baroque Rome, the city of the Counter-Reformation. From the Egyptian obelisk in the centre of the piazza three streets fanned out, separated by the twin churches of Santa Maria dei Miracoli and Santa Maria in Montesanto. The central street was the Corso, the thoroughfare where aristocratic ladies promenaded in their best carriages, but the English party took the Via Babuino on the left which led straight to the Piazza di Spagna. This was the quarter where the English usually took their lodgings. It was convenient to the Caffe Inglesi, a regular meeting place of English gentlemen, who received letters there and congregated for rum punches, a drink the Italians found disgusting. This quarter rose up the hill of the Trinita dei Monti, providing cooler air, views of the city and better light for painting. As they drove to their lodgings, Maria was no doubt struck by the rather dull appearance of those afoot. Indeed, there were scarcely any women in the streets, for women were not permitted to go out unaccompanied and there must have been twelve times as many men as women in public. Of those, most all appeared to be clergymen, although many were not, being garbed in black for the court or to make economies. At last, they gained their apartments on the third level, always considered the best in Rome, of a small palazzo.

The next day Mrs. Gore may have taken Maria to meet the two foremost English *cicerones*. These men were more than simple travel guides, but had pretensions to be antiquarians, authorities on all the antiquities and ancient customs of Rome. James Byres was an irascible Scot, but a bit more serious than his great rival, Thomas Jenkins. Both conducted the English around Rome. Both became dealers, suspected of 'aging' their antiques with such agents as tobacco juice. It was said that Jenkins had an atelier in the Colosseum where cameos and antique gems were made. Byres was a Jacobite and a Catholic, but Jenkins became so close to one Pope, Clement XIV, that he could arrange private visits and do favours at the Papal Court. Finally, Jenkins became a banker, amassing a great fortune, and receiving royal visitors. He acted as a *de facto* English ambassador in Rome, in the absence of an official envoy, withheld in protest of the Pope's protection of the Stuart Pretenders. By the time Maria came to Rome, Jenkins had become very grand and not too interested in young artists, although he did organise Christmas dinners for them. Mrs. Gore knew both men, but probably preferred one of Mr. Byres' courses. He required his charges to prepare a chapter from Venuti's *Descrizione topografica delle Antichita di Roma* the night before a visit. However, after learning that he asked twenty sequins, which was ten guineas, for a six-week course, Maria would have been obliged to decline. With her copy of a guide book by Guiseppe Vasi, which told travellers how to see all of ancient and modern Rome in eight days, she was able to organise her own tours and she began drawing in earnest. There was so much to see and copy.

It would take several days to understand the different ways of the Romans. The Roman *sequin* was worth about the same as that of Florence, but when they went to look at silk for dresses they must remember that a Roman *braccio* was eleven English inches longer than a Florentine arms length. Papal rule was stricter in some ways than Austrian: no theatre or opera except in the Carnival, but quite liberal toward the violence of the people. Stabbings and murders went unpunished and criminals often received more sympathy than victims. Usually these crimes were only the results of quarrels, so did not represent a real danger. Florence was well-lighted, but Rome had no lights in the streets except the occasional lamp put before the picture of Virgin and Child at corners. It was so dark at night that they could not venture out after sunset. When they did set out in the day, in five minutes they would have two dozen fleas on their stockings, and if they passed through the quarters of the common people their legs would be black with vermin. Instead of killing them, the Romans shook their sheets and shifts every morning out the windows so that the fowls could eat the fleas. Modern Romans had built a system of aqueducts in imitation of the ancient ones, giving an abundance of water, but this did not benefit the cleanliness of the city. When they went to see the richest, most exquisite treasures such as the Sleeping Faun in the Barberini Palace, they were obliged to wade through disgusting filth under the portico. Even the staircases of the princely palaces were used by passers-by as latrines. After a time one ignored the odours, relying heavily on a silver *vinaigrette* held to the nose and averting the eyes, for there were so many objects of beauty to be admired.

The days rushed by like a magic lantern of delicately-tinted pictures: calm Greek faces, tiny incised cameos, Bernini's swirling draperies, vaulted frescoes, powerful muscles in marble, Guido's pining saints, Raphael's golden heads. It was too much to absorb, and then suddenly one day in late November, several months after Maria's arrival, she had to confront a searing emotional pain, the first of her young life. On a cool November day with charcoal burning in the brass pan used to heat her apartment, she received a letter from Florence. Her mother had written to announce that her father had been ill and then the words she could not at first take in — he had died the previous week. There must have been a long moment before she could continue reading and learn of the surprising contents of his will. All of his estate had been left to her brothers and sisters with the exception of 100 scudi for her. Mother was guardian for all his minor children and had effective control of the estate. He then explained in the testament that he did not wish to slight Maria, that he loved her as much as the others, but felt that her talents would enable her to make her way in life. As a matter of justice, he further stated that he had already spent much on her education, even more than her just part of his estate and that she had many advantages that her brothers and sisters did not have. This was all a great shock. Was she to feel flattered and cherished or left as an orphan? It was too late for her to do anything for him now, so she stayed on in Rome to finish her studies as her father would have wished.

Fortunately, Ozias Humphry returned from Florence at this time, where he had been several months on commissions, one a portrait miniature of the Countess of Albany. Humphry must have been an enormous comfort, encouraging her to continue her visits. Through the patronage of King George's brother, the Duke of Gloucester, he had received letters of introduction to two of the finest collections in Rome, those of Cardinal Albani and Prince Borghese. She could have also profited from these introductions. Cardinal Alessandro Albani was a fast friend of the English, serving as an intermediary, obtaining export permits for works of art. After selling hundreds of his pieces of sculpture to Pope Clement XII for the Pope's museum on the Capitoline hill, the Cardinal's villa remained a temple of taste and riches, the finest achievement of any collector of that time.

Johann Winckelmann had been the Cardinal's librarian, an association which added the aura of scholarship to the collection despite rumours of excessive restoration and facile attributions.

Maria had been dazzled by the Grand Duke's palaces, but here in Rome there was a rare and unique luxury. In the Villa Albani, one walked on floors paved with slabs of every sort of fine marble, even lapis lazuli or verd antique. There were columns of *giall antique* and *paglia*, a straw-coloured marble from the Apennines and one from a single piece of alabaster. Pilasters were ornamented with hundreds of antique cameos, one wall with a red marble mask three and a half feet in diameter. The most celebrated room in the villa was that of the Antinous, a bas-relief portraying the Emperor Hadrian's favourite, discovered at the site of the imperial villa near Tivoli. Winckelmann had pronounced it one of the three most perfect specimens of antique sculpture after the Apollo Belvedere and the Laocoon. Cardinal Albani had appropriately made this piece the centre of a large salon on the noble floor, where it was placed over the mantelpiece. He had further enhanced the glory of the setting by asking Mengs to paint the ceiling in fresco with the subject of Apollo and the Muses on Parnassus. This work had become an example of the purity of classical style although some thought it had a somewhat stiff and static quality.

The Villa Borghese, outside the walls of Rome, was just a short walk from the Villa Albani on the Via Salaria. The Borghese family had also amassed a treasure trove, especially rich in sculptures: the Borghese gladiator, the Death of Seneca, the Hermaphrodite, Centaur with Cupid, Bernini's Apollo and Daphne. The Borghese princesses slept in a bedchamber with a chimney-piece carved out of amethyst, and the princes hung Titians over their beds. The door frames were of agate, porphyry, or onyx. Maria was deeply influenced by one particular frieze, an antique *bas relief* of five dancers, tunics gracefully swaying to a frozen rhythm. They were widely known as the 'Borghese dancers', an image which later inspired one of her most successful paintings *The Hours*.

Apart from the strong visual impressions garnered from collections like those of Cardinal Albani and Prince Borghese, the young Miss Hadfield greatly benefited from joining in study with other artists. Most evenings Humphry held what he called an 'academy' in his apartments. A group of artists met to discuss the day's drawings and improve their knowledge by

9. Henry Fuseli *by James Northcote, 1778.*

sharing. If Mrs. Banks, the wife of the sculptor Thomas Banks, accompanied her husband to these meetings, Maria could join them. The Banks had been in Rome some years and were well liked by most all the British artists. The couple showed Maria much kindness, and Mrs. Banks was an amiable companion for her. At these gatherings Maria was able to renew her friendship with Henry Tresham, who had begun to neglect his painting after discovering the advantages of selling antiquities. But the artist who dominated the group by his personality and original-ity was a little Swiss painter, Henry Fuseli, who had been living in London before coming to Rome six years before. Fuseli was a strange and magnetic man. He was then some thirty or forty years old with white hair and trembling hands, the results of a fever. Although most artists still preferred the calm majesty of Raphael, Fuseli was fascinated by Michelangelo and the frescoes of the Sistine Chapel. There was something passionate and wild in Fuseli's drawings. They expressed deep emotions of terror and grief. His subjects were often taken from literature, especially tragic scenes from Shakespeare or Greek plays. Many of the young artists who knew this strange man with his sardonic sense of humour were profoundly influenced by his innovative style. Thomas Banks and Fuseli became great friends. They were fond of comparing figures drawn from five points at random. The Swiss painter made a great impression on Maria, which was not flattering to Fuseli. One of Maria's artist friends from Rome, James Northcote, told William Hazlitt in an interview years later that, '…you could not put Fuseli in a greater passion than by calling Maria Cosway an imitator of his…'

Other artists who contributed to Maria's education were those already prominent in Rome: Pompeo Batoni, the leading portrait painter of tourists, Anton von Maron, the Austrian brother-in-law and student of Raphael Mengs, whom she had met in Florence, and of course Mengs himself. Younger artists were allowed to visit their ateliers with the hope of observing the masters' techniques or colour secrets. These visits had to be conducted with discretion for Batoni and Mengs were great rivals. The former had a natural gift for painting and for making portraits that were very like their subjects, while the latter enjoyed a greater reputation, largely due to the praises of Winckelmann. She also found inspiration from visits to the new museums created by Popes Pius and Clement: the Capitoline and the Pio-Clementine Museum in the Vatican. But most important she faithfully practised drawing and painting every day.

Life in Rome was not all work and study. It was also the scene of a certain social freedom and the development of every young girl's favourite skill – flirtation. One of the English artists that Maria met during that winter in Rome was Mr. Prince Hoare, the young son of the artist William Hoare of the Royal Academy. Mr. Hoare was a charming, rather delicate young man, a bit timid, but with an enchanting, mirthful laugh which made his eyes weep as if he were crying. Soon after they met, he became a frequent caller. Some days both Humphry and Hoare would ask her to go out to see some new wonder. This was an agreeable situation, which she allowed to continue, being careful not to offend either of her friends.

In March of 1777 Maria received surprising news about William Parsons, the music student with whom she used to sing in Florence. Unbeknownst to her he had asked the Hadfields for their daughter's hand in marriage,

10. Self portrait *by Prince Hoare, 1779.*

but Isabella Hadfield had not seen fit to speak of it to Maria. Practising the eternally moving calculation of a mother with daughters to marry, she had decided to wait and see if they received a better proposal. Since Parsons would not have been Maria's choice, her mother's reticence was not too troubling. Now at Parsons' urging Mrs. Hadfield broached the subject by letter, enclosing one from Parsons, but she left her daughter free to decide. She assured her that she was not pushing the marriage:

> I would not have you think I want to get rid of you. On the contrary I shall think it the greatest happiness of my life if you will live with me always.

Isabella also gave Maria a series of admonitions:

> I would have you think before you promise for once done it cannot be undone – and you are young enough – in case I should die I would advise you to marry by all means – as a girl without a parent is liable to many things…you may give him an answer as you think proper – but don't make him hope if you have no intention for that will make you talked of as Angelica was for I don't believe half to be true as they say of her.

Her mother was warning Maria not to be a coquette like Angelica Kauffman. A story went round that Angelica led Nathaniel Dance on for a long time and was even seen in a Roman theatre between Dance and another artist simultaneously encouraging each of her suitors.

There was one piece of advice that Maria did not follow. Her mother asked that she keep Mr. Parson's letter and her own absolutely confidential and not show them to anybody. However, she must have shown them to one person, who eventually ended up with the letters in his possession. At some time after receiving them, she was with Ozias Humphry.

Perhaps it was the day they visited the Palazzo Rospigliosi. As they walked toward the Quirinale Hill, Humphry the older teacher would have described what they were to see: first a loggia decorated by Guido Reni and Paolo Bril to resemble the interior of a garden pergola and then Guido's famous Aurora fresco in another casino in the garden. Was it the enchantment of the painted pergola? What made her break her resolution to follow her mother's counsels? She must have come to rely upon Humphry's friendship in small ways. They conversed in Italian. It had now been almost two years that they had shared their interests in painting and music and ancient history. He had given her instruction in miniature painting. He was older, having the maturity of his thirty-four years. As they gazed upward at the leafy canopy in trompe l'oeil they felt enclosed in this silent aviary where owl, heron, eagle, peacock, falcon, even turkey and rooster paused to rest. This feeling of intimacy, of being sheltered and unseen but for the eyes of the playful putti above each pilaster, must have caused her to say it.

'*Mr. Humphry, may I have a word with you in confidence?*'

'*Of course, Miss Hadfield, you may rely on my discretion.*'

Without preliminaries, she went directly to the matter. '*William Parsons has asked my hand. Indeed, it seems he asked it of my mother over a year ago, but she chose not to inform me of this. He is willing to take me without a fortune and now presses her for an answer. I am to reply directly to him. I have letters to that effect here.*' *Without reflection she swiftly extracted the letters from the openings in her skirt and the embroidered pocket tied around her waist.*

At that moment, two gentlemen entered the loggia to look at the ceiling. Without a word Humphry took her arm and escorted her into the gardens, through the green geometry of boxwood and gravel to another pavilion. They were again alone, this time under Apollo in his chariot following Aurora, the dawn.

'*Ah, Guido must have seen Cardinal Borghese's bas relief of the dancers,*' *Maria said. She had noticed the similarity of the women escorting Apollo's chariot, symbolising the Hours. As on the classical frieze, these graceful figures, hand in hand, moved rhythmically forward, some looking backward over their shoulder.*

'*Are the Hours moving forward too swiftly for me, Mr. Humphry?*'

'*My dear Miss Hadfield, that is not the question. What are your sentiments towards Parsons?*'

'*The truth is I find him rather odious. I do not wish to accept his offer, but perhaps I should. You know that my mother has four young children besides me. She is alone. I shall not even have a portion of my father's estate as he felt he had invested a large sum in my education.*'

Mr. Humphry fell silent as both gazed at the ceiling, contemplating the swirling clouds around the sun god.

At last, clearing his throat, he said, 'Miss Hadfield, or may I say, Mary, had you ever considered that I might be a suitor? Had you ever considered that we could be agreeable companions? I have a nice reputation as a painter of miniatures and am improving as a history painter. You could return with me to London and continue your studies there.'

Had she an intuition that speaking of the letters would provoke a proposal? Perhaps, yet she was probably surprised. She feared that Ozias had never forgotten the disappointment of losing Miss Payne. Also surprised because money and connections were important to him, and she had nothing material to offer. Although she preferred Ozias Humphry to William Parsons, there was another that she preferred to them both. By the time of this interview Prince Hoare's youthful gaiety and wit had turned her head away from Humphry's melancholy charm. It was true that the older man was better looking; Hoare did have a rather large nose. But he was closer to her age, being about twenty, and she felt more comfortable with him. Given the success of his father, he was confident and easy about his circumstances and did not seem to be overly ambitious in his choice of relations.

'Mr. Humphry... . Your offer is unexpected. Are you certain of your sentiments?' Attempting to fill the air with words, she twisted the gauze ruffles of her left sleeve nervously.

'I am extremely fond of you. You are a most charming young lady and one of the most accomplished that I have ever known. You would be a wife of whom any gentleman could be proud.'

'But you, Mr. Humphry, are not any gentleman. Can you sincerely say that you wish to forego a settlement and ally yourself with a family consisting of a widow and five young children?'

His answer was silence and lowered eyes.

'I fear we are not destined to spend our days together, Mr. Humphry. I am honoured by your proposal, but I must refuse it. We are two artists who must have something more, something infinitely stronger and more binding to hold us together and protect us from a precarious existence. I am not speaking of a fortune, although that is one barrier against adversity, but a conviction that we must be together. I do not sense that conviction in you, and I do not feel it in me. It is wiser for both of us to remain friends. That is my dearest wish.'

All sweet reason and wise beyond her years she must have seemed. Everything is simple when one's emotions are not deeply engaged. Her sensibility had not yet been tested.

A month later Humphry left Rome to begin his journey back to London. Maria must have sincerely regretted that, contrary to her wish, they did not remain friends. Indeed, his great animosity toward the man who became her husband would separate them forever.

Prince Hoare and Maria spent a delightful summer visiting the churches of Rome, as well as continuing their study of pictures and statues. There was a new discovery to instruct them. Henry Tresham had made an excavation in the gardens of the Villa Negroni where frescoes, still freshly coloured in blue, tawny yellow, and Roman red, had been unearthed. Tresham thought them so important he had bought them. To be present at the unveiling of new hallmarks of taste, whose influence would soon be felt all over Europe, was a further excitement of the Grand Tour.

When the Pope left Rome to escape the heat, the art students had easier access to the collections of the Vatican. There Maria may have sometimes seen a serious young Frenchman, who railed against the rigidities of French official art, in spite of having won the *prix de Rome,* which entitled him to a stay in the French Academy. Jacques-Louis David knew a few British artists, but the French students kept to themselves, living in their academy in the Palazzo Mancini on the Corso, where they followed a formal program with daily classes and rigorous artistic exercises. David became a good friend of Maria some years later and must have told her how much that Rome had been an overwhelming shock to his art. When he was confronted face to face with so many ancient and modern masters, he realised how feeble his perception of true art had been, glimpsed but faintly through the tradition handed down by French painters.

Every artist discovering Rome felt at first the weight of his previous ignorance and then a tremendous lift of taste and ability. Maria's drawings also improved. Hoare complimented her in a letter to Humphry that summer:

> Miss Hatfield is here still as diligent as usual & has painted some very clever things lately infinitely superior to what she has done before. I am very happy in having the pleasure of seeing her

frequently, the only society to which I aspire in this place. I have had the honor of making almost the whole giro of churches with her according to your list.

As they were always together, Maria must have had the impression that he was fond of her. Others certainly had the impression that she fancied him. Years later their flirtation was remembered by a mutual friend in Florence who wrote to Hoare about the portraits of their circle (Hoare, Maria, William Hadfield, James Northcote) all hanging in the same room of the Accademia di Disegno:

>...closer to you but towards the door is the one of Signorina Maria which continues to make a wonderful effect in that place, certain 'doctors' said that she had been placed close to you because you were her 'darling' from Rome.

11. William Hadfield
by Pietro Labruzzi.

Maria's daily excursions with Prince Hoare gave the summer of 1777 a glow of romanticism. But this idyll was not to last. Her mother and brother William came to Rome. The Gores were returning to England, and William wished to have the same benefits his sister had enjoyed, for he aspired to be an artist as well. Mrs. Hadfield could not take time away from her responsibilities as an innkeeper. When she felt that she had been away long enough, she prevailed upon Maria to accompany her back to Florence. Thus began a difficult and rewarding year. Of course Maria was happy to embrace brother George and her little sisters Charlotte and Elisabetta. They had grown, now being thirteen, eleven, and eight years of age. They were thriving, but then William – or 'Melmo' as everyone called him – caught a terrible fever in Rome, from which he could not seem to recover. It was thought best to send him home, and with Isabella's and Maria's care he finally responded and regained his strength. That winter in Florence was not a happy one for Maria. It was difficult to adjust to her home without Charles' voice and cheerful presence. Above all she missed her friends in Rome. She thought constantly of her excursions with Prince Hoare. Elizabeth Banks reported to Ozias Humphry now in London that Maria was depressed over her separation from Hoare:

> Miss H…is very melancholy and does not pursue her studies. She tells her Mother she shall not unless she returns to Rome. It is the opinion of many that she has left her little heart in the possession of Mr. H…nor do they scruple to say that his appearance occasion'd the refusal of you…her mother says if we were to stay another year in Rome she would let Mary return. I think by that then is no sign of their going to England this spring, but I find Mary's head is slackened, she has no such wish now.

Maria had begun copying a picture in the Pitti Palace by Rubens which portrayed the artist and three scholars. She decided with a new confidence that this picture could be much improved. Her efforts were rewarded beyond any expectation, for it was this picture that convinced the members of the Accademia di Disegno of Florence that she was worthy of being elected one of their members. The Accademia was considered the oldest academy of artists in the world, being the continuation of the Company of St. Luke, a corporation of artisans which went back to the fourteenth century. When reorganised as an Academy of artists in the sixteenth century, the first academicians were Cosimo I di Medici and Michelangelo. The members were Florentines and foreigners, artists and aristocratic *dilletanti*. Very few women had ever been elected to membership, and now at eighteen she was to be one of them. If only her father had been there to see the day, 27th September 1778.

Life seemed more promising than it had during the winter. Maria received some interesting callers. One of the most frequent visitors was a young Florentine named Giovanni Bastianelli. He was related to Pietro Bastianelli, Keeper of the Grand Duke's Gallery. His brown eyes sparkled with malicious wit, and his dark hair, pulled back in an elegant catagon, had the lustrous shine of ebony. Mercurial and quick, he could be bitingly disrespectful, a trait which both shocked and amused.

In November there were more amusements. A young Scot, Joseph Mercer, came to stay at the *locanda* on his Grand Tour. He was immensely good company. Maria and Joseph spent hours together drinking tea and telling each other droll stories about her aunt Molly Pocock or Mr. Caulet's uncle (a relative of Thomas Patch) – the sort of nonsense young people like to chatter about. They sat next to each other at the opera at the Pergola, where she could whisper to Mr. Mercer that the man in the velvet great coat with the decorations of the Order of the Garter, who lay sleeping in his box during the entire performance, was none other than the Pretender, Prince Charles Edward Stuart. For a Scot this must have been a sadder sight than for Maria, who was used to his debilitation.

After dinner Maria sometimes sang for Joseph Mercer or they took long walks together. Once they went as far as the Grand Duke's country house at Poggio Imperiale, about a mile from the Porta Romana. The most amusing promenade was in the Boboli Gardens behind the Grand Duke's palace in the town. They started out with Mrs. Hadfield, but the gardens were so vast, filled with statues, all sorts of walks between green corridors of privet, several pools well stocked with gold and silver fish, and fine prospects of Florence from the higher points that after three or four hours they lost Isabella and could not find her again. When they returned home, Maria received a harsh scolding despite their sincere excuses.

Maria's family did not have the means or the time for dressing and undressing ceremoniously. However, about this time Maria began to take more time with her appearance. Mercer was especially complimentary one day at dinner when she wore a new frock caught up in two places in the back to form a sort of bustle, called a *polonaise*. He even noted in his journal,

> Miss Hatfield looked very pretty today at dinner…dressed in a Nightcap and something of a polonaise Quaker colour and pea

green satin…*bella ragazza* – She is going in a day or two am sorry as well as everybody else was it not for many matters I certainly should go with her to Rome…

William and Maria departed on 13th December without Mr. Mercer. A week before Christmas they were in Rome, installed in the Banks' high apartment on the Piazza Mignatelli with views over Rome, just a short walk from the Trinita de Monti. Renewing her friendship with Prince Hoare and Henry Tresham, they had a jolly dinner on Christmas Eve, where she saw Mr. Hoare's friend, James Northcote. He was a plain and serious young man, earnest, ambitious and known for his sharp tongue. He had been elected a member of the Accademia the same day as she had been on the strength of his reputation as a portrait painter and pupil of Sir Joshua Reynolds. Fuseli, who could be equally biting, said that Northcote looked like a rat that had seen

12. Self-portrait *by James Northcote.*

a cat. Northcote's judgement of Maria was unsentimental although he did admire her and became a lifelong friend. Later he remembered her as too ambitious, an unacceptable trait in a woman:

When she first came to Rome…she was just eighteen years of age, not unhandsome, endowed with considerable talents, and with a form extremely delicate and a pleasing manner of the utmost simplicity. But she was withal, active, ambitious, proud, and restless: she had been the object of adoration of an indulgent father, who unfortunately for her had never checked the growth of her imperfections; she had some small knowledge of painting, the same of music, and about the same of five or six languages, but was very imperfect in all these.

After all the rain of early December, January brought the coldest weather for decades. The ladies were forced to stay inside as the snow was a foot deep in the streets with sheets of ice everywhere. Many died in the freezing nights. Towards the end of the month Joseph Mercer came to Rome. The day after his arrival he came to call late one evening. The next evening he took Maria and Mrs. Banks to the Teatro di Valle where they heard some fine music between the acts of the comedy. Mercer found the Roman theatre very peculiar since women were forbidden to play. He said that he certainly should have taken the men playing the women's parts for women by their voices, dress, and movements, but he was not so easily deceived by the ballet! He behaved strangely during the performance, shifting in his seat as if he were ill at ease, and mumbling his responses to Maria's comments. After the theatre, it was well past midnight, but they ordered the carriage to drive to the Colosseum, to see it looming up in the cold moonlight. There were so many in the carriage that they feared it would turn over at any moment. Mercer confided in his journal the reason for his unease that night:

> Found myself very uncomfortable. Miss Hatfield spoke to me several times & I gave her very awkward answers. I can account for my behaviour in no other manner than that I am certainly in love with her and don't like her to xxxxxx

Two days later Joseph Mercer left Rome for Naples without taking leave of Maria. After all the attentions that he paid her in Florence, he left without calling or sending a word. She was learning that gentlemen were attracted to her, quite interested in enjoying her company, but that she should not interpret this warm interest in a serious way, for they could also suddenly disappear, leaving behind nothing but the scent of insincerity. It was baffling; she had received two offers of marriage recently, giving the expectation of others to come, but life was more complicated than she had first believed. Of course she tried never to reveal the slightest interest in any young man, for it was not expected of young ladies to show their sentiments. Indeed, they were not expected to have them. Passions were considered most unseemly in a lady of delicacy and modesty. Having no strong attachment for the young Scot, she did not mind his absence, although she must have found his behaviour impolite.

These were her last months in Rome. Isabella Hadfield was more and more determined to take her family to London. She had been managing her houses well and continued to have enough lodgers, but must have found it tiring and incompatible with her ambitions for her children. She thought Maria would have more success as an artist and, more importantly, would find a better husband in London. William had no desire to take over the houses in Florence, and Mrs. Hadfield did not wish George, her younger son, to do so either, for she felt it was beneath him. She thought he should have a finer profession. It was decided that he should study architecture.

In April Maria's Grand Tour drew to its close with a splendid voyage to Naples. She went with a large party: Mr. and Mrs. Banks, Mr. Hoare, Mr. Tresham, Mr. Northcote, Mr. Alexander Day, a miniature painter, and others. They most likely left by the *procaccio*, a mode of travel with a Captain in the lead chaise with a passenger, and two passengers in each of the other chaises. The same drivers and mules were used throughout the journey. The fare included beds and one meal a day. The inns were miserable, but they were sure of not being robbed.

On the four-day journey they first passed the still mirrors of Lake Albano and Lake Nemi, reflecting the forested flanks of the Alban hills. Thick groves of oaks, chestnuts, and plane trees, interspersed with the ever-present cypresses and pines, created the same magical prospects which had inspired the landscapes of Claude. Later they suffered the sulphurous stench of the Pontine marshes before confronting flinty, dry mountains, where peasants pulled them up the hills with buffaloes. As they passed along the seacoast, masses of orange and lemon trees mixed their perfume with the salty air. When hours away from Naples, they could see Mount Vesuvius belching smoke, trailing out into a long cloud as far as the eye could see. Toward six in the evening, they entered a labyrinth of narrow, filthy streets full of *lazzaroni* or half-naked beggars, but then emerged into a better quarter on the sea and took apartments near the Mole with a fine view of the harbour.

Naples, twice as populous as Rome, was said to be the third largest city in Europe. Only Paris and London had greater populations. Houses were crowded together down the hills in the centre of its immense curving bay. Those better off lived in white villas on the northern hills of the cape of Posillipo. Their residents had before them the perpetual spectacle of smoking Vesuvius across the bay. In spite of dark and dirty slums, Naples' centre was embellished by the Royal Palace and the largest opera house in Europe, the Teatro San Carlo. The palace was now the seat of King Ferdinand IV, a Spanish Bourbon, and his Austrian wife Maria Carolina, daughter of Empress Maria Theresa. If the travellers went to the opera they might have glimpsed the king, who had a rough, uncultivated appearance. It was said that he only enjoyed the company of *lazzaroni* and footmen, spent all his time in hunting, was completely uneducated, and had no interest whatsoever in affairs of state. It was also said that the Queen had stepped into the vacuum and taken the reins of government into her hands, sharing power with the King's ministers.

If the opera was not in season some of the best music in Naples could be heard at the British Envoy's home. Sir William Hamilton, kept an impressive establishment in the Palazzo Stesso, overlooking the Bay of Naples. The artists' party must have asked for the privilege of viewing Sir William's amazing collection of paintings, antique vases, objects of *virtu*, engraved gems, and curiosities. If so they could have heard the best harpsichord player in Naples, Catherine, Lady Hamilton. This lady, who was only to live a few years more, was the epitome of grace and discretion. Delicate of constitution, she was shy and retiring, but a most exquisite musician. She held weekly concerts in their home, where she played the harpsichord with a skilful light touch and great expression. How opposed she was in every quality from the second Lady Hamilton, whom Maria was to meet more than a decade later.

Sir William was tall and distinguished with an aquiline nose that gave him a profile like those etched on his ancient gem stones. He was a passionate *connoisseur*, avid collector, and man of science. He had become an expert on volcanology, having observed and ascended Vesuvius dozens of times. He proudly showed visitors his four sumptuous folios which he had published to illustrate his collection of Etruscan, Greek, and Roman antiquities. He was eager to share his findings with young artists and apologised that these volumes were too expensive for them to own. More recently he had published a more beautiful work the *Campi Phlegraei or*

Observations on the Volcanoes of the Two Sicilies. Sir William had written the text and supervised the painting of forty lavish illustrations, portraying Vesuvius night and day.

After seeing these stimulating works and hearing Sir William's enthusiastic accounts, nothing would do for Hoare and Tresham until they could see Vesuvius for themselves. They decided immediately to organise a party to see the rumbling mountain as close as possible.

The next day chaises were hired. Mrs. Banks may not have been too keen on this expedition, but Maria must have persuaded her to accompany them. Dressed in travelling habits and their oldest shoes with broad-brimmed Leghorn hats against the sun, they set off with Messrs. Banks, Hoare, and Tresham, arriving after an hour's ride at the seaside village of Portici.

There they hired asses and five ciceroni or guides. They were told that a guide was necessary during the last stages of the ascent. Perched on donkeys, each led by a guide, they could see fine vineyards, then vines burned and submerged by a recent lava flow. The ragged lava, composed of black congealed curls, cut their shoes to pieces, but the beasts were able to pass through without too much slipping. A bit higher, a wide stream of melted rock oozed slowly down the slope, large black blocks of scoriae floating on a glowing red-gold river. This lava stream came from a fissure well below the summit of the cone. Following the burning river up without coming too close, intrepid tourists came to steep terrain impossible for the animals. Continuing on foot, climbers understood the role of the guide. He pushed or pulled them with a sash as they sank halfway to the knees in a mixture of stones, cinders, and loose ashes. It was difficult to keep their shoes on, which filled with ashes at every step. After an hour of this and an immense fatigue they approached the summit, which consisted of a small cone which had formed within a larger one. If the wind was blowing away, taking with it the towering column of smoke, visitors could see billowing fumes within the crater.

Taking some oranges to assuage their burning thirst, they turned to admire the prospect of Naples, its bay and the islands beyond. If one heard rumbling sounds in the bowels of the crater deeper in tone than thunder, the guides would insist that everyone hurry back down the slope. Sliding down took only a quarter of an hour. Hastily remounting the asses, sightseers often had to avoid the red hot stones thrown hundreds of feet into the air. As they shook and slipped on the asses' backs, the riders could look over their shoulders to see the most terrible fireworks any human could see.

The displays of Maria's childhood in Florence, or even over the Castel San Angelo in Rome, were candle flickers in comparison with this supernatural eruption from hell. At night from Naples they could see a fiery plume rising straight up over the dark cone, and a wide burning ribbon running down one side.

13. The Ascent of Vesuvius *by Henry Tresham. Since Tresham was one of the artists in Maria Hadfield's party visiting Naples, it is possible that this drawing portrays the day that she ascended Vesuvius.*

After such excitement more peaceful excursions were a welcome change. From the overwhelming energy of the earth, they passed to those traces of its victims, whose life had been choked out by showers of ash in the space of a beautiful day. Herculaneum and Pompeii were being uncovered. Pompeii was the more interesting as rooms with coloured wall paintings were exposed to the open air after many centuries. These discoveries, like the excavations at Rome, were having a profound influence on taste. Decorators, painters, sculptors, cabinetmakers – all artists were renewing their dedication to classical principles, using the colours, the arabesques, the Greek and Roman deities, to embellish palaces and fine houses all over Europe. The day Maria was tramping over the rocks and fragments of broken marble in Pompeii with Hoare and Northcote, she may not have fully realised that she was seeing at first hand one of the important sources of European taste. Many painters and architects yearned to see what she was seeing, to drink of this inspiration and here she was, a young girl of modest means, receiving a princely education. On that particular day she was probably not appreciating her privilege, being more concerned with a young girl's typical frivolities. Now Prince Hoare, for whom she had secretly pined and wept in Florence, seemed just another friend. With a bit more maturity, she may have realised that she had no business becoming entangled with a Protestant. Perhaps her rational approach had been inspired by the appearance of the young Bastianelli. A much more fitting choice for her, for it was Italian that she felt, spoke and wrote. Italy was her home.

The manner of passing MOUNT CENIS. August 1755.

3

Journey to London

A darkly handsome young man gave Maria his hand. It was one of the few times that Giovanni Bastianelli conformed to a gentleman's rules and gallantly helped her into the chaise. It was 25th June 1779, the day of the Hadfields' departure for London. One month had gone by since her return from Rome with Thomas Banks and his family. The young Bastianelli had called at their house every evening. This regularity in his attentions had stirred the hope that he would not be able to bear her leaving. Maria's desire to remain in Italy was reinforced by his attractive company. As each day passed in June, he paid his visits, he laughed and amused; his wit was irresistible. Yet he never looked into her eyes with a serious, knowing look. It became evident that he was unresponsive to her efforts to be charming. His indifference and her unhappiness at leaving led to a desperate act. One evening she slipped away to Il Conventino and asked the Mother Superior if she could stay. She pleaded that after being pulled away from her earlier vocation by art and other distractions, she now sincerely wished to lead a cloistered life. Her seclusion was a model of brevity. The next morning Isabella Hadfield was jangling the bell at the convent gate with angry energy. She demanded that the sisters return Maria to her care, and the law was on her side. One of Grand Duke Peter Leopold's reforms had been a 1775 decree that no young person could choose a religious vocation before the age of twenty. It was also decreed that no young girl could be put in a convent for the pretext of education before the age of ten. It was clear that the very early influence of convent life left a deep inclination in young girls' minds. Now Maria was almost nineteen, and felt certain of her desire to retreat from the world but she was not old enough to decide her destiny.

At least this version of events was the one Maria wanted to have remembered in the history of her life. Another variation of the story is suggested by Giovanni Bastianelli's gossipy letters to Prince Hoare after Maria's departure from Florence. In one he expresses cynicism over her motives:

> Truly last night was wonderful because my pain was alleviated by a piece of news which made me laugh a lot – this was when a person incapable of telling a lie told me that the Signora Maria entered the convent because of falling in love with a Florentine, whose name is unknown to me, who lives in Florence, and he being so indifferent and not returning this feeling…she, out of rage at not being able to explain herself made up all that beautiful monastic silliness, for the love of God, help me to laugh because with all the pain I have in my knee, from all the laughter I cannot hold the pen in hand. Oh! Oh! Oh! What a lovely thing.

Although he could be repeating rumours concerning someone else, Bastianelli's attitude suggests that the unnamed Florentine loved by Maria was himself. The tone of the correspondence is light and mocking, at times bordering on the vulgar, suggesting that neither the Florentine nor by that time Prince Hoare were particularly enamoured of Miss Hadfield. But there is also a youthful bravado which could be covering up the truth. The letters give evidence that Maria wrote to Bastianelli from Paris and that he had written two rather 'indifferent' letters to her which remained unanswered.

Whatever Maria's sentimental dilemmas may have been, Mrs. Hadfield's resolve to take the family to London had been firm. By the middle of June 1779 she had obtained passports for herself, four children, and a maid. William was not going, as he still wished to study in Rome. She sold the business and furniture to John Megit, a former servant to Lord Maynard. As an innkeeper's wife, she no doubt had some experience with the coach owners and post house keepers in Tuscany. She probably received good terms for the rental of at least two carriages drawn by four horses. Since they were nine or ten with the Banks family, she may have also negotiated with a *vetturino*, someone with a small chaise and one horse which he rides, leaving the chaise to the client. One of the small girls, Charlotte or Lisabetta, could ride with Maria or George in the chaise, so that the horse did not pull more than a heavy man.

Maria left Florence under duress probably strongly resenting her mother's authority. Isabella Hadfield refused to hear talk of a religious vocation, only conceding that if Maria truly did not like England she could always return to Florence.

As they were leaving and Maria took her place in the chaise beside Charlotte, there remained one touching farewell. An old friend approached the carriage in front of the chaise and thrust his arm inside to take Isabella's hand. It was Thomas Patch.

'Well, Mrs. Hadfield, we shall all miss your family. What will this place be without Carlo's? How many years has your house been welcoming the English here? Is it thirty years?'

'Perhaps, just a shade more, Mr. Patch. And I thank you for coming to bid us farewell, but you have Mr. Megit to carry on.'

'Yes, but the merry evenings at Carlo's and your dear husband's hospitality

will live in our memories. As well as your charming family. I wish you much prosperity and good fortune and a safe journey. Godspeed.'

This was too hard for Maria. Patch had been painting in Florence since before she was born. So many childhood memories welled up at the sight of him. She could do nothing but take his hand as their chaise brushed by, and then wave without looking back. Tears kept making spots on her travelling costume well past the Porta San Gallo, even well into the mountains as they took the road for Bologna. Charlotte chattered and amused herself while Maria relived the past. They were on the road, but her mind was still fixed in Florence and she must have been sorrowful until Turin.

Did she take advantage of her opportunity to see the works of the Bolognese painters she had so admired and copied: the Carracci brothers, Guido Reni, Domenichino, and Guercino? Or to stop at Parma to see the magnificent paintings of Antonio Allegri, *Il Corregio* or Francesco Mazzola, *Il Parmigianino*? There was also the amazing wooden theatre in Parma, which had a row of Ionic pillars around the hemicycle instead of boxes and in place of a pit an enormous lead-lined basin where ancient sea fights were enacted on water with ornamental boats and stands of floating candles. She left no record of her impressions of this first voyage across Europe.

Already before Milan they were obliged to enter and leave three states: the Papal Dominions, the Duchies of Modena and Parma, which meant incessant questioning by soldiers and customs officers. Officials would even come to their lodgings to pursue their interrogations. They had to take care not to have purchased anything of value as the customs officers or *rats de cave* as the French called them, did not want them to export products. After five days they crossed the Po by ferry and entered the Duchy of Milan. The vast plains of Lombardy were rich and unending, broken only by rows of elms or mulberry trees on which vines had been trained to grow.

Surely by the time they reached the Alps Maria's taste for travel had re-awakened. She liked entering the small upholstered room of a carriage, settling in for a long journey, filled with new vistas and stimulating conversation. Rattling wheels, dusty winds or muddy ruts, sleepless nights and wretched food, the perils of broken axles or highway thieves, rainwater leaking round the windows – nothing discouraged her. She always loved travelling. At many crises in her life, the journey was her answer. This time was no exception.

The view of the Alps must have lifted her spirits. Their peaks rose in frightening majesty above Turin's flat lands. Maria had travelled in Italy's mountains, but their contours had been worn down, rounded off, eaten away. These mountains were of another dimension, jagged, ice-capped, other-worldly. As they approached by a straight, wide avenue, planted with shade trees on either side to cool the King of Sardinia as he travelled to one of his country houses, the scale of the Alps changed. They became larger and larger until the carriages were in their deep shadow. Most parties stopped in the village of Susa at their base. Here they lodged in order to rise early on the morrow and have a full day for an ascension to the high pass of Mont Cenis.

The travellers would now be in the hands of three *vetturini* to take them to Lyons. They no longer had large carriages, for it was easier to dismantle the small post chaises and carry them through the high passes than a larger vehicle. The Hadfields' knowledge of the language would help them resolve disputes between their *vetturini* and the muleteers with whom they were negotiating the passage of baggage over Mont Cenis. In the morning everything was packed on the mules – trunks, valises, the chaises in pieces, and finally the Hadfields and the Banks.

At the village of Novalesa they were obliged to transfer from the mules to chairs to be carried to the summit by porters. Charlotte and Maria, being small, may have shared one of the wicker armchairs extended in front so that their legs were straight before them. Two long poles on either side permitted the two bearers to carry them up an extremely steep and stony path. Massive but delicately poised boulders and roaring cascades of water accompanied them all the way, and at times the path fell away to an abyss at the side. The poor men had to stop and rest many times. Perhaps youthful insouciance made the girls forget the danger and find the passage exciting, although the adults refused to look, especially behind. Everyone was relieved to arrive at the summit, a surprising plateau of some three miles long where a pure cold lake provided trout for the travellers' dinner. Then they made a bouncing descent in less than an hour, the porters practically running, but always surefooted. It was awful to look down, but soon the lurching and plunging was over and they entered Lanselbourg, where they retrieved baggage and chaises from the mules and resumed a calmer method of travel. During the next four days they would wind their way through the most striking scenes of the Savoy – dark, blue green rivers sliding over white rocks, mountain sides of chestnut, walnut, and fir, craggy escarpments, white villages huddled around church spires. There were also ugly sights. Over half the peasants suffered from grotesque goiters. Many had red, irritated eyes. Wretched, shoeless beggars in rags implored the passing travellers from the side of the road, signs of the difficulty of life in this poor and rugged country.

At Pont Beauvoisin they were in France and after a day's journey of easy travel over a flat, rich cultivated country in Lyon. This was the first time in Maria's life that she entered a truly foreign land. She could speak the language awkwardly, but had difficulty with the accents and dialects of the postillons and innkeepers. In the *diligence* which took them to Paris, they might have practised their French with one of the provincial notables travelling to Paris. The *diligence* was a public carriage, which offered a voyage of five days, lodging and meals included, for fifty-five livres a person. It was more economical than hiring carriages.

After many leagues of boredom, staring through the dust-coated panes of the coach's windows and listening to the droning conversation of the French, their lumbering vehicle began its laborious descent down a steep proclivity, past several windmills into the vast bowl-shaped plain of the Seine. Spread before them was Paris, the largest city Maria had ever seen. At the time London had more inhabitants, some 800,000 to 900,000, but Paris was the largest city on the continent with over 600,000 souls, almost twice the size of Naples and four times larger than Rome.

The *diligence* lurched to a stop before the barriers to the city to be, yet again, harassed and searched by the customs agents. A young man in a redingote approached and abruptly opened the coach door. '*N'avez-vous rien contre les ordres du roi?*'

One of the passengers replied, '*Voyez.*'

Some of the travellers stepped down into a thick, black mud to watch the searching of their baggage.

The 'magnificence' and 'splendour' of Paris were not yet evident. Passers-by navigated the filthy morass with wooden sabots like peasants; children romped naked in kitchen waste and foul-smelling water. One impressive building stood out from the general shabbiness. It was the Hotel Royal des Gobelins. The manufacture of the world's finest tapestries had been placed here on the banks of the River Bièvre, where the road from Italy and Lyon entered the city.

Unfortunately they could not spend their hour of waiting to visit the artists' ateliers or the looms of this wonderful manufactory. Maria could not have imagined, amid the heat and smells, that she would one day receive a sumptuous set of Gobelins tapestries as a gift from the King of France. Such a future was inconceivable as she helped her mother to repack their carelessly rifled belongings after obtaining the necessary cachets in the customs bureau.

At last they slowly rolled down the rue Saint-Marcel. Numerous beggars approached the carriage, only to be driven back by the threats of the coach driver. They penetrated deeper into a city whose extremely tall houses and narrow streets created hot, dark passages. The smell of a turgid stream of mud, kitchen water, and chamber pot waste in the middle of the street was stifling. Out came the *vinaigrettes*. Rome had been more disagreeable in this respect than Florence, but Paris was in another dimension of grime and human effluvia.

Compared with the enlightened administration of Grand Duke Peter Leopold, the powers who regulated Paris were far less vigilant in matters of sanitation. Cemeteries and church crypts spread their infected miasma within the city gates. There were no *abattoirs*. Cattle were being slaughtered in the butcher shops or in the street. As the English party turned into the Rue des Boucheries, their carriage wheels were stained in puddles of blood.

After arriving at the *Bureau de Diligences*, they transferred to several of the black *fiacres*, the common transport of Paris. The drivers of these shabby vehicles were reckless creatures, who took them careening into the Quarter of Saint-Germain, where their lodgings were located. The rue Jacob was in shadows as they halted before the Hotel de York. This house was, like Carlo's, a stopping place for the English where one could find clean lodgings, and a proper bed with curtains. The rooms overlooked the gardens of the Augustins and not the impossible clamour of the street, composed of rattling wheels and vendors hawking mackerels or cabbage, rabbit skins or old hats, most anything one could imagine. How good it felt to slide between stiff, cool linen sheets, close their eyes, and dream of Italy.

Maria was not letting go of the past so easily. Tomorrow she would go to the stationer's and replenish her supply of paper to write an important letter.

Mornings in Paris were not quiet. Between the water carriers who brought two pails of river water to all floors of the house, the milkmaids selling their daily milk, and the waiters bringing coffee in silver pitchers guests were always awakened by bustling activity on the stairs. They were careful not to drink the water of the Seine before adding some vinegar because it caused strangers to have stomach troubles. The hot, black coffee and fresh milk were welcome.

Maria would have been allowed to explore their quarter as long as she was accompanied by at least George and Elisabetta, their servant. The streets were daunting, so full of carriages that it was too dangerous to take a chair, and no dry place to walk in the mud, rendered black by the iron particles of hundreds of wheels. French gentlemen, powdered and impeccable in silk suits and white stockings tiptoed their way through the filth with hardly an accident, protecting their crimped wigs with parasols against the unpredictable ejections from high windows. If spattered by a passing vehicle, they had recourse to the 'decrotteurs', who were on most corners, ready with brushes to clean shoes and stockings. One could enter a salon with an old frayed shirt or worn elbows, but never a spot of mud. One paid a *decrotteur* two sous for the right to cross his little bridge on wheels, delicately placed across the fetid stream in the middle of the pavement. If walkers took the direction of the *quai* to see the river, they were in for a disappointment. It was quite a contrast with the dry and clean promenade by the Arno. After discovering that many Parisians used the quais for a public latrine, while laundresses beat linen and shirts to shreds in the washing sheds nearby, they would renounce this itinerary.

If Maria needed writing paper she was only a few steps away from No. 26 Rue Dauphine, where she could find one of the best stationers of the capital – *Sieur Salmon, Marchand Papetier*. As an artist, she would be especially sensitive to the look and touch and smell of her missives. At Salmon's one could fall into a reverie before the riches of a kind of commerce never seen in smaller cities: gilded paper from Holland, great sheets of English ass skin, velin for maps or drawings, paper from China in sheets of five feet, blue paper for pastels, ruled music paper, black-bordered sheets for mourning, parchments – no corner of the earth was too far for Parisians to beckon their luxuries.

Such letters could not be written on a humble table. Small writing desks in the form of books, fitted out with a candlestick, an ivory knife, an ebony ruler and inkstands of crystal or silver were sufficiently precious for tender redactions. For drawing there was English lead or pastel crayons and for writing there were pots of Chinese ink into which one dipped the finest Dutch feathers or the plumage of crows. One's most intimate thoughts laid on paper were then dried by the sprinkling of brilliant powder, fixing them for years beyond the lifetimes of the correspondents. Secrets or the banalities of everyday life must be sealed with a cachet of Spanish wax. Not only coats of arms or enlaced initials revealed the personality of the writer but the colour and scent of the wax. This evocative seal, whose breaking rendered the recipient either breathless or indifferent, was often red or brilliant black, but could also be bronzed, gilded, pistachio, plum, puce, or crimson and could smell of bergamot, lemon or vanilla, pot pourri or tuberose, lavender, or jasmine. These dazzling refinements must have tempted her greatly. If she had come for writing paper, she must have wished much for a small writing desk, trimmed in red morocco. Its locked drawer was garnished with paper of *peau d'âne*, plumes, wax, envelopes, and the latest novelty, small tablets of portable ink. On a limited budget Maria could only have afforded several sheets of velin letter paper, a small box of portable ink tablets, and a stick of crimson wax.

While in Paris Maria penned a letter to Giovanni Bastianelli, in which she no doubt described the events of her voyage thus far and a pretended satisfaction to be on the road to England. She may have written of her ambition to enter a convent or to be a painter. She asked him to reply to her at Paris, or failing that, at Mr. Water's Tea Warehouse, Old Bond Street, London. A chapter in her life was closing. She had to admit it and look to the possible attractions of a new identity as an English girl.

After a week's journey on wide paved roads to Calais and a Channel crossing, seeing England must have been a novel experience for Maria. This was her country, but it was so strange to her. Healthy fat cattle and sheep grazed before thatched cottages in a green and groomed landscape, neatly outlined with hedgerows, giving an impression of rich tranquillity. Yet the roads were bustling with carriages. There was so much traffic on the road from Dover to London that the grass and trees beside the highway were coated with a whitish dust. One felt immediately the atmosphere of activity and energy in the way people went about their work. The coachmen had a sense of purpose and were always hurrying, at least on the roads. When they approached London the animation and excitement intensified. Swept up with anticipation, the Anglo-Italian children were approaching the largest city in Europe, perhaps the largest in the world, the city thought to be the most modern, the wealthiest, and the freest of any great capital in any kingdom known to civilised man.

Following the Thames by the Dover Road, the little party of weary, dusty travellers approached London from the southeast. Palladian villas in soft green parks guarded the river's banks. Like Rome the city's profile was overpowered by one great dome, that of St. Paul's, on another scale to the numerous church spires piercing the sky. They continued on to Westminster Bridge to avoid the congested City and entered the aristocratic West End. Skirting Saint James Park, they proceeded up Pall Mall, then Piccadilly Street, past the Chelsea Waterworks Reservoir in St. James Park to reach their lodgings with a Mrs. Reilly in Chapel Street, Mayfair. Their street ended in Tiburn Lane, the Western boundary of London, beyond which stretched acres and acres of Hyde Park.

If one wanted to be at the centre of modernity, London was the place to be. The latest inventions were quickly put to use. Raised paved platforms on each side of the roads protected those on foot from mud and dust. The architecture was plain and modern. Many streets were lined with uniform yellowish-brown brick or stucco houses, each with the same number of unadorned windows. Wooden trim and shutters were reduced to avoid the risk of fire. The only decorations came from the shop windows. There was no city like London for shops. Their large bow windows displayed a profusion of conveniences – umbrellas, smokeless stoves, kitchen ranges, alarm clocks which automatically lit candles, oil lamps, Pears soap, Mr. Schweppe's mineral waters, printed cottons, broadcloths – and of most interest to Maria – the prints papering the printsellers' windows with the latest portraits, landscapes, historical events, and political satires.

14. Print Shop in St. Paul's Churchyard.

SPECTATORS at a PRINT SHOP in St PAUL'S CHURCH YARD

After a few months, Mrs. Hadfield found a house, one of the brick boxes in the fashionable Hanover Square estate, 9 George Street. After becoming settled, they began a series of calls with letters of introduction from Lady Penelope Rivers. Her husband, George Pitt, Lord Rivers, had been Envoy Extraordinaire in Turin during Maria's childhood. Poor Lady Rivers, a widow and almost deaf, spent most of her life travelling alone in Italy and France. She had been kind enough to give Maria letters to Sir Joshua Reynolds and Angelica Kauffman.

Sir Joshua, President of the Royal Academy, was showered with commissions, prestige and critical praise. Armed with one of her letters and accompanied by her mother, the young artist ventured to call on the great man in his studio. He had constructed a long gallery behind his house, which led to an octagonal painting room. The gallery cleverly served as a reception room for clients, where they could admire examples of his work and see prints engraved after his paintings. As President of the Academy,

Sir Joshua had by his exceptional politeness and amiability elevated the status of artist to that of gentleman. Since the day Maria first saw his self-portrait in the Grand Duke's Gallery, he had been a model to follow in portraiture. Now she saw the professional way in which he organised his painting, taking four or five sitters a day and demanding one half the price in advance. Laying eyes on this prestigious figure, she saw a short man, whose large nose, thick upper lip, and cleft chin did not match his distinguished reputation. He was obviously addicted to snuff-taking, if one could judge by the tobacco littering his studio floor. Middle-aged, already rather deaf, he did not hear unless one shouted, a demeanour not befitting ladies. In his favour, Sir Joshua had an extremely modest manner, pleasant and good humoured. He willingly agreed to look at some of Maria's work. She showed him her copy of Lord Cowper's *Raphael*, the *'Niccolini' Madonna*, which he examined with great care through silver spectacles, commenting that he judged the original must be worth four to five thousand pounds. A few kind remarks on Maria's painting turned out to be the limit of his assistance. James Northcote, having been Sir Joshua's assistant for several years, had said that the great man would be lavish in praise and patronage if he felt unthreatened by another painter. Perhaps Maria should have been flattered that he never offered to help, but he probably did not feel threatened by a young girl who could not pursue painting in his manner. He no doubt subscribed to his friend Dr. Johnson's view that it was not proper for a lady to do men's portraits: 'Publick practice of any art, and staring in men's faces, is very indelicate in a female.'

Curiously, Angelica Kauffman had overcome such disapproval and earned the respect of Sir Joshua and other painters. It was even said that the Royal Academy president had fallen in love with Miss Kauffman twelve years earlier when she first arrived in London. Angelica and Mary Moser, a flower painter, had been the great exception to the rules against women in the professions. The two had been the only women elected to the Royal Academy as founder members, although their admission was only agreed after the strong insistence of Queen Charlotte. Since their election no other women had been so honoured. Maria was surely impressed with Miss Kauffman during their interview. Mrs. Hadfield had met her in Italy some fifteen years ago, but Maria had been too small to remember. Angelica was now a mature woman, attractive if not beautiful. Her manners were charming and gracious as she showed visitors round her painting and exhibition rooms in her house on Golden Square. She had begun work on allegorical designs for the ceiling of the Academy in Somerset House, representing Invention, Composition, Design, and Colour. This visit certainly kindled Maria's hope that she too could become an artist whilst retaining the position of a lady. Angelica was able to do this in part because she was not considered a portrait painter, but a history painter. Portrait painting was a business, but history painting, considered the noblest form of art, had a superior moral function, requiring a superior education. To excel in this genre one must draw on knowledge of history, literature, scripture, and mythology to portray noble deeds which were models for virtuous conduct. Through pursuit of the highest art, Maria thought she might have a vocation almost as pleasing to the Lord as that of religion. She surely

hoped to become Angelica Kauffman's friend. Unfortunately a year and a half after their meeting Angelica married the Italian painter, Zucchi, and they settled in Rome, where Maria only saw her many years later.

That first winter in London left a memory of damp and gloom forever associated with that city. Maria had not wished to go there and did not wish to be there. The endless dark, wintry days began in a thick fog, blackened by coal smoke, and often ended in a worse haze, choked with

15. Self-portrait *by Angelica Kauffman.*

the smoke from dozens of brick kilns around the city. For her it was a cold and depressing place, whose vaunted liberty was of little use to her, whose riches came at very high prices compared with the easy life they had enjoyed in Italy, whose modern conveniences did not feed the soul and spirit. Some days the only warmth was to be found by staying very close to the fire while painting. Unable to accustom herself to the chemical smell of coal-burning in the house, she would soon fling her brushes down. Adding weight to her melancholy was a constant longing for Italy. Despite a hope that her letters to Giovanni Bastianelli might elicit a response, might give her a reason to return to Florence, his indifferent replies cut off that possibility.

Her family's lack of connections painfully exposed the social aspirations Isabella Hadfield might have had for her children. London was unforgiving to those of modest means living on the fringes of polite society. The respectability of women living alone hung by a slender thread if they had neither wealth nor family behind them. To remedy their precarious finances, Maria attempted to have some commissions for pictures, but this was extremely difficult. Sir Joshua thought that London could only support eight painters. There were already many fine ones – Romney, Gainsborough, Zoffany, Fuseli. Northcote returned from Italy in the spring of 1780, but unable to earn a living in London he was obliged to return to Plymouth. Ozias Humphry had difficulty as well, and sailed to India to try to make his fortune. Even a painter as well-connected as Zoffany, who had enjoyed the patronage of the Queen, could not regain his former position after returning to London and went out to India three or four years later. When Zoffany exhibited his painting of the Tribuna at the Royal Academy Exhibition of 1780, the Royal family did not hide their disappointment. They could not understand why Zoffany had cluttered his picture with all those people they did not know when they were only interested in the room and its works of art. As opinion often followed the Royal lead, the picture did not enjoy the success that Zoffany expected and deserved.

After a winter of struggle the Hadfields experienced a more frightful shock. In early June of 1780 London was shaken by public disorders of an extreme violence. To their horror the riots were fuelled by hatred of Catholics. After Parliament and the King gave some relief to Catholics by passing an act to improve their civil position, one member of Parliament, Lord George Gordon, was radically opposed. He inflamed the rabble in the City with cries of Popery, urging the drunken hordes to violence. The

West End was invaded by vicious mobs, pillaging and burning the houses of Papists, public figures, or prominent Whigs. For seven days the constables were overwhelmed, night skies were lit with fires on all sides. Lord Mansfield's house was sacked and burned, Westminster was almost attacked by an angry crowd. Catholic chapels of foreign ambassadors were burned as well as Newgate Prison. London was given over to anarchy. Fortunately the Hadfields' house escaped unscathed. After over three hundred deaths the King finally acquitted himself honourably and sent in soldiers to put down the riots. Isabella Hadfield immediately took out an insurance policy of £300 with the Royal Exchange to cover their furniture and clothing. This episode gave the measure of the gulf separating Maria's education from English society. She could not freely worship. One could only discreetly visit a private Catholic chapel. However, towards the end of that year, when their circumstances were financially the most desperate, it was a prominent Catholic acquaintance who indirectly became the means to the family's salvation. They had sent a note to Charles Townley, the collector whom they had known well in Florence. Townley had recently completed a splendid townhouse overlooking St. James' Park with rooms specially designed for the finest collection of antiquities in England.

On the day they called on Townley they would have only seen an unpretentious brick house on the outside, hiding a museum of the Grand Tour inside. The large entrance hall and dining room overlooking the garden were sculpture galleries, crammed with treasures. Maria must have felt she was back in Rome. After the Hadfields had seen the ground floor, Townley took them up the curving staircase to his small library, which had no windows, but was well-lit from above. There were heads, statues, bas reliefs covering the walls, urns on the bookcases, a true connoisseur's cabinet. After the tour of his collection Townley introduced Maria to some London artists and antiquarians of his acquaintance.

Two characters stood out from the rest. The first was a French antiquarian, who called himself Baron d'Hancarville. It was he who had published the sumptuous book on Sir William Hamilton's collection. Now Townley was engaging him to help organise and catalogue his collection. This curious person was erudite and did have a deep knowledge of ancient civilisations, but he also had strange theories about influences on the Greeks from India and Persia. Isabella Hadfield may have remembered his financial problems during his residence in Florence some years earlier. He put off his creditors by obtaining the Grand Duke's patronage of a wild scheme to reorganise the fishing industry in Leghorn. Nothing ever came of it, and it was a mystery how he persuaded the Grand Duke that he, an antiquarian, knew anything about fishing. He had now re-emerged in London. As destiny would have it, this eccentric person would be a witness to important events in Maria's life.

The second character was equally eccentric. He was a tiny individual – immaculately coiffed and elegantly dressed in embroidered satin. His waistcoat was a feast of red silk strawberries. The little man strutted and preened, was very lively, and made others laugh. He painted portraits in miniature, like himself. His name was Richard Cosway.

THE MINIATURE MACARONI

Pub.d accord.g to Act Sep.r 24 1772 by MDarly (39) Strand.

4

The Macaroni Painter

Maria Hadfield was amused by the scene in Charles Townley's study. In walked a very small man dressed in the latest fashion. Every detail was studied – the wig with black silk bag holding a pig tail inside, the well-cut grey silk coat, and the extravagant waistcoat profusely embroidered à la française with crimson strawberries. In spite of his high scarlet heels the little man was not as tall as Maria. Personages like this were mockingly called macaronis because their refinements of dress were identified with the Continent, especially Italy. The man before her had been the subject of numerous satires sold in the print shops, calling him the Macaroni Painter. He was a rising artist, and his name was Mr. Richard Cosway.

'Townley,' the little man exclaimed after they were presented, 'you know my weakness for Italian beauties. Where have you been hiding this charming lady?'

'Cosway, I urged you to join me in Italy, but you were too occupied with important business.'

'A business which seems less important now that I see what advantage the Grand Tour can procure. Miss Hadfield, are you residing in London for some time?'

'Mother says we are, although I would have it otherwise. I desire to return to Florence.'

'No, my dear lady. You must not leave our society. I understand that you are superbly accomplished – excelling in painting and in music. The English need these refinements, especially when cultivated, like yours have been, in the seat of civilisation. We need beauty…both ideal beauty of the ancients and of course the natural sort.' He looked at her with a slight smirk. Mr. Townley and the other gentlemen began to laugh as if they knew something she did not.

When Maria Cosway was introduced to Charles Townley's circle, her innocence may have prevented her suspecting that she was in a circle of cultivated and learned men who not only shared various intellectual passions but a pronounced taste of the carnal variety. None was more assiduous in pursuit of the latter than Richard Cosway.

Miss Hadfield would soon understand that this small painter of fashionable miniatures did not have small appetites. He was never improper, for above all Mr. Cosway was a gentleman with exquisite politeness of manner, sometimes deformed into obsequious behaviour with his betters. Beneath his natural vivacity lay a refined sensuality. Animated in conversation, his best qualities were wit and good humour. Maria once told a French friend who asked what Mr. Cosway was like that he was always gay, always laughing. One was rarely bored in his presence. He had overcome a physical deficiency by force of character and an overweening self-confidence.

After Maria met Richard at Mr. Townley's, he came to call at George

Street. He seemed to appreciate the portraits and other pictures in her painting room, offering helpful criticism, proposing lessons in miniature painting. Isabella Hadfield encouraged his visits. All London was talking of Cosway's success with his first portrait of the Prince of Wales. Earlier that year he had pleased His Royal Highness much with the young man's likeness. It was also said that Cosway's portraits were not very *like*, but were flattering enough that his sitters did not mind. Portrait painters lived or starved according to one criterion. Were they fashionable? Was it necessary to be painted by the artist of the year to maintain one's rank in society? It seems to have been the case. It was not that talent had no role in the fickle choices of fashion. An artist must have talent. But he also had to have the art of *pleasing*, as did Sir Joshua. His personality must please. His studio must please. His likenesses must please, corresponding to the desires of the sitter. If an artist pleased a member of the Royal Family, his reputation as a fashionable painter was almost assured. Richard Cosway had a secure success with noble families before he met the Prince of Wales, but he was now at the beginning of a more glorious period in his practice of the arts. He had a nice fortune, to judge by the way he lived, among a growing collection of paintings, sculpture, *objets d'art*, and curiosities.

When Cosway came to call in late 1780, the Hadfields had just received a shocking report from Florence. Charles Edward Stuart's wife had escaped from her husband and sought the protection of a convent. Maria may have attempted to explain the reasons for this scandal to her caller, but Cosway had more pressing matters on his mind. He asked to see Mrs. Hadfield in private. Maria could not have been pleased. She realised that this interview must have her future as the subject. She had entertained the idea of marriage when young men pleased and amused. Now in what was for her a foreign country, she wanted nothing to do with the little painter and still hoped, somehow, to escape – like the Countess of Albany – from an unhappy marriage to a quiet retreat.

After the interview Mrs. Hadfield had a relieved expression on her face. Nothing was said about their conversation until Cosway had left. Then she soothed Maria's curiosity.

'Mary, as you must have divined, Mr. Cosway has asked me for your hand. He is ready to marry you without settlement or fortune. He ardently wishes to do so. There is more, for he is a generous man. Recognising the straitened

circumstances of our family, that you and I are struggling to educate your brothers and sisters, he has gone so far as to make himself responsible for the family. He has proposed to settle on you the sum of £2,800 upon your marriage – a princely sum, dear! You know that he has gained the favour of the Prince of Wales and has outstanding prospects. In spite of these arguments in favour of his proposition, I told him that I must speak to you before giving him a response. You are a minor child and the decision is mine, but I shall not give a favourable reply without your consent. What is your sentiment on the matter?'

*'You know well my sentiments now on marriage and especially this marriage. I do not wish to marry. I do not wish to marry a Protestant. And if I did I would not marry Mr. Cosway. He is a gentleman, a kind and amusing man, but he is also the target of all the vicious wits in London, a ridiculous figure to many. Do you truly wish me to be **MRS.** Cosway, the Miniature Macaroni's wife? Is that your desire?'*

'Mary, I know he may not be the best choice. You deserve better, but you refused Mr. Parsons, who would have been, in my eyes, preferable to Mr. Cosway. We cannot retrieve lost opportunities now.'

*'Nor do I wish to retrieve them. I do **NOT** wish to marry!'*

'Ungrateful child,' Isabella Hadfield's face was now reddening. 'You know what your father sacrificed for your fine education. Your talents and graces are such that one of London's leading artists, a Royal Academician, is willing to do anything to have you, even support your poor family. And you will have none of it? What are we to do if you refuse this offer? Do you not see that we shall soon be in the streets? Take the measure of the consequences of your decision. It is not just your selfish destiny in the balance. 'Tis the lives of your sisters and brothers. If you are truly a Christian, think of them and not your childish dreams of convent life! Now pray over what I have said, and we shall continue our talk tomorrow.'

The ensuing days were filled with more painful interviews, followed by long nights of tears and agonised praying. Maria was a sacrificial offering, who must have no will or desires of her own. If she stood her ground, her mother incessantly repeated her argument about saving the family. Against that, there was no defence. She was right. It was the eldest child's responsibility to sacrifice personal happiness, to restore the security and position of the family honourably. As to the particular attractions of the gentleman in question, she could console herself with the reflection that few young ladies were able to choose a husband according to their inclinations especially in the world of property and rank. She would only be imitating the propertied classes by agreeing to a marriage of reason. A small consolation. Cosway enjoyed the luxury of being terribly fond of a pretty, talented young girl. Indeed, he had fallen in love with her. This became apparent the day around the New Year, when he came to call. This would be their first interview tête à tête. By this time Mrs. Hadfield had eroded all resistance; Maria was prepared to give him the reply he sought.

Nonetheless, she did not expect to see this elegant little man spring from his chair, take her hand, and formally make his demand.

'Maria, would you do me the honour of agreeing to become my wife? 'Tis my profoundest wish.' Sitting down beside her, grasping her hand, he began to whisper. 'My dear Maria, do you have an answer to give me?'

She would have liked to order him away. But what could she do? In several seconds this man would be her betrothed. Eager to legitimise the painful situation, she rushed to the denouement without coquetry.

'Yes, Mr. Cosway, my reply is yes.'

'Maria.' She felt the embroidered buttons of his waistcoat pressing against her as she waited patiently for him to finish his embrace. Soon he returned to his more characteristic behaviour. In rapid conversation he fairly bubbled over making plans for the forthcoming marriage.

The Hadfields' financial worries were no secret nor the reason for Maria's marriage. James Northcote later reminisced:

> She [Maria] came over to England after the death of her father in company with her mother, two brothers, and two sisters, filled with the highest expectations of being the wonder of the nation like another Angelica Kauffman. But alas! These expectations failed; the money which the father had gained in Florence was quickly spent in England, and the family were soon in some degree of distress. This change, to her so very great, she bore with admirable fortitude and magnanimity, but in the end, after having refused better offers in her better days, she from necessity married Cosway, the miniature painter, who at that time adored her, though she always despised him.

Northcote exaggerates a bit. Maria did not always despise Richard and was reasonably happy with him at first.

⊹══•══⊹

The marriage ceremony was no doubt hastily arranged. It was to be solemnised in private before the family and a very few friends. Mrs. Hadfield and Cosway wished to see the union consummated before the bride found the energy to oppose their scheme or before she reached the age of majority in six months time, after which her mother's permission was no longer essential. The date of the ceremony was 18th January 1781.

On the morning of her wedding, Maria was awakened early when Lisabetta her maid came in with a silver pitcher of steaming tea.

'Signorina, signorina…we must begin dressing now…the hairdresser comes at eleven, then Mr. Cosway, the Banks, and Mr. Townley.'

'Lisabetta, do not remind me. I have been here in the dark, imagining we were in Firenze, that today was only a bad dream. Now the dream continues, I am in London and it is the day of my marriage. At least the ceremony will be brief, briefer than the ceremony of dressing.' She glanced at the accoutrements of her ordeal – the gown of pale lilac and silver brocade hanging on pegs in the recess of the wardrobe, its matching petticoat, and the most sumptuous of all, a heavy grey satin pelisse, with cowl lined in ecru silk and bordered with marten fur.

'But, Signorina, you are so fortunate to have a rich husband. No worries for you. I shall fetch the hot water for your bath while you take your tea.'

The ritual began. Sitting on linen sheets, lining a copper tub, Maria was slowly scrubbed, dried carefully and helped to don a long cotton chemise which served as an undergarment. While still able to move freely, she pulled on embroidered silk stockings, tying the tops down with pink silk garters, whose ends were ribbons, embroidered with the inscription: 'La vertu m'attache.' Marital chains, she must have thought, while defiantly and firmly tying the knots. Slipping on mauve satin shoes, embroidered with grey and silver gilt threads in arabesques around small satin rosettes, she had now done all that was possible without assistance. Lisabetta helped her tie the false rump of cork around the waist, and then the two large pockets suspended on each hip, hidden from view but convenient for handkerchiefs reached through openings in the side of her gown. The pockets were delicately embroidered with birds and flowers, souvenirs of Il Conventino.

1. Thomas Patch, A Punch Party. Painted in 1760, the year of Maria Hadfield's birth, this caricature portrays a group of Englishmen dining at Carlo's inn in Florence. Maria's father, Charles, holds the punch bowl aloft. Her godfather Sir Brook Bridges is sitting in the centre, facing right. Earl Cowper in profile is standing at the far left.

2. *Johann Zoffany painted the growing family of the Grand Duke of Tuscany, Peter Leopold, during his stay in Florence between 1772-1778.*

3. *One of Thomas Patch's vedute of Florence. The Hadfields' house can be seen on the left opposite the Palazzo Corsini on the right bank of the Arno.*

4. Zoffany's Tribuna of the Uffizzi, painted to show Queen Charlotte the many treasures assembled there. She did not appreciate the portraits of people she didn't know added to the picture. On far left stands Earl Cowper. The head of the artist Zoffany is fourth from the left. Thomas Patch has his right hand on Titian's 'Venus of Urbino' in the centre. Standing to his left is Sir Horace Mann with sword and the Order of the Bath.

5. A Distant View of Florence *by Thomas Patch. Il Conventino, the convent where Maria Hadfield was educated, is probably the white building in the angle of the city walls.*

6. Zoffany's group portrait of George, Earl Cowper and the Gore family, *painted in Florence c. 1775. Maria Hadfield went to Rome with Mrs. Gore and became a friend of Hannah, the Gore's youngest daughter, who married Lord Cowper in 1775.*

7. *(right)* Charles Townley and friends *in the Townley Gallery by Zoffany. 1781. This portrait of Townley seated at right in the midst of a part of his collection suggests his obsession with antiquities. The man seated in the centre is Pierre-Francois d'Hancarville, the antiquarian who helped Townley catalogue his collection and became the Cosways' friend. The other two gentlemen are Thomas Astle, another collector, standing right, and Charles Greville, Emma Hart's lover, who presented her to his uncle, Sir William Hamilton.*

8. *(below)* Charles Townley's Dining Room *by William Chambers. The ground floor of Townley's Park Street house was the setting for the display of his collection, often visited by connoisseurs and visitors to London.*

9. Dicky Causeway, *a satirical caricature inspired by Cosway's romantic self-portrait* Rdus Cosway armiger, R.A., *both appearing in 1786.*

10. Mariano Bovi after Richard Cosway, *Rdus Cosway armiger, R.A., 1786.*

11. Self-portrait in miniature, *Richard Cosway, 1790.*

12. What is this my son Tom? *Caricature illustrating the difference between the typical Englishman and the exaggerated elegance of a 'macaroni', 1774.*

13. The Macaroni Painter or Billy Dimple sitting for his picture, *1772. The Macaroni Painter is thought to be Richard Cosway.*

The MACARONI PAINTER, or BILLY DIMPLE sitting for his PICTURE.

14. Hanover Square. *In the centre background rises the spire of St. George's Church in St. George's Street, where the Cosways were married.*

15. The Eidophusikon, *1781-1784, invented by Philip James de Loutherbourg, one of the earliest forms of 'moving pictures'.*

As Lisabetta tugged and struggled with the laces of taffeta stays, Maria could feel her back straightening, waist tightening, breasts rising. Her body had found its familiar position for public presentation.

'There, Signorina Maria, we are ready for the hairdresser,' Lisabetta announced with a pat of satisfaction. She threw a loose, ruffled deshabille around her lady's shoulders. They moved to the dressing table for the second phase of the ordeal. During the hour's crimping, curling, and combing, her naturally dark blond locks rose higher and higher, mounted on a small hidden cushion and anchored behind with four vertical curls above three smaller ones at the nape of the neck. The young French hairdresser, his apron and breeches whitened with powder, began to apply flour to his creation.

'No, no, no, Monsieur, no powder please. I prefer the natural colour.'

'But Mademoiselle, this is your marriage day!'

'What better day than to present oneself naturally and simply! Please, no powder.'

Disapprovingly, he proceeded to the final decoration of plumes, ribbons, and a string of pearls which Mr. Cosway had given her, all draped and pinned artfully in and around her towering locks.

As the hairdresser retired, a bustle at the door preceded the noisy entrance of her little sisters Charlotte and Lisabetta, followed by their mother, anxious to inspect the results of the morning's work.

'Oh, Mary, Mary,' Charlotte exclaimed. 'Hurry, please put on your gown so we may admire you.'

'Yes, Maria, let us see you, please. Your hair is so high. You shall be much taller than Mr. Cosway, I fear.' Lisabetta, covered her mouth with her hand at this audacity.

'Quiet, children, No more silly remarks about Mr. Cosway, ever again. Now, Mary, let us see you. Yes, the coiffure is becoming, but Mr. Cosway may take exception that you have no powder. Well, let's get you into your gown.'

Lisabetta lifted the lilac taffeta petticoat from its pegs and helped her mistress step into it without treading on the costly band of lilac and silver brocade which bordered the hem. Maria slipped her arms in to assume its weight and she fastened it in the front of the bodice, leaving the skirt open to show the petticoat. Mrs. Hadfield busied herself arranging the folds behind over the false rump, and spreading out the train. As Lisabetta pinned lace ruffles inside the bottom of each sleeve, Isabel delivered her obligatory maternal advice.

'Now, dear Mary…'

'Mother, you know my name is Maria and Mr. Cosway prefers it too.'

'If you prefer, but you've always been Mary to me. In any case, you know that you are entering a new life, and must not look back to the old one. We must accept that this change is God's plan. It will be easier for you if you do. If you obey Mr. Cosway in everything, you will find marriage more pleasant. He is, I think, a kind man at heart, despite his worldly manners, and he seems genuinely fond of you.'

'Yes, Mother,' she assented, knowing that her true sentiments weighed little in the balance against £2,800 sterling.

'Maria, you are such a fair bride. No one could be more fortunate than Mr. Cosway.' Charlotte tried to cheer her.

'Yes, dear sister,' Lisabetta added, 'please be content with this day.'

'Yes, why not,' the bride responded, 'why not be content?'

At that moment the arrival of the Banks, Mr. Townley, and Mr. Cosway was announced by brother George. Maria gathered up gloves and fur-trimmed cloak, prepared to face this turning point, when her mother remembered what was missing.

'Mary, you have forgotten Mr. Cosway's gift.'

'So I have. We have narrowly avoided the certain disaster were I to appear without it.' Lisabetta fetched the precious pieces of jewellery: an amethyst and pearl cross on a string of large pearls, a pair of earrings of large amethysts and pearls. Two bracelets and a brooch of amethysts completed the parure. 'It does not go well with this brocade, but that's not to be helped, is it?'

As they descended the staircase, Mr. Cosway came out of the drawing room and stopped, apparently in admiration.

'My pretty…pretty child, come, let me see how fair you are.' He stretched out a soft hand to grasp Maria's fingers.

It was difficult not to withdraw her hand when she looked into a whitened face, whose strangely disembodied rouged lips spoke to her. Was there a trace of surprise flickering on her countenance when she realised that the groom was more painted and powdered than his bride. His bag wig was high and white, large curls at the side. He held the required small black three-cornered hat under his arm. A sword gleamed at his side, its length making walking hazardous in spite of the extra height of his scarlet shoes. His dove-coloured, silver-embroidered court suit was as rich as Maria's gown.

'*What a fine lady you will be, my Maria. Such natural beauty and innocence needs but the slightest refinements to render native charm irresistible. I can give you what you need – instruction in the ways of the world – so that your considerable gifts will be properly appreciated by others. 'Tis not enough to have talents. One must know when and how to exercise them…Townley, is not my bride splendid?*' He turned to see his friend emerging from the drawing room. '*You know how I have always fancied Italian women.*'

'*Yes, indeed, Cosway. A treasure I admired in Italy, but was not wise enough to collect.*'

'*Mr. Townley, Father told me that you collected every fine object that you could get your hands on if the price was right. Surely a collector's passion has everything to do with opportunity. If an opportunity was missed, I suppose the price was not right,*' Maria now dared to say.

Happily Mr. Townley was not offended; he even smiled slyly. As for Cosway, he would let nothing spoil his wedding day.

'*Come, come, Maria, we should be off. The Banks are here. Ah, Mrs. Hadfield, my dear lady. I owe you everything.*' He kissed her hand and patted the heads of Charlotte and Lisabetta.

The small party had only to cross the street from their house in Great George Street to St. George's Church, Hanover Square, the scene of many fashionable marriages. Catholic marriages being forbidden, Maria had the added sorrow of bowing to the sovereignty of the Church of England. She must have found the ceremony itself brief and the church austere – stone floor, high oak pews, galleries on three sides – the painting over the altar of the Last Supper in the manner of Poussin. Did her artist's eyes study the painting and see the figure of Judas stealing away from the disciples at the Passover table? She was doing the same that day, betraying her faith. Thomas Banks and Isabella Hadfield were the official witnesses, signing the parish register after Maria and Richard Cosway. It was extremely easy and quick to change one's life irrevocably.

Maria's older and worldly wise husband must have easily controlled her at first. He held strong opinions, insisting on his way. He now held rights over the little property she might have had. What was more unsettling, he had the right to make all decisions concerning her life, her art, and her person. Her apprehensions over the latter rights soon dissipated. What did it matter if this stranger wanted to take his pleasure like a nervous little dog, often not waiting for her to undress, just pulling up her skirts when it suited.

Despite her early awe or distaste, they soon settled into an easy relation that was at times a happy one. In the beginning of their marriage Richard wished to please his young wife in all things. He was kind and generous, and could be agreeable. The side of his character that was most pleasing was the good humour that he maintained in most circumstances. He was cheerful, always seeing the amusing side of life's daily events. He loved to recount anecdotes and had his ear cocked for gossip. Sometimes he extravagantly exaggerated, but everyone knew that was part of his charm. His eccentricities made life interesting; his constant banter kept her spirits up.

His rooms, where the couple first lived, were at No. 4 Berkeley Street, right off Piccadilly. Cosway complained about their dull view. The windows faced the side wall of Devonshire House, where the Duke and Duchess were the centre of a fast, brilliant and politically important set. Nonetheless the Cosways had a fashionable address, where their house was often the meeting place of the painter's aristocratic and wealthy sitters. The view might have been dull, but upon entering the house one discovered a marvellous world, fairylike, exotic, bizarre. Their house was not only a home and work room, but a collector's cabinet. Maria had not seen such a profusion of art and curiosities piled up in disorder since she visited the Grand Duke's galleries. Cosway was not only a collector of pictures, drawings, and books as most artists were, but of every imaginable class of object – armour, porcelain, sculpture, furniture, antique bronzes, marbles, terra cottas, curiosities like stuffed mummies or birds, old bones and skeletons, screens, tapestries, Persian carpets – anything which he fancied to be either strange or beautiful. Their apartments in Berkeley Street had nothing of the magical quality of later residences, as their smaller dimensions did not lend themselves to a magnificent display and Cosway had not yet acquired all that he would when at the apex of fame and fortune. Yet, one was immediately struck by his singular taste and originality. He had specially prepared their home like a scene from a theatre to welcome Maria, having gone to live with his friend Cipriani, a fellow Academician, while the painters and plasterers finished their work according to his designs.

Richard Cosway's life as an artist could be read in the pictures around them. If Maria wished to know more of his past, she had only to point to a mysterious portrait or print and wait for her voluble master to begin a monologue.

The portrait of that kindly, old-fashioned man?

'Ah, my beloved drawing master, Mr. Shipley, with whom I lived for five years from the age of twelve. This quiet and generous gentleman took in the untried boy from Devon and put me to drawing casts of classical sculptures. I might add that each year of study in his institution, the Society of Arts, I won a prize for drawing, twice the first premium.'

The erotic Leda and the Swan on a gold snuff box?

'Not for you, my girl. I painted many of these bibelots for London jewellers after leaving Mr. Shipley. One had to get on in life and portrait commissions were not frequent in the beginning.'

The mezzotint of Zoffany's painting of the members of the Royal Academy?

'There we all are in a life class, all except Miss Moser and Miss Angelica of course. No ladies admitted, but you can see their portraits on the wall. You know, my dear, I was the fourth member elected to the Academy after the original founders in 1768. My election took place only two years after entering the Academy school. Zoffany, the scoundrel, could not resist making a criticism of my penchant for the fair sex by posing my cane on a cast of Venus.'

The satirical prints of 'The Miniature Macaroni' and 'The Macaroni Painter'?

'Worthless daubers' mockeries. They think to ridicule me with this rubbish, but it only shows the ignorance and cupidity of the print sellers. These people engaged in trade have no understanding of the noble calling of an artist, nor do they care to have it. They feed the public's suspicion of people of taste, especially those who, like you, have had the privilege of seeing Italy. As the rabble only think of their stomachs, going to Italy means eating macaroni. You must learn to defend yourself, my dear Maria. As my wife you must not let the mob's attacks ruffle your sweet disposition. I have learned this: their buffoonery does me no harm; in fact the notoriety has helped spread my name in the profession.'

This was said carelessly and bravely. Maria must have sensed that despite Mr. Cosway's serene self-confidence in all circumstances, he was inwardly

16. Members of the Royal Academy c. 1771–1772. Richard Cosway is at the far right with his cane placed on a torso of Venus, a reflection of his provocative personality. Reynolds is in the centre with a hearing trumpet. Angelica Kauffman and Mary Moser, the only female members, not being admitted to a life class, are given places as portraits on the wall.

wounded when reminded of his small stature, or worse, when his visage was likened to that of an ape. His self-portraits had no simian traits, nor did portraits of him by others. Cosway's extreme refinement gave no such impression. Perhaps it stemmed from the fact that before their marriage Richard kept a baboon as a domestic animal until the beast bit a great piece of his master's leg and had to be put down. Or perhaps from a well-known incident at a Royal Academy meeting in the Turks Head Tavern, when two of the rougher-mannered Academicians, Francis Hayman and Richard Wilson, insulted their more elegant colleague rudely. When Cosway arrived late to a crowded room, Hayman taunted him, asking if the little monkey could find no place to sit. The coarse and slovenly Wilson added some well-chosen jibes in the same vein. With his usual aplomb and good humour Cosway turned aside the jest and conciliated his attackers. One account says he replied, 'It would not be the first time the monkey rode the bear.' Unfortunately, the 'monkey' accompanied them throughout Cosway's life. Once the public journals have found an amusing caricature for a personality, as far from life as it may be, the poor individual is doomed to carry this ridiculous baggage as long as he is the subject of public discourse.

'And why so many Rubens' paintings, dozens of Rubens' drawings, hundreds of his prints?'

'To me Rubens is the master, and perhaps Michelangelo. I do indeed imagine myself a century ago in Flanders – you know my family emigrated from Flanders to Devon, being important in the wool trade – I imagine working in the time of Rubens, Van Dyck. That was a heroic age. Come into my painting room, child.'

As they went into his studio, Richard opened a large trunk in the corner. He began to pull out all sorts of fancy dress, gowns of rich stuffs, large plumed hats, men's doublets. None of these costumes was modern; all were in the fashions of a hundred years before.

'Pray, Maria, choose one of these gowns…this one should suit. I should like to paint you in this.' He held up a Renaissance costume with a stiff, high collar and quilted sleeves. 'Here is charming hat to go with it. You see, similar to the one worn by the lady in Rubens' Le chapeau de Paille.' He held up a large-brimmed black hat with sweeping black and white feathers.

'Yes, shall I try the hat. Am I handsome in it? I would like to paint myself. Do you think I might be able to do it?'

'Why not, my girl? You may after I have done with mine. Then I propose to do a portrait of both of us together in our ancient costumes, as artists of the last

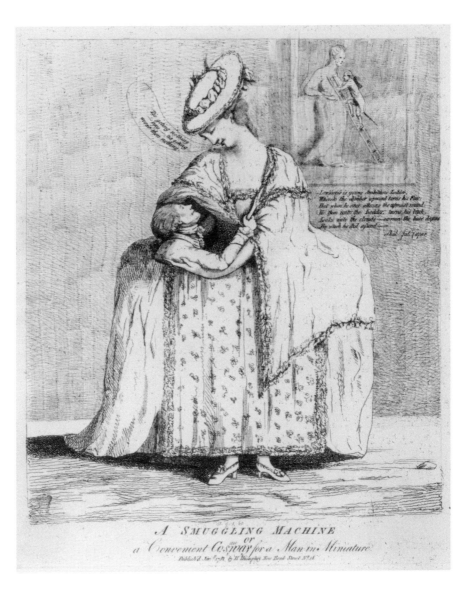

17. A Smuggling Machine or a Convenient Cosauway
for a Man in Miniature.

century, the Golden Age of Art. That was an age of taste, not like today with the pandering to the masses and all these manufactures. You have seen in Italy the remnants of beauty. In this country of vulgar tradesmen and uncultivated country squires it is difficult to make John Bull understand what refinement is. To him the least mark of taste becomes the occasion for crude jokes or public satires of macaronis. 'Tis surprising that one of the English artists most resistant to foreign influence...I am speaking of Mr. Hogarth...strove to understand the essence of ideal beauty. I believe him to be right in his analysis that the sinuous, curving line

18. Maria Cosway *by Richard Cosway after Rubens's* Le chapeau de paille.

gives motion and life, and is therefore the most beautiful. From this the great interest of a woman's body... from the standpoint of art of course.' He began to slide his hands down the sides of his wife's waist and hips, while she pulled more rich stuffs out of the trunk.

"Mr. Cosway, we can have a masquerade every day! What elegant dress for our painting!"

'You must address me as Richard when we are alone. No more of this "Mr. Cosway". And you are right. Every day I am going to dress you up and paint my Maria with her ravishing S curves.'

He pressed her roughly against him, but she turned and flung a cloak of Genoa velvet around his shoulders with a laugh.

'Richard, we must get on with the painting. You have many coming to sit for you this afternoon.'

'No matter, you know that I work swiftly as Hermes. I can do twelve or more sitters in a day and do a miniature of some merit in an hour, if not wholly finished.'

L'ALLEGRO.

19. Maria Cosway in seventeenth-century dress.

'*You are quick in all respects. Let us see if you can capture a likeness of me in an hour. I lay down the gauntlet.*'

'*So, I shall, my lady, so I shall.*'

And so their days passed, both of them dedicated to taste and elegance in the slightest details of daily existence. Cosway never tired of painting Maria in all types of fancy dress, posing in scenes of antiquarian splendour, pretending they were living in more heroic eras. He was proud to reveal the secrets of his painting room: how he pressed ivory tablets between papers and heated them with an iron to remove grease, how he mixed his palette, especially the Antwerp blue, prepared for him by Newman's in Soho, how he applied masses of blue and white, then took them away with a squirrel's hair brush in rapid, deft strokes. How he often viewed his sitter through an oval cut out of paper the same size as the finished miniature. How he drew so rapidly but precisely, saying that many painters tried to cover up their inadequate limning with paint. He was accused of flattering his sitters; many had longer necks and larger eyes than in life, but he could do a good likeness. He was obliged to please and he did please. For him it was not only flattery of his subject, but homage to his ideal. The sinuous line which he advocated was one of the keys to the grace, elegance, and lightness of his portraits.

During the first months of their marriage, Maria remained somewhat cloistered as her poor English and limited understanding of the ways of London society impaired her ability to be a proper hostess. Cosway preferred to keep her for himself, and this time together did permit them to become better acquainted. As Maria learned more about the true talent that lay behind his professional success, her initial fears were transformed into respect. She was rarely seen in society that first winter but they surely went to see the invention of one of Cosway's colleagues and dearest friends, Philip Jacques de Loutherbourg.

A native of Strasbourg, Mr. de Loutherbourg had settled in London and married one of the prettiest women in England, Lucy Paget. Endowed with

PAINTING

20. Miniature painter and sitter.

extraordinary imagination, this friend of the Cosways was one of the most original of his circle. Terribly ingenious, he designed scenery for the theatre. That winter, all London was talking of the mysterious illuminations he had created for a Christmas fête at William Beckford's gothic country house, Fonthill. There had been labyrinthic decorations and an exotic masquerade of Oriental and Egyptian imagery lasting three days and nights.

Then Loutherbourg advertised his latest invention in the newspapers. He called it the Eidophusikon, a miniature theatre, which imitated natural phenomena with moving pictures. The Cosways surely hastened to the Loutherbourgs' house in Lisle Street to see one of the performances.

A fine large room had been arranged for the performances, much more comfortable than a theatre, and decorated with richly painted and gilded flowers and musical instruments. At one end of the room a small stage of about six to eight feet wide had been created, much like that for marionettes. As the Cosways entered, heads must have turned to see the striking new couple. Half the London art world was present. Taking their seats on the small gilt chairs, Maria and Richard could see Thomas Gainsborough. As the panorama of paintings moved to portray a setting sun, then a rising moon, hidden by a passing cloud, followed by effects of rain, wind, thunder and lightning, Gainsborough interjected enthusiastic comments like 'By Jove!' and 'Capital!' After the storm the gradual coming of dawn was portrayed by rosy clouds, beautiful gradations of light and another sunrise. The audience then saw the most amazing rural employments — a ploughman, milkmaid, a country wagon, and hay-making — while birds and hunting horns sounded. After the performance, Gainsborough turned and exclaimed, 'Never saw anything like it. This is my fourth performance! How does he get those natural effects? Well, Cosway, are you going to introduce me to your fair bride?'

'You have done so yourself, my friend. Maria, this is my esteemed fellow member of the Academy, of whom you have heard so many fine compliments, Mr. Gainsborough.'

'My sincere congratulations, my dear lady,' Mr. Gainsborough bowed graciously.

'I thank you, Mr. Gainsborough, 'tis...'

Before she could finish her phrase, another Academician, Cipriani, came to greet them, and then a third, and then several others. They were soon surrounded by a circle as curious to see Richard Cosway's bride as the Eidophusikon. The slightly incredulous expression on some faces could be read as evidence that they were confronted with an incongruous pair. At that moment Cosway took his wife's arm, 'Come away, Maria, there is work to be done. We must depart.'

5

Mrs. Cosway

'I kept very retired for a twelve month until I became acquainted with the society I should form.' So Maria Cosway described the first year of her marriage. Surely the new Mrs. Cosway must have ventured out to the Royal Academy Exhibition in the spring of 1781, where she exhibited three paintings. Richard Cosway's artistic and professional life revolved around the Academy, established by the King as an institution to cultivate and improve the Arts of Painting, Sculpture and Architecture. Sir Joshua Reynolds, the Academy's president, aimed to elevate the arts from the status of craft or trade to the more noble function of forming taste and forming it to appreciate history paintings, which were rarely commissioned. A proper school was necessary. The 1781 exhibition was held in handsome new rooms, specially built for the Academy, the Royal Society and other public offices. Sir William Chambers, R.A., the architect of this new Somerset House, had lavished taste, talent, and money to create a monument to beauty. Maria had no doubt visited the 1780 Exhibition, but it was more amusing to participate in this great annual event as an Academician's wife and, for the first time, as an exhibitor.

The silk ruffles of her gown were trod upon as she lifted her skirts to ascend the elegant curving staircase amid a crush of visitors. The stairs were extremely steep, obliging ladies to expose their ankles to the gentlemen below, prompting

21. Rowlandson's The Exhibition Stare-Case.

one journalist to observe that some visitors to the exhibition came to view the heads while 'others remain at the bottom of the stairs to contemplate the legs'. It was always necessary to rest on the landing and take time to admire the screen of Corinthian columns leading to the Antechamber of the Great Hall where the pictures were displayed.

As they were about to enter the magnificent top-lit gallery, Richard Cosway paused and pointed to a Greek inscription above the door with his cane.

'Do you know the importance of this inscription, Maria?'

'I was told that it means "Let no stranger to the Muses enter".'

'Perhaps that is the exact transla-

tion. I think it better expressed by "Let none but Men of Taste presume to enter here." This states succinctly the purpose of the Academy, although you shall soon see, my dear, that this rule of admission is more honoured in the breach,' he said with a knowing look.

As they entered the crowd, noisily tramping over a sawdust-covered floor, Richard grumbled, 'Where has the Hanging Committee hidden our pictures?'

There was always keen competition among the painters to have their work hung on or just below the 'line' which ran around the gallery on a level with the top of the door frame. Otherwise the pictures were so high that they were hardly noticed and the details impossible to see. Miniatures were also poorly displayed. Grouped around the fireplace, the small portraits were hidden by too many viewers with their noses up against the wall. For this reason, Cosway preferred to exhibit his larger paintings. That year he was showing two: Sigismunda, *from Boccacio's* Decameron *and a full length portrait of the Duchess of Cumberland, the pretty wife of the King's brother. The Cumberlands' marriage as well as the secret marriage of the King's other brother, the Duke of Gloucester, had prompted the Royal Marriage Act, requiring Parliament and the King to give permission for any marriage of a Royal family member under the age of twenty-five. The Cosways made their way over to view the portrait and also to listen to the observations of a small group gathered before it. As they approached, Maria recognised a familiar voice, a voice she had known in Italy. It was Prince Hoare.*

'Ah, 'tis Mrs. Cosway, I believe. My sincerest compliments and congratulations.' Her old friend bowed. 'I have been charged by your many amiable friends in Italy to convey their congratulations: Mr. Plura, Mr. Bastianelli, and others.'

'My thanks, Mr. Hoare, I believe you have been presented to my husband, Mr. Cosway?' She hid her embarrassment with a formal tone of address.

'Sir,' he bowed to Mr. Cosway, 'I have had the honour to be introduced by my father, your fellow Academy member.'

'Yes, yes, young man, how is your esteemed father?'

'Quite well, sir. Thank you for inquiring. I must also compliment you on your marriage. Mrs. Cosway is a lady of many accomplishments. I found her paintings exhibited here today rich in colour and significance.'

'Pray tell me your meaning.'

'If we examine that one.' Mr. Hoare led them to Maria's picture of Rinaldo, high over the line. 'Rinaldo, a crusader from Tasso's Jerusalem Delivered, *is tempted by the enchantress Armida, whom he loves and abandons to her great sorrow. The dramatic power comes from an impossible love, yet Mrs. Cosway has not chosen to portray the Enchantress, only the hero of the epic, as if to deny the temptation and its consequences. We see only the triumph of virtue.'*

'Mr. Hoare, please, you see much that I never saw,' Maria protested. 'I thought of Rinaldo for no other reason than the popularity of Mr. Sacchini's opera on this theme. You may have seen it at the King's Theatre.'

'Yes, Hoare, what are you constructing? Please excuse me. I see one of my sitters with whom I must have a word. Will you accompany Mrs. Cosway? I shan't be long, my dear.'

'Sir, my compliments...Mrs. Cosway, I invent. Shall I continue? Take your portrayal of Creusa and Aeneas across the room. This is a curious view of another tragic separation. Creusa, Aeneas' beloved wife, has been lost in the flames of Troy. He returns to the burning city, searching everywhere for her, when her ghost appears and tells him to search no more, that the gods wish him to start a new life in a new land without her. Your Creusa is pretty, graceful, feminine, and somewhat exalted, not sad and tragic, as if her heart is breaking. Oh, oh, I go too far with my interpretations. Please do not be offended.'

This was too much. Mr. Hoare saw that his criticism of Mrs. Cosway's pictures was causing distress. Her face could not hide hurt feelings. He did not like her pictures nor did he seem to like her. She thought their friendship had been preserved.

'Let me tell you, my dear lady, I did not wish to offend. I do admire your other picture called Patience on a Monument, Smiling at Grief. But I do not understand the subject. Will you cast light on my darkened understanding?'

'Willingly, Mr. Hoare. It portrays the virtue of Patience as a young woman. The text was taken from Shakespeare's Twelfth Night. Viola, disguised as a manservant is speaking to her master Orsino with dramatic irony, describing her secret love for him as if it were the love of another woman. She says that this other woman was capable of deep feeling, even though still and quiet as a statue of Patience. You seem to see an avoidance of feeling in my pictures. I shall answer you with these words of Viola:

She sat like Patience on a monument,
Smiling at grief, was not this love indeed?
We men may say more, swear more, but indeed

Our shows are more than will, for still we prove
Much in our vows, but little in our love.

'*Do you see my meaning now, Mr. Hoare? Good day, sir.*'

A few days after the Cosways' visit to the Exhibition, the newspapers began to give their criticism of the paintings. This was Maria's first experience as the subject of public comment. It seemed exhilarating at first taste.

'Mr. Cosway, Richard, listen to this paper: "This lady promises to rise high in her profession: her Creusa and Aeneas *is very classically told, and embellished with tints of uncommon softness and harmony.*"'

'And this one.' She picked up another newspaper. ' "*Like* Patience on a Monument *– Well conceived, and a spirited, bold clear effect.*"'

'Yes, my dear, and what did they say of my portrait of the Duchess of Cumberland: that it was inanimate, formal, void of life and spirit. That the colouring of my Sigismunda's arms was "dirty and muddy"! Hah! Those scribblers should know about dirt and mud. They deal in it!'

'Yet another paper said your Sigismunda was a work of great genius, marked with a poetic pencil, and the colouring would not disgrace the most celebrated master of the Italian School.'

'You see, confusion confounded, a hopeless muddle. Maria, you would do better than to read the newspapers. They are a two-edged sword. One day you are elevated to the Olympus of the Gods, so that the next you may be gleefully thrown out of heaven into the raging inferno of public ridicule!'

'I must confess that it is infinitely pleasing to have one's work praised after working so hard to be worthy of public approbation.'

'Yes, yes, but "public approbation" is not to be won by honest effort. You are young, Maria. You do not understand what parties are behind the critics. Did you know that the Reverend Henry Bate Dudley, proprietor of the Morning Herald, *always supports Gainsborough and abuses all others, or that Reynolds has his claque of supporters in rival papers? Or did you know that the papers often print scandal as a form of blackmail? They know that some will pay anything to have unpleasant gossip suppressed? Or that others pay shamelessly to place paragraphs of praise to themselves?*'

'No, I suppose I was unaware of those things.'

'Of course. Remember that being famous may be necessary for an artist to attract custom, but fame's price is high – constant carping of the envious, the *unkind arrows of the satirists. Do not believe the critics, my dear Maria, for one day they will wound you deeply if you believe them. Furthermore, the characters they create and the dramatic conflicts they write about are a form of theatre which has some relationship with real people and real lives, but more often than not 'tis only a fantastical tale.'*

Listening dutifully to her husband, Maria must have still glowed with pleasure that her three pictures had not only been accepted by the Royal Academy, but seemed to please the public and the newspapers. She would have been loath to admit that the Academy's Selection Committee might not have as readily admitted 'Maria Hadfield' to the Exhibition as they had 'Mrs. Cosway.' A lady alone without the connections of a family was rarely recognised, whatever her talents, Angelica Kauffman being the great exception to this rule. Once a lady acquired the name of her husband, who had a place in society, she could surpass her husband in acclaim if she possessed intelligence, artistic gifts and, above all, beauty. Marriage served to spring her onto society's stage. If she was fair to look at, possessed of grace and good manners, the masses found feminine attractiveness the object of its idolatry. The power of the goddess was magnetic. This phenomenon seemed to be Maria's lot. Once married, she became famous partly because

22. Mr. and Mrs. Cosway in the character of Damon and Phillis, *engraving after Richard Cosway, 1788.*

of novelty – a very young woman who surprised by being able to paint, to sing, to play harp and harpsichord with almost uniform excellence – and partly because the notoriety of her husband became attached to her and was then enhanced by feminine attraction.

In the early years of the Cosways' marriage the attention of others helped to fill the empty space in her heart, a vacuum that she could not acknowledge without the experience to realise that something was absent. In reflecting upon the subjects she painted, one could conjecture that they revealed unspoken longings. Motivated by her ambition to be considered a history painter like Angelica, she looked for themes in literature and classical history. But on a deeper level, one does not choose a text and then spend hours in the studio, labouring to give it visual expression if the subject has not touched some fibre of the heart. No matter how others interpreted her pictures or however badly they may have been painted, she had been aware that the history of Rinaldo and Armida was one of tragic separation, of love sacrificed to duty. She was also well aware that the ghost of Creusa told of the same separation, the same sacrifice ordained by the gods, the same desperation as Aeneas tried three times to embrace the vision of his wife and found 'her phantom melted in my arms, as weightless as the wind'. She knew that Patience often quietly masks a world of inner turbulence and longing, for it was patience she needed to face a life she had not chosen. These pictures were indeed history paintings. Not the history of moral dilemmas, noble choices, or glorious feats. They told the history of an inner life, attracted to moments of intense feeling and deeply drawn emotions, expressed on canvas and there alone, for the scenes she depicted had not been measured by experience, except for Patience. She was quietly hiding the strength of her feelings, as she would continue to do.

Except when she painted. The next year Maria exhibited *Aeolus Raising a Storm*, showing the King of the Winds, high on the mountain where he stood guard over the raging and howling winds, kept chained deep in caverns. In her picture, Aelos releases the winds in a black whirlwind over the sea to pursue Aeneas and the Trojans. This violent, dark scene was not appreciated by the critics. Curiously they accepted such subjects from Fuseli, at least some of the time. Everyone was immensely shocked by his picture exhibited that year entitled *A Nightmare*. It portrayed a lady swooning on her couch with a grotesque beast squatting on her stomach and an eyeless

ÆOLUS RAISING A STORM.

23. Engraving of Maria Cosway's Aeolus Raising a Storm, *exhibited at the Royal Academy in 1782.*

horse head hovering over all. Most viewers found this picture abhorrent, but it did no permanent damage to Fuseli's reputation as much as Maria's milder Aeolus did to hers. A portrayal of power and violence was repelled as improper if it came from the pencil of a slight girl. Nor did the papers like her picture taken from Macpherson's *Tales of Ossian,* the Scottish bard. One said that her portrait of the face of Darthula was so utterly deficient of beauty that it occasioned the fearful start of her lover Cairbar. No one seemed to see the romantic content in Ossian's poetry which had moved her. The Exhibition of 1782 might have been her first failure had it not been for the great success of her large full-length portrait of the Duchess of Devonshire, which overshadowed the unenthusiastic reception of the other pictures.

Lady Georgiana Spencer had been married to the 5th Duke of Devonshire at seventeen. This young, inexperienced girl immediately became the queen of London society in no small measure because of her utterly beguiling personality. She was tall, with reddish hair and not beautiful, but possessed of such a natural, spontaneous and infectious good humour that she captivated both men and women. Everyone was mesmerised by her energetic charm. Many Londoners were as happy to catch a glimpse of this dazzling young aristocrat in her carriage as a member of the Royal Family. Her set, second only to the Court in social importance, included the Prince of Wales, Richard Brinsley Sheridan, Charles James Fox, the Whig politician, and a cluster of beauties: Mrs. Crewe, Lady Melbourne, Mrs. Bouverie, Lady Diana Beauclerk, and Mrs. Anne Damer. The success of Sheridan's *A School for Scandal* was partly due to the fidelity with which he transposed the wit and vivacity of the Devonshire circle into the mouths of his characters. The Duchess and her friends had a way of speaking exclusive to them. It was a nasal drawl, occasionally lapsing into a lisping baby talk.

Having seen Maria's pictures at the Academy, the Duchess inquired if she might do a portrait of her. Although Richard did not wish his wife to paint professionally, this was a request not to be refused. Maria's first interview with the Duchess may have surprised a young, unsophisticated girl. She would have been awed to enter the wrought-iron gates of the very high wall which hid Devonshire House from Piccadilly. This house was supposedly a great achievement of William Kent some fifty years ago, but had a plain, unornamented facade with small second-floor windows. Yet the marble halls and sumptuous collection of Old Master paintings inside were suitably grand.

As Maria was ushered up the grand staircase to the Duchess's sitting room, she was unprepared to see someone of the Duchess's rank receive her so simply, naturally and in a genuinely friendly manner.

'Mrs. Cosway, 'tis so good of you to come to me. I do hope you do not object to my sitting for you here. I have not been well of late, my complexion is all "yaller", but none of that. Now, tell me what you propose? What costume should I wear? Before we start, would you like a cup of "tay"? I shall ring for some.' Her peculiar pronunciation did not seem affected.

'Thank you, Your Grace, I should like tea very much.... As to the costume, I would like to paint you as Cynthia, the moon, emerging from the clouds as a

personage in Grecian dress, vaporous and flowing. Would you like to hear again Spencer's verse on Cynthia? I have brought a copy of The Faerie Queen.'

'*Yes, yes, that would be pretty. Please do read it to me.*'

'*Spencer compares the brightness of the beauty of his heroine, Britomart, with that of a full moon. He writes,*

> *As when fair Cynthia in darksome night,*
> *Is in a noyous cloud enveloped,*
> *Where she may find the substance thin and light,*
> *Breaks forth her silver beams, and her bright head*
> *Discovers to the world discomfited.*

'*I see you breaking through the clouds suddenly, illuminating the skies. You are in motion, not sitting still.*'

'*Ah, my dear Mrs. Cosway, I was told that you were original. Are you certain that would not be too "gulchy"?*'

'*"Gulchy", Your Grace? I fear I do not understand?*'

'*Oh, of course, that is a private little word. It means sentimental, excessive.*'

'*I should hope not. It seems to me an attitude which would best capture your éclat, your personality.*'

'*Well, let us try it! By all means. Let us begin at once. Would you mind coming into my bedroom and giving your suggestions to my maid as to the stuff of the costume, my hairdressing, et cetera? I would be so pleased if you could.*'

Thus began a brief, but agreeable collaboration between Maria and the young Duchess during the winter of 1781-1782. They must have cheered each other. Although the Duchess hardly ever spoke a complaining word and was of a uniformly sunny disposition, she was going through a low period brought on by the contemplation of eight childless years.

Many satisfactions came from Maria's portrait of the Duchess. First was public acclaim. One paper said: 'The fair artist has unquestionably a claim to a *poetic* fancy. In the personification of Cynthia, she has evidently introduced the Duchess of Devonshire. The sprightly *air* which distinguishes that *Beauty* is admirably hit off in the advancing step of the *Regent* of the night. The different shades of *azure* diffused through the piece, is an argument of consistence much in favour of the artist.'

Unfortunately the same critic added, 'She has certainly left one of the hands in an imperfect state.' And he was right. Even more enthusiastically, the *Morning Chronicle and London Advertiser* noted the painting's 'originality and delicacy' and even said that Maria Cosway was 'the first of female painters and among the male sex only inferior to her husband and Reynolds'. More rewarding than public praise was the news Maria heard in the autumn that the Duchess was expecting her first child. Right after the Exhibition, she had gone to Bath for her health. There she had been introduced to Lady Elizabeth Foster. They had passed an extremely happy summer together, and Georgiana had conceived shortly thereafter. One might imagine that the portrait of *Cynthia* was symbolic of the Duchess's emergence from dark and depressing clouds into her new life as a mother. She would have other grave difficulties: her slavery to gaming, the eventual *ménage à trois* that evolved when Lady Elizabeth, her dearest friend, became the Duke's mistress. Yet the Duchess would always have the tender compensation of two daughters and a son and heir to her husband's titles and fortune. This son, the 6th Duke, later wrote of Maria Cosway's portrait that 'the head…is very like my mother and it is almost the only likeness of her that reminds me of her countenance.' After all the portraits of Georgiana by Reynolds, Gainsborough, Lawrence, and Downman, this opinion of her son was a special compliment for such a young painter.

Each year the Academy's exhibition had its stars, one or several painters who were the talk of London. Sometimes a new prodigy appeared. In 1782 everyone was talking of a young rustic from Cornwall named John Opie. Although it was not widely known at the time, the mechanism of promotion in the papers was highly organised just as Cosway knew. Opie came up to London with Dr. John Wolcot, a crude but cultivated, man who variously practised as a physician and even a priest. He was determined to make the young Opie a success. They shared lodgings and, it was said, even their earnings. Once in London Dr. Wolcot changed professions again and became a satirical writer, the better to assure the fame and fortune of his protégé, Mr. Opie. Writing under the pseudonym Peter Pindar, Dr. Wolcot published regularly his *Odes to the Royal Academicians*, in which he savagely lampooned almost every artist except Opie, who was effusively praised as a young genius. Both Richard and Maria were the objects of his gibes. The satirist counselled her to stay in the kitchen in these words:

'Fie, Cosway! I'm asham'd to say
Thou own'st the title of R.A.;
I fear, to damn thee 'twas the Devil's sending.
And bid thy wife her kitchen mind,
Some honest calling quickly find;
Or shirts and shifts be making or be mending.

If Madam cannot make a shirt,
Or mend, or from it wash the dirt,
Better than paint, the poet for thee feels;
Or take a stitch up in the stocking
(Which is for a Wife very shocking,)
I pity the condition of thy heels.

'What vanity was in your sculls,
To make you act so like two fools,
T'expose your daubs, though made with wondrous pains out?
Could Raphael's angry Ghost arise,
And on the figures cast his eyes,
He'd catch a pistol up, and blow your brains out.'

Then after such nonsense, knowing he had gone too far, Wolcot repented:

'Muse in this criticism, I fear,
Thou really hast been too severe:
Cosway paints miniature with truth & spirit,
And Mistress Cosway boasts a fund of merit.'

But the very next year he attacked another of Maria's paintings, *The Hours*:

No, no with all my Lyric powers,
I'm not like Mistress Cosway's Hours,
Red as cock-turkeys, plump as barn-door chicken:'

If the young girls who symbolised the Hours' progress across the heavens were too strongly-coloured, it was only her excessive fidelity to Gray's

'Ode on the Spring' which begins 'Lo! Where the rosy-bosom'd Hours,/ Fair Venus' train appear'. Remembering Guido Reni's fresco, visited so long ago in Rome, she had laboured to catch the same graceful dancing movement, and despite Peter Pindar's snide mockery, *The Hours* has been considered one of her better efforts.

Despite these attacks her reputation as a painter was not too tarnished. Encouraged by the success of the Duchess's portrait, for the next two Exhibitions of 1783 and 1784, she exposed four pictures each time and half were portraits. One, a self- portrait, was thought to be wanting in expression and force. Her natural reserve prevented a fuller revelation. When she attempted another scene from Ossian, *Althan Seeing a Ghost*, it was no better received than her earlier portrayal of the Gaelic bard's poetry. Turning for the first time to the Bible, she showed Samson pulling down the temple as recounted in Judges, Chapter Sixteen. Again, her technique in designing masculine sinews and destructive power was not only deemed inadequate, but ridiculous. Peter Pindar mocked that Samson was 'Between two Garden- rollers staring'. More successful were two works of 1784, *A Persian Going to Adore the Sun*, a little picture she had done as a gift for Elizabeth, Lady Lyttelton and *Astrea Instructing Arthegal*. This last was a portrait of Mrs. Braddyll and her son in the character of two figures from Arthurian legend. According to Spenser, Astrea, the mother of the knight Arthegal, teaches him in secret,

> So thence him far she brought
> Into a cave from company exiled
> In which she nurs'd him till years he wrought
> And all the disciplines of Justice thence him sought

Both these pictures were available as prints in the print sellers' shops as were many other of her works. Valentine Green, one of London's leading mezzotinters, was the most assiduous in reproducing her paintings. He came out with a new print or two almost every year. Francesco Bartolozzi, one of the few engravers admitted to the Royal Academy as an Associate, also did some lovely stipple prints of her work including a very fine one of *The Hours*. An artist could often earn much more from prints at a guinea a piece than from clients' commissions. Although, as Mr. Cosway reminded her, she was not in trade, he thought the selling of her prints good publicity for him. Prints greatly enhanced public recognition and awareness of an artist as they travelled everywhere, outside London, even the Continent, where many European collectors were avid buyers of English prints. The circulation of prints of her pictures, the comments of the newspapers, the thousands of viewers at the annual Academy exhibitions – all this exposure of the name of Maria Cosway meant that the most profound effect of her marriage had been the elevation of a penniless and unknown girl into a public figure and member of fashionable society. Her husband's predictions of public criticism had not proved completely true. In fact, the following extract from the news of 1783 was typical:

24. *Engraving of Maria Cosway's* Clytie, *exhibited at the Royal Academy in 1785.*

'If the Parisians boast of their Madame Le Brun we have our Maria Cosway, born of English parents, but nursed in the schools of Rome and Florence. This young artist (yet *very* young) promises to be one of the luminaries of the approaching age. Her figure delicate, and feminine to a great degree, is accompanied by a mind that emulates the boldest subjects, the grand and the terrible. Her stile is nearer that of *Fuseli* than any other modern artist; yet it possesses a distinguishing character that, to a discerning eye, proves her to be no copyist. …There is a noble wildness enough, but little consistency or nature. It is worthy remarking, that her taste in music seems to be essentially different from that which governs her pencil in painting. In music her compositions are tender, elegant, and persuasive; in painting strong and commanding. The *Cosway* is perhaps the only lady, not only in England, but in Europe, who possesses an excellence so superior in the two sciences of music and painting.'

6

The Goddess of Pall Mall

Just as the Royal Academy had been the theatre for the display of her paintings, Maria soon had a suitable backdrop for her musical performance. In the late summer of 1784, the Cosways moved into the centre part of a red brick mansion on Pall Mall called Schomberg House. The name came from a previous resident, the third Duke of Schomberg, who had extensively rebuilt the house in 1698. Cosway had long wished an establishment larger than his house in Berkeley Street. Now his success as a miniature painter and his private dealing in Old Master paintings had made it possible. They had a home worthy of Richard's aspirations. He oversaw the transport of their furniture and pictures to their new house with his usual meticulous care.

'My good fellow, please take care with that harp on the stairs. 'Tis an instrument of extreme delicacy. My wife will thrash us both if it does not arrive safely.... . Maria, come, let me show you how I intend to arrange my studio.'

'I do hope that you are not going to have it on the top floor like Mr. Astley. That twisting, narrow staircase will discourage all but the most agile sitters.'

'No, never, my dear. I have a better idea. Here on the ground floor there is the gallery to the staircase where I shall hang Poussin's series of Rinaldo and Arminia from the Aldobrandini Palace and other choice pictures which my sitters may admire. Then if they wish they may cast a glance in the Eating Room to see some of my best Rubens, some Giorgione, a Van Dyke portrait or two. Then just look at the Grand Saloon, perfect for a studio as well as being an elegant reception room. There is enough space to hang my cartoons of Julio Romano.'

'And the painting room on the top floor?'

25. *Original staircase leading to the Breakfast Room, Schomberg House.*

'That is for you, my dear. You can use it for painting or dining or reading, whatever you wish. And you have access to a little roof garden if that pleases you.'

'It has such a lovely view to the south over the gardens of Marlborough House. I think it should be our breakfast room, where we can try to capture the few rays of English sun available to us.'

'So it shall be, Mrs. Cosway's Breakfast Room!'

'And my bedroom shall be next to it on the top floor. I certainly do not wish to have it in the room where Dr. Graham had his notorious Celestial Bed.'

'No chance of that. I think he used the first floor for his special cures.'

'I hope the newspapers will forget that we are living in the Temple of Health and Hymen.' Their house had formerly been the scene of a bizarre cure for infertility. Dr. James Graham charged fifty guineas a night for a couple to use his magnetised Celestial Bed. The bed's brass columns were bathed in coloured lights whilst organ music serenaded the lovers. These various stimulations of the senses were guaranteed to produce procreation.

'We shall make London forget Dr. Graham…although a night in his bed might have been interesting! … Ah Maria, this house corresponds exactly to my desires. It was built in the Great Century, over a hundred years ago and is perfectly situated, overlooking the Royal domains between St. James Palace and Carlton House. We have excellent neighbours – Gainsborough in the West part of the house; he enjoys the patronage of the Queen and receives visits from the Royal Family. And I can easily advise the Prince of Wales on his new decorations at Carlton House We are only two doors from Mr. Christie's so I can pop over whenever he has a sale. I am going to make this house a palace with you enthroned as reigning Muse.'

'Yes, but before I can reign there is much work for both of us. You may have a collection of royal proportions, but it must all be unpacked, dusted and hung. We do not have scores of royal servants to do it.'

'We have Ottobah to help you. He is most efficient.'

'But he is only one. These days you must release Andrew from your service to help me until all is in place. 'Twas I who engaged him when you did not wish a helper. Now he is monopolised by you.'

'True, young Plimer surprised me by his cleverness. He shall be a miniaturist himself one day. He may help you until everything is arranged. When shall we be ready to receive visits? I am anxious to show this house. It will make a splendid stage for your musical performances, and I shall be the scenery designer. You can give one of your concerts. Everyone finds your playing and singing equal to the standard of the King's Theatre.'

'No, they surely do not. I think they find my music simply a match with my appearance – soft, feminine, romantic. This offers a contrast with my painting, which is considered unseemly in its fantastical energy.'

'For my part, I have not seen enough of this energy, Mrs. Cosway. Nor of the dark passion attributed to you by your critics.' Probably seeing no response, he continued, 'Well, I must be off to Berkeley Street to see that all has been removed. Good afternoon, my dear.'

26. Schomberg House in Pall Mall.

Maria was left amid the arriving boxes and barrels, clocks and chamber pots, trunks and carpets, harpsichord and harp to contemplate the rising *crescendo* of life as Mrs. Cosway. It had started quietly, almost intimately, then had become amplified with public appearances at the Academy and their obligations to receive a great number of the 300 or so who made up the *bon ton* of the West End in Mr. Cosway's painting room. An artist's studio was a place where the smart set could meet informally without protocol, to take tea, look at pictures and prints, or watch one's friends being painted. The freer atmosphere of the studio had a racy reputation, but now that they had a grand house, a coach, and even Ottobah, a black servant, the lords and society beauties, actresses and rakes, writers and politicians could move from Mr. Cosway's studio to Mrs. Cosway's decorous drawing room.

Maria's first experiences as a Mayfair hostess may not have pleased her. The English dinner could be a protracted, overly formal and boring affair – at least for the ladies. For the gentlemen, it could be uproarious and stimulating when they discussed political news or told licentious stories over wine after the tablecloth was removed. Starting around five o'clock in the afternoon, Maria would lead the lady of highest rank, followed by the other ladies, into the dining room to be seated at one end of the table, and her husband would do the same with the gentlemen. The continental custom of alternating ladies and gentlemen at table did not begin until several years after their marriage, rendering the conversation more interesting for the ladies and more polite for the gentlemen.

After two hours of eating, mostly roasted and boiled meats, perhaps a flounder or a salmon, potatoes, turnips, or carrots, followed by apple pie or currant tart, small bowls of water would be brought to the table. More fashionable guests would rinse their hands in the water, but many still followed the custom of rinsing their mouths, gurgling loudly and spitting into the bowls. As napkins were not provided, greasy hands and mouths were then wiped on the edges of the damask table cloth. Happily the cloth and all the bowls of dirty water were then removed, revealing a mahogany table polished to metallic brilliance. Decanters of claret and port and silver baskets of biscuits were enjoyed for several minutes by the ladies before they retired to the drawing room to escape the heavy drinking which followed. Thereby delicate sensibilities also avoided the spectacle of gentlemen not bothering to interrupt their animated conversation whilst they used the chamber pots provided on the sideboard.

These dinners were costly and took up so much time that they were reserved for a closer circle of friends. What became one of the most talked-about entertainments in London was Maria's Monday evening musical assembly or *rout*. On those evenings carriages and sedan chairs pulled up before Schomberg House, obstructing all the traffic on Pall Mall. Card-playing, gaming, and drinking tea were the principal activities on these occasions, but her assemblies became known especially for their music. At first Maria performed the music, either playing the harp or harpsichord and singing airs from the Italian opera. As the reputation of her musical assemblies grew and her little invitations, written in Italian, became more and more sought after, she invited great singers such as Rubinelli, Tenducci,

27. Mr. and Mrs. Cosway in their garden *after Richard Cosway.*

and Marchesi to perform for their guests. What a reversal of fortune when she received Earl Cowper in her drawing room on one of his London visits! She had not been invited to his grand concerts in Florence.

Sir Horace Walpole found so many foreign diplomats at these concerts that he called them 'Mrs. Cosway's Diet'. Being a polyglot herself Mrs. Cosway favoured a mix of Europeans in society. Another foreigner, Tiberius Cavallo, the scientist, described her parties in a letter to Prince Hoare:

> Mrs. Cosway, alias Mary Cosway, alias Lady Mary Cosway, alias the Goddess of Pall Mall, alias la decimal Musa, alias the Magnetic Muse, and her sister Charlotte were very glad to hear something of you.... In evenings in the week, viz: on Monday and Thursday, Mary the great sits in state; ... On Monday last amongst a great variety of people she had Mr. de Calogne [Calonne], and the French Ambassador, persons peculiarly remarkable for being in one room at the same time. The performances in those stated evenings consist of music, flattery, scraping, bowing, puffing, shamming, back biting, sneering, drinking tea, &&

Later, Maria remembered the variety of her guests:

> My exercise in Music made my Evenings very agreeable. Lady

Lyttelton, the Honourable Mrs. Damer, Countess of Ailesbury, Lady Cecilia Johnston, the Marchioness of Townsend were my most intimate friends...Lady M. Duncan, Miss Wilks & General Paoli, the Foreign Ministers, the distinguished foreigners, Lord Sands, Mr. Erskine, the most distinguished talents & many such formed the agreeable evening society. Until they became great Concerts...of the first professors. H.R.H. the Prince of Wales honor'd constantly.

The fashionable did not flock just to hear the music. They came to catch a glimpse of the Prince of Wales and other prominent members of the *bon ton*. Shortly after the Cosways' installation in Schomberg House, the Prince named Richard Principal Painter to the Prince of Wales. Patronage by the great was absolutely indispensable for an artist's success, and no patronage was more desired than that of the Royal Family. Although the Prince was on very poor terms with the King and Queen because of his dissolute behaviour, he was still the heir to the throne and had the aura of glory and potential favour about him. Cosway had been in his good graces since the time of his mar-

28. George, Prince of Wales *after Richard Cosway*

riage, but the events of 1785 made him an indispensable accomplice of the Prince's adventures, notably with Mrs. Fitzherbert. After the Prince had fallen in love with this young, pious widow, she escaped to France, absolutely refusing to become his mistress. Being Catholic she had no hope of marrying a member of the Royal Family. Marriage to a Catholic was grounds for exclusion from succession to the throne. A respectable and well-connected widow, she had no intention of sacrificing her reputation and material advantages for the precarious and scandalous existence of a Royal mistress. The Prince, only twenty-two, was spoiled and unaccustomed to having his wishes thwarted. He threatened suicide, stabbing himself to prove his intentions. Seeing no other recourse, Mrs. Fitzherbert spent most of 1785 in exile in France. While there she received great attentions from the Prince's friend, the Duc de Chartres (later Duc d'Orléans or Philippe Egalité, who voted the death of Louis XVI). When the Duke was criticised for his regard for a simple gentlewoman, he replied that she would soon be a great lady and possibly one of the greatest. During his love's absence the Prince wanted her all the more intensely and lost himself in the most riotous conduct imaginable. He drank astounding quantities of alcohol with his friends for the express purpose of becoming disgustingly drunk. The Cosways' could well have been awakened by the Prince's revels. After one evening's consumption of some forty bottles of wine, the Prince and his friends decided to leave Carlton House to go out into Pall Mall on a rampage of breaking all the lamps and windows they saw.

Despite this behaviour, the Prince was an intelligent and charming young man, fair-haired and considered handsome. Cosway's portraits of him always captured the grace, elegance and romantic side of his character, and represented the expanding girth of the Royal silhouette in miraculously reduced proportions. Although no one dared comment upon his corpulence, the Prince was fat, even when young. His dissipation showed in his person at an early age. This was sad, for the Prince was a man of taste, a collector of paintings, and appreciator of all that was refined and beautiful in the decorative arts. He adored fashionable clothes, richly gold-braided uniforms, fancy masquerades. One evening he went to a costumed ball with a group of friends disguised as singing barefooted friars, save one who elected to protest the window tax, by dressing as a house with all the windows stopped up.

The Prince's set were merry and it was difficult not to be swept up in this merriment, even if Maria did not approve of everything she witnessed. Their dependence on the Prince's patronage meant complicity in his amorous adventures. Cosway's brush recorded their history. Presenting miniatures of oneself to mistresses and commissioning their likenesses as tokens of remembrance were part and parcel of the rituals of dalliance. Before Mrs. Fitzherbert, Cosway painted the actress Mary 'Perdita'

Robinson, the Prince's lover when he was eighteen. Then came a more discreet liaison with Elizabeth Milbanke, Lady Melbourne, a member of the Devonshire set, who being married, presented her youngest son, George Lamb, as being that of her husband, when he was generally thought to be the son of the Prince of Wales. Maria, too, was drawn into this intimate world, painting portraits of little George Lamb as a child and Maria Fitzherbert, both exhibited at the Royal Academy, albeit tactfully in two different years.

For an artist, the flawed character of this royal patron – expressed in self-indulgent extravagance and monumental debts of hundreds of thousands of pounds – was a cornucopia of benefits. There were no limits to the Prince's spending. The only hardship for artists was that he did not pay his bills. Yet he attracted other sitters who did. The ever-present possibility of adventurous schemes and new intrigues gave his presence a magical quality, persuading the Cosways to forgive his many failings.

The musical parties at Schomberg House were illuminated by the white flames of wax candles in the Gallery, their reflection glistening in the polished mahogany stair railing and the oil surfaces of Rembrandts, Van Dycks, Rubens, and Jordaens. The effect was doubled in intensity by great mirrors, momentarily darkened by passing clouds of rich coloured stuffs – brocades, velvets, silks, mousselines. As Maria greeted guests at the door of the Grand Saloon, she could hear the rustle of painted taffeta against embroidered satin, and the click of ivory-ribbed fans shutting to punctuate a feminine caprice. When she heard an excited bustle in the entrance hall and the raised voices of young men out on a lark, she knew the moment had arrived that her guests had been pretending not to expect – the Prince had arrived.

He would stride across the hall where Cosway had artfully displayed Grecian heads, porphyry urns, and bronze figurines on marble-topped consoles. He was a fleshy young man, tightly fitted into a well-cut suit of dark blue velvet, gold-threaded embroidery on lapels and pockets. His shirt of fine linen and lace puffed out over a grey-striped silk waistcoat with buttons under great stress. Blond, lightly-powdered ringlets framed a reddened face; his eyes glistened with drink.

As he approached, Maria could see a tiny, diamond-studded locket tied round his neck by a pale blue silk ribbon. It held Cosway's portrait of Mrs. Fitzherbert. Maria curtseyed deeply before him.

'Mrs. Cosway, my dear lady. Are you in fine voice this night? I should like to hear your singing. I need to have it, but pray choose a mournful air to suit my humour.'

'If one is low, is not the remedy a contrary dose of cheerfulness. Shan't I sing gay and lively airs to help us forget this dreary fog. I should like to bring the warmth of my beloved Tuscany to London. 'Tis ambitious to pretend that I could cure your melancholy, but I am used to being called overly ambitious. May I try to lift your spirits?'

'My lady, your accomplishments are known throughout London…now I see that we can add another talent to your tableau of honours. You are a kind attendant to the sick. Mr. Cosway is damned fortunate to have found you. Where is the fellow?'

'My husband is there…in conversation with Le Chevalier d'Eon and Sir Horace Walpole.'

'Aha! Two old women together. A fine pair! One – a gentleman in petticoats, the other a crone in knee-breeches. Look at the arms of "Mademoiselle" d'Eon. Sinewy, covered with black hairs. What an embrace she could give, eh St. Leger?' The prince turned to his companion, Colonel St. Leger, giving him a wink.

'I shall conduct you to them, Your Royal Highness.' As they passed though the drawing room, the ladies closest to him curtseyed, the gentlemen bowed. The Prince motioned casually with one hand for the assembly to rise. He preferred not to have protocol at their house. Mingling with artists, foreign ambassadors, Whig politicians,

29. La Chevalière d'Eon.

writers, actresses and a few of the smartest among the aristocracy was an adventure. He preferred the stimulating mix of company to be found at Schomberg House to the dull courtiers and staid family life of his parents.

Midway through the crowd, the Prince saw Charles James Fox, whom the Prince had vigorously supported in the recent campaign for the House of Commons. Mr. Fox was engaged in serious conversation with Lord Erskine, the celebrated advocate.

'Fox, not at Brooks's yet?' the Prince stopped to ask. 'The tables are warming up now.'

'Your Royal Highness, the gaming may be hot, but Fortuna, that fickle goddess, has turned cold. My purse is quite flat. So I must seek consolation among more warm-blooded divinities.'

'I know your plight, Mr. Fox, know it well. But lack of means has never stopped your wagering before, nor mine. That's the interest of the whole game. The sword of Damocles tickling the back of the neck! The higher the stakes, the keener the pleasure. A perverse law, but there you have it! Lord Erskine, my compliments.'

Leaving the Whigs, they hurried past John Wilkes and his daughter Mary, whose backs were turned. Wilkes' form of democratic politics, beginning with his opposition to the American War, was too extreme even for Whigs like Fox who also opposed the war, but disdained Wilkes' dependence on middle-class opinion.

The Prince, looking over his shoulder, whispered to Colonel St. Leger, 'God, that Wilkes girl is ugly – a real Medusa!'

Just as they reached Richard, still with the two 'old women', Monsieur de Barthélemy, the French Minister, approached. After waiting for the Prince to acknowledge him before speaking, he informed him, 'Your Royal Highness, I have received word that the Duc de Chartres is returning to his house in Portland Place for a private visit. He wishes me to inform you that he would be honoured to have your company for the Newmarket races during his stay. He wishes me to inform you also that the Governess of his children, Madame de Genlis, was extremely pleased with her recent visit to London where she received every courtesy.' M. de Barthélemy continued, 'Mrs. Cosway was most gracious in arranging with our friend Sir Horace,' he nodded toward the older man, 'for Madame de Genlis to visit Strawberry Hill. And last, Monseigneur has asked me to tell you that he has seen that a certain friend of yours now in Paris has been well received.'

'This is a wealth of good news, my friend. I am obliged to you. But tell me, is it true that your Ambassador, Comte d'Adhémar, is leaving London because of health?'

'Yes, your Royal Highness, I shall be the chargé d'affaires until his successor arrives.'

'Congratulations, but I shall miss Adhémar. He suffered from too many midnight excursions with me, too much wine, too much exposure to the damp. London is a dangerous posting. But your diplomatic colleagues at the other end of the room seem to be thriving.' The Prince nodded toward a group of the 'foreigners' who were known to be an important constituency of Maria's assemblies. These emissaries from Southern Europe found a congenial remnant of Italian culture at Schomberg House, and several, Marchese Francesco d'Ageno, the Genoese Minister, Marquis del Campo, the Spanish Minister, Count Soderini, the Venetian Minister, and Ambassador da Pinto of Portugal, became part of the Cosways' intimate circle.

'Who would not thrive in this warm atmosphere where Mrs. Cosway surrounds us with her beautiful works of art and enthralls with a delicious Italian accent?' Monsieur de Barthélemy, usually reserved and serious, surprised Maria with his gallantry. She suspected the compliment was designed to impress the Prince more than his hostess.

At this moment Mr. Cosway, having spied his Royal guest, greeted him with exaggerated reverence, bowing low. His excessive politeness, although sincere, was accepted with a certain amusement.

'Mrs. Cosway and I are deeply honoured that Your Royal Highness has deemed our invitation worthy of your interest. Your presence gives us and our guests infinite pleasure.'

'Et cetera, et cetera, Mr. Cosway. 'Tis my pleasure to be here. Yet this evening I do not see many younger members of the fair sex. Where is the Duchess of Devonshire? Or Mrs. Damer?'

Maria replied, 'The Duchess sent word that her mother was ill and Mrs. Damer is abroad.'

'Yes, yes. I heard that. Well, we shall have the fresh beauty of Mrs. Cosway and as for the rest, we shall have to make do with Lady Lyttelton and Lady Townshend.' Turning to Richard, 'May I have a word with you in private, Mr. Cosway? Will you pardon this intrusion of business, Madame?'

'Please consider your Royal Highness at liberty to do as he pleases, as if he

were in his own home. I shall attend to my other guests, if you will excuse me.'
'Madame.' He bowed.

The Prince wished Cosway to execute another miniature of himself as a gift for Mrs. Fitzherbert, who was returning from Paris. He excitedly confided in the artist that he expected the lady that very day and had left word with her servants at her Park Street house that she must come at once to Carlton House. Furthermore, he had instructed his household that if she did appear they were to escort her through his garden to the alley which adjoined the garden of Schomberg House and from thence into the Cosways' house. He wished urgently that Mr. Cosway would post a servant outside to escort her properly.

Ignorant of this conspiracy, Maria moved across the drawing room to speak with her best friends, Elizabeth, Lady Dowager Lyttelton, who was of an older generation, and Anne, Viscountess Townshend, still young and handsome. She told them a bit spitefully and indiscreetly that the Prince was very drunk although still clearheaded. His condition became embarrassingly evident during the musical part of the assembly. Sprawled in a large gilt armchair, he nodded off in the midst of Mrs. Cosway's singing – at his request- a sad air, 'Tacite Ombre' or 'Silent Shadow'. All pretended not to hear his snoring accompaniment to the *song for fear that the princely guest would awake and catch them in flagrant lèse majesté. The Prince's incapacity compromised his planned tête à tête, arranged to take place on the Cosways' premises without their consent.*

Such assignations were the price of patronage, not a heavy one for Richard. He participated in amorous intrigues with gusto. Maria's sentiments were probably more nuanced. It was exciting, in a certain sense flattering. Yet in her heart she would be uneasy. She knew that those of high rank could do exactly as they wished, while observing a special code of discretion and maintaining the facade of respectability. Those of the middle rank, although elevated by the attentions of the mighty, did not truly enjoy the luxury of their special morality.

And this proved true. The unsavoury reputation of Schomberg House persisted after the Cosways' death. *Fraser's Magazine* commented in 1840:

> He [Cosway] was a great collector of paintings by the celebrated old masters; and every apartment of the parlour, drawing room and second floor was crowded with Raphaels, Titians, Rembrandts, and Tenierses; and those, as the Duke of _____ asserted, were convenient furniture for a first rate house of assignation.

Furthermore, the character of the Cosways' patron had serious defects. He was self-centred and careless of others. After his secret marriage to Mrs. Fitzherbert, performed on 15th December 1785, without the monarch's permission, therefore illegal under the Royal Marriage Act, he let Fox defend him in the House of Commons with a blatant lie. Referring to the rumoured marriage, Fox declared to the House that it '…never did happen in any way whatsoever, and had from the beginning been a base and malicious falsehood.' If the Prince would do this to the son of Lord Holland, what would he not do to artists? During their years in Schomberg House, the Cosways were not abandoned, but later it was a different story.

Inevitably the social ascension of the Cosways, like a highly placed lightning rod, attracted the flashing bolts of gossip, jealous spite, and vicious newspaper attacks. The first Royal Academy Exhibition after their move to Schomberg House, that of 1785, was not a happy experience. There were not many nice comments about Maria's six pictures except perhaps by her friend Mrs. Harriet Cowley, authoress of many successful comedies for the theatre. She was flattered, that Maria illustrated several lines from her 'Maid of Aragon' and returned the compliment by praising the artist's self-portrait.

The papers were not so kind. One critic in the *Saint James Chronicle* was audacious enough to suggest that Maria's self portrait was a joint production of husband and wife. The *Morning Chronicle* apparently disliked her dramatic style, cautioning:

> ...a dark room and her pencil to be no longer suffered to go loose.
> In short, 'Heaven help the lady, she has caught the Fuseli.'

Peter Pindar, in his habitually derisive tone, came out with new *Lyric Odes to the Royal Academicians*. He found Mrs. Cosway's paintings too exaggerated and certainly too violent for a lady's brush.

> Maria Cosway, from old Ossian's tone,
> Will bring a tale of Rawhead – so tremendous!
> So full of beef, and blood, and guts, and gore.
> So stuff'd with storms and tempests – heav'n defend us!
> That honest folks will shudder in their beds.
> Is this too little for her: She'll do more,
> And ghosts with monstrous arms, and men with monstrous heads!

The most savage attacks, however, appeared in the *Morning Post*, hardly surprising as that paper was the biggest purveyor of scandal, gossip, and calumny. In this particular case, it was not a writer defending his protégé as with Wolcott and Opie, but the artist himself attacking his peers. The darts directed toward the Cosways and the American artists, Copley and West, were launched in unsigned articles by none other than John Hoppner. This young artist had won the R.A.'s gold medal for history painting two years before, but had not been satisfied with his progress. No one could explain his particular vindictiveness toward Maria, especially his tasteless comments on her picture *The Deluge*, in which she portrayed Jupiter in violent mood. Having thrown Cybele, the earth goddess, out of heaven, he returned to his wine, which he spit out upon the poor goddess. Hoppner described this picture almost in scatological terms, suggesting unspeakable vulgarity. He summed up his opinion by saying of Maria's self-portrait:

> She seems here as much out of humour with the spectators, as they in all probability will be with her performances in the present exhibition.

The very paper in which these notices appeared commented that they were in Mrs. Cosway's case 'vulgar' and in the case of poor Copley and West 'abusive'.

An artistic sensibility does not always have strong defences against public attacks. This ridicule may have affected Maria's health. During 1785 and again in the winter of 1786, she suffered from illness and sometimes from depressed spirits. In one of these low periods she made a bad impression on the daughter of the American Envoy to the Court of St. James, the young Abigal Adams.

30th January 1786

> This evening Mamma, myself, Mr. Smith & Mr. Humphreys went to visit Mrs Paradise at one of the evening parties…arrived rather late, no choice of seats. I took one next to a Mrs. Cosway an Italian who is rather a singular character. She paints and her subjects are the most singular that one can imagine – I saw the last year in the exhibition of painting several of her performances. One was a <u>dream</u> – another the deluge…the most extraordinary that imagination could form. She speaks English, Italian and French vastly well …plays and sings well but has nevertheless the *faibles* which attend those accomplishments – I mean – I sat by her the evening and was witness to solicitude from almost every person…to her to play and sing and of her absolute refusal, she was sick, had a violent cold and had not sung for a fortnight – at last after every one had given over their solicitude she followed her own inclination and played and sung 'til she came away – now I think a woman is never excusable for such a conduct

unless…she has an inexhaustible fund of wit and good humour to display upon the occasion – which this lady had not. She is one of those soft, gentle, pretty women whose compliance with the request of the company would please more than her airs could possibly give her importance.

It is possible that Maria had succumbed to a touch of self-importance after the attention she attracted while still young. But another of her critics, James Northcote, who did not hesitate to accuse her of ambition, also gave her the highest praise. He told the artist James Ward that he had only known two individuals who seemed superior to circumstances. One was Sir Joshua Reynolds, adding:

Mrs. Cosway was just the same. I knew her when she was in the greatest distress. I knew her afterwards when she was in high prosperity and visited by the Prince of Wales, but at both periods her behaviour was exactly the same.

30. Angelica Schuyler Church.

7

Friendship

'*Cicisbeo*' signifies 'whisperer' in Italian. Intimates whisper to each other, so the word came to mean 'lover' or 'intimate companion', but not necessarily in a carnal sense. To understand the subtlety of the role of a *cicisbeo*, one must know Italian language and poetry, which over the centuries formed manners and relations between the sexes. Being an ancient society, Italy in the eighteenth century still remembered the tradition of Platonic love expressed in Petrarch's poetry. This love was a guiltless passion between a married lady and an adorer. The gentleman who felt such an affection never dissociated a lady's virtue from her beauty, and considered his feelings to be praiseworthy, for they moved him to display heroic courage and virtue.

The English, having little acquaintance with any other nation's cultural attitudes, never understood this. English travellers to Italy filled letters, journals, and published accounts of their voyages with scandalised descriptions of the debauchery of Italian women who publicly paraded with their *cicisbeos* and institutionalised adultery. The truth was considerably more nuanced. It was true in Florence that almost every Italian lady of rank had a *cavalière servante* or *cicisbeo*. Since marriages were arranged, it was also true that husbands preferred to be free to spend time with their mistresses and allowed their wives to be accompanied daily and publicly by other gentlemen recognised by all as their companions. Although there most certainly were those who used this widely approved custom of a Platonic relation to hide lawless pleasure, the existence of a *cicisbeo* was by no means evidence of infidelity — except to the English. One tourist, Samuel Sharp, published such a violent attack on the practice, and on Italian manners in general, that an Italian friend of Dr. Johnson's, Giovanni Baretti, felt compelled to publish a defence of the honour of Italian women.

Feeling as much Italian as English, Maria was not shocked by the idea of having other gentlemen pay court to her or even express affection if their attentions observed the rules of courtly love. Perhaps she was too quick to impose foreign attitudes on London society; many thought that she had lovers. Some even linked her to the Prince of Wales. No doubt most suspected that she had taken the national hero of Corsica, General Pasquale di Paoli, as her lover.

The relation that existed between them was more likely to be what the French call an *amitié amoureuse* or loving friendship. It began about the year 1782. They first met either at the Royal Academy or perhaps at Mr. and Mrs. Paradise's, who were mutual friends. They were immediately drawn to each other in assemblies because they could converse in Italian with greater elegance than in an awkward English. Having heard of the

General as a great man, a noble defender of the liberty of his country, everyone was impressed by the softness of his manners. Well-bred and polite, he never tried to impose himself or loudly proclaim his views on politics in an egotistical way. He was calm and natural, though possessed of extraordinary vitality. He loved to converse while walking and said he could not sit and write for long periods. Many, knowing his reputation, upon meeting him for the first time were surprised that he seemed more ordinary than one would expect. Yet, he had a compelling presence. He was tall and strong with well-chiselled features. His reddish-blond hair was turning to white when Maria met him not long before his sixtieth birthday. A great part of the charm of Paoli's company was his wit, for his mind was so quick that he always had a *bon mot* appropriate to the subject of conversation, sometimes drawn from his vast knowledge of classical literature. He preferred Homer, Virgil, Livy, Plutarch, and Tacitus, but could also recite the poetry of Tasso, Dante, or Metastasio.

31. General Pasquale Paoli.

This amiable companion was not only pleasing, but he was a man of noble and solid character, a man upon whom one could rely. As Richard Cosway was often caught up in his painting, in the decoration of Carlton House and in Academy business (he was elected a member of the Council in 1785), Maria naturally spent much time with General Paoli. Cosway was not in the least troubled by her friendship with the General. He understood that her sentiments for the older man were like those one has for a father. After Maria explained to her husband the true significance of a *cicisbeo*, he must have thought it rather smart that his wife should have such a distinguished *cavalière servante*. Paoli meant more to Maria than a fashionable appendage. He was one of her truest friends, giving her the gift of loyalty for over twenty years. He offered a quiet haven in the midst of a demanding worldly existence where the formal display of a gay façade and exposure to public ridicule were her lot. He wrote many amusing letters to his 'Tenth Muse'; perhaps he chose this name because he was a member of the Lodge of the Nine Muses or because the year Maria arrived in London a painting of the 'Nine Living Muses of Great Britain' was exhibited at the Royal Academy. It portrayed noted bluestockings, actresses, writers, and painters such as Angelica Kauffman, Elizabeth Montague, Elizabeth Linley, Hannah More and others. The General wished to flatter by adding his own tenth muse to the group. The two shared literary tastes, exchanging books often; he lent her his copies of Euripides and Alfieri. He often put his carriage at her disposal. During Dr. Johnson's last illness he took Maria to see the great man:

> Your servant will either fetch you with the carriage or will be at the Doctor's as if by chance.... Your servant desires ardently to see the first impression that this person, who some find bizarre, will make on you; they see in him the true portrait of Caliban in *The Tempest*...but don't make eyes at him, for though he may be Caliban, or divine, I am sure that you will conquer him.

They went to Mass together in his carriage. On these occasions she could share confidences that she could not make to others. At some point, she must have complained to him that Richard did not let her paint professionally. Later she blamed her lack of progress in art on her husband:

> ...had Mr. C permitted me to paint professionally I should have made a better painter but left to myself by degrees instead of improving I lost what I had brought from Italy of my early studies.

Paoli held traditional views on the role of women, but he could have comforted her by giving the reason that he remained a bachelor. On one of their carriage rides he could have wisely explained:

'I shall tell you what the matter is. You see, dedication to a profession, even for a gentleman, requires much energy and the total concentration of his mind. For a gentlewoman who has domestic responsibilities, there is little time left for consecration to an art. In either case, marriage and the accomplishment of a great life's work are at odds. That is why I have not, nor shall I ever marry. I could not give all my thought and my life to the people of Corsica and be the head of a family.'

'I did ask myself why you had never married. Do you find marriage incompatible with your life's work?'

'Yes, it is impossible. The commander of a nation may be distracted by private matters and the cares of his family. I have no conjugal virtues. The only woman who could tempt me into marriage would be one with an immense dowry, which I could give to my country.'

'Men... always after a fortune, even patriots. But I should not speak ill of a custom which I followed with the same motives – not to save my country, but my family. Without Mr. Cosway's settlement, would I have married? I think not, at least my mother would have not arranged it. I only wished for the quiet of the cloister.'

'No, no, Maria was not made for the cloister. You can be sure of that. You should not regret your marriage. Marriage is a noble and necessary state, the best assurance of happiness and the general good of society.' He continued with a softer, encouraging tone. 'As for your painting, you have attracted great praise at a young age. Everyone speaks of your accomplishments. You are a 'bella donna' with infinite charm and a husband who does not oppress you. Of more importance, you have a good heart and many friends who love you. Do not let melancholia assail you now.'

'You are kind truly. I shall try to follow your counsel to fight against these low periods.'

'Ah, I have just the remedy! Mr. Boswell and I shall invite you to see Astley's Dancing Dogs! I hear they offer a droll spectacle. Something frivolous is in order. I wish to see these intelligent dogs, for I have often speculated that beasts must have a language.'

'My dear friend, that is a medicine which I shall swallow with pleasure.'

'Excellent! Such an outing will be a good distraction for Boswell. I fear his hypochondria contributes to an overindulgence in wine, a weakness which mightily impedes his affairs. I have begged him for years to find the manly courage to *defeat this vice, but he does not listen. He seeks to hide his condition by stealthily going to bed after I have retired and avoiding my company in the morning when he feels ill. Dr Johnson told him that it would be better to drink water for then he could be sure not to get drunk, which was never the case with wine, but he replied that drinking wine was a pleasure that he was unwilling to give up. I told Dr. Johnson of my concern over Boswell's drinking, that it would cause him to go mad.'*

'Poor Mr. Boswell. He can be a charming companion, tho' sometimes a bit forgetful. I do wish for him a better mastery of his inclinations, and I hope he will join us.'

32. James Boswell *by Reynolds.*

Perhaps this is how they conceived the project of going to see Mr. Astley's dogs. Mr. Boswell, who resided at the General's house in Portman Square when in London, was able to be of their party. He and Paoli had been firm friends since the young Scot's famous interview with the hero some twenty years earlier, before the General's defeat by the French and his forced exile to London. Boswell's book about Corsica and its national hero was a great literary success, bringing fame to the author and to Paoli. The two friends saw the Cosways regularly during the spring and summer of 1785. The Cosways often dined at Portman Square on Sunday evenings and Boswell often attended the 'musick' at Mrs. Cosways on Monday. In his journal Boswell notes that one evening when he was feeling 'dreary...Mrs. Cosway came and played on the piano forte and sung. I grew easier.' Another evening at the General's Boswell notes that they had a 'choice concert' of three violins, a bass, and the singers, Tenducci and Mrs. Cosway. As an amusing 'ambassador' bearing 'dispatches' from the General, Boswell wrote playful notes to Maria such as this one:

> 'I left my note (my <u>dispatches</u> I should say) where I supposed you would most certainly cast your eyes on your return home. For I found upon your table an old translation of Homer lying open. But I assure you the place <u>then</u> was not <u>Penelope's Industry</u> but the <u>Battle of the Frogs and Mice</u> which being a burlesque upon all battles I hope will make you laugh away the war which I am sorry to think still subsists between two powers which should ever maintain the strictest alliance. I pray you let my first <u>diplomatick</u> attempt be successful & come and dine with us tomorrow which will highly honour and oblige your most obedient and most humble servant James Boswell'

The evening of their visit to Astley's Amphitheatre, General Paoli and Boswell came to fetch Maria and her sister Charlotte in the General's coach while Cosway chose to walk through St. James Park and then across Westminster Bridge to Astley's Theatre the other side of the Thames. Astley was an outstanding horseman, who had distinguished himself as a cavalryman in the 15th Dragoons. He first established an equestrian centre where he performed trick riding – standing on one leg, or balancing on two or three horses in parallel. Soon he organised spectacles with an intelligent horse who could compute, feign death, fire a pistol, and do mind-reading. By the time they attended his circus, Astley had added Fortunelli the clown, Signor Colpi the acrobat, Breslau the conjurer, tumblers who formed the 'Egyptian Pyramids', and the 'Original Dancing Dogs and Vigorous English Bull Dog'.

The afternoon of the spectacle Boswell had addressed the following note to Mrs. Cosway in Italian:

> In my character of Ambassador, I beg you, Most Serene Princess, to let me know at what hour this evening we shall attend your court to accompany you to see Astley, who, unlike you, makes dogs resemble human beings, while (if I may revert to English) treat men like dogs. Please excuse my barbarous Italian!

Astley's ROYAL GROVE & AMPHITHEATRE RIDING HOUSE

When they arrived at the theatre, called the Royal Grove and painted inside with vines and trees, they found that they were to share a box with some members of the Duchess of Devonshire's set: Lord and Lady Melbourne, Harriet, Lady Duncannon, the Duchess's sister, and Lord William Gordon. All in the party were much entertained by the exhibition and by conversing with their neighbours. Later they took tea at the Cosways where Boswell was bored, confiding to his journal that they had passed the evening at Cosway's rather insipidly.

General Paoli was part of a circle of intimate friends that Maria saw more often than some of those who attended her Monday evening concerts. This circle included the Marchese d'Ageno of Genoa, Count Soderini of Venice, Elizabeth, Lady Dowager Lyttelton, Anne, Marchioness Townshend, and Mr. and Mrs. Henry Swinburne. Swinburne, like Charles Townley, was a rich Catholic gentleman excluded from public life, but rather famous after writing about his Italian travels. Swinburne had been a guest at Carlo's in Florence. Mrs. Swinburne was friendly with the Queen of Naples from whom she had received a letter of introduction to the Queen's sister, Marie-Antoinette and thus the Swinburnes became intimates of the Court of Versailles.

Another of Maria's dearest friends was an American, Angelica Schuyler Church. Her husband, John Barker Church, was a wealthy Member of

Parliament who had sided with the Americans in the recent war, serving under Lafayette. When in America, he met and married Angelica, a member of the old Schulyer family of Albany. Upon their return to London, the Churches became prominent members of the social scene with a town house in Sackville Street and a country house, Down Place, near Windsor. Angelica welcomed many Americans in London – the American Minister, John Adams, his wife and daughter, the painter John Trumbull, and Mr. and Mrs. John Paradise. The Cosways also knew the Paradises through Mr. Paradise's links to literary and artistic circles. He was a member of the Royal Society and a respected friend of Dr. Johnson and Sir Joshua. Gentle and scholarly, he was ill-matched to his beautiful, but erratic American wife, Lucy Ludwell of Virginia. Unlike the pretentious Lucy, Angelica was not only young and lovely, but gentle in manners and natural. She was one of the few friends of Maria's age. They could speak together easily and freely, as they must have after the Sunday evening at Mrs. Paradise's, attended by Maria and General Paoli and the Adams. As they took tea in Sackville Street, Angelica would have been eager to hear about the Paradises' assembly.

'Now, Maria, how was last evening? No scandals I trust?' Angelica stirred the embers in the hob-grate of her drawing-room fireplace without calling a servant to do it.

'Oh no, she was well-behaved and looked pretty, I must say. Her small, fine figure was shown to great advantage by an elegant robe à la polonaise'.

'I hope Mary Moser was not present to provoke one of her famous rages,' Angelica mused.

'No, never, after that notorious dinner when Mrs. Paradise took Miss Moser's compliment for an insult. Poor ignorant Lucy thought being called a "sylph" was some terrible slur,' she laughed.

'Then she hurled back a barb, aimed at poor Mary's short-sightedness.' Angelica imitated the Virginia accent of Mrs. Paradise: 'Bettah to be so, than to be as dull-lookin' and blind as a mole!'

'Dr. Johnson had to intervene and separate the hellcats! No, last evening was calm, but I was feeling ill after my violent cold of the last two weeks. It was my first outing. Almost all those present were most solicitous of me, begging me to play and sing, but I had not sung for a fortnight and hesitated much. At last, later in the evening, I ventured to play; the music proved curative.'

'I know the company appreciated your little concert.'

'Except your friends, the Adams, I fear. There were some thirty or forty of us crowded into two small rooms. When Mrs. and Miss Adams and two American gentlemen arrived, there were few seats left. Miss Adams took one beside me. She is a handsome young girl, but she and her mother showed by their demeanour that they did not approve of me.'

'My dear friend, be patient with American ladies. We are educated by books and have not had the same advantages as you. I believe that the Adamses are a bit severe towards what is different or new. They are virtuous and intelligent, perhaps too virtuous for London society. But they should be careful in their criticism; I can tell you that in Court circles much ill is spoken of the Americans. Lady Mary Coke goes so far as to call them low, vulgar people raised to a high station.'

'Yes,' Maria laughed, 'but you know that Lady Mary Coke never consorts with anyone below the rank of Duchess. Speaking of Lady Mary, I am having her friend Lady Cecilia Johnston to dine and must take leave of you. Look out the window, 'tis mid-afternoon and quite dark. What we must spend in candles this winter!'

'Yes, English winters are hard to bear, especially for one used to an American sun in cold, pure air.'

'Or an Italian sun in hot, languishing air. I have been in such ill health these past two winters that Mr. Cosway has promised me a voyage to the Continent, if not to Italy, at least to France. I wish so much that it will be possible this year.'

'And I wish this change of climate for you, my Maria. You are a flower that follows the sun, and you will find its warmth this year. I am certain of it.'

Maria did find her spirits lifted by a voyage that year. In that spring of 1786, Cosway was invited to Paris by the Duc d'Orléans. The Duke was frequently in London for parties of pleasure with the Prince of Wales when they indulged their similar tastes in horse-racing, women, and all-night drinking. On 29th of April of that year the two princes honoured the Royal Academy by accepting an invitation for dinner. The Duke, accompanied by the Dukes of Fitzjames and Lauzun, was placed immediately beneath the portrait of himself by Sir Joshua (the same portrait later burnt at Carlton House). It was about that time that Richard Cosway did a whole length of the French prince, engraved and published by Maria's brother George. The

Duke's satisfaction with Cosway's work prompted him to urge Richard to journey to Paris to paint his wife and children. That is how Richard Cosway decided at long last to fulfil his wife's desire to leave London for a more congenial climate.

The Cosways must have been mightily sick at that time of the satires and public ridicule that continued to harass them. A complete change would be a relief. Maria may have been too tired to make a great show at the 1786 Exhibition, only presenting one little picture. Nonetheless, the print sellers came out with two new views of Mr. and Mrs. Cosway, satirising two fine portraits that Richard had done of them. They were harmless and amusing except for the reminder in the caricature of Maria that the paintings surrounding her – *The Deluge, Samson, Aelos* and *Ossian* – were those which were failures with the public.

MARIA COSTIVE.
at her Studies.

More wounding, because scurrilous and vulgar, was an attempt at humour in a satirical play by Anthony Pasquin, a *nom de plume* for John Williams. This rogue was an unreliable attention-seeker who, like Wolcot, relished attacking the Academicians. In his farce, *The Royal Academicians*, seven R.A. members and Maria Cosway were characters with ridiculous names like Sir Varnish Dundizzy (Sir Joshua Reynolds), Monsieur Lethimhumbug (Mr. de Loutherbourg), Thomas Daubborough (Mr. Gainsborough) Rev. Mr. Priapus (Rev. Mr. Peters) and Tiny Cosmetic (Mr. Cosway). The most humiliating parts were the lines of Tiny Cosmetic, using crude innuendo to describe The Prince of Wales and Maria drawing together with pencils and brushes representing various parts of the anatomy. July of 1786 was a good time to prepare for their departure. Shortly before leaving, another friend, John Wilkes, came to breakfast. They spoke of his daughter, Mary Wilkes, who was already in Paris.

Maria had no news from her, so she chided, 'Miss Wilkes has forgot me Mr. Wilkes, but you have not. How we did relish the fine haunch of venison you sent us.'

'Never could she forget you, Mrs. Cosway, but she has not been that well and asked for a particular smelling bottle. Do you think I could trouble you to carry it to her?'

'I would be pleased to bear her such aid. What a shame that her days in Paris should be spoiled! What could we send to cheer her? What if my husband does a drawing of you that we could give Mary?'

'Oh no need, my good lady. All she has to do is look into Buffon's Histoire Naturelle *and she will find a great likeness of me among the Sapajous and Sagoin apes.'*

'Mr. Wilkes, she will not find you there at all. But what else could we take to your daughter?'

'Just your company, I know your presence will cheer her.'

'You are eminently kind, Mr. Wilkes. We shall miss you and our friends here, but we need this change of clime and habit. It has now been seven years that I have been in England, and I am longing to travel again. I have this happy feeling of anticipation.'

After this breakfast, Wilkes wrote to his daughter Mary, '...Mrs. Cosway has taken charge of the smelling bottle, which you desired: she is truly amiable & attaches her friends more & more by her virtues & graces.'

His most SERENE HIGHNESS LOUIS PHILLIP JOSEPH DUKE of ORLEANS.

8

Paris
1786

The perfume of roses and carnations filled the Cosways' carriage. They were passing through fields of rich red, salmon pink, and gold blossoms, cultivated just north of the city for the Paris market. The straight road, lined with tall poplars, seemed to end in the open skies of the Parisian valley.

Maria must have been relieved to be on the continent again where manners were gentler, the atmosphere a bit more refined than the games of Blind Man's Buff at Brighton. The Cosways had just left the Prince of Wales there. Richard had been retained by the Prince several days until he finished a commission. The couple had departed London on July 16th, and now it was the end of the month. The always fashionable pair had well chosen their moment to visit Paris. That year anglomania was at its height. Parisians had a passion for English carriages, gardens, tea, whist, redingotes, horseracing even '*lieux a l'anglaises*' or water closets. Maria no doubt wore a simple white gauze dress with sash called a *robe à l'anglaise*.

The Cosways also had the highest patronage, the Duc d'Orléans. The House of Orleans, the younger branch of the Royal Family, represented a rival power to Louis XVI. It was said that the Orleans' estates represented at least half the kingdom: most of the Ile de France, Lower Normandy, Picardy, Champagne, Bresse, Auvergne, and naturally the Orléanais, bringing in millions of *livres* of rent. Louis-Philippe-Joseph, Duc d'Orléans, enjoyed wealth almost equal to that of the King, but bore none of the burdens of a sick kingdom, crushed by war debt and mismanagement.

Behind the Duke's demeanour of polished manners and elegant speech lay the character of a rake of mediocre intelligence, who lacked the redeeming wit to render his excesses amusing. Maria could not have measured then the extent of his caprices – none too bizarre to be left unexplored if it excited his senses. The timely death of the previous duke had enabled this self-indulgent prince to wipe out his debts and pursue pleasure unfettered by material cares.

The Cosways chose lodgings not far from the Duke's *Palais Royal* and the Louvre. It is known that they stayed in the *rue Coqheron*, probably at the Hotel *Parlement d'Angleterre*, which would have been recommended by their friend, Anne Damer. Mrs. Damer and her half-sister, the Duchess of Richmond, favoured this hotel as did Sir William Hamilton. That summer there was a regular English colony at their lodgings. Mrs. Damer arrived from Italy shortly before the Cosways. Lady Elisabeth Foster was just leaving, and the Duchess of Kingston arrived at their hotel the last week of August.

After approving the situation and furnishings of their rooms, which looked out over neat boxwood gardens, Mr. Cosway sent word to the Palais Royal that he awaited the Duke's orders. If they did not come right away, the Cosways had much art to see and would have soon taken a dirty Parisian fiacre, directing the driver to the Royal Academy in the Louvre. Having sent a note to Charles Townley's antiquarian friend, Pierre-François Hugues, Baron d'Hancarville, now returned to Paris, they were greeted by him in the antichamber of the Academy's apartments.

'My dear friends, how delighted I am to see you. The charming members of Mr. Townley's circle remind me of that esteemed gentlemen. How can I be of service to you?' The hunched little figure bowed deeply.

'You may pilot us around a bit, my fellow,' Mr. Cosway replied. 'And interpret for me sometimes, if you would be so kind. Of course, Mrs. Cosway has been improving her French and needs no intermediary, but I am not a linguist.'

'I shall be honoured to conduct you through the Royal Academy apartments and then the Grand Galerie, where the King intends to install his collection and create his museum.'

As they began a visit of the Royal Academy rooms, their first impression was the contrast of the gilded boiseries and over-painted frescoes of these former royal apartments with the simple elegance of Somerset House. The 'presentation works' of the Academicians — those pieces presented upon admission to the Academy — were randomly placed on easels or against the wall, all overlaid with a thick coat of dust. As artists, they were interested in each work, although disappointed by the extreme disorder on every side. The Galerie d'Apollon was in the same condition, yet shabbily glorious, for one could see A Death of the Virgin by Caravaggio and a magnificent series of LeBrun, portraying the battles of Alexander. His drawing and composition were beyond compare, but the colouring of dirty red flesh tones unpleasing. They then passed through the large Salon Carré, reserved for the Academy's biannual exhibitions, to the Grand Galerie. Its length, over 800 feet long running parallel with the Seine, took their breath away.

Monsieur d'Hancarville explained, 'Monsieur le Comte d'Angiviller, le Surintendant des Bâtiments, has the idea to create a magnificent Museum in this gallery where all the King's pictures, now in storerooms here in the Louvre or in Versailles, will be reunited and displayed.'

'What a grand scheme!' Richard exclaimed. As their footsteps echoed over the creaking parquet, the emptiness of this enormous space caused Cosway to make an amazing offer. 'Such a great gallery should have large, grandiose works like my cartoons from the hands of Raphael and Guilio Romano. You know, I shall give them to the King's Museum! There is no better place. What do you think of this idea, Mr. d'Hancarville?'

'That is a noble sacrifice, Mr. Cosway, which attests to your true fidelity to the fine arts.'

'The four cartoons, pillaged from the palace of the Duke of Mantua, were taken to London, where I had the good fortune to acquire them. They show four scenes from the Triumph of Camillus, the Roman hero. Being about twenty by fifteen feet each they are one of the glories of Schomberg House, but this great gallery is where they belong! How shall I go about proposing my gift?'

'Well, I suggest that you write a letter to the Comte d'Angiviller, and I shall transmit it to him, with my own introduction to impress upon him the prestige of the donor and the elevation of his motives.'

'Yes, yes, please stress that I am not picture-dealing. Absolutely no sums, employment, or any other advantage do I seek.'

'The French nation will be flattered that you have honoured us with your largesse.'

'Yes, Mr. Cosway,' Maria added, 'and I am flattered that my husband should have made such a gesture. Your generosity is more a source of pride to me than your connoisseurship.'

'My dear, let us not be sentimental,' he whispered. 'Those cartoons are too large for our house. They'll be shown to better advantage here.'

Baron d'Hancarville followed Cosway's instructions and wrote to Comte d'Angiviller stressing that:

> Nothing is more disinterested than this offer, for he would refuse any sum, any employment, any advantage that could be presented to him. His ambition is to contribute to the good of the Arts, he himself is a very distinguished artist, member of the Royal Academy of London and first painter of the Prince of Wales, which promises him the charge of First Painter of the King, if this prince arrives to become that.

The King's Director of Buildings and the Arts wasted no time in putting

Cosway's offer directly before the King, who accepted with alacrity within a week.

That is how Richard Cosway became the benefactor of the King of France. The artist did have a worthy dedication to all that promoted the fine arts, but he must have nourished secret pride. By his possession of objects desired by royalty and by his philanthropy, he had elevated himself to a higher rank.

Below the Grande Galerie on the ground floor of the palace lay a warren of small ateliers and cramped apartments, much sought after by artists as privileges offered by the Crown. Other artists were lodged in temporary buildings in the courtyard or in the wing of Perrault's grand colonnade. Continuing their first visit to the Louvre, they visited the atelier of Jacques-Louis David.

When they entered David's studio, the painter did not seem to mind being interrupted, and welcomed them to see two pictures which he had exhibited in previous Salons, Belisarius Asking Alms *and* The Oath of the Horatii. *They were considered to be extremely well-conceived and well-painted, pure, austere, perfectly conveying the antique. Yet they expressed an atmosphere of aggression, of implacable virtue, something terrifying in their aspect. While d'Hancarville was discussing the literary sources of the pictures, Livy and Plutarch, Maria engaged David in conversation. He appeared to be under forty, pleasant-looking, although his right cheek was slightly drawn, deforming the corner of his mouth and giving him a slight lisp.*

'Do you remember your English friend, Mr. Northcote, with whom you sketched in Rome? I was in Rome at the same time for studies. He used to tell me about his talented companion from the French Academy. Mr. Fuseli and Mr. Banks also spoke of you. I was living with the Banks at the time.'

'Madame, you are very kind, but how did I miss meeting you? That is a pity. And how is Mr. Northcote? I should like very much to visit London to see him and other English artists. You are fortunate to breathe freer air than ours.'

'Freer, perhaps,' Maria smiled, 'but blacker with soot and fog. I believe Mr. Northcote gets on well with his portrait business although he had some difficulties at first. Do you find commissions for your history paintings?'

'Yes, this one, The Oath of the Horatii, *which shows three brothers swearing*

allegiance to their father and to their civic duty, is a royal commission, and I have some enlightened friends, the Trudaine brothers, who have asked me to paint the death of Socrates. So, there is enough work with some portraits here and there. But what brings Mr. and Mrs. Cosway to Paris?'

'Mr. Cosway has been asked to paint the children of the Duc d'Orléans and the Duchess, although we have not yet been presented to them.'

'They are charming children. Madame de Genlis asked me to participate in their artistic education. I have little time for that, but I do pass by when I can. She has engaged a Monsieur Mirys to give them drawing lessons. I understand the little Duc de Montpensier acquits himself rather well.'

'And is Madame de Genlis as formidable as they say? When she was in London I arranged for her visit to Sir Horace Walpole, but was not able to accompany her. My friend Miss Wilkes found her conversation most stimulating.'

'Most stimulating, indeed, and persuasive. The Comtesse de Genlis convinced Monsieur le Duc that she would be the best educator of his children. 'Tis unheard of for a woman to have total authority over the upbringing of Princes of the Blood, but Madame de Genlis is no ordinary woman. Never short of ambition, she has gradually transformed her status from mistress to author and educator without losing the Duchess's confidence. But I have been indiscreet. You must not repeat what I have had the imprudence to say. For one thing the Duchess is such an extremely naive character that she appears to be totally ignorant of her participation in a ménage à trois all these years.'

'Do not be concerned, sir. I was aware of that history. Besides, I would not betray you. Be assured of that.'

'Madame, this brief meeting gives me confidence in your word. You radiate a natural sincerity.'

'You may pay Madame Cosway gallant compliments,' Monsieur d'Hancarville having overheard, approached. 'But you do not know the breadth of her talents. She is an accomplished painter herself, exhibiting her work at the Royal Academy and a musical performer of the first rank, singing, playing harp and harpsichord.'

'Madame, I can only add to all these virtues the most honourable, that of incomparable modesty, for you never spoke of your art. Monsieur d'Hancarville should present you to our estimable lady of the arts, Madame Vigée Lebrun? Her atelier is not far. I fear you shall have to excuse me, but I must finish my instructions to my students. With your permission I shall speak to my friends, the Trudaines. They always wish to meet persons of talent.'

'That would be most kind of you. I am sorry that we have interrupted your work; we know how precious an artist's time is. Good day, Monsieur.'

A short passage down a narrow, winding staircase and they were soon in the feminine atmosphere of the famous Madame Vigée Lebrun, the Queen's preferred portraitist. As the Academy schools maintained a strict separation of the sexes in their instruction, two young ladies were the only students. Madame Lebrun was, however, showing her drawings to two gentlemen as they entered. Her chestnut hair was bound up by a large ribbon, and she was originally dressed in a loose, Grecian-style garment. This informal attire was flattering to her delicate-featured beauty. She looked younger than her years, for she was about forty then. The two gentlemen presented a striking contrast – one tall and richly dressed in a silk waistcoat and velvet coat, the other a very young man of short stature in a plain blue costume, unpowdered dark hair and dark eyes. The Cosways were introduced to the older as the Comte de Vaudreuil, a friend and patron of Madame Lebrun, and the younger was Mr. John Trumbull, an American painter.

'Mr. Trumbull,' Maria inquired, 'are you the young painter that I have heard so much praised by Mr. and Mrs. Church in London?'

'I cannot say, Madame, if they have been complimentary, but Mr. Church has been most generous in aiding me with my studies. I am ever in his debt.'

'I am happy to make your acquaintance. Mr. Cosway, this is young Mr. Trumbull of whom we have heard many good things from the Churches.'

'Well, my young fellow, you are beginning with one of the best models of excellence if you see how Madame Lebrun is working. But what else brings you to Paris, other than your general edification?'

'I am principally here to take the portraits of the French heroes in the American War, Count Rochambeau, Monsieur de La Fayette and others, for I am hoping to paint the history of our Revolution. I have brought two of my paintings of important battles to Paris to be engraved here.'

'A splendid project, which must find more favourable reception here than in London.'

'Indeed, Mr. Cosway.'

'Mr. Trumbull is also visiting all the fine monuments and collections of Paris,' Madame Lebrun added.

'As are we,' Mr. Cosway replied, 'perhaps we can make a party one day.'

'It would be an honour for me to join you in your visits, and now I must take leave of you to dine with my host, Mr. Jefferson.'

'Is he another of your countrymen?' Maria asked.

'Of course, Madame, one of the most learned of our statesmen. You must have heard of his authorship of our Declaration of Independence, and now he is the American Envoy to the French court.'

'Oh yes, of course. He did know how to irritate our King, but my dear late father supported the American cause, which made him unpopular with some of his fellows. We shall look forward to seeing you again, Mr. Trumbull.'

'Madame, your servant.'

'What a polite young person,' Madame Lebrun commented after Mr. Trumbull's departure.

'Yes, he is,' the Comte de Vaudreuil agreed. He had kept silent during their brief conversation, studying several drawings as they spoke. 'I understand Mr. Cosway is in Paris to paint the Orleans children.'

'The principal reason for our voyage is to distract Mrs. Cosway, to give her a change of scene and improve her health. I have also been asked by the Duke of Orleans to do a few portraits of his family, but that should not take more than a few days. We are most keen to be able to see the great collections including that of the Duke. To me Rubens is the great master, and I hope we shall have permission to see his decoration of the Luxembourg Palace, but I understand the King does not often allow it.'

'I might be able to arrange that, Mr. Cosway, as I know several persons at Court. And I have a few Rubens that may be of interest to you. You must come to see them. Well, I must be taking leave as well. Mesdames, my respects. Gentlemen.'

'Well, Mr. Cosway, you certainly expressed your wish to see the Luxembourg Palace before the right person!' Madame Lebrun exclaimed. 'Monsieur de Vaudreuil is the intimate friend of the Comtesse de Polignac, governess of the Royal children. In fact, the Queen is sometimes jealous of him, but Madame de Polignac can obtain any petition she wishes, so I should say your chances of seeing your Rubens have considerably increased.'

And so they had, for in about ten days' time, the Cosways visited the Gallery of Marie de Medici to see the twenty-odd large allegorical paintings of Rubens. They took along young Trumbull and were also accompanied by Monsieur de Belisart, the King's Architect. It was then apparent why few were allowed to visit. The gallery was so decayed that it had to be supported by large props of wood, and the varnish of the paintings was old and cracked. The entire palace and garden was in a complete state of disrepair, but they were thrilled by the power of the colouring and the composition of Rubens, which shone through all the neglect.

The Orleans' household probably took its time in arranging sittings for Cosway. The children had to be brought from the country, where they spent the summer with Madame de Genlis. It was September before arrangements could be made. Whilst in Paris, Mr. Cosway was asked many times to paint likenesses of many great persons but he always refused. The only portraits he accepted were those of the Duchess of Orleans and her children, the Duchess of Polignac, requested by the Duchess of Devonshire, and the Duchess of Kingston.

In the meantime the two painters were left free to pursue their avid interest in the arts and architecture, leading them to new acquaintances and the beginnings of lifelong friendships. Almost daily they toured artists' ateliers in the Louvre and had soon entered into intimacy with the architectural fantasies of Hubert Robert, the romantic scenes of French seaports by Joseph Vernet, and moments of French history recorded by François André Vincent. John Trumbull often joined them for an excursion. The Sunday they all went to Versailles, Trumbull brought along the engraver of his history paintings, Antonio di Poggio, and an American architect, Mr. Bullfinch. D'Hancarville was again their indispensable guide, able to show them the private collections of Charles Labillarderie, Comte d'Angiviller, the Director-General of the King's buildings, gardens, manufactures, and academies. This title meant that its possessor controlled all the King's palaces, collections, patronage of the arts and manufactures, and promotion of artists. To French artists, Comte d'Angiviller was God and master. His position also meant that he lived in a treasure house, where he surrounded himself with the choicest objects of the kingdom. Monsieur d'Angiviller's summer pavilion graced a little park near the Gobert ponds. There he kept his collections of art and minerals and a fine library.

After seeing d'Angiviller's house, they wandered in the gardens among bowers of hornbeam, admiring the ingenious fountains: Apollo's chariot arising from water instead of sky or the giant Encelade, half emerging from a rock in a still green pool.

Two days later Trumbull invited the Cosways to view his paintings *The Battle of Bunker Hill* and *Attack on Quebec*, along with a party consisting of the Comte de Vaudreuil, Monsieur LeBrun, Monsieur Menageot, the painter, and the faithful d'Hancarville. The paintings were located at Thomas Jefferson's house, but the Envoy was in Versailles with other ambassadors for one of their regular days at Court. His house was located at the Grille de Chaillot, the Western gate of Paris on the Avenue des Champs Elysées. It was a quiet, leafy neighbourhood, far from the murmur of the city. In this classically-designed villa, there was something original, even peculiar, which may have been compatible with its inhabitant. It was asymmetrical, the wing on the Champs Elysées, longer than its opposite. Thus, the central, oval salon was angled to face the northeast, overlooking a French parterre, which slid off to the left into a sinuous and very large *jardin anglais*. The upper story with its small windows was like that of a mezzanine, for the noble second story had never been built.

The house was sparsely though tastefully furnished with new chairs of pure lines, suitably simple for the representative of a republic. Traces of the cultivation of the master of the house were seen in the oval music room – a violin and music-stand, ready with music open, calfskin books lying about on console tables, or in cabinets, wherever they had been put down or could easily be picked up. Jefferson was an inveterate book collector and had begun to buy pictures in Paris. Those hanging in the house were copies with a religious theme, a Guido Reni of Saint Peter, Herodiade with the head of John the Baptist by Simon Vouet and a Virgin lamenting Christ.

While the Cosways' visits of the day were instructive, their evenings were devoted to society. They were introduced to the most agreeable of institutions, the Paris salon. Each hostess and her circle of friends had a distinctive character. Some were literary; others a mix of men of arts and letters who mingled with aristocratic patrons. Many were openly political. The great difference between the *haut monde* of Paris and London was the important role of Parisian women in the politics of the day. The Duchess of Devonshire's campaigning in the parliamentary election of 1784 was a novelty in England. In Paris many salons were known to be centres of support for a particular minister. Madame de la Reynière was known for her support of all ministers except Monsieur Necker. She was more renowned for her sumptuous feasts, provided by a rich husband, whose family had once been sausage-makers. Madame de Polignac supported the Minister of Finance, Monsieur de Calonne. The Cosways were not too interested in this sort of gathering. They found the conversation of artists and connoisseurs more soothing than the effervescence of the liberals who animated much of Parisian society. That innocent summer of 1786 Maria may not have realised that the Duke of Orleans and his household formed one of the poles of opposition to the King, and that the underground press which circulated calumny and rumour against the Royal family distributed many of its libels in the public gardens of the Palais Royal, the Duke's palace.

After David's introduction the Cosways frequented the house of the Trudaine brothers on the Place Louis XV. These young, enthusiastic patrons of the arts and letters, Charles-Louis and Charles-Michel, were only one year apart, the elder but twenty-one. Already Counsellors to the Parliament of Paris and immensely cultivated, their grandfather, the 'Grand Trudaine', had built France's admirable network of roads for Louis XV and begun the family fortune. Inheriting one of the richest libraries in France, the Trudaines attracted classical scholars, poets, and painters to their evening parties. These evenings were not like the stiff and formal assemblies of London, where the ladies were together on one side of the room, sipping tea, and the gentlemen, if not sitting in Parliament, were apart, discussing politics and professional matters.

In Paris, one did not need a formal invitation. It was known what houses were receiving. About nine o' clock, the most interesting people might appear and fall into easy and graceful relations and demonstrations of wit, which never excluded ladies. On the contrary their society was sought by gentlemen, which explains why feminine opinions on political subjects were not scorned. About ten or even later, a *souper* would be brought in. A table would be set up in the drawing room, the cloth laid, where without ceremony everyone who wished could sup on cold fowl, a roast, salads, pastries.

It was one of these evenings that Maria first laid eyes on a small young man with an enormous head. His forehead appeared larger than it was, for his cropped, dark hair had disappeared in front. But his eyes were deep and kind, his manner soft and polite. Although modest, he could not hide his

33. André Chénier (Monsieur de Saint André).

vast learning. He read and spoke Greek as his first language. Some considered him ugly, but this passionate olive-skinned youth, introduced to the Cosways as Monsieur Chénier de Saint André, could exhibit a mesmerising charm. His true name was André Chénier, but he added 'de Saint-André' to give himself a noble air, more in keeping with his wealthy friends. When he was presented to Maria, he was immediately interested by her Italian origins.

'Madame, an Englishwoman born on the banks of the Arno inspires me with fascination. Your Mediterranean accent is a delicious surprise, offset as it is, by an aureole of golden curls.'

'Monsieur, as a child of the Greek culture of your mother and that of France, you understand well what contradictions come from disparate sources.'

'Without contradiction, life becomes tepid, dull. Our emotions are stirred by contrary winds. Our most beautiful effects by happy accidents like your captivating voice and its Southern melody.'

Without warning Monsieur de Saint-André began to declaim verses, a technique he used to fascinate Parisian society. His voice vibrated:

> *Abandoning the flowers,*
> *The sonorous bees come humming on her lips of vermeil*
> *To alight and leave this sweet and flattering honey*
> *Which flows with her voice and penetrates the heart.*

He paused and smiled, waiting for a response. Incapable of replying in his language, Maria could only recite a few words of Thomas Gray:

The insect-youth are on the wing
Eager to taste the honied spring
And float amid the liquid noon.

'Ah, Madame, I shall begin my English lessons at once to understand what I perceive already, by the music of your lips, to be a wonderfully inspired answer to my poor verses.'

'Chénier, my friend,' Charles-Louis de Trudaine approached and broke the intensity of Monsieur de Saint André's gaze. 'Do not keep Madame Cosway for yourself. I want to present her to other friends. I must warn her that you are totally devoted to Venus and always worshiping at her altar.'

'You are unjust, Trudaine. I appreciate the chaste virtues for they are surer. For proof:

The fleeting torch of beauty alone
Ignites the sense with a fire, quick then passed,
But the gentle virtues and the modest graces
Inspire in pure hearts only flames that last.'

'Just so! I should like a companion like the Trudaines' dear Hermes!' Maria nodded toward Charles-Louis' little whippet, peering up at them through white silken legs. 'He would always be of a perfect loyalty. No chance of his fire waning. Never would he tire of me. Never would his ennui destroy our affection.'

'If my brother and I could so easily satisfy your desire for fidelity, Madame, we would be honoured to find you a cousin of Hermes and offer him to you as a token of our sincere admiration.'

'Would you be that kind? I would love to have a friend with me as a souvenir of your charming company. Dear little Hermes.' She reached down to stroke his fine, satin head. 'Would you send one of your brothers to sit through long winter evenings with me?'

'He replies, "Yes! I should go even to the cold Terre Neuve to have the exclusive right to warm the feet of such a beautiful mistress." ' Monsieur de Saint-André spoke for Hermes.

'Chénier, you see Madame Cosway is not used to your badinage. You cause her to blush.'

She replied for him, 'The conversation of English gentlemen isn't so *cold…but expressed with far less elegance. I fear that I hear what I feign not to hear more often than not.'*

'My friends, you have importuned Mrs. Cosway too long. Now I must present her to a serious gentleman of talent. Monsieur de Non has been waiting patiently for the privilege of knowing her.' Charles-Louis de Trudaine whisked Mrs. Cosway away to another group in conversation.

34. Vivant Denon *1792.*

Dominique Vivant Denon, or de Non, as he was known at the time, was a diplomat turned artist-engraver. Like many opportunists who knew how to move with the times, he dropped the particule '*de*' when it became a dangerous appendage a few years later. Maria's other young friends – the Trudaines, André Chénier – enlightened, liberal, amusing, and kind – were cut down by bloody, illiberal forces, permitted to thrive by the victims' naïve optimism. Monsieur de Non would survive and would be a friend she would keep over many years. She could never have imagined this sombre future in those evenings of insouciance.

9

The American Envoy

On the first Sunday of September – after the Cosways had been in Paris for a month – they planned to meet John Trumbull for a visit close to their lodgings. It was one of the last days of summer. The tourists were going to see the new *Halle aux Bleds et Farines* or Grain Market, which had the highest dome in Paris, comparable to the Pantheon in Rome. An obvious point to rendezvous was the Medici Column, built for Queen Catherine de Medici's astrologer to better observe the stars. This relic of the sixteenth century was now only a decorative ornament beside the domed circle of stone where grains were traded.

Upon approaching the column, the Cosways saw another gentleman talking with young Trumbull. They heard the stranger speaking English in a low voice with a peculiar, soft accent that reminded Maria of Lucy Paradise. They were soon introduced to Mr. Thomas Jefferson, the American Envoy, whom Trumbull had so warmly praised during their previous excursions.

After presentations were made, they stepped inside the hall to a dazzling sunlight, magnified by the elongated glass windows, ingeniously placed in the dome to give the enormous space a light, airy atmosphere.

Jefferson, having studied the architects' model of the structure, was guiding them through the intricacies of the method of construction, explaining that the builders had revived a technique of Philibert Delorme, a Renaissance architect. He seemed deeply absorbed in his subject. Listening to this soft, intense voice, Maria could observe him with an artist's eye. He was of a fair, pinkish, slightly-freckled colouring. His un-powdered hair, carelessly tied back, was reddish-brown. His eyes of a green shade were slightly deep-set with a bright light in the pupils, which by moments suddenly became veiled and his thin lips clamped shut. The line of his jaw was firm, prominent, and manly. He was simply dressed in pale tan breeches, a blue coat with no ornament but brass buttons, and carried a bamboo walking stick. He held himself perfectly straight, nobly so. But when he walked his gait was a sort of slow lope, for he was very tall, almost too thin. His hands appeared strong, but the long fingers were delicate. Beside Richard Cosway he seemed a giant, and Maria noticed that Richard did not let the two of them be seen together for more than a few seconds before he moved away. On the contrary, when she stood beside him, his height gave her a new and pleasant sensation. She felt his manly strength as a foil, bringing forth, for the first time, a feeling of her own femininity.

For a time the three men forgot her presence as they discussed the technical tour de force of the rotunda. Ah yes, she must have thought, an Englishman and two Americans — that is how it is in London. The gentlemen go off to themselves and leave the lady to her own devices since she would not be interested in their serious business. A month's stay in Paris in the polite society of French gentlemen, who treated ladies as if they were Princesses of the Blood, had caused Maria to forget the separation of the sexes in Anglo-Saxon countries. When Maria heard Jefferson compare this grain market to the Pantheon in Rome, she spoke up.

'Sir, I find this space vastly agreeable because of the light, but the Pantheon is even more imposing, with its marble interior and its superior dimensions.'

'Madame, have you had the good fortune to inspect the Pantheon at first hand?'

'It was my privilege to sojourn twice in Rome as my beloved father had decided that such study would be beneficial for my improvement in the arts.'

35. Halle au Blé, *1786.*

'Anyone who has seen those highest attainments of the antique has certainly a privileged rank above those from wilder climes.' Jefferson looked down into her eyes intently.

'Mrs. Cosway has not only studied the highest attainments of the arts. She and Mr. Cosway are considered among England's finest practitioners, exhibiting their paintings annually at the Royal Academy to great acclaim,' Trumbull added.

'And we are often exposed to the satirists' barbs,' Richard jested.

'The price of fame,' the ambassador commiserated. 'Mr. Trumbull has enlivened our dinners with his compliments to the many talents of his English companions, and it is certain that he has not exaggerated. I have an invitation to

dine this afternoon, but 'tis too fine a summer's day to spend at an endless, boring meal indoors. If I can find an excuse to extricate myself from this obligation, would you like to take the water coach down the Seine to Saint Cloud and see the chateau's collection of pictures? We could dine rapidly at the Palais Royal. Do you know the Mechanical Restaurant? It is amusing and clever, if not the finest cuisine.'

'How kind of you, but we, too, are invited to dine. We would be honoured another day,' Cosway declined.

'Mr. Cosway, you did express the wish to see the Chateau of St. Cloud, and it is such perfect weather for an expedition. Don't you think we might dine with those other friends on a rainy day?' Maria implored.

'Perhaps, my dear, perhaps. Oh why not? It seems a capital idea! Let us fabricate our various excuses and organise an escapade. Yes, yes, why not?'

Jefferson was expected by the Duchess d'Enville-de la Rochefoucauld at dinner, but preferred to send word to her that newly arrived dispatches required his immediate attention. After sending disingenuous little notes by the post – conveniently distributed nine times a day – the tourists were free to explore Paris together. The Palais Royal, close by, may well have been their first destination.

Seat of the Duke of Orleans, the palace was more than a royal household. Before the Duke's inheritance of almost one half of France, he had resorted to building speculation to pay his debts. To the consternation of his neighbours, who had long enjoyed an unobstructed view of the ancient trees in the palace gardens, the Duke decided to enclose these green spaces on three sides with arcaded galleries of several stories, which he then rented out to restaurants, boutiques, gaming houses, theatres, and hotels. The neighbours' woe became the joy of other Parisians, of high and low rank, which flocked to this centre of commerce and pleasure.

As the Cosways and their friends walked carefully through jostling coaches and light cabriolets, Jefferson extolled the convenience and originality of this urban innovation, which he hoped to introduce to his native Virginia. Maria's impression – on aesthetic grounds – may have been less enthusiastic, primarily because the work was not yet finished. When they passed through the second courtyard of the palace, they saw the passage to the garden barred by an enormous wooden structure, thrown up temporarily. This shopping gallery of two corridors and three rows of boutiques was called the 'Camp of the Tartars' after some of the lower ranks of ruffians who frequented it. After escaping the 'tartars,' they did see a harmonious ensemble of arcades bordering the garden, only marred by the building site in the centre where the Duke was constructing a partially subterranean riding circus!

Strolling through the covered arcades, Jefferson pointed out various shops and amusements. Richard became more and more animated, chattering gaily. Each of them began to exclaim: 'Oh look at that automat of Mr. Pelletier!' or 'The watches of Le Roy,' or 'the wax statues of the Royal Family by Mr. Curtius!' For light-hearted amusement, there were several marionette theatres – one called the 'Chinese Shadows' – as well as a popular theatre of varieties, gaming clubs for gentlemen and other rooms for unsavoury rogues. One could see the latest fashions in hats or costumes in the shops or on the ladies promenading in the gardens in early afternoon. Later in the day only 'girls' walked alone. On such a warm day there were many taking ices and lemonade under the trees at the Cafe de Foy. More important meals could be had at the best restaurant in Paris, Brauvilliers. At Jefferson's suggestion they chose the 'Café Mecanique'. They were served by a dumbwaiter, which arrived up a column forming the leg of their table and dispensed with the need of catching a server's eye. They dined amid hilarity provided by Cosway's wit as the dishes appeared mysteriously from the depths below with much grinding of cables.

The English couple must have felt at home with the two Americans and at the same time introduced to a New World. Cultivated and polite, their new friends were visibly unimpressed by notions of nobility and rank, a refreshing contrast to the carefully-regulated European society. To them, merit and honesty were the great values. Maria could perceive a new way of thinking and feel a freer spirit when with them. Her studies of the antique, of the history and art of Greece and Rome, which inspired much of the creative endeavour of their times, were like worship of past virtues. These men were living them in the present.

After dining, they glided slowly down river to St. Cloud on a flat-bottomed boat, boarded at the foot of the Pont Royal. Leaving the city, they saw fine villas on the hills of Passy, wooded islands in the river's midst, Bellevue, the chateau of the King's aunts, and after an enormous bend, St. Cloud, recently purchased from the Duke of Orleans by the Queen. The chateau was a feast for the eyes inside and out. From the terrace they surveyed all of Paris and

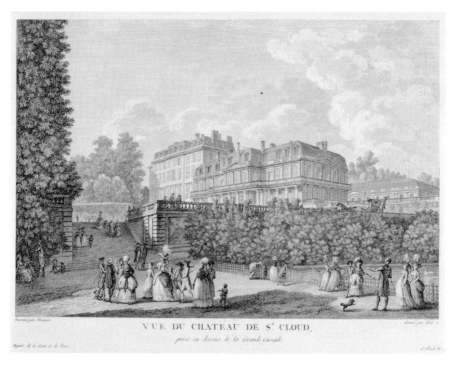

VUE DU CHATEAU DE S.ᵗ CLOUD,
prise au dessous de la Grande Cascade.

36. Château de St. Cloud.

its silver river sliding below the palace gardens. Inside, the great ornament of the building was the Gallery of Apollo, its ceiling decorated by Mignard with glorious scenes from the god's life and its walls covered with dozens of pictures by masters.

As they gazed at nine views of Venice by Canaletto, Jefferson could query Maria on her knowledge of Italy.

'Have you also seen Venice, Mrs. Cosway?'

'No, sir, that is one city which I have never visited.'

'Is it possible that you have not? At last, we can share ignorance. I think you must have seen much of the architecture, the statues, and the pictures that I have longed to see. Tell me, in Rome did you see the Dying Gladiator or the Farnese Hercules or the Apollo Belvedere?'

'Yes, yes. They were objects of study for all the artists.'

'And most naturally, you saw the Venus the Medici, the Dancing Faun, the Knife sharpener in the Tribuna in Florence?'

'Oh, I could not miss them. Mr. Zoffany was painting them when he became my teacher.'

'One day would you be kind enough to give me your impressions of the mass of wonders you have seen. I have heard of them from my friend, Dr. John Morgan of Philadelphia, but you have lived with them from childhood.'

'Mr. Jefferson, surely you will go to Italy yourself. Now that you are in Europe, it would be a shame not to see at first hand all that has filled your imagination.'

'I shall, I shall. You know I have built my home on Italian models. Its name is "Monticello" for it is on a little mountain.'

'Monticello, Monticello.'

'I have never heard the word spoken so perfectly, with its essence in the intonation.'

Maria laughed, 'It is not difficult. Mr. Cosway tells me that I shall never lose my accent.'

'You must not lose it. That would deprive others of an indescribable charm.'

The compliment surprised, coming from one whose reserved manners could be taken for coldness in character.

'I suppose we should think of returning to Paris,' Trumbull mused.

Jefferson looked momentarily unhappy. Then he suggested, 'Yes, but the day is still warm. The evening promises to be perfect. What if we took advantage of our good fortune and visited Ruggieri's garden? I know 'tis not as fine as Vauxhall, but they say Monsieur Ruggieri is clever with fireworks and music.'

They needed no persuasion. At dusk they entered the large pleasure garden on the northern outskirts of Paris, owned by the Ruggieri brothers. As they promenaded along tree-lined walks, their easy conversation with Jefferson continued. During the course of the evening Maria may have been intrigued by the delicate balance of his character. Under the surface of an apparent timidity, there were signs of an ardent nature. He was at the same time humble yet dignified, reserved yet easy of manner, diffident yet warm and engaging. As he warmed to one in conversation, he had such a kind expression on his face that one was soon induced to converse with him as an old and trusted friend. She felt as if she had known him always.

'Mrs. Cosway, I suppose the little spectacle of Mr. Ruggieri does not compare with the Roman feasts you may have seen.'

'On the contrary, I am told that the Ruggieri brothers surpass all others. In truth I did not see any grand Roman feasts, only the celebrations of Florence. The greatest display of fire I ever saw in my life was that of Vesuvius, which proves the superiority of nature over artifice.'

'*What have you not seen? This evening's portrayal in sparks of the "Forges of Vulcan Beneath Mt. Etna" and the "Combat of Mars" will be pathetic exhibitions to you.*'

'*Oh, not at all, sir. This evening all concurs to make a joyous outing — a pleasant garden, bouquets of fireworks, music, and, above all, congenial company.*'

'*Yes, but one element lacks. The music played here is not the best. Mr. Trumbull has told me of your concerts, your fine singing and skill on the harp and pianoforte. Have you heard the new harp, invented by Mr. Krumpholtz for his wife? They are both among the finest harp-players in Europe. I believe she can be heard this evening with her husband accompanying her on the violin.*'

'*We have been wishing to hear them. If Mr. Cosway and Mr. Trumbull are agreeable, shall we perfectly conclude our day with music?*'

The evening seemed to go on and on, as Jefferson thought of new amusements. But the time seemed short, composed of hurried moments of pleasure, which vanished all too quickly. During the harp concert they must have spoken of their favourite composers. He told her of his fondness for Italian music and particularly that of Campioni.

'*Mr. Jefferson, what a remarkable coincidence of taste! Forgive me if I seem immodest, but I once had the honour to be directed by Signore Campioni at the Court of the Grand Duke of Tuscany. What a privilege it was to know and make music with him.*'

Jefferson fell silent. He looked into her face deeply, and she saw a flicker of recognition in his eyes.

From that day, their new American friend began to accompany the Cosways on frequent excursions. Although these outings probably numbered no more than a half dozen, the memory of those few days seems to have remained clear in Jefferson's mind. Strong feeling is the engraver's acid, incising an entire scene with all its sensory power – a look, a word, an aroma – on the heart. Almost all their visits were escapes to gardens and chateaux, nestled in the gentle hills west of the city's noise. Jefferson had a need for the country and a passionate interest in gardening. He often walked four or five miles a day, invariably heading up the Champs Elysées to the Bois de Boulogne. Two days after their first meeting, the Cosways took a carriage to his house where he suggested that they take his habitual route to

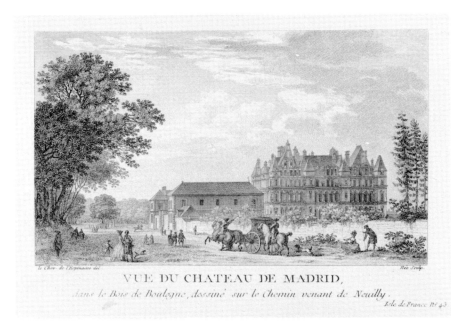

VUE DU CHATEAU DE MADRID,
dans le Bois de Boulogne, dessiné sur le Chemin venant de Neuilly.

37. Château de Madrid.

the Bois to see two chateaux – one very old, the Chateau de Madrid, and the other, Bagatelle, modern and original. Madrid, built by François I after his liberation from prison in that city, was almost falling down, curiously decorated by coloured tiles which reflected the sun light. In spite of its dilapidated state, the King gave the Marquis de Rosanbo, President of the Paris Parliament, the right to live there.

Bagatelle was the latest in fashion, especially the Anglo-Chinese garden, laid out by the Scottish gardener, Thomas Blaikie, for the King's brother, the *Comte d'Artois*. English gardens of sinuous lines and sentimental symbolism had been eagerly adopted by the French. Bagatelle was a park of amusing follies – an Indian pavilion, a tower of the Paladins on a little mountain which served as icehouse, an Egyptian obelisk mounted on the backs of tortoises, a Gothic philosopher's house, from whose balcony one had views in all directions, artificial lakes and rivers, cascades and Chinese bridges.

The most rustic was the Hermitage, a house entirely made of tree branches and reeds. As they climbed its moss-lined staircase, Jefferson may have thought

38. l'Hermitage de Bagatelle.

that the Scottish gardener had been inspired by the wild imagery of the Gaelic bard Ossian. He began to recite:

> *O thou that rollest above, round as the shield of my fathers!*
> *Whence are thy beams, O sun! thy everlasting light?*
> *Thou comest forth in thy awful beauty;*
> *The stars hide themselves in the sky;…'*

Maria continued,

> *'the moon, cold and pale, sinks in the western wave;*
> *but thou thyself movest alone.*
> *Who can be a companion of thy course?*

'Or do you know this from Darthula:

> *He brought me weeping to Selama.*
> *He spoke the words of love, but my soul was sad.*

I saw the shields of my fathers; …
I saw the arms of the dead, the tear was on my cheek!'

'Or this?' he responded,

'…ye are laden with grief.
The darkness of age comes like the mist of the desert.
My shield is worn with years! my sword is fixed in its place!
I said to my soul, Thy evening shall be calm; thy departure like a
* fading light.*
But the storm has returned. I bend like an aged oak.
My boughs are fallen…I tremble in my place.'

A spark passed between them. Was it a rush of literary enthusiasm?
'The greatest poet that has ever lived,' Jefferson exclaimed. 'At periods of
my life I have read him every day.'
'Truly sublime!'
'Yes, yes, that's it! The sublime! The deepest grief becomes beautiful in its
passion, increases the power of the intellect, elevates the imagination, sharpens
the feelings.'
'Mrs. Cosway has painted scenes from Ossian which were not justly appreciated
by hardened critics,' Richard loyally said, not seeming to perceive the changed
atmosphere.
'They were not my best pictures. I suppose I failed to capture the elevation or
the depth of feeling of the bard because I lacked tragic experience.'
'I wish that you should never know it,' Jefferson said.

After the fantasies of Bagatelle, the scientific side of the American
asserted itself. Nothing would do now but visits to the great repositories of
the intellect – the King's Library and the King's Garden. It was during
these visits that they could appreciate the immense curiosity and learning
of Mr. Jefferson. The Cosways had an extensive library, but they both had
poured their energies into the practice of the arts. Their imagination was
continually exercised, without the intellectual passion to measure and
classify, to establish the science of nature. The King's Garden was renowned,
even in America, as the centre of the study of natural history after its

Intendant, the *Comte de Buffon*, had published his description of the King's collection of plants, minerals, and animals.

Jefferson led them through the gate of the King's Garden just before noon. He was eager that they witness a demonstration of Monsieur Buffon's ingenious sun dial, which marked only the hour of twelve noon. Hurriedly they ascended a spiral path around a little hill to find a kiosk of iron and copper at the summit. This construction was crowned by the curious solar meridian which struck the hour of twelve every day. The hammer was a globe of the earth, which dropped on a Chinese tambour when the cord holding its counterweight was burned through by the sun's rays focused through a magnifying glass .The angle of the glass determined the exactitude of the hour.

Jefferson read the Latin inscription around the frieze of the meridian: ' "I count only the sunny hours." That is how time should be measured, by the clear hours, as it must be in eternity when time is stopped.'

Cosway replied to his dreaming friend, 'Time is stopped, my friend. With these dark clouds the sun will not mark its appointment with midday, and you shall have your wish.'

39. View of the King's Garden.

'Perhaps I shall. Well, there is no point in waiting for the globe to fall. Shall we take a tour around the garden before the rain comes? Monsieur de Buffon receives at dinner those who ask to see his house and grounds. He is an amiable dinner companion if you would like to dine with him.'

Again Richard answered for them: 'I fear we have an invitation to dine, but if you do stay, a word of advice, if I may. Do not speak of Buffon's son or daughter-in-law, for she has virtually left her husband for the Duke of Orleans. The Duchess is not au courant, but I am told the elder Buffon is understandably vexed.'

'Mr. Cosway, you are more Parisian than Trumbull and I. We shall not be treading on such delicate ground, you may be assured.'

As they parted that day, regrets were appeased by the promises made on all sides that they should profit from the next fine day by making an excursion to Marly and St. Germain.

The day they rode out to Marly was as warm and clear as that first Sunday. Their carriage passed over the river by the Pont de Neuilly and then followed a country road to the next large bend in the Seine to see the famous Machine of Marly. They did not follow all Mr. Jefferson's explanations of how this assemblage of water wheels lifted many tons of water into the pumping system, feeding all the reservoirs and fountains of Versailles and Marly. The Machine made an impossible racket and tossed up a foul-smelling mud, which must have been a nuisance to its neighbours. That day, however, they took the aesthete's view and felt transported by the rainbows glistening in the droplets of spray hovering over the wheels. After giving vent to his passion for mechanics and science before the groaning Machine, Jefferson showed his sensibility to nature from the high terrace of the Chateau of Saint Germain. As they surveyed the pastoral scene of the entire Seine valley and Paris in the distance, Jefferson spoke more to himself than to his companions.

'What is it about living on the heights? One is windswept, chilled and sometimes barren, exposed to all nature's buffeting. Yet that is where we wish to live. That is where I have built my house. Only on the heights can we truly see, can we rise up out of the muck and give ourselves the illusion of dominance.'

Maria must have come to the realisation that their friend harboured unspoken sadness. This side of his character was touching. Trumbull would have told her about the personal losses — a beloved wife four years ago and a young daughter more recently. The darkness he had passed through surfaced again later that

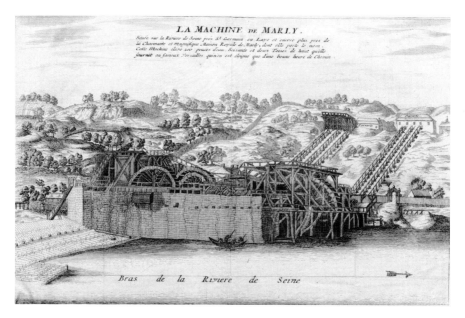

La Machine de Marly.
Située sur la Rivière de Seine pres St Germain en Laye et encore plus pres de la Charmante et magnifique Maison Royale de Marly, dont elle prend le nom. Cette Machine élève 200 pouces d'eau Soixante et deux Toises de haut qu'elle fournit au fameux Versailles qui en est éloigné que d'une bonne heure de Chemin.

40. The Machine at Marly which pumped water from the Seine into a reservoir, which then watered the gardens of Versailles.

day. They were in the gardens of the Chateau of Marly, created in a low, marshy basin to become a jewel among Louis XIV's homes. Marly was a small Palladian pavilion for the King, representing Apollo the Sun. In two rows either side of a long sunken pool were twelve small guest pavilions, decorated with Italianate frescos in trompe l'oeil to economise on the cost of real statues. The effect was that of a theatre design to which the comfort of the King's guests was sacrificed when he ruled that flues would spoil the pavilions' rooflines and guests would have to live with smoking fireplaces. While Trumbull and Cosway examined a strange chariot on a wooden track —conceived by Louis XIV as a toy, which he drove hurtling through the garden with several ladies — Jefferson and Maria were enjoying the shady tunnel of honeysuckle and clematis, which arched from one pavilion to another.

Was it this moment at Marly when Maria sensed something unknown behind Jefferson's kind eyes? The possibility that he could have more than a feeling of friendship for her was unsettling. Yet she had not discouraged the attentions of General Paoli when she suspected that he cared for her in a deeper way than she for him. That was distinctly different. He was older than her father; he was like a cicisbeo who understood ambiguity. An American was far from understanding *such a relation. These confused sentiments were no doubt in her head as they dined at a rustic inn in Marly, where Jefferson had arranged for his servant Petit to lay out their dinner. Was her tongue paralysed during the meal, always watching, watching, the tall Virginian, listening to his low voice? This was unlike her.*

After dinner they had one last visit to make before returning to Paris. Again it was Jefferson's interest in architecture which took them to see Madame du Barry's music pavilion at Louveciennes, built by the architect Ledoux. It was a charming Neo-classical structure with sumptuous interior frescos and luxurious furniture, created only for the private visits of Louis XV. Madame du Barry found the main chateau too cramped and unworthy for him. When they paid the concierge the usual pourboire to visit the pavilion, they were told to be discreet for Madame was in residence. Madame Lebrun had told them about her recent visit to paint the middle-aged former favourite, who lived quietly at Louveciennes.

'I should like to have a glimpse of Madame du Barry. Perhaps she will walk in her garden,' Maria wished aloud.

'My dear, she is not going on parade for a group of Anglo-American tourists like an exotic bird of the Royal Menagerie,' Cosway reasoned.

'Yes, yes, but Madame Lebrun did say that she was really simple and direct, kind and generous. She would certainly not be disdainful.'

'No, but we also heard that she was a bit of a coquette. We cannot let these two bachelors be exposed to the dangers of a wily Royal courtisane.'

'We might like to be exposed to such a danger, at least to have known the temptation of kings,' young Trumbull spoke up.

'Mr. Trumbull, a republican of the New World, could hardly be tempted. I am persuaded that you would be as marble before the coquetry of an old royalist,' Maria interjected.

Jefferson answered for him: 'Madame, a man may be made of ice, but never of marble. Even the coldest disposition melts before the sun, whose very virtue renders her irresistible.'

'I did not know that Royal favourites were known for virtue.'

'The most desirable, if not virtuous, were no doubt able to create an illusion of aloofness, of inaccessibility – even if submission was inevitable, as we know it is in absolute regimes.'

'Is it not then the unattainable, rather than the virtuous, which attracts?'

'Mrs. Cosway, that is a topic for the philosopher on which we might discourse all month.'

'Sir, your superior science would be too much for a poor woman.'

'A lady of your accomplishments does not need science. Indeed, the disputatious manners of French ladies, their continual interest in political matters, to say nothing of their pretensions to learning, render them singularly unattractive.'

'Mr. Jefferson, you mean you are alone in Paris, and you find the French ladies unappealing! My good fellow, you must have some exceptional specimens in America to render you so indifferent,' Cosway said, perplexed.

'We do have exceptional women in America, but 'tis more a question of manners. I am accustomed to greater simplicity, less affectation, the charm of honest interchange.'

'I have found greater naturalness and grace in social relations in France than in England. Here manners seem easy and soft to me,' Maria ventured.

'Madame, on that we can agree. I pray you to excuse me, Mr. Cosway, if I seem harsh on your countrymen, but I was not well received in London this spring. You may have heard that when I was presented at Court, your King simply turned his back on me without saying a word. I can understand his displeasure with our political differences, but ten years later I would have thought him above stooping to rudeness.'

'Quite right, quite right. He can be narrow in his opinions.'

'But no political subjects. Nothing is more impolite in society than the introduction of topics that lead to contention. Please forgive my ill-considered commentary on your Sovereign. We must not leave these places of harmony in a mood incompatible with their atmosphere. Dusk is falling. I hope I may have your promise to return with me to an enchanted garden nearby, which we have not ample hours to see – the Desert de Retz of Monsieur de Monville.'

'We shan't fail to see it. I have heard of Monsieur de Monville's Desert and have been longing to visit it.' Maria seized upon the suggestion.

'Madame, consider your wish fulfilled.'

That first week of the Cosways' acquaintance with Jefferson they saw him every two days and after St. Germain every day. They were not always outdoors. They also shared a love of music and enjoyment of the theatre. He accompanied them to a *concert spirituel* and to an evening at the *Comédie*

Italienne. The *concerts spirituels* were no longer devoted exclusively to sacred music. Originally they were organised to provide music when the Royal Academy of Music was closed on Sundays or religious feasts. Over the years profane music was included in the programmes, performed in a hall of the Tuileries Palace. They heard two Haydn symphonies and Madame Mara singing Italian airs. Although some of the best music could be heard at these concerts, the performers and their listeners suffered nuisances from other inhabitants of the Tuileries. The Royal Family had long preferred other residences and hired out apartments in the palace, including the concert hall. Between concerts a lock-maker installed his furnace in the hall; others left slabs of meat on the stage. Odours from numerous kitchens discouraged some concertgoers from frequenting the hall, although the night the Cosways attended the diplomatic corps was well represented. Jefferson noted the presence of the Ambassadors of Sardinia, Venice, Malta, Denmark, and the Minister of Genoa.

The next evening they went to the new Theatre des Italiens built, strangely enough, with its back facing the grand boulevard. Jefferson had seen the light opera *Richard Coeur de Lion*, the main offering of the evening, but gallantly proposed that an Italian lady would surely not wish to miss the theatre named after the *commedia dell'arte* tradition.

After they were seated on the red velvet benches in their loge, Jefferson leaned over to ask if Maria had heard Madame Dugazon sing in Nina ou la Folle par Amour, *one of the Italians' most successful productions.*

'Well, yes, I have, although I did not wish to tell you that we had attended the Theatre Italiens before,' she whispered.

'Why ever not?'

'Perhaps it would have spoiled your pleasure in showing us another aspect of Paris, and I know it would have spoiled mine if we had not come.'

'Then you have saved two of us from needless distress.'

'Whispering, whispering,' Richard muttered.

'Mr. Cosway, you know I have the habit of whispering to my cicisbeo; you know how innocent these secrets are.'

''Tis bold of you to presume on Mr. Jefferson's politeness by referring to him thus.'

'Never fear, sir, Mrs. Cosway has too good a heart to offend me.'

Later in the evening, during the second spectacle, a one act comic harlequinade entitled Les Deux Billets, *Maria must have decided that Jefferson could never be her cicisbeo. He could be a friend or something else, but never her cicisbeo. She knew this when she stole a sideways glance and saw him doing the same. It was during a scene when Harlequin reads and spells aloud a letter from his beloved Argentine: He spells out slowly, as if he did not understand, J E T 'A I M E, je t'aime, then he says, 'this word is too short, I want it to use the entire alphabet.' And Argentine replies, 'I shall say it to you all my life.'*

Vue Perspective de la Colonne.

10

'Le Désert de Retz'

It was now mid-September. Richard Cosway was taken up with his sketches of the Orleans children at the Palais Royal or at the convent of Bellechasse. The children and their governess, Madame de Genlis, spent most of their time at Bellechasse in a special pavilion Madame de Genlis had ordered to be constructed in the convent grounds. In her transformation from *coquette* to bluestocking, she had become a highly original person. It was said that she had refused marriage with the rich, handsome, young and talented

Monsieur Racine de Monville simply because he was not 'of the Court'. Now she had abandoned all luxury — no trimmings, no laces, no painted face, no powdered hair. Dressed in severe dark clothes, wide-brimmed hat and veil, this authoress of several treatises on education was a tenacious pursuer of culture. Her rejected suitor, Monsieur de Monville, a splendid flutist and harpist, continued his regular visits to her drawing room to play the harp, an accomplishment to which Madame de Genlis also pretended. He never married, dedicating his prodigious fortune and considerable learning in botany, horticulture, and architecture to one of the most inventive and fantastical gardens in France, called his *désert* or place of solitude. Fashionable *anglo-chinois* gardens — romantic and sinuously laid out parks, punctuated with *'folies'* — were springing up everywhere: the Count d'Artois' Bagatelle, the Baron Saint-James' *folie* at Neuilly, Marie-Antoinette's garden at *Petit Trianon*, the Duke d'Orléans' Parc Monceau. Many incorporated the taste for the exotic with Chinese bridges or pavilions. All included temples or ruins inspired by the Antique. The originality of Monsieur de Monville was that he actually lived in his *folies*. When he purchased a farm on the site of an abandoned village, St. Jacques de Retz, he began designing his house and a garden dotted with twenty or so ornamental constructions. The first, elevated on the highest prominence of the garden, was a neoclassical Temple of Pan. Then Monsieur de Monville added the indispensable *chinoiserie*, a gaily-painted wooden Chinese House beside an artificial lake. He was perhaps the first European actually to reside in such a garden structure where he kept his library and organised readings of Rousseau. The imagination of this gifted amateur, still not satiated with novelty, undertook a few years later to build the most unusual residence in Europe; his new home was a giant reproduction, some four stories high, of a ruined Doric column, whose contrived fissures concealed the windows of the highest level.

It was to this enchanted place that Thomas Jefferson took Maria Cosway on what was probably their last long excursion of the summer. It is not known if they were alone together. But it is possible that Richard was sent for by the Duchess d'Orléans at the last hour. In which case Maria would have most probably donned some of the new fashions that her elegant husband purchased for her chez Mademoiselle Bertin, the Queen's milliner. The *Cabinet des Modes* for 1786 illustrates what a fashionable lady might be

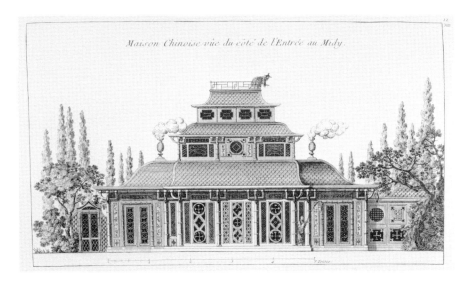

Maison Chinoise vue du côté de l'Entrée au Midy.

41. Chinese House in the Désert de Retz.

seen in: a *caraco* – a short waistcoat of straw-coloured and chestnut stripes – worn over a corset and petticoat of watered pale green taffeta. The ensemble is finished with a gauze fichu around the shoulders, a gauze pouf on a large coiffure, adorned with pink, white, and green feathers, and gloves of lemon-coloured calfskin.

As their carriage retraced the road to St. Germain and Marly, taken only some days before, so much had changed. The last time their party had been carefree and unthinking. Now there was a certain tension in the atmosphere as they conversed about news of the day, things of little consequence. As they passed through the Forest of Marly and approached the entrance to the Garden, Mr. Jefferson must have served as guide: 'Now, dear lady, we shall pass through the gates of a grotto, for that is the first folie of Monsieur de Monville. An artificial cavern forms the introduction to his park, as if we were entering primeval chaos. I believe many of the constructions are inspired by the symbolism of the Freemasons. Are you prepared for this adventure, this journey into other realms, ancient civilisations?'

'Oh, yes, I am.' Mr. Jefferson took her gloved hand and helped her alight from the carriage. They stood before two massive oak gates. After he rang the bell, a footman soon admitted the tourists. They passed through the deep shade of a grotto where they could scarcely make out two satyrs holding torches – a dramatic entrance when aflame.

Peering through the tunnel, they could see the great curiosity of the garden, framed in the light: 'Oh, that must be the Column House!'

'So it is. What a whimsical idea! Shall we take a closer look?'

They made their way towards a grassy open space between two rows of elm trees. It was an open air theatre. The stage was marked by a carved frieze, portraying Bacchus being pulled in his chariot by numerous little Cupids. As they approached it, a temple came into view opposite the great broken column, but in the same axis.

'I believe the Temple is dedicated to Pan, representing the pure paganism of Nature,' he suggested.

'Is the pagan pure, sir?'

'Some of them were surely still innocent. Was it not the Christian Saint Paul who said sin came with the law?'

'A serious contradiction with the story of Adam's Fall.'

'Madame, you will not be able to drag me into a theological debate. I respect the beliefs of all and am reluctant to judge. If judgment be necessary it should be on the basis of acts, not professions.'

'The words of a wise man. Let us turn our backs on Pan and look at this sublime Greek ruin.'

'Yes, but pray do not brush against Bacchus, who appears to be led by love not drink, lest you partake of his intoxication.'

'*Would that be tragic? Not one taste of forbidden wine? At least once? I know strong sentiments do not befit the modesty of a lady. I should not speak to you of these subjects, but I have confidence that you will not think ill of me. I feel so easy with you. I feel as if you would not judge my weakness harshly.*'

'*Judge you? If I were to judge it would be only to praise. There is much to praise: accomplishment, taste, gaiety, loveliness…I see I have made you uncomfortable. Forgive me. Would you enjoy seeing the hothouses? I am told Monsieur de Monville has over 4,000 plants, including many exotic ones, in his botanical collection.*'

'*Before the plants, shan't we ask the concierge to let us see the interior of the Column? I am longing to see how one lives in a ruin.*'

They were not disappointed. The staircase in the centre of the house was a spiral of wrought iron turned into a brilliant swirl of colour as pots of geraniums pushed between the posts of the balustrade stretched toward a glass skylight. The rooms were finely furnished like any gentlemen's house. There were many mirrors, beds hung in toile de Jouy, gilded fire surrounds, clocks, leather armchairs – all giving an appearance of comfort. Jefferson was fascinated by every detail and every innovation of the house's plan.

His absorption in architecture was matched by that in horticulture when they entered the overwhelming display of plants in Monsieur de Monville's greenhouses. Among hundreds of bright blue periwinkles, purple heliotropes, white lilies, Arabian jasmines and Indian fig trees, the reserved Mr. Jefferson may have finally opened a gate and let Maria see past his wall of diffidence. He appeared to be reading the neatly-lettered plaques identifying the exotic species when he turned and said, 'While we were in the theatre you paid me a great compliment to say that I had earned your confidence. It would not only be ungracious but unfeeling if I were not able to

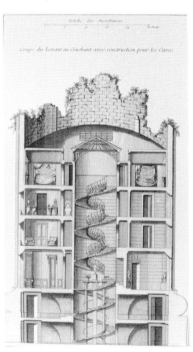

42. *Cross-section of Racine de Monville's house.*

return your trust. And I wish to say that I do. I perceive your honest heart, your capacity for friendship, your reliable affection, and though it is considered impolite to compliment a lady on her physical person, I shall break that rule and tell you that your innocent beauty causes something inside one to melt. Since my wife died no one has been able to replace my solitary thoughts with happy ones. You have done it. I shall ever be indebted to you for that alone. Forgive me if I have troubled you with this effusion, but your sweet sincerity called it forth.'

'Mr. Jefferson…Mr. Jefferson. I am indebted to you. What has it been? A fortnight ago that we first met and now we seem to be friends for life.' She could hardly say more. Even had she been unmarried, a lady could not declare her feelings to a gentleman too openly. In her position what could she have said? That she had never felt such a pressure in her heart? That she was bursting with contradictory thoughts? That she felt possessed with a strange energy? All, all impossible to say. She could never admit that she wished him to read her secret thoughts.

'Yes, friends for life, each inhabiting a whole continent, thousands of miles of ocean between us when I return to America.'

'It may be better that way, easier.' She overstepped her own boundaries.

'Better perhaps, easier never.'

'This hothouse has become terribly warm. Shall we walk a time in the garden?'

They left the humid, fragrant glass houses and entered a path leading through a wood. They soon emerged on the grassy banks of a large pond and before them a bridge of wooden planks leading to an island in the centre of the pond. Monsieur de Monville's imagination, never idle, had erected on the island a wonderful Oriental tent of tole, its large yellow and turquoise stripes and tasselled trim painted in trompe l'oeil as if the curtains of the tent had just been pulled back. A small wooden sign placed nonchalantly at the end of the bridge announced the name of the island: Isle de bonheur.

Leading Maria by the hand as they carefully stepped across the narrow bridge, Mr. Jefferson echoed her wish: 'We cannot refuse to explore such an island.'

'No, I am anxious to see the inside of this folie.'

The interior of the tent was wonderfully lined in real, not painted, toile de Jouy, and apparently served as a salle d'armes or place to exercise the art of fencing. 'Oh, I see it is a place of combat, not a place of happiness, as the island pretends to be,' she reflected.

'Yet happiness must often be won, fought for, secured by arms. I have seen this in my life. Happiness requires a certain boldness of action.'

'True for gentlemen, they are soldiers, knights, conquerors. They must win through adversity. A woman must wait, must watch, must hope, must submit. I do not see where boldness of action shall win her much but scorn. She depends on the boldness of others to secure her fortune.'

'Yet it is she who holds the destiny of others in her hands, if she did but know it.'

'She only holds in her hands what is first given her to hold.'

He did not reply, taking her gloved hands in his. Slowly he unfastened the pearl button of one, then the other. Gently he pulled off each glove, letting them fall to the ground. Taking her hands in his, he pressed each one in turn to his lips.

'Oh, I feel short of breath. Am I ill?'

'No, your innocence mistakes happiness for illness. You appear so young. 'Tis difficult to believe you are a married lady. Forgive my curiosity, but there is much I would know about you. Are you long married?'

'Five years now.'

'Have you children?'

'No, no children.'

'Are you content? I would wish you always content.'

'Content? I have thought so at moments. I have received more in many ways than other women. Yet all was done in spite of my wishes. I wished to stay in Italy, but we came to London. I wished not to marry, but I married. I have found comfort in religion, which teaches me to be meek and not to resist.'

'I would wish more for you than resignation.'

'What more is there?'

'Are you not aware of more?'

'I do not understand your meaning...I am feeling uneasy. Could we please begin to make our way back?'

'Of course, I beg you to forgive my apparent indifference to your indisposition.' He picked up her gloves and put them absentmindedly in his pocket.

They left the tent in silence, treading gingerly across the planks of the bridge and turning towards another smaller pond beside which was the marvellous

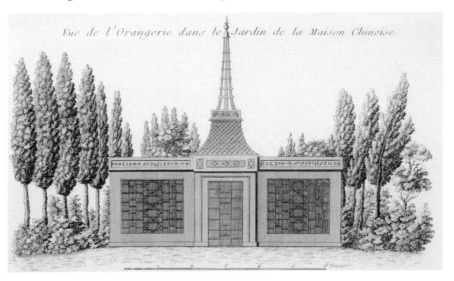

Vue de l'Orangerie dans le Jardin de la Maison Chinoise.

Chinese House. In its garden was an orangerie in the Chinese style. As they passed by she may well have begun to feel very tired.

'Mr. Jefferson, before returning, do you think there might be a bench in the orangerie where we might rest a moment?'

'We shall see of course...yes, there is. Please let me assist you.'

When they were seated, the power of the mingled jasmine and orange scents invaded the senses. She tried to explain her fatigue. 'I am not ill. Do not be concerned. It is worse than illness. It is because...because of...'

He placed a finger on her lips, leaned over and kissed her neck softly. In France it was thought vulgar to kiss a lady on the mouth and rouged cheeks prevented any kisses on the face. He took her hands and pressed them tightly. She felt his mouth on her throat, then moving down, above the heart.

'Please, sir, please no.'

'My dear girl, can you know how I feel?'

'I think I do. For the first time, yes.'

They sat together in silence, her hand in his two, for a very long time. The perfume of orange flowers infused the air. With thoughts tumbling, they must have understood why the Isle de Bonheur was an island. They were isolated from the rest of the world, from society. If they stayed on the island, there was no bridge back. The brightness of the windowpanes began to dim with the twilight outside. They rose and made their way past the theatre, the Column House, and then saw another folie. It was a stone pyramid, which also served as an ice house. It was then that Jefferson spoke.

'I believe the pyramid is the Freemason's symbol for perfection, the achievement of the quest for truth, the harmony of each with universal knowledge.'

Too confused to know what sort of truth she had found that day, Maria did know that she was profoundly changed. The first change, not altogether comfortable, was her state of unrest. During the next days thoughts of the Desert were her nourishment and rest. She did not know when she would see him again. After two eternal days, he passed before the Cosways' lodgings in a cabriolet and asked if they would like to walk in the Champs Elysées. Maria accepted with alacrity, only pausing to take her gloves, a large, straw hat festooned with plumes, and a parasol.

18th September was a glorious day, warm and sunny. They had not had such a day since August and it was now mid-September. As it turned out, it was the last day of summer. They wished to profit from every minute of warmth. Jefferson may well have proposed that they leave his carriage at the Hotel de Langeac and set out from his house for their promenade. If so they could head straight for the Seine, using a country road that cut through pastures and gardens, intending when they reached the river to walk down the Cours de Reine to the Grand Cours or Champs-Elysées. While walking, Jefferson's usual dignified reserve and soft politeness had occasion to give way to a more animated manner. He could joke:

Vue de la Glaciere.

43. *Ice House in the form of a pyramid, thought to be a Masonic symbol. Most of the follies of the Desert de Retz seem to trace symbolically portions of the Freemasons' initiation rite.*

'Did Mrs. Cosway lose part of her fashionable new ensemble the other day?' he asked with a mischievous smile.

'Whatever do you mean, sir?'

'I found these.' He pulled a pair of citron yellow gloves from his pocket. 'Do they belong to you?'

'You know well that they do. How kind of you to return them!'

'To tell you the truth, I do not wish to return them. I would keep them, if it were possible, as a souvenir of our days together.'

'Is that all we are to have: souvenirs?'

'One cannot have souvenirs without first living, without all the fortuitous encounters of life. We have that and cannot be robbed of it. Now life will have its way with us. Let us not be troubled by depressing thoughts on such a day as this.'

'No, no melancholy today.' She wished to be brave, although filled with apprehension. She could not fear that this new friendship would end, for this friend was surely not one to betray. Perhaps she feared that she would be the traitor, refusing to admit that treason had already been committed, imagining that the fatal decision lay somewhere in the future. There was no honourable issue, but resisting the force of her inclinations was unimaginable.

'You must never let melancholy tarnish happiness. You must always remember these days with the knowledge that my sentiments are composed of true affection, that I shall always think of you and never with anything but love.'

She could only lower her head and gaze at the tips of her silk slippers. Neither spoke for several minutes. When they approached the midpoint of the Cours la Reine, the heat of the day began to be felt. She created a current of air with her fan. When it snapped shut, she failed to notice that the silk cord of the fan looped round her wrist gave away. For a while the fan must have rested in the folds of her petticoat and then slipped to the ground. They continued across the stone bridge which led to the Champs Elysées where they could find chairs under the trees and sellers of lemonade and pastry. As they settled down to take refreshment, she must have realised she had no fan.

'Oh, I appear to have lost my fan! How careless of me! And it was one that I had painted myself.'

'I shall fetch it for you. Can you tell me what I should look for? It must not be far. You had it by the river.'

'It was cream silk, with three divisions. In the middle is a lady with a hat, copied after one of my husband's portraits of me, on the right is a gentleman, and on the left another lady. I dislike troubling you like this.'

'It is the least a gentleman can do for his lady, and I shall relish the opportunity to retrieve yet another souvenir. I shall not be long,' and he hurried away toward the Cours la Reine.

Jefferson was gone a very long time. Someone must have fancied the fan. Then he approached with a much changed demeanour. He was walking slowly with a pained look. He seemed to hold his right hand, covered with a handkerchief, in his left.

'Oh dear, what is the matter? You look so troubled.'

'Such a foolish accident, but here is your pretty fan, no worse for its adventures, which I cannot say for mine.'

'Are you wounded? What happened?'

'I was so eager to get to the Petit Cours before a carriage crushed your fan or a thief absconded with it that I took the shortest way and avoided the bridge, crowded with people and vehicles. Then too imbued with my illusion of youth I decided to leap across the stone-paved ditch that serves as a fence along the Petit Cours. I beg you not to imagine the rest. I seem to have done harm to my right wrist, which is not surprising considering the force of my weight upon it.'

'Oh dear, does it pain you much? Do you wish to return home?'

'I think I must, but I do not wish to leave you and spoil our outing. Shall we try to forget about this little mishap as we make our way to my house?'

As they walked through the Champs Elysées more was broken than Jefferson's wrist. (It did turn out to be severely injured.) The spell was broken. Their happy mood was dissipated. She could tell that he was very uneasy. Despite his bravery he could not hide the discomfort. By the time they reached the Hotel de Langeac, he begged her to forgive him for not accompanying her further and asked his coachman to see her home. He called two surgeons that day, but they were unable to relieve his suffering.

Although Mrs. Cosway lived in London, the freest city of Europe, where thought was liberated and her mind had been forced to accept many modern ideas, she must have remembered the superstitions of Italian peasants, who would have seen this unfortunate accident as a sign from heaven. It was an unwelcome augury at the critical moment when she wished to embark upon an exciting journey. Be that as it may, she was not prepared that day to believe in superstitions, and would not yet give up her unreasonable hope.

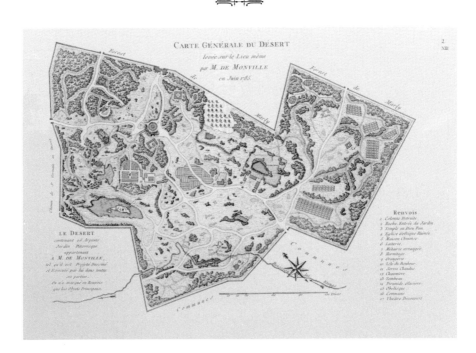

The Cosways' final fortnight in Paris was unlike the carefree summer of the previous two months. The climate became autumnal, mostly damp, heavy skies and cold grey light. Jefferson was injured far more seriously than they had suspected and was unable to keep any engagements, often staying in bed. Two days after his accident he sent word to Maria that he was greatly indisposed. She was apparently desperate to see him and know how he was. She tried to persuade her husband that they must visit their invalided friend. He agreed, but then spent hours looking at pictures in the collection of Monsieur de Beaujon in the Hotel d'Evreux. Maria felt he was being deliberately slow, but could not say so. Then they had no time for a visit; the Duchess of Kingston was expecting them at dinner at her house in St. Cloud. They could not disappoint her. She had been exceedingly gracious to them, receiving them in her large apartments in the same hotel where they were staying, the Parlement d'Angleterre. She had lived outside England since her scandalous trial for bigamy in 1776 and had a reputation for extravagance and eccentricity, but was known for her stimulating conversation. She had been Lady-in-Waiting to the Queen, a friend and confidante of Frederick of Prussia and the Czarina, and was still accorded much favour by many Europeans. Most impressive to those who knew her was the great generosity of spirit she showed toward her late husband's nephew, the cause of all her troubles. It was he who had provoked the trial for bigamy in order to gain her inheritance. The ploy failed, except for legally taking away her title, which she continued to use on the continent. As soon as the Duchess discovered that this nephew was penniless in France, she interceded with Louis XVI to have his debts forgiven, found him a house near Paris, and gave him a pension.

The Duchess's brilliant conversation must have seemed excessively long that evening. It was dark and late when the Cosways finally entered the courtyard of the Hotel de Langeac to have news of Jefferson. They rapped on his door for a very long time and finally saw the head of a servant who asked with a sleepy voice whatever could be their business, that the entire household had gone to bed. Again disappointed, Maria could only write a note that night:

> …I have appeard a Monster for not having sent to know how you was [sic], *the whole day.* I have been More uneasy, Than I can

express...I came home with the disappointment of not having been able Make My appologies in propria *persona*. I hope you feel my distress...[We will] come to see you tomorrow Morning.... Oh I wish you was [sic] well enough to come to us tomorrow to dinner...I would Serve you and help you at dinner, and divert your pain after dinner by good Musik.

The next day the Cosways paid their visit. They found Jefferson in a large oval upper room, which served as his study and bedroom. The windows overlooking the garden were draped in heavy blue silk as was the bed. Books were, of course, everywhere – on his writing table, piled beside the bed, in bookcases. It was sad to see him so low, resting on his couch in his dressing gown, dark half moons under his eyes from little sleep. His arm was bound up and suspended in a sling of cotton, from which swollen fingers hung.

After they were seated, Richard asked in a cheery voice, 'Well, my dear fellow, what mischief have you been up to?'

'I imagined that I could race about like a green boy, whose bones were not green at all.'

'Does your arm pain you enormously?' Maria asked.

'Honestly, Madame, a great deal. Since the bone pierced the skin, the surgeons were forced to employ brutal manipulation to align it properly. But that is finished, ...I have only to await nature's work.'

'I wish you could be attended by Dr. de Mainaduc. He was introduced at Versailles by the Duke of Manchester and was to have a royal appointment as Physician to Louis XVI. When he could not afford the price of his predecessor's practice he settled in London. He uses no potions of any kind, but depends on the inner powers of the patient. He says that all corporeal activity is dependent on mental influence.'

"Tis kind of you to think of me, but I would be a poor adept of mesmerism. I can not credit it. Dr. Franklin was a member of the Royal Commission, here in France, which investigated Mesmer's theories of animal magnetism. These learned gentlemen found no evidence for the so-called universal fluid, which supposedly affects animals as a lodestone does iron.'

'But of course, Dr. de Mainaduc would be in complete agreement with their findings,' Richard chimed in. 'He says the magnetic poles of Mesmer are ridiculous, that Mesmer pillaged the ideas of Sir Robert Fludd, stumbled over

an unknown power, but instead of attributing it to the divine Spirit of our Maker, he substituted lodestones and magnetic ideas.'

'I must say that I was surprised to see my friend La Fayette enamoured by this fashionable cure. There were so many carriages before Mesmer's house, they blocked the rue Coqheron, near your lodgings.'

'Did you venture inside to see the vats with their magnetic rods?' Maria asked.

'No, but we heard about the methods: dimly lighted rooms, soft music, ladies swooning from holding on to rods in giant vats. It's all a matter of suggestion.'

'Dr. de Mainaduc pretends that cures can be effected by suggestion, but if the motives of the healer are not moral and his understanding not dependent on the Divine Will, then eventually his powers will be lost,' Richard continued.

'We have tired Mr. Jefferson with our talk. Perhaps we should try to let him rest.'

'My dear lady, you do not tire me. I always learn something new and amusing from the Cosways, tho' I do not wish to suggest that your doctor's cures are amusing. He must offer something of substance or you sensible people would not listen to him.'

'We cannot stay longer. Indeed, we must be off. Maria is being received by the Duchess d'Orleans and must prepare her toilette.'

When Maria was finally presented to Louise Marie Adelaide de Bourbon-Penthièvre, the Duchess of Orleans, she had witnessed enough of the Duke's dissipated life in London to have made her uncomfortable in the Duchess's presence. Although dignified, the great lady could also be described as humble. Still a young woman, she was blonde and gentle. The picture of contentment, she was surrounded by her ladies-in-waiting at a round table where they busied themselves with embroidery. While everyone knew the reason that Madame de Genlis had such influence over the Duchess's husband and children, the Duchess saw the governess as nothing more than one of her most intelligent ladies in attendance. Now Madame de Genlis was almost as old as Mr. Cosway and had given up the world to the younger generation like Madame de Buffon. The Duchess seemed blithely unaware of her husband's current mistress as well. But who could tell what she knew? In these circles morality was considered saved if its outward forms were respected. Whatever she knew, Maria would have had sympathy for the young Duchess, who appeared to like the talented young artist. Madame d'Orléans would have asked many questions about painting, about the Cosways' impressions of the Duke's collections and Paris. Finally before leaving, she made Maria promise that she would return to Paris next year and come to see her.

Maria needed no encouragement to give her word to return. Now that the sketches of the Orleans family were completed, Mr. Cosway began to think of their departure. As they made their round of farewells, they were solicited on all sides to promise a speedy reprise of, what must be admitted, was a success in every way. Maria's satisfaction with these rewarding days was now tinged with dread at the approaching separation. Jefferson's accident kept them apart.

The best that could be arranged was one more visit on her own whilst Mr. Cosway visited the Academicians in the Louvre. She took one of the nasty black fiacres to the Hotel de Langeac. As the coachman hurled oaths, trying to push his way through the mass of carriages, carts, and people clogging the streets, she must have had feelings of elation, alternating with anxious doubts. Her misgivings vanished when she was shown up to his room and saw that he was genuinely pleased. The comfort one always felt with him, the naturalness of their relation came back, and they began to chat in an easy manner.

' 'Tis so good of you to come to see me, but I have nothing of excitements too offer a lady who has conquered all Paris.'

'A lady cannot live on excitements. She needs something more substantial.'

'Yes, she needs a lasting devotion, a permanent attachment.'

'Is not a true attachment always permanent? Is it not as long as it is sincere?'

'That ratio should hold, but the world has a cruel way with our sentiments. It does not give us an easy road and buffets us so that we are sometimes obliged to bend to circumstances.'

'And not be faithful to our affections?'

'And not be faithful to our affections.' He replied affirmatively, but his actions belied his words. His left hand took her right and lifted it to his lips.

She could not bear the tension. This man was a mystery to her. He changed his mind often, alternating between ardent affection and a sudden reticence. This did not seem a stratagem, for he exuded kindness. Something deep inside caused him to waver. Sensing that she was perplexed, he spoke of his apparent contradictions.

'To give you but one example of how I have been unable to be faithful to my affections. My great passions in life lie with literary pursuits and domestic life, tending my garden, building my home. I have been obliged to leave all that brings pleasure and devote my time to matters of state and politics. The crisis which arose in my country was such that I could not refuse to play a role. It was the obligation of all men of education to step forward and contribute whatever meagre talents they had to assure our mutual security.'

'You do not seem to be like most men in politics. You seem genuinely interested in the arts, in music, in architecture and not solely occupied with playing for power.'

'Let us say that I am truly interested in the ideas of governance, of how our social organisation can best render men happy.'

'I know nothing of politics, but I don't believe governments can make men happy. Only men and women can do that. I wonder if the Lord believes happiness is so important.'

'It is in the nature of man to aspire to happiness. Do we not have glimpses of bliss even here?'

'Yes, undeniably.' During their conversation, he had continued to hold her hand, a simple pressure dominating her thought more than philosophical questions.

To prolong their time together she proposed cheering him by reading. Her injury to the English language with an Italian pronunciation caused them both to laugh many times. The afternoon passed gently. She went downstairs and played his pianoforte with the drawing room doors open so that he could hear. When she entered his room to bid him farewell, he was dozing quietly, so she wrote a little note and placed it beside his pillow before slipping downstairs and asking Monsieur Petit if the coachman could take her back to the Rue Coqheron.

It was far past the hour for dinner and was almost dark when she arrived to find her husband waiting in ill humour.

'Where have you been, Maria, gallivanting about Paris alone?'

'I went to call on Mr. Jefferson to see how he was.'

'Alone? Do you think that proper?'

'To visit a sick man? I don't think appearances enter into the matter. After all, it has been a week without news of him.'

'Hmmph! And how is the Envoy?'

'As well as can be expected. He is still resting most of the time. He was not able to attend the ceremony at the Hotel de Ville to present Houdon's bust of Monsieur de la Fayette to the City of Paris. 'Twas such a shame. He had to send Mr. Short in his place.'

'Speaking of diplomats, d'Hancarville gave me an invitation from the Comte d'Albaret. He asks us to a concert for several ambassadors on Saturday the 30th. This will be one of our last appearances before leaving so I told him we accepted with pleasure. Perhaps we shall be departing next week.'

'Next week? The summer has passed so swiftly.'

'Indeed, and I cannot be away from my work any longer.'

'Of course not.'

The Comte d'Albaret was an exceptional music lover and host. He kept his own musicians in his house and gave some of the best concerts in Paris. A Maecenas for all the arts, Monsieur d'Albaret spent his considerable fortune on people of talent, which made his salon one of the most amusing of the capital. Physically he had the face of Saint Ignatius and the bearing of Don Quixote, but it was said among his intimates that his comic imitation of Voltaire was irresistible. The Cosways did not have the pleasure of seeing him in this mood, but his concert was their last opportunity to see many of their new friends. Beside the Ambassadors of Sardinia, Portugal, Venice, Denmark, and the Minister of Genoa, they would have said farewell to the Marquis de Cubières and the Marquis de Bièvre, whose puns called *calembours* were famous all over Paris. It was said that Louis XVI asked him to invent a *calembour* on the subject of his royal person. Bièvre replied, 'But His Majesty cannot be a subject.' Madame de Bonneuil, who was absolutely adored by André Chénier, despite the fact she was years older, was also present. Maria was beginning to know the true life stories of those whom she had met in society. Perhaps she sang one of her compositions, *'Mormora il fumicello'*. Many of her friends were kind enough to make her promise to send them some of her own music.

Three or four days after the concert, Jefferson found a pretext to see the Cosways. He proposed one last tour by cabriolet around the city. Perhaps he suspected that Richard had tired of touring, his mind being occupied only with their return to London. This proved to be the case and so she found herself alone with her friend the next day as they headed again toward the Bois de Boulogne. After they passed through the gatehouse of the Etoile and were outside the city, Jefferson must have felt both the liberty of the country and the short time that was left to them. He began to speak more frankly than before. First he enquired about Maria's plans.

'Have you fixed the day of your departure?'

'No, Mr. Cosway will not say, but he says we must leave within a day or two.'

'Will you go straight to London?'

'No, we shall pass through Antwerp and Flanders. My husband must make his pilgrimage to the home of Rubens.'

'Yes, yes, for an artist that would be obligatory ... . As this may be the last moment we shall have together, there is more I wish to say, much I wish to know about you and now there is no time ... but you must know one thing.' He spoke in low tones.

'Yes, pray what is it?'

'You must know that if you were free and had no attachments, I could not let you leave.'

'And I would most likely not wish to leave.'

'But you must, and I suppose that I must keep my promise.'

'Promise?'

'When my wife was dying, during her last moments, she asked that I promise never to oblige my children to have a stepmother. Of course, I did as she wished. Until I met you, it was not a difficult promise to keep. No other woman could replace her, and I wished no other. My dear Maria — may I call you that, I cannot say Mrs. Cosway — my dear Maria, you have changed all that. If you were free I would have to reconsider my promise, perhaps ask you to wait until my daughters were older ... . But this is only daydreaming, a mirage, for you are not free.'

Maria turned her face towards the window. After a long moment she tried to say something encouraging. *'You have given me something extraordinary that I might have missed, had I not known you. Now I have it. Even if we cannot be together, we have a secret knowledge of a bond that cannot break. Our hearts cannot be separated by space.'*

'Your affections are pure.'

'And yours are not?'

'For you, yes, but you are a temptation at every moment. The atmosphere of libertinage here does nothing to calm my ardour. You are an innocent, surrounded by the worst sort. One has only to cite the Orleans circle.'

'Except for the Duchess. Everyone acknowledges that she is Virtue Personified.'

'She is the exception, not the rule.'

'Because she is extremely fond of her husband and has no idea of his infidelity, the poor woman. 'Tis easy to be virtuous in such a condition. I cannot say the same for my circumstances. They are the opposite. As you may have guessed, my marriage is not a union of hearts. Any virtue I may have is a form of ignorance. 'Tis not to my credit. A lady who has not loved cannot be tempted. When I met you I realised that I may be well married, but on the level of the sentiments I was in a virginal state. Now I am no longer in that state. See what you have done, Mr. Jefferson!'

'I must receive the accusation without the benefit!'

'And I must lose my virtue without the benefit!'

'Yet the benefit is easy to have.' He lifted her chin with his uninjured hand: 'Despite what the French think I wish to kiss your lips.' And that is what he did.

The morning after this last ride together, Maria received an alarming, badly scrawled note from Jefferson. Apparently written with his left hand, he wished to tell her that he could not see her again before her departure, that their rattling over the cobblestones the day before had aggravated his mending arm.

I have passed the night in so much pain that I have not closed my eyes. It is with infinite regret therefore that I must relinquish your charming company for that of the Surgeon whom I have sent for to examine into the cause of this change. I am in hopes it is only the having rattled a little too freely over the pavement yesterday. If you do not go today I shall still have the pleasure of seeing you again. If you do, god bless you wherever you go. Present me in the most friendly terms to Mr. Cosway, and let me hear of your safe arrival in England. Addio Addio

Let me know if you do not go today.

Maria asked the servant to wait and hurriedly scratched a reply.

> I am very, very sorry indeed, and [blame myself?] for having
> been the Cause of your pains in the [Night]; Why would you go?
> And why was I not more friendly to you and less to Myself by
> preventing your giving me the pleasure of your Company? You
> repeatedly said it wou'd do you no harm, I felt interested and did
> not insist. We shall go I believe this Morning, Nothing seems
> redy [sic], but Mr. Cosway seems More dispos'd then I have seen
> him all this time. I shall write to you from England, it is impossible
> to be wanting to a person who has been so excessively obliging. I
> don't attempt to make Compliments, they can be None for you,
> but I beg you will think us sensible to your kindness, and that it
> will be with infinite pleasure I shall remember the charming days
> we have past together, and shall long for next spring.
>
> You will make me very happy, if you would send a line to the *post
> restante* at Antwerp, that I may know how you are.
>
> Believe me dr: Sir your Most obliged affectionate servant,
>   Maria Cosway

Mr. d'Hancarville, faithful as ever, came to the Cosways in the rue
Coqheron and offered to accompany them as far as the Barrier of St. Denis.
They were preparing to set out when, to their great surprise, Jefferson came
clattering up.

'Mr. Jefferson, poor fellow, we thought you were ill. Do you think it
wise to be out?' Richard asked.

*'I am better here than shut up in my room with nothing to think of but my
pains. Besides the surgeon was useless, could offer no explanation nor remedy. I
decided the best medicine was to see my friends one more time.'*

*'Hancarville here was kind enough to do us the honour, but I fear we have so
much baggage that there is not a place in our carriage to take you farther.'*

*'That makes no difference. I can follow you in mine to the Pavilion de Saint
Denis and see you off from there.'*

'As you wish, ah, this damned rain, we had best be getting underway.'

It began to rain at midday as they climbed into their carriages, a weather of circumstance, as the Parisians say. They began their slow progress northward. Maria was longing to be in the carriage behind, but it was comforting to know that he was still with them. All too soon they arrived at the Pavilion Saint-Denis or gatehouse at the Farmers-General's wall, where taxes were collected on goods entering the city. They descended from their carriages to take their farewells. It is easier to be the one departing than the one left behind, but this time Maria felt a wrench as Jefferson kissed her hand one last time, and asked when he might see them again.

'I think we may return next summer,' replied Mr. Cosway.

'Or in the spring,' Maria suggested.

'You must return as soon as possible,' Monsieur d'Hancarville added. 'You have too many friends here now, and you mustn't disappoint us. You know, Madame, I am not exaggerating when I say that you have made a sensation in Paris, a sensation! We shall not forget you. Promise that you will return.'

'If it were my decision alone, I promise you I would return. But one is not always at liberty to do what one likes.'

'A charming person can assuredly find a way to do it. I trust you to find a way. Now Madame, Monsieur, I pray you shall have a safe journey. All my compliments to Mr. Townley and General di Paoli, and au revoir until next year.'

'Au revoir, Monsieur, and all our gratitude for your many kindnesses. You have done so much to make our stay agreeable and pleasant. We are in your debt.'

The little man disappeared with a curious shuffling gait into the pavilion. The travellers could delay no longer. Mr. Cosway took his seat in the carriage. Jefferson handed Mrs. Cosway in beside him and shut the door with a click. Despite the rain Maria pushed the window down, and he put his left hand on the open window edge as if to keep the carriage from moving. She leaned toward the window so that her husband could not see their faces. All they had left to share was one more meeting of the eyes.

'My dear friends, I hope to see you in the spring. Please write to me to tell me that you have arrived safely home. May God speed.'

Mr. Cosway tapped on the carriage wall with his stick and the wheels began to turn. Maria watched the tall, nobly straight figure standing under the vaulted portico waving with his good arm. Then he turned and walked into the pavilion.

Jefferson wrote to Maria that evening:

> Having performed the last sad office of handing you into your carriage at the Pavillon de St. Denis, and seen the wheels get actually into motion, I turned on my heel, and walked, more dead than alive, to the opposite door, where my own was awaiting me. Mr. Danquerville was missing. He was sought for, found and dragged down stairs. [We] were crammed into the carriage, like recruits for the Bastille, and not having [sou]l enough to give orders to the coachman, he presumed Paris our destination…. After a considerable interval, silence was broke with a *je suis vraiment affligé du depart de ces bons gen.* This was the signal for a mutual confession [of dist]ress. We began immediately to talk of Mr. and Mrs. Cosway, of their goodness, their [talents], their amability, and tho we spoke of nothing else, we seemed hardly to have entered into matter when the coachman announced the rue St. Denis, and that we were opposite Mr. Danquerville's… . I was carried home. Seated by my fire side, solitary and sad, the following dialogue took place between my Head and my Heart.

A VIEW from M.R COSWAY's BREAKFAST-ROOM PALL MALL,
WITH THE PORTRAIT OF M.RS COSWAY.
The Landscape Painted by W.m Hodges RA and the Portrait by R.d Cosway RA.
& engraved by W.Birch Enamel Painter.
Published Feb.y 2,1789 by W.m Birch,Hampstead Heath,& sold by T.Thornton,Southampton Str.t Cov.t Garden.

11

'The Next Year'

'Heart. But they told me they would come back again,
the next year'

'Mr. Trumbull, how lovely to see you! Is not London gloomy after our little jaunt in Flanders?'

Maria was sitting in her first floor study the day after the Cosways' return from the continent. 'Please sit down by the fire. What a change from the warm days in France! I miss them already.'

'Then you will be comforted by the parcel I bring you from Mr. Jefferson. I found it waiting for me.'

'Mr. Jefferson? You have something from him? But we left Paris after you.'

'Yes, but he has decided to use me as a courier between yourselves. His excuse was that he did not have your address this time, but he wishes to continue using me or other friends, for he is certain that all his letters sent by the post are read by the police both in London and in Paris.'

'Oh, do you think that is true? Does he have to be so careful?'

'Yes, Madame, any diplomat can be certain his correspondence and his movements are closely watched.'

'We have no secrets of state, no secrets of any kind for that matter.'

'Of course, Madame.... And how is Mr. Cosway?'

'He is well and busy as ever in his studio.... How fortunate we were to find you in our hotel in Antwerp! After our horrible journey in a furious rainstorm, I thought we would both be in bed. But my husband was revived by his passion for Rubens. We so enjoyed our fortnight with you in Antwerp and Ghent. Mr. Cosway is never happier than when buying pictures, and how pleased he was to find that merchant who sold pictures by weight. With his knowledge as a connoisseur, he is sure to find something of interest in that lot. But enough of telling you what you know. Do you also have news of Mr. Jefferson?'

'Only a short letter enclosed with your parcel. He says his arm is set now, and he has only to wait. He is able to write with his left hand. 'Tis not a pretty scrawl, but legible.'

'I feel anxious for his pain and sad that he will be deprived of his violin.'

'That is certain, alas. Well, I must take leave of you now, Madame. I wished to acquit myself of my postal duties as promptly as possible, but I am expected by Mr. West. Please give my compliments to Mr. Cosway.'

'That I shall do. Pray call on us soon Mr. Trumbull. We have many happy memories to relive together.'

She could scarcely *wait* for Trumbull to bow and leave the room so that she could open her parcel. It consisted of two letters, one less than a page, another of three folded sheets or twelve pages. There was also a copy of the air *'Jour heureux'* from Dardanus. He remembered! The short letter was only a note, explaining why he was confiding letters to Trumbull. In a jesting tone he counselled her not to read more than a half page at a time of the long letter lest she be too bored. He mocked his own sentiments as if to say that she shouldn't take them too seriously or perhaps he was embarrassed by what he had written. This was his introduction to a very long essay, laboriously written in an awkward, irregular script.

The dialogue between his Head and his Heart was a debate about whether a friendship fated to end in separation should ever be undertaken. In the course of the dialogue, he relived the moments of their days together, when he had been happiest, and revealed the depth of his grief at their separation. The night before their separation he had been thrown into agonies, tossed from one side of the bed to the other,

> no sleep, no rest. The poor crippled wrist, too, never left one moment in the same position; now up, now down, now here, now there; was it to be wondered at, if its pains returned?

He wrote that he was 'overwhelmed with grief', was 'the most wretched of all earthly beings' and that 'my mind…broods constantly over your departure'. In spite of his careful reference to 'they', meaning both Cosways, she knew that he was not overcome with sorrow by his separation from Mr. Cosway.

As she sat reading every line over and over, she relived the day they had first met at the *Halle aux Bleds*, from within his mind. He had thought that 'we' were worth all he had seen in Paris, that he had contrived 'how to prevent a separation from them'. When he came home at night '…it seemed to have been a month agone'. After they had gone to Marly and St. Germain he thought, 'What a mass of happiness had we travelled over!' and he had felt as happy with her company as she did with his:

> Hills, valleys, chateaux, gardens, rivers, every object wore its liveliest hue! Whence did they borrow it? From the presence of our charming companion. They were pleasing, because she

seemed pleased. Alone, the scene would have been dull and insipid: the participation of it with her gave it relish!...that the lady had, moreover, qualities and accomplishments belonging to her sex, which might form a chapter apart for her; such as music, modesty, beauty, and that softness of disposition, which is the ornament of her sex...

Although Maria did not wish him to suffer, how reassuring it was to hear his Head berating his Heart:

> you rack our whole system when you are parted from those you love, complaining that such a separation is worse than death... that the separation would, in this instance, be the more severe, as you would probably never see them again.

Indeed the problem of protecting himself from the pain of separation was at the core of his wrestling. Almost half the letter explicitly dealt with the problem of separation and loss; the two-horned dilemma – Maria's marriage and his inevitable return to America – created the tension underlying the dialogue. Nothing could be said about her marital obligations – although there was a curious passage in which he imagined that he would like to comfort either her husband or her in some future grief and, again, she could not envisage him saying to Mr. Cosway:

> I would open every cell of my composition, to receive the effusion of their woes! I would pour my tears into their wounds... . Fortune can present no grief of unknown form to me! Who, then, can so softly bind up the wound of another, as he who has felt the same wound himself? But heaven forbid they should ever know a sorrow!

As the vast Atlantic was the great obstacle upon which he could wax eloquent, he wrote a long passage portraying his dream that they would come to America and be able to draw all its naturally beautiful landscapes and see for themselves what a tranquil and lawful country it was. His Heart clung to this slender hope and justified his pain with philosophy declaring:

We have no rose without its thorn; no pleasure without alloy…. It is the condition annexed to all our pleasures… . True, this condition is pressing cruelly on me at this moment. I feel more fit for death than life. But when I look back on the pleasures of which it is the consequence, I am conscious they were worth the price I am paying…I comfort myself with expectations of their promised return…'In the summer,' said the gentleman; but 'in the spring,' said the lady; and I should love her forever, were it only for that! … I have taken these good people into my bosom …. I have lodged them in the warmest cell I could find;…I love them, and will continue to love them through life; that if fortune should dispose them on one side the globe, and me on the other, my affections shall pervade its whole mass to reach them.

The dialogue ended on this more hopeful note. The last lines brought suddenly to mind the happy feeling she had in the Theatre Italiens:

If your letters are as long as the Bible, they will appear short to me. Only let them be brimful of affection. I shall read them with the dispositions with which Arlequin, in *Les deux billets,* spelt the words '*je t'aime*' and wished that the whole alphabet had entered into their composition.

She picked up the music of '*Jour heureux*' and read the words to the song as a message:

Happy day, enchanting hope!
Charming price of a love so tender!
I am going to see her, I am going to hear her,
I am going to find happiness again!
In this hidden place where she is late in coming!
I feel troubled by a new fear
The moment that I have so longed for
Ah! do not linger more!

Did he have the same dispositions? Did he truly love – not admire, but love? Was she imagining? Or was he saying what he dare not say? As soon as she had read this wonderful gift, she went to her writing table and in spite of feeling a complete incapacity to respond in kind she scribbled a page in awkward English and then gave up and finished the letter in Italian. It was the usual length of four pages on a single folded sheet. At first she tried to convey her confused feelings.

> How I wish I could answer the Dialogue! but I honestly think my heart is invisible & mute, at this moment more than usual it is full & ready to burst with all the variety of sentiments which a very feeling one is Capable of; sensible of My loss at separating from the friends I left at Paris.... My thoughts Must be contrasted by the joy of Meeting my friends in London. It is an excess which Must tear to pieces a human Mind, when felt.

Then her convent education dictated that she must mask any gratification that she might feel by professions of unworthiness. This sense of inferiority was sincere when she wrote:

> You seem to be Such a Master on this subject, that whatever I may say will appear trifling, not well express'd, faintly represented …but felt…I could write a volume, but I could wish that my selfishness was not reproaching to Me, for with difficulty do I find a line but after having admired it, I recollect some part concerns Me. Why do you say so Many kind things? Why present so many opportunities for my feeling undeserving of them, why not leave me a free consolation in admiring a friend, without the temptation…to my Vanity?

When she lapsed into Italian, instead of more freely expressing herself she became conventional, telling him that London amid the fog and smoke was full of people with sad faces and the only way to resist the melancholy of the climate was in meeting agreeable friends and practising the fine arts, for 'one can often avoid sadness, even if something is lacking for perfect happiness'. The rest was not a true reply to his letter, but the usual compliments to Mr. Short and Mr. d'Hancarville, that they were still contemplating a voyage to Paris or Italy the next year, and that she would never forget his attentions to them. Jefferson was to receive much less in their exchange than she had received. But what else could she write? It was not a lady's place to express her sentiments openly.

After this unforgettable opening to their correspondence, Maria could not have imagined that she would soon be disappointed. The methods of conveying his letters – sending them to Trumbull or confiding them to some traveller to London – resulted in unforeseen obstacles. If he employed the regular post, a letter could be received within five days from Paris, but he chose not to do so. Days, weeks, the entire month of November passed without a word. What an agony to survey the post every morning with hope and meet with disappointment!

As often happens, one receives the letter one is not expecting, in this case, a long note from General Paoli postmarked Bath. This was a surprise. After meeting Jefferson, Maria had reconsidered her relation to General Paoli. Platonic it may have been, but in her mind it had an intimacy she no longer wished to share with him. Paoli had written to her regularly while she was in Paris, and she had responded. In her last letter, written on the eve of her departure, she told him as gently as possible that he should forget her, although she gave no explanation for this change of heart. Perplexed, Paoli wrote to Boswell later:

> …she hasn't written to me since her return to London, and as I don't know whether she has come back from France as a friend or as an enemy I have no wish to precede her, all the more for her telling me the last time she wrote to me from Paris not to think of her any more… . If you go to see her, do not convey my compliments but rather my disappointment…

He decided to test her mood. From Bath he wrote:

> You will recognise that although you stayed so long in France in the midst of my enemies, I hope still a bit of your friendship remains; if you save it, it will only be a merited reward for the most constant attachment and respect that I profess for you for so many years.

It is not known if Maria replied to the General, but after days of waiting for a letter from Paris, she could not resist taking up her pen again to complain:

> But what does this silence mean? I have awaited the post with so much anxiety and lo each time it arrives without bringing me any letters from Paris. I am really worried, I fear lest it be illness or that your arm is worse, I think of a thousand things at once except that my friends should so soon have forgotten me. If you were contemplating making me another big gift of a long letter, I shall beg you to send them to me shorter but more frequent. I no longer have the patience to wait and I am venturing to take up the pen without being sure whether I am to complain, whether I am to reprove, whether I am to implore patience, to express my mortification and anxieties of this disappointment…when we separate, after the pain of separation is past, one lives in continual anxiety, one does not receive letters, one imagines a thousand misfortunes, if some mishap occurs one cannot run with succour or comfort, nor receive news of it.

She partially attributed her anxiety to the climate, always the London climate which so weighed on her spirit:

> …there is something so heavy in this air…this climate imposes upon us…Night Thoughts, before the fire, and when the imagination is well warmed up, one could go cool off in a river … so much is the air darkened by the fog and smoke that it prevents the celestial inhabitants from penetrating with their gaze the human foibles of this island.

After another ten days of impatient waiting without letters she took the pretext of sending Jefferson a book of her songs, as well as the air from Nina, *'l'attendo e mai non vien'*. How fitting were the words, 'He does not answer, He does not answer, He no longer cares for me.' The occasion arose when Trumbull told her that Colonel Smith, the young Abigail Adams' new husband, was going to Paris. She sent her songs with a hasty note:

…Every post-day I have waited anxiously. I fear lest your arm is worse, but even that would not prevent your writing me. I take this occasion to send you a couple of lines to ask if you have received my letters, to beg you to send me news of yourself…

At last, over a month after receiving the Dialogue, she had a second letter, sent through the regular post unsigned and with his seal disguised. He had indeed received two letters from her and claimed that this was his third. His second had gone undelivered, still being with a gentleman who promised to depart immediately for London but was still in Paris. He repeated his fear that all his letters were opened in the post office.

I send thro' that channel only such as are very indifferent in their nature. This is not the character, my dear madam of those I write to you. The breathings of a pure affection would be profaned by the eye of a *Commis* of the *poste*. I am obliged then to wait for private conveyances…

Most of the rest of his letter echoed the Dialogue:

When those charming moments were present which I passed with you, they were clouded with the prospect that I was soon to lose you… . Thus, present joys are damped by a consciousness that they are passing from us… . I am determined when you come next not to admit the idea that we are ever to part again.

The last line leapt up from the page. She saw that he suffered from the same anxiety as she:

But are you to come again? I dread the answer to this question, and that my poor heart has been duped by the fondness of it's wishes. What a triumph for the head! … May your heart glow with warm affections, and all of them be gratified! Write to me often. Write affectionately, and freely, as I do to you. Say many kind things, and say them without reserve. They will be food for my soul. Adieu my dear friend!

Those were the last words she had from him in the year 1786. It was early December, and it was her only letter that month. She had this short note and the Dialogue to cherish during that Christmas season, and even into the New Year.

New Year's Day, 1787, was one of the low points of the winter.(She could not know then that he had written to her on Christmas Eve.) Perhaps in two letters he had said and done all he could at the beginning, and there was nothing left to say. Nevertheless, following the custom of New Year's greetings, she penned a sad note, which was not affectionate as he wished, but anguished and sorrowful. She could not believe he could have cared so much at the beginning and so little now. Surely if he realised how tormented she was, he would respond.

> Esteemed friend, I have awaited with infinite anxiety the long letter which you announced to me, but I do not know for what crime I must experience the punishment of Tantalus, every day I believe it near, but that day never comes; …what concerns me still more you do not tell me how you are, whether your arm is cured, whether you have received a book of music which I sent you some time ago… . I am the worst person in the world for sending news since I never enter upon that subject; I am sensitive to the severity of the season; to this unpleasant climate, and to the melancholy of this country; perhaps it seems more severe now, after the gay months I spent in Paris where everything is gay, I am susceptible and everything that surrounds me has great power to magnetize me. If I am more endowed by nature with any one sense, it is that of melancholy, according to the objects which surround me, it may be dissipated or increased. Such is the influence upon susceptibility…

Her petulant complaints seemed to meet with no response, but she did not realise this at once because the two long-delayed letters of November 19 and December 24 arrived towards the end of January. They nourished her affections, partly out of sheer relief. The first was very short for it was the first written with Jefferson's right hand: 'I write with pain and must be short. This is good news for you; for were the hand able to follow the effusions of the heart, that would cease to write only when this shall cease to beat.' He told her that his friend Madame de Corny was coming to London and 'I wish she could put me into her pocket, when she goes, or you, when she comes back.'

The second, written on Christmas Eve, was more forthcoming, still full of wishes and hopes for them:

> I was so unlucky when very young, as to read the history of Fortunatus. He had a cap of such virtues that when he put it on his head, and wished himself anywhere, he was there. I have been all my life sighing for this cap. Yet if I had it, I question if I should use it but once. I should wish myself with you, and not wish myself away again. *En attendant* the cap, I am always thinking of you. If I cannot be with you in reality, I will in imagination. But you say not a word of coming to Paris. Yet you were to come in the spring, and here is winter. It is time therefore you should be making your arrangements, packing your baggage &c. unless you really mean to disappoint us. If you do, I am determined not to suppose I am never to see you again. I will believe you intend to go to America, to draw the Natural bridge, the Peaks of Otter, &c., that I shall meet you there, and visit with you all those grand scenes. I had rather be deceived, than live without hope. It is so sweet! It makes us ride so smoothly over the roughnesses of life.... Think of me much, and warmly. Place me in your breast with those who you love most: and comfort me with your letters. *Addio la mia cara ed amabile amica!*

He added at the bottom: 'After finishing the letter, the gentleman who brought yours sent me a roll he had overlooked, which contained songs of your composition. I am sure they are charming, and I thank you for them. The first words which met my eye on opening them, are I fear, ominous. "*Qua l'attendo, e mai non viene.*" '

'I wait and he does not come.' But she would come. Somehow she would. Mr. Cosway said they would still be returning to Paris in the summer. She was happy to have these letters. For once she sat down at her writing table with contentment and proceeded to write a long, seven-page letter

completely different from the others. She made an effort and wrote in English. Wishing to make amends for the scolding tone of her other letters, she considered her attitude and did not like what she saw.

I must confess that the beginning of your correspondence has made Me an *enfant gatée* (a spoiled child). I shall never recover to be reasonable in My expectations, and shall feel disappointed whenever your letters are not as long as the first was. Thus you are the occasion of a continual reproaching disposition in Me. It is a disagreeable One. It will tease you to a hatred towards Me, notwithstanding your partiality you have had for Me till now. Nothing disobliges More than a dissatisfied Mind.

She realised that women's complaints were little tolerated so she wished to recognise this before he did.

Of all the torments, temptations, and weariness, the female has always been the principal and most powerfull object, and this is to be the most fear'd by you at present, from my pen. Are you to be painted in future ages sitting solitary and sad, on the beautifull Monticello tormented by the shadow of a woman who will present you a deform'd rod, twisted and broken, instead of the emblematical instrument belonging to the Muses, held by Genius, inspired by wit, from which all that is pleasing, beautifull and happy can be decrib'd to entertain,

Then to make her letter long and amusing she most uncharacteristically gave him political news of the House of Commons.

16. Mrs. Cosway's Fan: *this hand-painted fan is attributed to Maria Cosway. The centre portrait repeats the pose and costume of Richard Cosway's portrait of Maria, engraved by Bartolozzi, which appears as the frontispiece.*

17. *A plate from* Cabinet des Modes, *a Parisian revue, which illustrates ladies' fashions in 1786.*

18. *Engraving of Maria Cosway's picture*, Like patience on a monument, smiling at grief, *exhibited at the Royal Academy in 1781 and inspired by a scene from Shakespeare's* Twelfth Night.

19. Creusa appearing to Aeneas *by Maria Cosway, oil painting exhibited at the Royal Academy in 1781.*

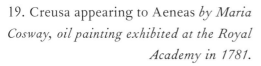

CREUSA APPEARING TO ÆNEAS.

20. *Valentine Green engraving of* Creusa appearing to Aeneas, *1781.*

21. *Engraving of* A Persian going to adore the Sun *by Maria Cosway, exhibited at the Royal Academy in 1784. Originally painted for Maria's friend, Lady Lyttelton, this picture is now in Sir John Soane's Museum.*

22. A British Minister worshipping the Meridian Sun, *1786. A rude satire on 'A Persian going to adore the Sun'.*

23. Georgiana, Duchess of Devonshire as Cynthia from Spenser's 'Faerie Queene', *exhibited at the Royal Academy in 1782, is probably Maria Cosway's most successful picture. Georgiana's son considered it to have captured his mother's likeness, or perhaps her essence, better than her other portraits.*

24. *Engraving of* Astrea instructing Arthegal *by Maria Cosway, exhibited at the Royal Academy in 1784, illustrating verses from Spenser's* Faerie Queene.

25. Portrait of George, Prince of Wales,
engraving after Richard Cosway, 1787.

26. Portrait of Mrs.
Fitzherbert, *engraving after
Richard Cosway.*

Vue du Jardin du Palais Royal
de ses Batiments et Galleries

27. *View of the gardens of the Palais Royal showing the shopping arcades.*

28. Self-portrait *(bottom left) by Elisabeth Vigée Lebrun, 1791.*

29. Self-portrait *(bottom right) by Jacques-Louis David.*

30. Portrait of the children of Louis Philippe, Duc d'Orleans *by Richard Cosway, 1786-87. This small portrait was the commission that brought the Cosways to Paris in 1786.*

31. Promenade in the Palais Royal Garden.

The Palais Royal Garden Walk.   Promenade du Jardin du Palais Royal.

32. *(Right) John Trumbull's portrait miniature of Thomas Jefferson was given to Maria Cosway in 1788. Trumbull painted a similar portrait as a gift to Angelica Schuyler Church. The Cosway version, which remained in Maria's school, was presented by the government of Italy to the United States on the occasion of the U.S. Bicentennial in 1976.*

33. *(Below)* Chateau de Marly and its gardens, *by Pierre Denis Martin.*

What do you think of a famous speech Sheridan has made which lasted five hours? ... Nothing has been taulk'd of for Many days but his Speech. The Whole House applauded him at the Moment.... Pitt Made him the highest encomiums, and only poor Mr. Hastings sufferd for the power of his eloquence; all went against him, though nothing can be decided yet.

Warren Hastings, the former Governor General of India, was accused by Edmund Burke, Charles James Fox, and Richard Brinsley Sheridan of cruel and abusive government in India, for which he was being impeached. The very day of Sheridan's brilliant speech, Hastings was with Cosway.

Mr. H. was with Mr. Cosway at the very Moment the speech was going on. He seemd perfectly easy, talking of subjects with great tranquillity and cheerfulness. The second day he was the same, but on the third seem'd very Much affected and agitated. All his friends give him the greatest Character of humanity, generosity and feelings, amiable in his Manner. He seems in short totally different from the disposition of cruelty they accuse him of.

Moving from parliamentary matters, she hastened to compliment Jefferson on his book, *Notes on Virginia:*

I have been reading with great pleasure your description of America. It is wrote [sic] by *you*, but Nature represents all the scenes to Me in reality. ... Oh how I wish My self in those delightful places! Those enchanted Grottos's! Those Magnificent Mountains rivers, &c. &c! Why am I not a Man that I could set out immediately and satisfy My Curiosity, indulge My sight with wonders!

She also shared her frustration with painting and the easier satisfactions of music and conversation:

All the Morning I paint whatev[er] presents itself most pleasing to Me. Some times I have beautifull Objects to paint from and add historical Characters to Make them More interesting. Female and infantine beauty is the Most perfect Object to see. Sometimes I indulge More Melancholy subjects…. . I attempt, I exercise and end by being Witness of My own disappointment and incapacity of executing the Poet, the Historian, or my own conceptions of imagination. Thus the Mornings are spent regretting they are not longer, to have More time to attempt again in Search of better success…[I devote my eveni]ng[s to] Music and then I am Much [visited by] the first Professors who come very often to play, every evening Something new… . And to add to Compleat the pleasure a small society of agreeable friends frequently Come to see me. In this Manner you see that I am More attached to My home, than going in search of amusement out, where nothing but crowded assemblies, uncomfortable heat, and not the least pleasure in Meeting evrybody [sic], not being able to enjoy any conversation.

Finally she told him that the Operas were bad, although she had not been, that the first singers were Rubinelli and Madame Mara. Ending with the eternal hope that they would meet again in Paris, she expressed her anxiety: 'I am in a Million fears about it. Mr. Cosway still keeps his intention, but how many chances from our inclinations to the execution of our will.'

Her joy in writing this letter would have turned to bitterness had she known that she would not hear another word from her affectionate friend for five long months. During the entire spring and into the summer not a word came from Paris. She heard from Trumbull that Jefferson had set out alone for a long tour of the south of France. One would have thought he could have sent letters through William Short in Paris, but no, he chose to forget her.

But she remained in touch with Paris through another correspondent. Baron d'Hancarville gave her a link to her friends there. His letters were mostly filled with compliments from the Countess of Albany or the Angivillers or the Marquis de Bièvre and much flattery from the writer.

The door of the Academy of Painting will open willingly to both of you; if Robert and Vincent have not offered to present you, David and Vernet would like to have this pleasure. Take all four.

True to his talent for making introductions, he sent letters with travellers to London. One of them, Francesco, Count Melzi d'Eril, later changed the course of Maria's life. When Melzi came to London as a young man of about thirty years, he had already charmed the Countess of Albany in Paris. A member of a prominent Milanese family, he won her friendship at once with his quiet cultivation and charming Italian manners. Melzi was young and idealistic. He was to become an enthusiastic supporter of French revolutionary ideas, seeing them as the way to end Austrian rule in Italy.

Princesse Lubomirska.

44. Princess Lubomirska.

Another friend presented by Monsieur d'Hancarville was a royalist to the core. An intimate of Princess de Lamballe and loyal to Marie Antoinette, the Princess Lubomirska was related to the King of Poland. As the widow of a Polish marshal, she was always called Madame la Marechale, and her character was worthy of such a title. Her courage was legendary. It was said that she and a servant were once attacked by a bear, after the angry beast had frightened their horse, overturning their sleigh. When the bear began to overpower her servant, the Princess Marechale coolly seized two pistols from the sleigh and shot the bear in the ears. Restless and commanding, she continually travelled across Europe, and had recently installed herself in apartments in the Palais Royal in Paris. Having no son of her own, she had informally adopted her nephew, Henri Lubomirski, a young, angelic boy, whose beauty enchanted all who laid eyes on him, including the Queen, Marie Antoinette. The Princess Marechale came to London with an entourage: her nephew, his tutor, an Italian abbé called Monsieur Piattoli, and Count Stanislaus Potocki, her son-in-law. Having seen prints of Cosway's portraits in Paris, the Princess was anxious to have her nephew painted by him. All artists loved to portray the young Henri. Maria also painted his portrait and Anne Damer sculpted a handsome head of the boy.

45. Henry Lubormiski *by Richard Cosway. The child, known for his beauty, was a favourite subject of artists including Maria Cosway and Elisabeth Vigée Lebrun.*

The Cosways introduced the Polish circle to General Paoli and took them to see Townley's antiquities. They naturally included them in their evening musical parties where so many foreign diplomats liked to gather. In return for their hospitality, Princess Lubomirska insisted that they should be her guests when they returned to Paris.

In spite of the diversions of these new friends, Maria's life was spent painting and making music. She had a new energy, which was reflected in the quality of her work. Before leaving for Paris, she had exhibited one insignificant picture at the annual spring exhibition of the Academy, but in 1787 she had five pictures hanging, all well-received. This critical success might also be attributed to a choice of subjects. No more gods, monsters, or great historical deeds. Perhaps she had youthfully overreached in earlier attempts to portray great and fantastical scenes. Now she exhibited portraits of women and children – in conformity with public expectations for women painters – and restrained her imagination to putting the portraits 'in character' except for a self-portrait. She painted the Ladies Charlotte, Anne, and Frances Villiers as Cybele and two nymphs. This picture was praised in the *World*, which kindly wrote 'Maria Cosway is a

warm and elegant Italian – and so are her two nymphs in No. 1 – the ladies
Villiers.' She portrayed the Countess of Jersey with her two children as an
enchantress. The *St. James Chronicle* praised this portrait, but vexed her
husband by commenting 'the productions of Maria are much superior to
those of her husband'. And vexed them both by its opinion of her self-
portrait: 'the portrait of herself, No. 251, though a symptom of the family
vanity, possesses considerable merit.' Other papers found this picture
'pleasing' or said that 'Mrs. Cosway excels' or that 'This Lady hath some
other pictures in the room that exhibit genius'. One of the most charming
pictures was that of an infant, young George Lamb as Bacchus. This little
boy of about three was Lady Melbourne's child and was rumoured to be
the son of the Prince of Wales.

It must have been a satisfying exhibition for Maria, but not for her
husband, who was criticised for not exhibiting miniatures and was thought
to be less successful in his large portraits. One picture in the exhibition well
represented Maria's mood that spring. William Hodges painted the view
from their breakfast room and asked Richard to paint Maria into the picture,
sitting beside a large window with her little dog, a gift from the Trudaines.
She is looking south over St James Park to the spires of Westminster Abbey,
and what the two artists did not know was that she was probably looking
far beyond the Abbey. She was looking toward Paris, and the wistful look
on her face was caused by thoughts of the past and the future, but not the
present moment.

After the Academy Exhibition they could begin to think of returning to
Paris. Cosway had finished the portraits of the Orleans family, and they
could be most safely transported by themselves. It was now June, but
Cosway could not leave London as he was to be called as a witness in a
court case. Two art dealers had quarrelled over the authenticity of a picture.
A Mr. Vandergucht had sold a picture entitled *La Vierge aux Enfants* to Mr.
Desanfans as an authentic Poussin. When this attribution was put in doubt,
Desanfans sued the picture's seller. Several artists testified on both sides.
Cosway gave his opinion that the picture as a whole was bad although certain
portions of it taken from a distance might be mistaken for Poussin.
Gainsborough and John Singleton Copley also testified that they did not
think it was authentic. Benjamin West, having first given Vandergucht his
opinion that the picture was the finest Poussin in existence, when called to

ΟΤΑΚΗ–ΑΜΟΥΣΟΣ–ΕΙΣΙΤΩ

The EXHIBITION of the ROYAL ACADEMY. 1787.

46. *The Royal Academy Exhibition of 1787. Maria Cosway exhibited five pictures in 1787 and was portrayed by her husband in William Hodges's* A View from Mr. Cosway's Breakfast Room.

47. Detail of RA Exhibition of 1787 showing Maria's portrait of George Lamb.

48. Detail of RA Exhibition of 1787 showing Maria's portrait of Lady Charlotte, Lady Anne, and Lady Frances Villiers in character of Cybele and two nymphs.

the stand wavered and refused to declare the picture an undoubted product of that master. Desanfans won the case and recovered his £700. But Cosway continued to dither about leaving London.

June passed. Then Maria had indirect news of Jefferson. Monsieur and Madame Ethis de Corny, intimate friends of the American envoy, arrived in London. As it turned out, they were guests of the Churches. Monsieur de Corny was a member of the Parliament of Paris and was taken round by John Barker Church, another parliamentarian. They also spent time in Bath and in Down Place with the Churches. Maria had given up hope of hearing from Jefferson when one day in early July his servant Petit appeared upon her doorstep to personally deliver a letter from Paris. When she asked if his master was in London, he replied that the Minister was so occupied after his long absence in France and Italy that he had not even felt it possible to come to London to fetch his young daughter, Maria.

'Maria?' I asked. 'He has a daughter named Maria?'

'Yes, Madame, however, the family always addresses her as Polly.'

'Oh, yes, I heard them speak of Polly. This child is in London now?'

'Yes, Madame. She was confided by the captain of the ship which brought her to England to Mrs. Adams. I shall accompany her back to Paris in the diligence the 9th of this month.'

'And Mr. Jefferson. He is well after his long voyage?'

'He seems to be quite recovered. I would say that he was benefited by his tour of France and Italy.'

'I did not realise he planned to see Italy.'

'I believe it was decided after his departure.'

'I trust Mr. Short is well. Will you please give him my compliments, and of course to Mr. Jefferson.'

'Mr. Jefferson asked me to inquire if you and Mr. Cosway would be coming to Paris this year.'

'Please tell him that is still our desire, but nothing is decided yet.'

'Yes, Madame. If you will excuse me, I must be going to Mrs. Adams now.'

'Of course, Ottobah will show you out. Goodbye Monsieur Petit.'

'Madame.'

It was hard to believe that she had at last a letter. As she broke the seal, she saw that this one was duly signed, no disguising of the writer. Yet it was so brief! After all these months only two short pages! He opened by telling her that he had been to Milan, Genoa, and Turin. When only thirty hours from Venice, he had not gone. He said he had no time to see Rome. How could he have gone to Italy without seeing Rome or Florence? How she wished she could be the first to show him these treasures. He had the same regrets too, for next he said,

> But I am born to lose everything I love. Why were you not with me? So many enchanting scenes which only wanted your pencil to consecrate them to fame…when are you coming here? If not at all, what did you ever come for? Only to make people miserable at losing you. Consider that you are but 4 days from Paris. … Come then, my dear Madam, and we will breakfast every day a l'Angloise, hie away to the Désert, dine under the bowers of Marly, and forget that we are ever to part again.

He closed with a half-hearted excuse that he had received her last letter at the moment of his departure and hoped that she would write another 'lengthy, warm and flowing from the heart'. Although still hurt by his long silence, she did not give in to artifice, making him wait and wonder as she had. Almost immediately she wrote a letter which flowed indeed from the heart, but was 'warm' from scolding.

> Do you deserve a long letter, My dear friend? No, certainly not, and to avoid temptation, I take a small sheet of paper… . How long you like to keep your friends in anxiety! – How many Months was you without writing to Me? And you felt no remorse? – I was glad to know you was well, sure of your being much engaged and diverted, and had only to lament I was not a Castle hanging to a cloud, a stream, a village, a stone on the pavement of Turin, Milan, and Genoa &c… . I wish you had given me a longer account of your voyage; your observations please me, your taste is good, your letters interest me, and I expected almost by right, that you would write me as many pages as you were days absent. … I am truly mortified. Nothing could pacify me, except that

these lines are yours, and then I do not measure the sparseness of the lines but the pleasure which they bring me.

She could not resist making him suffer a little, tantalising:

I do not know that we shall come to Paris this year. I fear not. My husband begins to doubt it, just at the time when one should begin to prepare to leave; You cannot believe how much this uncertainty displeases me, when I have everything to fear against my desire. Why promise? Why lead me to hope? It seems a dream to have been there and I now wish it to be real, because of the impression it left upon me. At least console me by receiving news of a place which so much interests me. Tell me what comedies there are that are new and good, what operas, what works of art &c. &c. everything that can induce you to write me long letters. You spoiled me in the beginning of our correspondence, I told you, you have not continued. …

I am sorry I have not had occasion to see your daughter who they say is presently here. I do not know Mrs. Adams, and I flatter myself that if you had believed that I might have been useful to her in any way at all, you would have gratified my desire to show you on every occasion how grateful I am for your friendship for your most affectionate and obedient servant, Maria Cosway.

This was their last exchange of letters for another five months, but this time the reason was that Maria persuaded her husband to let her return to France alone.

12

Alone in Paris

It was Maria's first long absence from her husband. His strong personality, his taste, his choices had completely guided her. She owed him much, but to be able to follow her own inclinations was a giddy experience. She had not been so free since Rome, but even then she was under the supervision of Mrs. Gore or Mrs. Banks. Now she was the absolute mistress of her time. This victory must have been the result of a long campaign of subtle suggestions to her husband that his portraits of the Duchess of Orleans and her children must be properly presented, that the Guilio Romano cartoons must be sent off and their safe arrival assured, that so many of their Parisian friends awaited them. The balance was tipped by the invitation to travel with the Princess Lubomirska on her return to Paris and be her guest once there. At last it was decided that Maria should go without Richard, since another long absence from London would not be advisable for him. He was, after all, the Prince of Wales' Principal Painter and had to stay close to his patron, who wished his advice on the decoration of Carlton House.

Two days after her arrival in Paris on August 28, 1787, she entered the grand Salon Carré of the Louvre to see the exhibition of that year, which had just opened. This was another reason she wished to visit Paris, for she had never seen the French Salon, held every two years When she entered the enormous hall overlooking the Seine, she realised how much larger and grander it was than the English Royal Academy's Great Room. Having one's picture hung too high here was surely to be doomed to obscurity. She was not searching the pictures, however, when entering. She was searching the faces of the great and the fashionable, scrutinising the back of wigs and catagons to see if he was there. She had sent word to Jefferson after arriving at the house of Princess Lubomirska. Would he be at the Salon? After a few minutes of experiencing the heat of the crowd and a feverish scanning of almost every corner, she could feel moisture building up at the back of her stays. It would surely stain their lilac silk and worse the white gauze of her robe a l'anglaise.

*' "Qua l'attendo, e mai non viene." I wait and she **does** come. I wait and she **does** come,' someone whispered behind her.*

'But how...who?' She whirled around in a rustle of skirts and saw him leaning over her. He had come. 'Sir, you are a clairvoyant as well as a diplomat. You have read my mind! I thought you had once again forgotten me.'

'No, my dear, dear lady. You know I shall never forget you, and I would never imagine that you could even consider the possibility. So, I was not reading your thoughts, just commenting on Madame Lebrun's picture of Madame Dugazon as Nina. Have you noticed it?' He took her hand and kissed it perfunctorily. His eyes had a sparkle in them. She took in the benevolent look, the sandy-coloured hair and erect carriage in a glance. Yes, he was here, right

MAD.^e DUGAZON. Rôle de Nina.

Pabx...il appelle... hélas! hélas!
Le bien aimé n'appelle pas.

49. *Madame Dugazon as Nina. A portrait of the same subject was exhibited by Madame Vigée Lebrun at the Salon of 1787. The scene is taken from a very popular entertainment at the* Italians Theatre, Nina ou La Folle de l'Amour, *which was certainly seen by the Cosways and Thomas Jefferson.*

before her, just the same. It was hard to believe after living through letters.

'No, where is it?'

'Across the salon, just there. Shall we look? Are you alone? 'Tis not possible.'

'No, I was with Monsieur d'Hancarville, but he seems to have disappeared. I believe he went to fetch a catalogue of the pictures.' They made their way through the assembly and came to stand before a lovely portrait of Madame Dugazon.

'You see, Madame, it is the moment when Nina believes she hears Germeuil.'

'Yes, but he does not come. It is the fervour of her emotion which makes her imagine so.'

'Our wishes construct worlds – our worlds destroy wishes.... . But tell me how you are. Did you have a good journey? Are you well settled with the Princess?

Will you be here long enough this time? If not forever, it will be too short. I want to know all.'

They moved away from Madame Lebrun's picture to the most talked about painting of the Exhibition, *David's* Death of Socrates.

'And how are you? How is your arm? You were so afflicted when I last saw you? I am glad to see you better. Are you playing the violin?'

'No, I fear I shall not be making music for many months, if ever. It is impossible to find the same suppleness in my wrist.'

'Oh, no. That must be hard for you. I know what joy you had in your music. I am truly distressed to hear that.'

"Tis not the worst of my losses. The important thing is I still have the faculty of my ears. So I have not lost music. You can amply satisfy my thirst for it if you will.'

'I shall do whatever is in my power to do for you.... . Oh, we are before the great picture. Do you have a catalogue?'

'Yes, I must ask you to read it for me. Upon leaving the Exhibition I must go to the Palais Royal and buy some reading glasses, without which I have become a poor reader. Perhaps you would care to join me and we could relive our happy adventure in the Mechanical Restaurant?'

'That would be charming. I think...'

'Ah, if it is not the belle anglaise, Madame Cosway, I heard you were coming to grace our society. How delightful to see you!' It was one of the Trudaine brothers.

'Mr. Jefferson, do you know Monsieur Charles-Louis... or is it Charles-Michel? Oh, your names are impossible. Now which is it?'

'Trudaine de Montigny, sir. A great privilege to meet the representative of America. My brother, Trudaine de la Sablière.'

'Gentlemen. It is I who is honoured to know such enlightened patrons of the arts. I believe we have you to thank for commissioning this noble picture before us.'

'It was my brother...Charles-Michel, sir...who is responsible for this great work.'

'Is it ? Yes, I believe it is – the charming Mrs. Cosway! Are you here alone? We must keep Chénier away from you.' It was the star of the exhibition, David, who joined their circle.

'Monsieur David, I am in awe of your picture...a great rendering of a

tragic moment.... May I present to you my friend, Mr. Jefferson, the American Minister in Paris.'

'Sir, I am honoured to be presented to a representative of republican virtue.'

'Please, sir, I am only one of a modest group of experimenters with liberty...'

Mr. Jefferson was rudely interrupted by the mischievous Chénier, or Monsieur de Saint-André as he preferred. He was declaiming again in a silky low voice,

> *The Seine and the Thames, Sisters united forever,*
> *Admire the daughter of the Arno, Endowed with a golden lyre...*
> *whose song is sweet and whose gifted hand*
> *Makes vibrate the harpsicord or the sonorous strings...*
> *O Cosway...cherished on the banks of the Seine,*
> *cherished beside the Thames.*

'My beautiful lady, you have come back to your admirers. We are transfixed with adoration.'

'No, no, no, Monsieur de Saint-André. You must not be. We are here to pay homage to art and to our friend Monsieur David, are we not?'

'Where does David turn to vivify his spirit with inspiration but to the Muse, and here before his eyes she descends from Helicon to inspire us all.'

'Monsieur Jefferson, may I present Monsieur Chénier de Saint-André.'

'Sir, I am honoured.' The young poet bowed low. 'I too have pretensions to the diplomatic service, but only as a lowly private secretary to Monsieur de la Luzerne in London.'

'The tyranny of protocol, Monsieur. I know what lowliness is. My young country finds itself wedged somewhere between Mecklembourg and the Bishop of Basel in the diplomatic order...at number twenty one I believe. At least you will be attached to the Embassy of an important country in the eyes of the English sovereign.'

'And you will be in London soon! That is excellent news for your friends there,' Maria added.

'To follow my Muse, wherever she may lead me. Will she and you, Monsieur, honour us with your presence at our table? We are dining with David at the Trudaines.'

'I fear I must decline your kind invitation. Several errands cannot be postponed, and then I must return to my writing table,' Jefferson refused quickly.

'And you my lady? Surely you have no urgent business that will deprive us of your charming company.'

'No, none at all. I shall be delighted to join you.'

Why did she thus reply when she was longing to accept the suggestion to dine en tête à tête with Mr. Jefferson? It must have been the prudence that always came to the fore as an unthinking reaction. With regret in her heart she distractedly heard Jefferson take leave of them and disappear among the preening crowd. This was their reunion. It only lasted a few moments and now he was gone again. She could have consoled herself with the thought that she must not give him the opportunity to pursue his inclinations. Yet wasn't he the reason Paris charmed her so?

The week following the Salon, Jefferson called on Maria in the Chaussée d'Antin, but she was out. The Princesse Marechale had moved to a lovely house there from her apartments in the Palais Royal. The next day she returned his call, only to be dismayed and disappointed for he had gone off to a hermitage on Mont Calvaire to spend several days in retreat. His servants could not even tell her when he would be returning. Those days of his absence were the most beautiful of September, warm and balmy with a liquid blue sky. She may have been longing to take another ride with him to the forested hills overlooking Paris, but he had gone to them alone. He often found refuge from the noise and dust of Paris by escaping to an abbey on Mount Valerian. An order of lay brothers or hermits kept a boarding-house on the highest hill overlooking the Seine valley. He may have been fleeing something other than the city.

It was not difficult for Maria to busy herself with the wide circle of friends made the previous year and especially with the Polish colony with whom she was now living. Count Stanislaus Potocki, Princess Lubomirska's son-in-law, reported to his wife in Poland that Maria was well integrated into their household.

> …your mother…has a charming house on the boulevard and a very amiable person with her. It's the famous Mrs. Cosway, painter or paintress… a woman of much talent and very amiable.

50. *The Salon of 1787 in the Salon Carré of the Louvre.*

Born in Florence, married in London, where she is hostess of an excellent house, and has come to Paris with your mother after having done I don't know how many portraits of Henri, which have brought a large fortune. Your mother lodges her. She does the honours of the house and everyone is accommodated, for she accommodates everyone.

When the Princesse Marechale Lubomirska had come to London in the spring, she and Maria discovered their shared tastes. Obviously the first was a passion for the arts. The Princess was a fabulous patroness of art and architecture. Her generosity was equal to her immense fortune. A widow, she exercised feudal authority over vast areas of Poland including some sixteen towns and over 300 villages. She managed mines, factories, glass works, paper mills, a private health spa and benevolently organised health care and education for those under her care. More interesting to Maria were the purchases of paintings, sculpture, and antiquities, which she made everywhere on her travels and shipped back to Poland.

The other interest that they shared was a new healing principle. The Princesse Marechale was attracted by all new ideas and fashions, and had probably become interested in the *animal magnetism* of Dr. Anton Mesmer because they were both Freemasons. The societies of freemasonry in France were not groups of atheists conspiring against King and Church, but a fashionable group who gathered to sing and converse freely about modern thoughts. Dr. Franklin had been a member of the Lodge of Nine Sisters, frequented by men of the arts and letters. Lafayette was a freemason as was the Duc d'Orléans and the Duc de Lauzun. The Princess de Lamballe, one of the Princesse Marechale's dearest friends was President of the Scottish Lodge of Adoption in Paris. When Dr. Mesmer came to Paris from Vienna he was easily introduced to his fellow freemasons, and soon gained prestige by healing the Princess de Lamballe with his magnetic techniques. With his usual enthusiasm Lafayette took a course of study from Mesmer and recommended this new discovery to General Washington. Before Maria's second visit to Paris, Mesmer had left the city. His teaching was past the height of its popularity, but the circle of the Princesse Marechale was still fascinated by this new scientific theory.

Dr. de Mainaduc, who taught a mental healing method in London, did not approve of Mesmer or his magnetic theory, finding it too materialistic. Mesmer wanted nothing to do with God or the Holy Spirit, which Mainaduc put at the heart of his teaching. The Austrian considered himself a man of science who had discovered a new universal principle, a magnetic fluid. These points were certainly debated between Maria and the Poles when they passed hours together in stimulating conversation. Potocki claimed that Maria had healed him of an ailment with her 'magnetism'. He recounted to his wife:

> I have for my account a charming magnetiser, Mrs. Cosway, a great person in magnetism as in painting, joking aside I am going to recount one of her miracles. I was one day very ill. She told me that I needed to take something to make me vomit. I replied that that wasn't the problem. With that she made I don't know what sort of gestures and I began to vomit as never in my life and an instant after I was entirely cured after having suffered more than ten hours like a wretch. This effect produced by a young, pretty and amiable person is … the strangest effect of magnetism that I have ever encountered.

The Princess may have let Maria do the 'honours of the house', receiving friends and playing hostess to a circle of artists and writers, but these diversions did not prevent her remembering the excursions of the previous September. At some point she did receive an invitation to dine with Jefferson, possibly when he was receiving the newly-named Minister from the French Court to America, the Count de Moustier. When she arrived at the Hotel de Langeac, she no doubt observed among the servants a very young girl, whose skin had the sheen of dark honey.

'*Well, Monsieur le Ministre, do you have children for servants in America?*'

'*Oh, the young girl. She accompanied my daughter Polly on the voyage from Virginia.*'

'*You mean she is a slave, but she is a white child. She looks very European.*'

'*Yes, well, she is not…exactly…her mother was a slave.*'

'*And so she must be also. What an injustice for such a pretty child! We have* an African servant, Ottobah, but he is paid wages, and is allowed to express his opinions freely. He has recently published a treatise against slavery. He pesters the Prince of Wales with letters, but we fully accept the reason of his views.'

'Yes, and so do I, but I have inherited a form of political economy which is too narrow to take into account the rights of beings who are different and foreign. I see the injustice of it, but feel helpless to overturn the entire foundation of a great part of my country. It is certain that the price of this wrong turn in history will be great for my descendants, and may lead to terrible violence.'

'Even if you cannot be expected to change the policy of others, can you not do something as an individual? Let some of your servants, like this girl, have their liberty?'

'I would be happy to give the greatest gift, liberty, to as many as possible, but I cannot condemn my daughters to destitution for the comfort of my conscience. It is a price I cannot pay.'

''Tis an awful conundrum. Let's talk of something else. Did your retreat to a hermitage do you much good? I hope you have profited from your retirement, for your friends have not. We have much suffered your absence, especially when our expectations were so high.'

'Mrs. Cosway, I fear you have not suffered as much as that. I have intelligence which leads me to believe you have been much occupied and much amused these last weeks.'

'And who could be your informer among the hermits?'

'Ah, it was not the good brothers who told me, but I have news from London. In fact, I have complaints from London concerning your conduct.'

''Tis not possible. No one in London could have news of me.'

'Precisely, my dear lady. Precisely. I just received a letter from Trumbull with a commission to scold you heartily with all due severity but with elegance.'

'To scold me! Whatever for? I would like to see that letter.'

'Here it is,' he unfolded a letter on his writing table and let her read Trumbull's report that not one of Mrs. Cosway's friends, nor her husband, nor her sister, had received a single line from Paris. Not only were they angry but anxious lest her silence was occasioned by accident or illness.

'You see, I have a commission which I cannot carry out,' Jefferson added.

'Why ever not? I am due to receive a scold from you after all mine.'

'I beg you to consider the scold still hanging over your head until I can invent *a machine for scolding, for it is a business not fit for the human heart and especially when directed toward someone such as you.'*

'You are truly kind.' She hesitated. 'Thomas…'

'What a charming sound when clothed in a delicious Italian accent!' He rose from his table and came toward her chair with some intention. As he reached her, the amber-skinned little girl came into the room to announce the arrival of the Count de Moustier and Madame de Bréhan. Abandoning his original impulse, he took her hand and escorted her into the drawing room to greet his guests.

In truth she was not deserving of too much scolding for she had written her husband the week before and given him news that all was well, that she received homage, certainly due to him, from many French gentlemen, and that she wished Angelica Church had been with her to share the charming company.

Another fortnight passed. She called at the Hotel de Langeac, and Jefferson called in the Chaussée d'Antin; each time they missed each other.

At last they agreed to attend a concert of the musical glasses or harmonica, an instrument that had been made popular after Mesmer used it as part of his treatments. Musically the concert was an oddity. Glasses of various sizes filled with liquids produced the tones of the scale when struck. After the demonstration they returned to give their impressions to the Princesse Marechale and her household.

As they entered her pale green and gilt drawing room, the gentlemen arose to greet them. It was a cultivated assembly – Count Stanislaus Potocki, connoisseur of art and antiquities and a politician, married to the Princess's daughter Alexandra; the Abbé Scipio Piattoli, a gentle and competent tutor to the Princess's nephew, Henri; and Julien Niemcewicz, a romantic young man, who later became a respected Polish historian. Seated in the centre and dominating all was the proud Princess Marechale, to whom all deferred. In spite of her small size, she spoke with authority.

'Welcome to my house, Monsieur le Ministre, I am honoured to have a defender of liberty under my roof.'

'It is I who am honoured to be your guest. Madame Cosway has told me of your enlightened charity and many good works.'

'I inherited many responsibilities. They had to be continued. So, what did

you think of the musical glasses? Did they put your nerves in harmony?' The Princess rose and began pacing in front of the windows, so the gentlemen remained standing.

'I must confess that I prefer the sweetness of violin strings for my nerves. The shrill reverberations of those glasses is troubling to my constitution.'

'Perhaps your constitution is in need of harmonising. Have you thought of the new theories of magnetism?' She looked out the window with searching eyes.

'Mrs. Cosway has mentioned her interest in new methods. Although I have little confidence in the efficacy of traditional medicine, I am perplexed by musical glasses, vats, and magnetised bars. I have not investigated these methods and cannot say if science is behind it.'

'Dr. Mesmer is a fine physician and scientist, who has discovered a principle of the universe.'

'Let us hope that he has, but I fear that my distinguished colleague Dr. Franklin and the other members of the Royal Commission who investigated his theories found no evidence of any magnetic fluid, and concluded that Dr. Mesmer was an expert in the powers of the imagination. I might add that Dr. Franklin did enjoy playing his own "harmonica" when he was living in Passy.'

'Sir, with all due respect to your friend, Royal Commissions are not always able to recognise genius! Even if there is no magnetic fluid, we know that certain persons are spiritualised enough to magnetise others through divine grace or the force of their faith and will. Your friend Mrs. Cosway may well have this power. At any rate she has gone far in the study of it.... Well, I shall retire now.... No, I think I shall take the air in the Palais Royal. Who will accompany me? My son? Abbé? Mrs. Cosway?'

Declining to join them, Maria begged off: 'I am rather tired this evening. After a little music I shall retire.'

'As you wish. Good evening, Mr. Jefferson.' She nodded curtly in his direction, then to the others, 'Mrs. Cosway…Monsieur Niemcewicz, Good evening.'

Young Niemcewicz said he had an engagement and left with the others. Unexpectedly Maria was alone with Jefferson.

'Please forgive the Princess,' she apologised. 'She was not considerate of you. I am truly sorry for it. She has a good heart, but is sometimes proud and hard.'

'I understand that. Did you see her restless pacing? In spite of all her luxury, she does not seem to gain satisfaction from it.'

'Tis true, but she is brilliant and can be quite interesting if one tolerates her eccentricities. And she has kindly taken me into her household.'

'For that I thank her and owe her much. I don't know if you have the power to magnetise others, but you have assuredly exercised a supernatural force on me.' Suddenly he took Maria's two hands and held them in his tightly. Still holding her hands, he led her to a soft damask canape. They sat down without speaking. They shared a long moment, immobile as the Greek figures in the room's sculpted frieze above. Almost imperceptibly he began to slide her hands to either side and press them into the silk cushion, while leaning toward her.

'No, no, sir. Please, you must not insist.'

'I shall not, but do you know how you have tempted me this past year? I have no right to speak to you this way. I have nothing to offer but dishonour when I wish to give affection, happiness, esteem. It is more than can be borne!' He released her hands with uncharacteristic anger.

'I do not know how to answer. I have no right to tell you my sentiments. I am uncertain that I know them. You have affected me as no other person. I was obliged to marry and was content enough with Mr. Cosway. He has been kind and devoted. My contentment now seems cruelly insufficient; you have been the measure of my loss. If my faith were less strong, my abhorrence of divorce not total, I might well have abandoned all. I often wish it, but cannot take the step...I wish it, but cannot.' Taking a large breath, she whispered, 'Will you not take it for me?' Her question hung in the air for a long moment without the response she longed for.

'You have the strength of the gods, Madame, and I a poor mortal have none before your divine powers. I can only render homage to them.' He rose wearily. 'And now the hour is late. I beg you to forgive me if I take leave of you without the soothing balm of your music.' He bowed to kiss her hand gently, turned on his heel and left the room without looking back.

During the next weeks he disappeared to Mont Calvaire. Again she called to find that he had gone away to his country retreat, leaving no word for her. This continual vacillation of interest in their friendship was perplexing. At times he was ardent and solicitous, and then just as often he was absent in body and in mind. In the former case she had the defence of her principles, and in the latter her principles weakened. The rhythm was never right. At last after a fortnight, she may have received invitations to two public events.

The first was an outing at the Palais Royal where they could spend a good time laughing at the ridiculous comedies of the Varieties. That evening three were given, but the most uproarious was *The Night of Adventures or the Two Living Dead.* Several days later they attended a *concert spiritual* at the Tuileries on All Saints Day where they enjoyed a symphony by Hayden, but the Italian singers were not good. Jefferson was as ever courteous and gracious, but distant.

In November Maria started to think of her return to London. She could not be a guest of the Princess for ever, and there was nothing to keep her in Paris but selfish insouciance. One bit of business was undone. The cartoons of Guilio Romano, promised by her husband as a gift to the King, had not arrived. She received a letter from her husband telling her that they had been carefully packed and shipped to Dover, addressed to Monsieur de Montmorin, the Secretary of Foreign Affairs and that Monsieur de Barthélemy of the French Embassy in London had written to the customs at Calais and asked that the package not be opened. D'Hancarville wrote to the Count d'Angiviller to assure him of these arrangements and to ask that the customs officers of Paris not disturb the cartoons, which were carefully protected by waxed canvas. All this was done, and Maria decided that she would not necessarily wait until the gift was received. Towards the end of the month, as she began to make plans for her departure, Jefferson decided that he wanted to give her a farewell dinner, and asked her to invite whomever she wished. The Poles accepted, but d'Hancarville had another engagement. The day before the dinner Maria wrote to Jefferson:

> If my inclination had been your law I should have had the pleasure of seeing you More than I have. I have felt the *loss* with displeasure, but on My return to England when I calculate the time I have been in Paris, I shall not believe it possible.

Was the dinner a compensation for the unsatisfactory way their relation had turned out? The relationship had turned out this way because of her contradictions as well as his. Yet there was a difference. He was rational as the Dialogue clearly demonstrated. She understood his reasoning, but was confused by the logic of love – the tangibility of a feeling that somehow should be able to resolve all contradictions. She was a woman used to abiding by the strictures of religion and society. He was a man and a rather freethinking one at that. He should have been able to cut through the obstacles and find a way to make the reality of their feelings permanent. He should have had the will to prevail, if he felt what he professed. She had expected more of him. Instead of a forward-moving man, he was a sort of ethereal spirit, who

51. *Garden side of the Hotel de Langeac, Jefferson's house located at the angle of the rue de Berri and the Champs Elysées.*

vanished if touched. Perhaps she would have vanished had he been the man she wished for, but she would never know.

The last Sunday of November was cold and clear. The fires were burning cheerily in the Hotel de Langeac when Maria arrived with the Princess, Count Potocki, and Monsieur Niemcewicz about four in the afternoon, a more fashionable hour for dinner than the usual three o'clock. The horizontal rays of winter sun gave a golden cast to the stone walls of the house. As the scene of a friendship that strained to be more, this house's atmosphere already touched Maria. It resonated with the personality of its resident.

After a short time of conversation in the oval drawing room, they were shown into one of the reception rooms overlooking the Champs Elysées where a table had been brought in and beautifully laid with silver candelabra of three branches, porcelain red-bordered plates, and a heavy white damask cloth. They were joined by Monsieur Chénier de St. André, Madame de Corny, Mr. Short, and young Miss Jefferson, tall and quiet, but surely perceptive, if one could judge by the attentive looks she gave each speaker. They were seated in the French fashion, which had begun to be followed in London, of alternating ladies and gentlemen. The Princess Marechale was on the host's right, and Maria on his left between him and Niemcewicz.

'Mr. Jefferson you have gone to too much trouble. You should not have done so much,' Maria protested as they were seated.

''Tis the least one can do for a friend whom we may not see for years to come. She should have a memory of our generosity.'

'The memory of your many kindnesses was assured before today.'

The Princess Marechale spoke up: 'Mrs. Cosway has recounted to me your excursions of last year, the houses and gardens you visited. I have undertaken important renovations in Poland. Mr. Adam has done plans for one of my houses…and I would like to hear about the house you have built…' With her unflagging curiosity and superior rank she managed to absorb Jefferson in conversation for most of the dinner. Since his French was slower he preferred to speak to only one person at a time. This left the rest of them to carry on animated talk across the table and Niemcewicz to pay her gallant compliments, occasionally overheard by Jefferson when the Princess interrupted her rapid monologue long enough to taste the pâté of turkey and truffles, the duck foie gras and the excellent wines.

Was that a pained look on Jefferson's face when Julien Niemcewicz whispered rather loudly, 'Ma chère Marie, I shall remember all my life the moments we have passed together. I shall remember you singing the air "I shed so many tears" and I shall shed them for we may never see each other again. But you don't feel all that for you have the philosophy of a man and I the sensibility of a woman.'

'Monsieur Niemcewicz, it seems we are quite complementary if what you say is true, although you are wrong if you think I have the intellect of a philosopher.'

'You have a virtue more important than intellect. You are a Stoic, calm before all discomfiture.'

'You have not seen me in all circumstances.'

'It is not necessary. One has only to read the unruffled innocence of your visage.'

'Niemcewicz, can you stop paying court to Mrs. Cosway for a few minutes?' Potocki interrupted. 'Madame de Corny was just recounting to me what her husband witnessed at the Parliament on Monday, how the Duc d'Orléans had the temerity to confront the King and tell him that his declaration of a Royal session was illegal. Louis, publicly humiliated, stuttered that the session was legal if he wished it, and, red with anger, he walked out of the Parliament. Philippe d'Orléans is already banished to Villers-Cotteret. This does not bode well for the royal reforms.'

'Full of surprises, Orléans. He is not a giant of oratory or intellect. That is the work of Brissot and that lot around him, who seek influence through opposition to the Court,' Niemcewicz observed.

'Gentlemen, no more politics. Our host must spend his days full of talk of politics and we must divert him with more amusing subjects on Sunday,' the Princess ordered, attributing her own desires to the American minister.

And so the dinner went on amiably – Madame de Corny entertained by the charming Potocki, Jefferson most likely bored by the Princess, Maria pursued by young Niemcewicz. Patsy Jefferson was left with her usual table companion William Short, and everyone was enchanted with the man of letters, André Chénier. After dinner Maria was obliged to play the harpsichord, specially tuned for the occasion, and they lingered into the candlelight of the early evening. When the host accompanied Maria to her carriage, she asked if they would see each other again and he assured her that they would.

True to his promise he called the next Friday, the eve of her departure. All week she had thought sadly of their *adieux* and it was possible that a reckless idea had germinated in her mind. If she was never to see him again, why not spend an hour doing what she wanted. After all she was in a marriage of reason and he was perfectly free. All that was needed was that he declare himself more openly and pretend that there was hope of a tomorrow for their friendship.

He was shown into her apartment whilst her hairdresser was still labouring over the mass of soft curls then the fashion. She received him in a dressing gown, a custom permitted when the ritual of dressing took hours.

'You need no adornments you know, no blond powders, no red powders,' he suggested.

'Yes I agree. The fashions are simpler these days. Ever since the Queen cut her hair after the birth of her last child, the French have dispensed with false curls, cushions and outrageous engines perched on the head. That will do, thank you,' she dismissed the hairdresser.

When they were alone, she expected that they would continue the conversation interrupted the night of the musical glasses, but they could not find the harmony.

'So, the dreaded day of adieux has come,' she lamented. 'I have seen so little of you. Three months have passed and we have hardly seen each other.'

She was standing before the window looking at a barren garden. She felt the bitter cold through the glass.

'You were so occupied with your many friends, my dear lady. You were always with your household or Monsieur de Saint André or the Trudaines or the many artists who adore you, David, Robert, Greuze. You are loved by everyone. It is natural. But that means that you have little freedom for long afternoon drives in the country or private meetings like this one.'

'But I wanted the freedom, I wanted to see you. You were always going off to be with the hermits. Mont Calvaire was my Calvary. I never understood why that each time I did come to you, you were in retreat. Why did you flee so often?'

'The press of business I suppose. The need to breathe purer air, to reflect on the proper course to follow.'

'Are you unable to follow your heart just once?'

'Madame, is it you who counsels me thus? The imperturbable Mrs. Cosway?'

'Don't be cruel, I am terribly perturbed. You can see that.' She turned swiftly to face him.

'Please I don't wish to see you troubled like this. What can I do to comfort you?' He took her hand.

'I believe there is nothing left but one small gesture.'

'I am your servant.'

Unable to say what she truly wished, she invented a pathetic substitute: 'I wish to hear you call me "Maria".'

'A service easy and painful, Maria…my dear Maria,' he said softly. Then he drew her close, put his arms around her shoulders and held her for a long silent minute. 'And now we have to mark the hour of parting or we shall never accomplish it.'

'We can't part like this, not yet…not yet.'

'I shall come to breakfast with you tomorrow and then accompany you part of the way. How is that?'

'Yes, yes. Please do.' She understood that their interview was drawing to its disappointing close. She felt as if he were fleeing once again. 'Are their commissions for you in London? Your harpsichord or other purchases?'

'No, it is kind of you, but Trumbull has all under his careful management.'

'Well then, I suppose there is nothing left for me to do but take my leave of you. Please give my compliments to Mr. Short and to young Patsy and little Polly. You are blessed to have such lovely daughters.'

'Indeed I am…I shall come to you in the morning then.'
'Yes, that's it. Addio, Addio, Tomaso.'
'Addio, 'til tomorrow.'

Tomorrow never came for them. That evening Maria was plunged into a fit of depression and certainly bouts of tears; she could not face another parting scene. Bitter and utterly disappointed, she gave in to petty vengeance or the desire to stimulate action in the inscrutable American. She may have cherished the vain wish that by fleeing abruptly Jefferson would realise how fond of her he really was, that he would finally do something. She hastily scribbled a note:

> I cannot breakfast with you to morrow; to bid you *adieu* once is sufficiently painful, for I leave with very melancholy ideas. You have given my dear Sir all your commissions to Mr. Trumbull, and I have the reflection that I cannot be useful to you; who have rendered me so many civilities.

At five the next morning in freezing darkness she set off in a post chaise for Calais, accompanied by Monsieur Chénier de Saint-André.

13

'Remember Me and Love Me'

1788-1789

The Channel crossing with André Chénier was rough and long, making the poet extremely ill. Upon reaching London Maria found her husband

and sister Charlotte also low with a winter malady. Remorseful over the rude parting with Mr. Jefferson, she penned a note of explanation:

> You promised to come to breakfast with Me the Morning of My departure, and to accompany me part of the way, did you go? I left Paris with Much regret indeed, I could not bear to take leave any More. I was Confus'd and distracted, you Must have thought me so when you saw me in the Evening; why is it My fortune to find Amiable people where I go, and why am I to be obliged to part with them! Tis very Cruel; I hope our Correspondence will be More frequent and punctual then our Meetings were while I was in Paris. I suspected the reason, and would not reproach you since I know your Objection to Company. You are happy you can follow so Much your inclinations. I wish I could do the same. I do all I can with little success, perhaps I don't know how to go about it.

There was no reply from Paris. The always serene Mr. Jefferson was letting his anger slowly dissipate with time. On Christmas Day Maria could bear it no longer. She had to know what he thought of her strange behaviour.

> How do you do My dear friend: You came to the invitation of my breakfast the Morning of my departure! [I presumed]…and what did you think of Me? I did it to avoid the last taking leave, I went too early for any body to see Me. I cannot express how Miserable I was in leaving Paris. How I regretted not having seen More of you, and I cannot have even the Satisfaction to unburden My displeasure…by loading you with reproaches.

Since Angelica Church was then in Paris and had surely been presented to him she inquired:

> Have you seen yet the lovely Mrs. Church?…what do you think of her? She Calls me her Sister. I call her My dearest Sister. If I did not love here so Much I should fear her rivalship, but no I give you free permission to love her with all your heart, and I

shall feel happy if I think you keep me in a little corner of it, when you admit her even to reigning Queen.

January passed. Still no word. Then Maria received his side of the story:

I went to breakfast with you according to promise, and you had gone off at 5 o'clock in the morning. This spared me indeed the pain of parting, but it deprives me of the comfort of recollecting that pain.

After giving news of the illnesses of Princess Lubomirska and Monsieur de Corny, he praised Angelica:

I find in her all the good the world has given her credit for. I do not wonder at your fondness for each other. I have seen too little of her, as I did of you. But in your case it was not my fault, unless it be a fault to love my friends so dearly as to wish to enjoy their company in the only way it yields enjoyment, that is, *en petite comité*.

His clever excuse was that he wished to see Maria away from society, that she was too sought after.

You make every body love you. You are sought and surrounded therefore by all. Your mere domestic cortege was so numerous, et *si imposante,* that one could not approach you quite at their ease. Nor could you so unpremeditately mount into the Phaeton and hie away to the bois de Boulogne, St. Cloud, Marly, St. Germains &c…Add to this the distance at which you were placed from me. When you come again, you must be nearer, and move more extempore.

The rest of his letter gave the usual reason for its delay – he did not wish to use the post because his letters were opened, that he was over a month looking for a private conveyance. What did Maria think if Trumbull told her that a certain Mr. Parker had delivered letters from Jefferson to the

Adamses in London? That Mr. Parker was not to be trusted with her letter? These little insincerities were Jefferson's usual way of smoothing the edges of relations.

When Angelica and Trumbull returned from Paris in mid-February, Maria was angry that they carried no letters for her. After smouldering a month, she expressed her spleen in a joking, yet passionate outburst:

> I have waited some time to try if I could recover my usual peace with you, but I find it impossible…therefore must address myself to you still <u>angry</u>. Your long silence is impardonable, but what is the Name I Must give to Mr: Trumbull and Mrs: Church not bringing Me a letter from you? No, My war against you is of such a Nature that I cannot even find terms to express it… . I believe that really you know how I value every line which comes from you, why will you add scarcity? But I begin to run on and my intention was only to say, *nothing*, send a blank paper; as a Lady in a Passion is not fit for Anything… . Will you give Mr: Trumbull leave to Make a Copy of a certain portrait he painted at Paris? It is a person who hates you that requests this favour. If you want private conveyance to send me a letter there are many, ask Abbé Piattoli, Madame de Corny, & many others. Tho' I am angry I can hardly end my letter. Remember, I do you justice by not thinking of you now.

As it turned out, this fit of *pique* had no effect. Jefferson had left Paris for another ramble, this time to Holland and the Rhine Valley. Her firebrand, lobbed over the Channel, burned itself out on his writing table. After many efforts to force a reply from a reluctant or busy gentleman, she was obliged to turn to other correspondents: the faithful d'Hancarville, the painter David, young Niemcewicz.

One of David's letters provided great solace to wounded pride, even if in another domain – art. He had seen a new print of her painting *The Hours*, beautifully engraved by Bartolozzi. She had sent several to Paris, among others to d'Hancarville and Madame d'Angiviller. The original painting, exhibited in 1783 at the Academy, was now being shown in Thomas Macklin's Poets' Gallery, a hundred works inspired by various poets.

Macklin also published prints of the exhibition in sets of four. After seeing *The Hours*, David wrote:

> …one cannot make a poetry more ingenious or more natural. Courage Madame Cosway, to glory, to glory, without genius one is nothing and with genius one is what you are. I regret to have known you, for I would have wished to have known you only to never leave you and to amuse ourselves in talking art together.

David never saw the original. Perhaps he would have agreed with the press review which said that her colouring of the 'rosy-bosomed hours' had been cheered up with <u>Cherry Bounce.</u> The reviewer gave all the credit to Bartolozzi, saying that he produced from Maria's picture 'one of the most beautiful prints we ever beheld'.

The importance of engravings to an artist's reputation was proved in the summer when Jefferson reported:

> Your Hours, my dear friend, are no longer your own. Every body now demands them; and were it possible for me to want a memorandum of you, it is presented me in every street of Paris. Come then to see what triumph Time is giving you. Come and see every body stopping to admire the Hours, suspended against the walls of the Quai des Augustins, the Boulevards, the Palais royal &c. &c with a 'Maria Cosway delint.' at the bottom.

Other distractions that spring were her usual receptions on Mondays and Thursdays. Richard was often at Carlton House, supervising the design of the ceiling frescos in the Grand Saloon and advising the Prince on the hanging of pictures. By April Maria was occupied with a portrait of Mrs. Fitzherbert to be shown at the Academy Exhibition, and two Parisian guests. One, the Duc d'Orléans, sullied the reputation of their house, and the other, André Chénier, endeared himself to Maria with his devotion.

After humiliating Louis XVI in Parliament, the Duke had become the rallying point for opposition to the monarchy. After his exile to the country, he obtained the King's permission for a pleasure-seeking jaunt to England. His closeness to the Prince of Wales meant that the Cosways could not avoid his company and worse, the company he kept. Cosway was not overly concerned, although Maria may have been displeased. The *Morning Post* seized upon the occasion, characterising Richard as Pandarus or a sort of pimp.

The more sympathetic Frenchman frequenting her house was the gifted Chénier. She took him under her wing but he was terribly unhappy in London. He had wished to come, admiring the political liberties of England, but the social reality was too cold. In Paris he had easy access to the best salons, where his talents and conversation opened all doors. Alas, without the golden key of language – his English did not flow – without rank and fortune, the English snubbed him. He became nothing but a poorly paid clerk to the French Ambassador in a foreign land with a dank, wretched climate. Maria welcomed him to her receptions, but they were not as stimulating and welcoming as the Paris salons. He repaid her loyalty with his verses. Inspired by her portrait, engraved in *intaglio* on an amethyst ring, he dedicated to her these lines:

> With Pyrgoteles' art his ingenious pupil,
> By a turn of the industrious iron
> Gives the features of young Marie
> To the veins of pebbles from the Ganges or Syria,
> Etched on amethyst or starred onyx,
> …O young Florentine!
> It is you, Nymphs of the Arno, who from the arms of Lucina
> Came to welcome her;…
> Queen with sparkling eyes, beautiful Poetry,
> Smiles on her and wets her mouth with ambrosia,
> Arms her weak hands with fertile brushes
> Which bring alive the canvas in magic pictures;
> And gives to her gaze this fire, this pure soul…
> Engrave all these brilliant gifts on her visage.
> Engrave, if you can, her soul and her speech,
> Her voice, powerful link which binds our days,
> The days of her friends, happy and faithful band,
> Who live all for her, and who die for her.

As often happens when one's attention is elsewhere, surprises occur. The unexpected arrival of a letter from Jefferson did not perturb her good humour even if it was mostly a travel journal about pictures seen in Dusseldorf, where 'I wished for you much', the castle of Heidelberg, where 'I led you by the hand thro' the whole garden' and Strasbourg, where 'I sat down to write to you' he said, but could think of nothing to say but a passage from *Tristram Shandy* about a man who provoked a stir in the city because of the size of his nose!

To this she replied the very day she received it,

> …how could you lead me by the hand all the way, think of me, have Many things to say, and not find One word to write, *but on Noses?*

His assurance that he had answered her last letter before all the others awaiting him was not comforting. To his blithe declaration: 'I do not think I was in arrears in our epistolary account when I left Paris. In affection I am sure you were greatly my debtor…' she replied dryly: 'I am not your debtor in the least.'

He considered her angry letter in March a proof of esteem.

> …but I love better to have soft testimonials of it. You must therefore now write me a letter teeming with affection; such as I feel for you. So much I have no right to ask.

To that she reminded him that if he preferred softer testimonials of her esteem,

> Give me the example if you please. Am I to address a stranger in such confidential terms? who writes to me so short and scarce as possible?

When he told her that the Princess Lubomirska had taken a house closer to his, he consoled himself:

> When you come again therefore you will be somewhat nearer to me, but not near enough; and still surrounded by a numerous

cortege, so that I shall see you only by scraps as I did when you were here last. The time before we were half days, and whole days together, I found this too little.

When would they see each other? She had great hopes and much repentance for past behaviour:

Oh I wish My dear friend I could announce to you our return to Paris! I am afraid to question My Lord and Master on this subject; he may not think or like to refuse, and a disappointed promise of this kind would be too cruel to me. I cannot bear it. I should be doubly Miserable all the Summer; but why dont you Come?… we shall not have a Numerous Cortege, I promise to Make Myself and my Society according to your own wish…if I come to Paris I may do more what I please this time. There are but four people I could wish to pass all my time with. Is this too great a Number? when *you* are One, even if you dont guess the others I am Sure you would not object to. I long to return. I left a bad impression in the atmosphere. I was worse than myself, and really so bad that Sometimes I hardly knew Myself. I am Much better now, and My Constant occupations for these three Months past keep me in better health or they keep me in better spirits, and that is the Most dangerous Malady I can have.

She closed by telling him that she was out of all patience with Trumbull for dawdling on the portrait of him and by sending her compliments to Mr. Short and Madame de Corny. Her last words were:

I Wish to deserve and nourish the good Opinion you have of me from your own Sentiments, enforce it by those you esteem, and oblige you from a return of the affection & friendship I feel for you to allow without bounds you will always be deficient to Maria Cosway.

If one judged by their correspondence, he would always be deficient in affection, for the pattern of his silence and her imploring was well-installed that year and would only change slightly when she matched his silence with her own. This became easier after her attention was captured by a musical sensation at the Opera. In the same letter chastising Jefferson's poor travel journal, she mentioned her enthusiasm for an Italian *castrato*:

> If you want to hear what Italian Singing is, come to London. Marchesi is here and the Most wonderful Singer I ever heard. The Opera is good but for want of equal performers with him it is rather dull as the whole spectacle depending on one person, makes the rest appear tiresome…'

Gaetano Luigi Marchesi was the most celebrated singer of his day, known and feted all over Europe, from St. Petersburg to Naples. In Vienna ladies attached miniatures of his face to bracelets, necklaces, and the buttons of their shoes. Everywhere he sang, even in London, he caused a sensation. He became Maria's friend, and, because of a certain imprudence on their part, was considered by some to be her lover. The truth of their relation was probably complicated and never understood by others. Part of the misunderstanding was caused by the exuberant personality of Marchesi. He was a creature of the stage, always performing, always creating excitement, and always profiting from his celebrity with feminine conquests. His susceptibility to the charms of the fair sex drew more attention than usual for this amorous success was the accomplishment of a *castrato*. Contrary to what would be expected,

LUIGI MARCHESI.
THE CELEBRATED SINGER.

many of the singers subjected to this grotesque operation as children were not prevented from having the normal reactions of a man. Other physical effects – the price of an angelic voice – varied. Some were given to corpulence. Others had extremely long limbs. Marchesi had escaped the negative results of castration. He was good-looking. Bright eyes illuminated a handsome face; his body was strong and well-proportioned. When he appeared on stage with his enormous presence, he knew how to create vibrant waves of excitement. Whatever the opera, he insisted on the same entrance. He appeared at the top of a hill carrying a sword, a gleaming lance, and wearing a helmet with towering red and white plumes. Giving the audience time to digest this magnificent sight, he would say, *Dove son io?* Where am I? A fanfare of trumpets followed. He then launched into his favourite aria, 'Mia speranza io pur vorrei' by Sarti. He liked bravura arias, *arie di tempesta*, where he could show off his incredible virtuosity. His voice was indescribable, clear and sonorous, from the soprano of high *d* down to the tenor *g*, a range of two and half octaves. He loved to improvise. Taking one breath he could sing a clear trill rising up over six or seven notes in succession or ornament passages of sixteen notes, vibrating every fourth note and giving nuances to the others. He controlled his voice as one would a violin. As tension mounted in the audience, he would slowly descend the steps to the stage, light reverberating from his weapons and plumes waving. Approaching the footlights, he basked in the glorious ovation which always rose up to meet him in a wave of physical pleasure.

His critics said that he 'pranced' on stage, was extremely vain and made impossible demands. They also complained that he was not convincing in tender, pathetic arias, and lacked the feeling which touched the soul. It was true that he was a man of excessive temperament. He had fallen into the trap which wealth and enormous adulation can lay for anyone, but especially for the young. Since his first success in Naples at twenty-three, ten years before coming to London, he had been showered with riches and praise by the courts of Europe. Apart from his amorous intrigues, he had been spared the experience of suffering the deeper emotions which would have nourished his interpretations of pathetic arias.

Maria first heard Luigi Marchesi sing in April of 1788. He made his London debut in Sarti's *Giulio Sabino*. The King's Theatre was so crowded that the spectators in the Pit were standing elbow to elbow. Every seat in the boxes was taken. Maria was most likely the guest of General Paoli, who subscribed to a box on the first row close to that of the Duke and Duchess of Cumberland, the King's brother and sister-in-law. Despite the criticism that Marchesi did not have sufficient feeling in his performance, she witnessed the effect he had on those present. Although London audiences were more attentive than those in Italy, there was still a great deal of conversation, bustling about, and late arrivals by the *bon ton*. That night everyone was rapt, eyes and ears fixed on the noble soprano, who transported his listeners with improvised embellishments or gave them shivery tears with the arias '*Cara figli*' or '*Come partir poss'io*', when the hero takes leave of his wife Epponina. Maria was present when the overheated air of the theatre was suffused with melting tenderness. The cheering 'bravos' demanded several encores; in each one the virtuoso changed his vocal ornaments. Marchesi was resplendent that spring night, a sort of demi-god, who attracted the spectators to his glistening person and provoked in all a desire to draw closer, to know him, to grasp a small part of this transient majesty.

After hearing him sing, Maria surely sent one of her Italian notes, inviting the man of whom all London was talking to one of her Monday evenings. As Pacherotti and Tenducci before him, the new sensation became a regular visitor to Schomberg House. He and his hostess sang together or she accompanied him on the harp. An accomplished harpist, he had written harp accompaniments for some of his favourite airs. For a musician like Maria it was an indescribable joy to play in harmony with this celestial voice when he sang '*Lungi dal caro bene*' from *Giulio Sabino* or '*Se cerca, se dice*' from *L'Olimpiade*. By July the newspapers were printing rumours. How could they not follow every step of a flamboyant personage such as Marchesi! He knew how to give them food for their insatiable maw. The night he came into Maria's box at the theatre caused a great public stir. She must have been the guest of Lady Mary Duncan, whose box gave directly onto the stage, open to the view of the entire assembly.

During the interval Marchesi opened the door behind them.

'Mesdames, may I join you?'

'Most certainly, maestro,' Lady Mary replied, as they made room with a rustle of taffetas and grating of chair legs.

Marchesi spoke little English. Naturally Maria was drawn into conversation with him in their native tongue, isolating them from the others.

'Bella donna, bella Maria, I could not stay away from you. The thought that you were beside me near the stage, your presence there just a few steps away—you cannot know how this inspired my voice. Every note was for you, my blonde Florentine. What a light in this cold country!'

'*You must not speak like this, even if others cannot understand. Surely they can read your ardent look, your face bent low toward mine. This will not do!*'

'*What can I do? You cannot wish me to renounce such happiness. I feel as if I have known you all my life, all my life!*'

'*We are of the same country, the same tongue. You find in me the home you are missing here. Well I know that longing. I pray you sir, do not confuse our shared history, our shared taste for music, with some destined familiarity.*'

'*No, no, no, it is you, you…gentilissima donna, bellessima…*' *He took her hand, leaning ever closer.*

'*Signore Marchesi, I beg you, please…look, others are observing us. Do not make a scandal.*'

'*Do you think it is of import what strangers may think?*' *His dark eyes glistened.* '*They do not exist…only you exist for me. No one else is in the theatre tonight. I sing for you alone, my private audience, my sovereign…listen to 'Lungi dal caro bene' and know it is addressed to you and no other. And now I must prepare for the next act. Mesdames, my respects.*' *He bowed low and disappeared, leaving the ladies gasping after the passage of this whirlwind.*

True to his announced intention, when he began to sing, 'Away from my dearly beloved' he turned towards their box and fixed his gaze on Maria. By the time he came to the last line, 'If my eyes may not look upon her, then let a sweet last sleep close them,' she dared not turn her head to look at the some two thousand pairs of eyes, focused on this tender scene with malicious glee.

The *Morning Post* was not long to spread the news:

…the charms of the fair Maria Cosway were so alluring in the eyes of Marchesi on Saturday last at the opera, that between the acts of *Guilio Sabino* he went into the same box with the seductive artist & remained there in tender homage till his theatrical duties called him again to the stage. The lady sat in the box next to the stage, so that this trip of the warbling hero being full in sight of the audience could not be deemed in the highest degree respectful.

Summer saw the close of the Opera season and Marchesi's departure for Turin where he received an annual subsidy from the King of Piedmont-Sardinia. Maria looked forward to the languid days of August, when she could profit from the hospitality of Down Place, the Churches' country house. Since Cosway was extremely busy with the decoration of Carlton House, she was accompanied by her sister Charlotte, now an attractive young lady of twenty-two. She had become an accomplished musician, excelling on the harp and harpsichord. Well-mannered and refined, she helped Maria with the management of Schomberg House and became a good companion. Mr. Cosway and all their friends were extremely fond of her quiet charm. Despite all her good qualities the poor girl was in the same situation as Maria had been – no connections or fortune – no prospects of a good marriage. She bore the situation with grace, enjoying the social advantages which her sister's house afforded.

Although Down Place, overlooking the Thames near Windsor, was only about three hours by carriage from London, Charlotte and Maria may have preferred the scenic detour, following the great loops of shimmering river upstream to Hampton. Maria had been enchanted by the thickly forested hills dominating the Seine, but had to admit that this part of the Thames Valley revealed the superior English genius for landscape. During the journey one never left a vast green park – lawns gently sloping to the water's edge, meadows of grazing sheep or cattle shaded by perfectly-formed oak trees. The Arcadian backdrop was a painterly stage for great houses, which in their turn enhanced nature as the highest attainments of human civilisation. A history of architectural styles could be read from the Palladian symmetry of Chiswick House, the Tudor turrets of Syon House, the Dutch House and Chinese pagoda of the Royal Gardens at Kew, the Gothic fantasy of Sir Horace Walpole's Strawberry Hill, to the red brick Tudor, then Wren baroque of Hampton Court Palace. In this immense garden the best English talents had worked. Lancelot 'Capability' Brown had created the tidal meadow for Syon House and the lawns of Kew Palace on the opposite river bank, before finishing his career in the gardener's cottage of Hampton Court. The view from Richmond Hill was famous, having been favourably compared with those painted by Claude and Poussin in the Alban hills. English painters were naturally attracted to the prospect. Reynolds and Gainsborough had chosen Richmond for their country retreats. Alexander Pope and his neighbour, Sir Horace Walpole, had created original gardens in Twickenham, depending on river views for their charm. After passing David Garrick's house and temple to Shakespeare at Hampton, they left their boat to take a carriage. Although they had added three hours to their journey, such beautiful prospects spared them the choking dust of the road.

Angelica herself greeted them at the door of Down Place, unaffectedly expressing her hospitality with no need to interpose servants. As she escorted them to their rooms, she inquired eagerly about London news.

'Dear Maria, and dear Charlotte, how good of you to come to be with us. But tell me, I heard dreadful news about your neighbour Mr. Gainsborough. Is it true?'

'Yes, he passed away in Schomberg House the second of August. You know he fell ill this spring while leaving the Hastings trial in Westminster Hall. As he wished to be buried privately in Kew Churchyard with only a few friends present, Mr. Cosway did not attend. 'Tis said that Sir Joshua visited him a few days before his death. Mr. Gainsborough desired to leave this world on friendly terms with his rival and to show him the little gallery of pictures which he had installed for the public after he refused to exhibit in the Academy.'

'Well, he was too well established to be damaged by that. These last years he has been as sought after as before, especially by the Royal Family.'

'Yes, and Mr. Cosway decided he too had no time to show pictures this year. I may soon follow his example. I had little success. One paper said that my portrait of Mrs. Fitzherbert showed her in a state of "jolly inebriety". I have no more patience with these critics.'

'Maria, that was the Morning Post. You know nothing good ever comes from that pestilential source!'

'True, but one clings to the illusory hope that the newspapers will improve.'

'My dear, you are an innocent. Tell me... to speak of a more pleasant topic...have you news of our friend, Mr. Jefferson? I received a letter from him this week, giving a good report of my daughter Kitty and Madame de Corny.'

'Yes, I have news as well. Two letters in fact, but one is only a reply to my constant scolding for his negligence. I had heard nothing since April, so in June I sent three lines by Mr. Trumbull in the vein of:

I will write two words to show you I can write if I please, but as I don't please I shall say no More, as I wait to hear from you. If my *silence is of consequence, you will easily be sensible that yours is very much so with me.*

I would not have written that much if Trumbull had not asked for a letter. Then in July Mr. de Saint André asked for a letter to Mr. J so I was obliged to write him again even though he had not responded to my last two! What could his silence mean? This was vexing. I could only express myself sincerely. I told him that I could not write to anybody that does not think of me; that a punctilious formality kept me waiting for letters to answer. I signed "Maria Cosway in waiting". Was it too bold to speak to him in these terms?'

'That rather depends on the intimacy of your friendship, does it not?'

'Yes, of course…. Well, shall we compare our news from Paris?'

'Indeed we shall. After you are settled in your rooms, come into the garden for tea and we shall read each other delightful lines from our reluctant correspondent.'

If Maria had not been so fond of Angelica, if she had not admired her greatly, she might have allowed a subtle jealousy to cloud their sincere attachment. Listening to her gentle voice under the elms' sheltering shade, Maria understood that Jefferson had taken an immediate liking to her. When she saw the letter he had written to Angelica, she must have seen certain similarities to his Dialogue of the Head and Heart, although this letter was much briefer and seemed less deeply felt. Trumbull had completed the miniature portrait of Jefferson for Maria, but there was also one for Angelica.

'So, Maria, I have told you all. What do you hear from Paris?'

'Not much more than you. He says that society has become more gloomy than usual because of the civil dissensions. Tho' they have not yet cost blood and he hopes they will not, conversation has become too serious and contentious. He says more flattering things, that if I were there my benevolence, embracing all parties, would disarm the party-disposition of my friends. That's because I have no interest in politics and – forgive me for I know it is a main occupation for Mr. Church – politics spoil society as gentlemen spend their evenings either in Parliament or closeted in political talk after dinner. Oh, I diverge from what Mr. Jefferson said. He says that someone has reported that I have become a recluse and that he approves. This is proof of my taste, for he thinks a great deal of love given to a few is better than a little to many, and that the world will benefit more from my talents if they are not dispersed by numerous visits…. Finally, he asks me to design a visiting card for him and suggests several themes such as*

Cupid leading a lion by a thread or Minerva clipping Cupid's wings. There is no doubt! The best symbol for him is Minerva clipping Cupid's wings!'

'Why ever for?' Angelica asked with amazement.

'Oh, it just seems so...my meaning is that...you know he is wise and dignified. It would not be fitting to have Cupid in the ascendant.'

'No, I suppose not. Is that all?'

'Yes' Her candour was compromised. He had also closed with three lines, speaking of the sketch for his card: 'I will put a "Maria Cosway delint." at bottom, and stamp it on my visiting cards, that our names may be together if our persons cannot. Adieu, my dear friend, love me much, and love me always. Your's affectionately,'

'You spoke of a second letter?'

'Oh that. No news in it. Only a brief note asking me not to chide him for not writing, that he was drudging over business from morning to night. That's all.' She could not repeat all that he had written or how it had touched her:

Cease to chide me...the only letter of private friendship I wrote on my return ...was to you. ... I am incapable of forgetting or neglecting you my dear friend; and I am sure if the comparison could be fairly made of how much I think of you, or you of me, the former scale would greatly preponderate. Of this I have no right to complain, nor do I complain. You esteem me as much as I deserve. If I love you more, it is because you deserve more. Of voluntary faults to you I can never be guilty, and you are too good not to pardon the involuntary. Chide me then no more; be to me what you have been; and give me without measure the comfort of your friendship. Adieu ma tres chère et excellente amie. Th: J.

'We must both write him at length. Madame de Corny wrote that he is planning to return to America soon.'

'Oh, no, for good?'

'I think not. He wishes to accompany Patsy and Polly back to Virginia. He thinks that they have been too long in France, especially Patsy. Then he intends to return to his post.'

'I must write him from Down Place.'

'Yes, do. Now, you must tell me all about Mr. Marchesi and the truth please.'

'My dear Angelica, there is nothing to tell you about Marchesi. You know that he pursues me shamelessly and makes no pretence to hide it and that is surely not a compliment. I forgive him for that is his character. Discretion is not one of his qualities. But he has many. He is warm and frank. He says precisely what he feels with little reflection. He is so delightfully UN-English that he cheers me enormously.'

'Take care, Maria, people are talking. You don't deserve that.'

'My dear, they have been talking since my marriage to Mr. Cosway. They have never stopped talking, whatever we do.'

'Yes, but I fear this is more dangerous, for on Marchesi's side, it is the truth.'

'Perhaps you are right. I shall try to calm him.'

What she did not tell her friend as they chatted away that summer afternoon was that Marchesi's attentions were probably a soothing balm for the erratic affections of Jefferson. The Italian was an easy companion with whom she shared many cultural affinities, but as humans are curiously made, it was the tension between insuperable differences and a deep moral and emotional recognition that rendered her attraction to the American so compelling. Maria's letter, written from Down Place, came from a new equilibrium deep inside. Bolstered by the flattery of a new admirer, she was able to express herself without whining. Since their relations were reduced to epistolary ones, she wrote,

> Next to the pleasure of seeing one's friends is that of hearing from them; I never think so much of the distance we are from them, as the length of time we don't hear from them. ... I have been Made very uneasy with the news that you intend to return soon to America, is it true? and is it possible! Oh then I give up the hopes of ever seeing you again; won't you come to pay us a visit first, it is but a little journey for so Much pleasure you will procure us, pray let me entreat you to Make me this promise. But we have hopes of going to Italy soon, I am doing every thing I can, use every argument, to make Mr: Cosway go next year, then My dear friend you should be of the party can you resist this proposition! I leave you to consider of it, and write to Me very soon... . Mrs. Church has told me to say many things to you; I

recommend My self to be admitted to half she deserves of affection from you, t'will be a good share but never so much as I have for you – adieu. Wish me joy for I possess your Picture. Trumbull has procured me the happiness which I shall ever be grateful for.

For once her pleadings resulted in a prompt response. Writing on 26th September, the day he received her letter, he confirmed her fears.

I am going to America, and you to Italy. The one or the other of us goes the wrong way, for the way will ever be wrong which leads us farther apart. Mine is a journey of duty and of affection. I must deposit my daughters in the bosom of their friends and country. This done, I shall return to my station. My absence may be as short as five months, and certainly not longer than nine. How long my subsequent stay here may be I cannot tell. It would certainly be the longer had I a single friend here like yourself.... But why go to Italy? You have seen it, all the world has seen it, and ransacked it thousands of times. Rather join our good friend Mrs. Church in her trip to America. There you will find original scenes, scenes worthy of your pencil, such as the Natural bridge or the Falls of Niagara. ... Think of this, my dear friend, mature the project with Mrs. Church, and let us all embark together at Havre. *Adieu ma tres chère et excellente amie* Your's affectionately, Th: J.

Sometimes the tiniest changes assume more meaning than they deserve. So it was with that French *adieu*. 'Goodbye my very dear and excellent friend.' The same closing as in his last letter, a formula. It was during the autumn of 1788 that she began to let go of the dream of going to Italy or going to America or going anywhere with Thomas Jefferson. For the first time it was she who remained silent for several months, only sending a letter of introduction for her friend the playwright, Mrs. Harriet Cowley, when she went to Paris in December.

That winter of 1788-89 covered Europe with a leaden cape of bitter cold. One could walk across the frozen Seine as early as late November. In

London black coal dust rendered the atmosphere more hellish. King George passed the winter as a madman with a strange illness which made him babble incoherently. He tried to throttle the Prince of Wales one evening at dinner, bashing his head against the wall. The Prince and his friends, the Devonshire Whigs, worked themselves up into a frenzied lust for power as they plotted for the Prince to become Regent. They were badly let down when the poor king's illness left him as mysteriously as it had come. These winter disorders were only a mild prologue to the gathering insanity in France. 1789 would prove to be a watershed in Europe, the beginning of years of political upheaval, war, and radical changes in morals and manners. It was also the beginning of a period of personal turmoil which affected Maria's health, her marriage, and her position in society. It may have begun in January when Marchesi asked Cosway to design costumes for the opening opera of the season, Cherubini's *Iphigenia in Aulide*. From this harmless beginning the newspapers began their usual drumbeat of gossip. Cosway was not normally jealous; he unconsciously imitated the *ton*, the leaders of fashion who thought a man and wife should not be seen in public together. Furthermore, he thought a certain amount of press attention was amusing and good for his professional success. The *Morning Post's* comments were just veiled enough: 'Maria Cosway has taken a *whole length* of Marchesi more successfully than any other artist in this country', or … 'the fair Maria [assisted] in decorating the person of the accomplished Marchesi' seemed innocent enough to her, but less so to the evil-minded. In February the *Morning Post* reported a scene of tension in the Cosway household:

Richard may have burst upon Marchesi and Maria one afternoon as they sang together.

'Signore Marchesi, would you be so kind as to excuse my wife. I must have a word with her on an urgent matter.'

'Mr. Cosway, Signore Marchesi has just arrived. Might we speak together later.'

'No, Maria, my dear. We must speak now.' He clipped his words firmly. 'I am certain that Signore Marchesi will understand that a wife has special duties and must sometimes tend to them when it is not convenient for her or her friends.' She translated her husband's curt phrases, trying to render them more agreeable

in tone. *Although Marchesi could not understand all that had been said, he read the stern voice perfectly.*

'Naturally, Signore Cosway, I would never impose my presence where my host found it not convenient. I shall take my leave from you and Signora Cosway at once. Good day,' *he bowed with a quick, sharp nod and left the room obviously offended.*

'Richard, how could you be so rude! Whatever has vexed you?'

'I shall tell you, Mrs. Cosway, that vain Italian has vexed me. You know that I have given you a total liberty. You see as many gentlemen as you like. You are escorted by General Paoli, or Mr. Jefferson, or your Polish friends. I have never questioned your choice of society for you have always conducted yourself with dignity and discretion. But this singer…this* castrato*…you know that people are talking about the two of you and I have at last heard what they are saying. You would not be pleased, and I am not pleased to be cuckolded by a…by a gelding! I will not have it, No, I will not have it.'

'Mr. Cosway, you DO NOT have it. You must understand that despite the appearances caused by Mr. Marchesi's exuberant nature, there is absolutely no cause for you to be upset, absolutely none. You could not credit such a thing. There is no reason to punish us all with this foolish gossip.'

'We have already been punished. The only way to escape this scandal is to bar him from our house. Appearance must accord with reality.'

'Oh no, now you go too far! Why should we give up his amiable company? Why should we give in to the malicious people who spread calumnies? You have surely injured Marchesi in an un-Christian manner by driving him out and I beg you to consider that we owe him our apologies rather than further ostracism. I most humbly ask you to reflect upon such a course before taking a final decision. Please wait until you may consider the matter with a cooler mind. Please do this as a favour to your wife.'

'If I give in to your entreaties, I shall most likely be a fool twice. But, you are a woman of principles and are to be believed. So I shall think about what course would be best. Until I have decided, I do not want to see him in this house.'

'Yes, Mr. Cosway.'

After the domestic storm blew over, Cosway must have thought better of his outburst. He never carried out his threat to exclude Marchesi from their company, and life soon went on as before. The damage had been done, however, for the newspapers had found a good story with famous characters, and they were determined to see the tale unfold. Imagining that this sensational news might make its way to Paris, Maria took care in her next letter to Jefferson to describe the way unfounded gossip was rampant in England:

> ...scandal which reigns without the least regard for personages, circumstances, humanity, and right or wrong: you cannot believe in this moment how much has been explained by a number of black and malicious hearts...of the things published daily, intrigues, calumnies, and injustices in which all comment as in a contest to see who can have superiority by force of atrocities, self-interest...

After not hearing from her, it was he who had renewed their correspondence in that terrible winter.

> It is very long since I have heard from you: tho I have no right to complain, as it long since I wrote to you...I have for two months past had a very sick family, and have not as yet a tranquil mind on that score. How have you weathered this rigorous season, my dear friend? Surely it was never so cold before. To me who am an animal of a warm climate, a mere Oran-ootan, it has been a severe trial.

He had news from America that Madame de Bréhan, widowed sister-in-law of the French Minister de Moustier, was 'furiously displeased with America'. He was too polite to say that the Americans were furiously displeased with Madame de Bréhan. She had been treated coldly and with open disapproval for her unconventional living arrangements with the Ambassador. Mr. J. closed with his eternal reverie of seeing Maria in America,

> Have you arranged all things for the voyage with Mrs. Church? We are so apt to believe what we wish that I almost believe I shall

meet you in America, and that we shall make together the tour of the curiosities of that country. Be this as it may, let us be together in spirit. Preserve for me always a little corner in your affection in exchange for the spacious part you occupy in mine. *Adieu ma chère et très chère amie!* Yours respectfully & affectionately, Th:J

His voyage to America filled Maria with anxiety. She replied:

…and your return when is to be? Why don't you announce me that as well as your departure? T'is cruel not to do it and you will not absolutely give us any hope of a visit here, how easy you Might do it! … Oh why am I never to achieve my great desire of finding myself in solitude with a small number of friends? That is the only happiness, it lightens a great deal the way to the unhappiness felt in a crowd which one despises and makes longed for solitude full of every pleasure.

The spring of 1789 brought more public attention. Scarcely a day went by when the papers were not talking of the Cosways. Two events stirred curiosity. The first was the arrival of sumptuous gifts from the King of France, Louis XVI, in gratitude for Cosway's gift of the Guilio Romano cartoons. The Cosways received a set of four Gobelin tapestries designed by Coypel, portraying scenes from *Don Quixote,* and a magnificent twenty-four-foot Savonnerie carpet. Richard displayed further generosity – or a desire to ingratiate himself with his patron – by offering the tapestries to the Prince of Wales for the embellishment of Carlton House.

The second unfortunate event may have been related in part to jealousy over the noise made over the tapestries. One evening at a Royal Academy dinner Maria's old friend, Ozias Humphry, having had too much drink, objected to Cosway's taking the President's chair and began a vicious verbal attack on him, which Cosway bore with patience, well understanding the condition of his adversary. Poor Humphry had never succeeded as he wished, had gone out to India to make a fortune and come home without it. Now he was reduced to attacking a rival pathetically and being ridiculed in the newspapers.

At the end of April reviews of the Royal Academy Exhibition began to appear. As usual Maria's choice of subjects – considered particularly eccentric for a woman – leaned toward the mysterious and frightening. She presented two pictures. One – a Medusa – merited little comment. The other meant more to her. She painted it for her dear friend, Anne, Lady Townshend, to record a tragic moment in her life. Lady Anne's sister, Elizabeth Gardiner, had died in 1783, leaving six children. Emily, one of them, fell ill in turn. Lady Townshend was present at the child's bedside when the girl saw her mother, called out to her and died. *The Times* gave a very sceptical account of this incident and confused the facts, substituting 'father' for 'mother'.

> Maria Cosway in her usual style has given something out of the common way. She has introduced the story of a ghost which she says is a FACT! It is the spirit of a deceased parent summoning the spirit of a dying child.... The child is supposed either to see or to hear this phantom of the brain & is painted to appear as if saying 'Coming Sir.' Such nonsensical subjects must always expect to be treated with ridicule when they are imposed on the understanding as if owing their existence to true facts.

News-sellers are victims of shallow means and minds. What appeared ridiculous to the world was a glimpse of Maria's inner convictions. Miss Gardiner's experience was not strange if one accepted the possibility of eternal life. On this ground Richard and Maria shared many ideas. Through his reading of Emmanuel Swedenborg, the Swedish philosopher, Cosway became convinced of the reality of the spirit world and of the possibility of communicating with deceased spirits. As Richard was an eclectic collector of ideas as well as art, he ignored Swedenborg's warning that speaking with spirits was dangerous and should not be permitted. In later life Richard believed that he possessed this power and unwisely told everyone he met about his conversations with spirits. Maria was not particularly interested in communicating with spirits, but she did share her husband's belief in mental healing power, as taught by Dr. John de Mainaduc. The couple's initial interest was primarily therapeutic, but they concluded – unlike Mesmer – that this therapy could not be separated from religious ideas. They took up these ideas as dilettantes, sometimes putting them into practice, but probably sincere in their belief that Mainaduc had discovered scientific principles in perfect accord with faith. The learned doctor was the first to say that such healing methods had been practised over 250 years earlier by other eminent physicians such as Paracelsus, Sir Kenelm Digby, and Sir Robert Fludd. He taught that this healing principle was behind the cures of Jesus and that the Almighty gave this power to all, but that to successfully cure the body one must first learn to cure his own soul.

Cosway made sincere if sporadic attempts to help others through this method, but his friends, Mr. and Mrs. de Loutherbourg, had an amazing success healing others. Their open generosity in employing such unusual gifts created a minor revolution in the spring and summer of 1789.

52. Philip James de Loutherbourg, *Self-portrait.*

Loutherbourg had painted the portrait of Swedenborg in the early 1770s. Through this acquaintance he became a follower of that teaching along with William Blake and John Flaxman. A man of spiritual gifts, Loutherbourg also followed a course with Mainaduc and began to practise healing by these techniques along with his wife. Word of these so-called miracles spread through London. The public healing room set up in their house on Hammersmith Terrace was besieged with sick people, clamouring for relief. Loutherbourg told a friend that through God's blessing he had cured some two thousand people during the first six months of the year. Huge crowds gathered before his house, necessitating a system of tickets offered freely to the poor. Some unscrupulous persons resold the tickets for two or even five guineas. Healings of all sorts of ailments were recorded: deafness, blindness, lameness, cancers, palsies. The reward for the couple's benevolence was ingratitude, denial of their cures, curses, threats on their lives, ridicule by the papers, and riots before their house.

The populace, seeing only the mystery of the supernatural, became fearful and began to oppose the goings-on in the artist's house. They did not believe that there was a natural principle at work. Public opinion became inflamed. Loutherbourg had to take refuge in the country until the heated atmosphere in Hammersmith cooled down. By the end of the year he decided to abandon his ministry of healing and went back to his paint-brushes, which pleased his neighbours if not the Lord.

Despite the opprobrium hanging over the head of the Loutherbourgs, the Cosways continued their friendship with them when others did not because the Cosways also believed in Mainaduc's teachings. They continued their association with Marchesi as well. Cosway must have decided that he was indifferent to criticism of the company they kept. During the spring they saw and heard much of Marchesi. Cosway designed a ticket for one of his benefit concerts. The male soprano generously sang at benefits for other artists. One – a concert given by the visiting harpist, Frau Krumpholtz – brought back the memory of the first evening spent with Jefferson in Paris. Towards the end of May Maria received a letter of farewell from the American envoy, still patiently awaiting his leave of absence. The reality of having an ocean between them loomed; this greater separation provoked him to view their relation beyond time or space.

Paris May 21, 1789

I have not yet, my dear friend, received my leave of absence, but I expect it hourly, and shall depart almost in the hour of receiving it. My absence will be of about six months. I leave here a scene of tumult and contest. All is politics in this capital. Even love has lost it's [sic] part in conversation. This is not well, for love is always a consolatory thing. I am going to a country where it is felt in it's sublimest degree. In great cities it is distracted by the variety of objects. Friendship perhaps suffers there also from the same cause but I am determined to except from this your friendship for me, and to believe it distracted by neither time, distance, nor object. When wafting on the bosom of the ocean I shall pray it to be as calm and smooth as yours to me. What shall I say for you to our friend Mrs. Church? I shall see her assuredly, perhaps return with her. We shall talk a great deal of you. In fact you ought to have gone with her. We would have travelled a great deal together, we would have intruded our opinions into the choice of objects for your pencil and returned fraught with treasures of art, science and sentiment. Adieu, my very dear friend. Be our affections unchangeable, and if our little history is to last beyond the grave, be the longest chapter in it that which shall record their purity, warmth and duration.

By the time Maria received his letter, she thought he must have been at sea beyond the reach of any reply. In any case, his last words better described their relation than any she could have penned, so she did not answer. She was taken up by the whirl of the June season, Marchesi's benefits, his last appearances at the King's Theatre, her own musical parties, now held on Wednesdays, and the demands of being a hostess for the *ton*. Mrs. Damer, one of the stalwarts of the Devonshire Circle, graced their house often that summer, not being able to go to Devonshire House in the absence of the Duke and Duchess, who were in Spa and Paris. She was with them the evening they all watched the towering flames of the King's Theatre from the roof of their house. The opera house burned to the ground two days after Marchesi finished his season there. The fire and the Loutherbourg riots were their topics of conversation until they began to hear the awful news from Paris. In early August Maria received a second farewell letter from Jefferson, still in Paris. It was delivered personally by another charming American, Gouverneur Morris, who was able to tell them what he had witnessed in the previous weeks. He came round with Trumbull one Sunday evening and immediately impressed the Cosways with his wit and urbanity. Maria told him that she hoped to see him often at Schomberg House and invited him for music on the next Wednesday. His short letter of introduction from Jefferson advised that the bearer was an intimate friend of the French Ambassador, the Marquis de la Luzerne. It also included a few lines on the Troubles in Paris,

...we have been here in the midst of tumult and violence. The cutting off of heads is become so much *à la mode*, that one is apt to feel of a morning whether their own is on their shoulders.

Whether this work is yet over, depends on their catching more of the fugitives. If no new capture re-excites the spirit of vengeance, we may hope it will soon be at rest, and that order and safety will be re-established except for a few of the most obnoxious characters… . But why should I talk of wars and revolutions to you who are all peace and goodness. Receive then into your peace and grace the bearer hereof Mr. Morris, a countryman and friend of mine of great consideration in his own country… . But do not let him nestle me out of my place for I still pretend to have one in your affection, tho' it is a long time since you told me so. I must soon begin to scold, if I do not hear from you. In order to be quiet, I persuade myself that you have thought me in, on, or over the Deep. But wherever I am, I feed on your friendship. I therefore need assurances of it in all times and places. Accept in return those which flow cordially from the heart of Your Th: Jefferson

Trumbull's departure for Paris was imminent; he hurried Maria to make a reply that very evening. She dashed off three lines of acknowledgment, saying she had longed excessively for a letter and would write a longer letter very soon.

Morris came often to the Cosways during his month in London. His worldly charm and dry humour were irresistible. This confirmed bachelor intrigued ladies with his wooden leg, the result of a carriage accident, and often seduced them it was said. He had enough sophistication to become the lover of Talleyrand's mistress, Madame de Flahaut, while maintaining cordial relations with all concerned: the ambitious Bishop of Autun and Monsieur de Flahaut. Admired by Madame de Chastellux, companion of the Duchess of Orleans, he was welcomed into their society at the Palais Royal on a daily basis. Cosway was easily won over when Morris complimented some miniatures without knowing the name of the painter, Mr. C. This showed the instinctive intelligence of the American. Maria was struck by the good sense and judgement of Morris, who was by no means shallow despite his social graces. His views of the Troubles in Paris proved to be perspicacious for he said that La Fayette and his friends were going to overshoot the mark with their romantic ideas about liberty, that the French nation and its National Assembly were not composed of the right materials for democracy. He reported that the anarchy of the mob reigned, there was no authority and a constitution would be difficult to form in such conditions. He found himself in the curious position of a republican who counselled his friends to keep the nobles as a protection against the total failure of a passage toward more freedom. By the time of his visit to London in August, he considered the Revolution over, for the *garde française* and the *garde de corps* had gone over completely to the Third Estate and the people. The King had no power, could not raise one regiment, and was willing to agree to anything to get out of the scrape he was in. In Morris's opinion it was too late for him to get out. He described a horrible scene in the Palais Royal when the head and body of a poor seventy-year old were paraded in triumph, the head on a pike and the naked body dragged through the dust. The crime of this Monsieur de Foulon was to have accepted a place in the King's government. After the body was shown to his son-in-law, Monsieur Bertier, the Intendant of Paris, that unfortunate was cut to pieces savagely. Morris reported that foreigners seemed to be in security for the time being and that Jefferson was well. His only misfortune was to have had his house robbed three times after the customs house, which formerly adjoined him, had been moved up the hill to the *Barrière de l'Etoile*.

On subsequent Wednesdays, when Morris returned for music, he proved to be an engaging gentleman in company, if sometimes too clever for his companions. Maria introduced him to Anne Damer, who liked chatting with the tall American. Morris found Mrs. Damer a bit slow and English society excessively staid. He confided to his journal:

> Visit by appointment to Mrs. Cosway's; a very genteel Company... . Music very good. The Arrangement of the Company however is stiff and formal... . I observe to the honourable Mrs. Damer that the French, having no Liberty in their Government have compensated to themselves that Misfortune by bestowing a great Deal upon Society but I fear in England it is confined to the House of Commons. She seems to suppose the latter Part of this Observation ironical and tells me with an animated smile that we enjoy Liberty in my Country.

In Maria's next letter to Jefferson, which was carried by her brother George, she exclaimed:

> I am quite in Love with Mr: Morris. Are all americans so engaging as those I know? Pray take me to that Country. Your description has long made me wish to see it, and the people I know confirm my desire.

Although she had promised a long letter, she apologised:

> I wish always to converse longer with you. But when I read Your letters they are so well wrote, so full of a thousand pretty things that it is not possible for me to Answer such charming letters. I could say many things if My pen could write exactly My sentiments and feelings, but my letters must appear sad scrawls to you… . I wish in your return to France you would come to England, since You will not in your way to America. 'Tis very cruel of you. I wish you would send me some account of their affairs in France. 'Tis so difficult to have true news… . Pray prepare a large parcel for the return of my Brother or Mr: Trumbull.

Through a series of contretemps, a mis-delivered invitation to George Hadfield's hotel and Jefferson's illness, they never saw each other. A month later Maria received an apology for this apparent inhospitality and another *Adieu,* as her friend made last-minute preparations to leave, expecting to return by the next May. Her long wait for the spring was now to be doubly long and difficult for at the same time that she received this last letter she discovered the most amazing news of the year, indeed of the decade: she was expecting a child! After eight years of marriage without children this news must have been a surprise to all concerned and there is no easy explanation for it. If Maria experienced an initial pleasure this was soon dampened by bouts of illness. At least this was her excuse for not journeying to say farewell to Jefferson one last time before he set sail. He was waiting at Cowes in the Isle of Wight before embarking upon his ship the *Clermont.* Trumbull agreed to take him her letter:

London 9 of October 1789

I did not answer your last letter, my dear friend, because I was in doubt whether it would find you at Paris, but now I shall profit of Mr. Trumbull's departure to send you a line to put you in mind of me in those still more distant parts of the globe, where your friends perhaps all your heart's sentiments are. It will be very flattering to me if you think of me some times. I was very near coming to see you when Trumbull told me that you was to be at the Ile of White but I have been very ill with a most violent cold, the weather is very bad & every difficulty opposes my desire of surprising you with a visit, but why don't you come. It would be so easy, so short & such pleasure to us. I think I could be angry with you for not coming, but perhaps you cannot you may have your reasons. Therefore, shall say no more. I will not take more of your time up now but expect a longer letter when you tell me where to write. I am too ill at present. I cannot write More. Please always I shall be your most affte. M. Cosway

The *Clermont* did not sail for another fortnight, but Maria received no visit. Just the following note which was the last *Adieu*:

Cowes, Octob. 14, 1789

I am here, my dear friend, waiting the arrival of a ship to take my flight from this side of the Atlantic and as we think last of those we love most, I profit of the latest moment to bid you a short but affectionate Adieu. … We have left a turbulent scene, and I wish it may be tranquilized on my return, which I count will be in the month of April. Under present circumstances, aggravated as you will read them in the English papers, we cannot hope to see you in France. But a return of quiet and order may remove that bugbear, and the ensuing spring might give us a meeting at Paris with the first swallow. So be it, my dear friend, and Adieu under the hope which springs naturally out of what we wish. Once and again then farewell, remember me and love me.

53. Maria Cosway in Travelling Costume *by Richard Cosway. This sketch seems to have been done during the period 1790-1794.*

14

Flight to Italy

1790-1794

The circumstances surrounding the birth of Maria's first and only child should have been a sweet period of expectancy, but her confinement seems to have been generally unpleasant. Not only was she feeling out of sorts in the early months, but in February she fell very ill and was only well enough to receive a few visits at home in the last two months before her lying-in. Angelica Church was a faithful friend during this difficult period as were Lady Townshend, Lady Lyttelton, and Mrs. Damer.

The gentlemen who had been her ardent admirers were far away: Jefferson in America, Marchesi in Venice for the Carnival, and General Paoli had embarked on the last great adventure of his career. The French National Assembly had pardoned him; his beloved Corsica was in effervescence. The Paolists had recalled him to lead them under the liberal principles of the hoped-for new French constitution. A week before sailing for Corsica at the end of March 1790, Boswell gave a dinner for the General to which only gentlemen were invited. Cosway was of the party as were the Ministers of Portugal and Sardinia. When Maria's *cavalier servante* called to bid her farewell, they both knew that years of separation lay before them.

Maria must have missed the General's company doubly because of a subtle change in her marriage, which seems to have become evident during her confinement. She and Richard had now been man and wife for nine years. Considering the fact that she had not wished to marry him, they had a pleasant, sometimes loving union. He was tolerant and kind to her and her family. He was amusing, gay, good company. They shared one great love – art. Few members of the Royal Academy were as knowledgeable and talented as Cosway, as devoted to the arts. The Cosways enjoyed the same friends; he had made Maria one of the most talked-about hostesses in London, but not always in the best sense. That was the rub. Her husband had a bawdy side that she did not share. Cosway, at some time in the marriage, began to seek elsewhere what he found lacking at home. In a letter written twenty-five years later, Maria associated their problems with her pregnancy.

> The moment he gave himself to <u>Hammersmith</u> by one to lead him from me and from his home. No one but God himself can know all I suffer'd when with child. My journey to Italy restored my health.

In another letter written a year earlier she had given a more precise sequence of events:

> Remember my good Mr. Cos. How many years we were happy … . Until you began to divide your thoughts, first with occupations in Bedford Square…a miss P ingrossed them. Afterwards with Hammersmith and the L. in this I found you immersed on my return from Italy…

Whatever the exact order of Richard's adventures, it seems that tensions in the marriage had arisen by 1789, which did not help Maria's health. Her later comments leave an ambiguity about the degree to which they were physical or emotional or both.

During the last month before her lying-in, she wrote a short note to Jefferson in which, strangely, she did not mention her approaching motherhood. He learned of it from their mutual friend in London, Lucy Paradise. Not having heard from him since his sailing, she lamented:

> I fear My dear friend has forgot me; not one line ever since your departure from this part of the world! I have heard of you, tho' not from you, don't let my reproches be too severe for I am willing to think you have been prevented by important reasons, however Silence from a person who feels the privation of your letters, would be impossible.

His response written from New York confirmed that he wouldn't be returning to Europe:

> I am now fixed here, and look back to Europe only on account of that circle, could it be transferred here, the measure of all I desire in this world would be filled up, for I have no desire but to enjoy the affections of my heart, which are divided now by a wide sea.… . They tell me *que vous allez faire un enfant, je vous en félicite de tout mon voeux.* … You may make children there, but this is the country to transplant them to. There is no comparison between the sum of happiness enjoyed here & there. All the

distractions of your great cities are but feathers in the scale against the domestic enjoyments & rural occupations and neighbourly societies we live amidst here. I summon you then as a mother to come and join us, you must tell me you will whether you mean it or no. *En attendant je vous aime au toujours.* Adieu, my dear Maria.

In the spring the expectant mother was well enough to receive visits and some comfort from American friends. Gouverneur Morris had returned to London and came to call one evening in early April with Angelica Church, who was recently returned from spending the winter in America. They were a source of sorely needed cheer when Maria welcomed them to her study on the second floor. Apart from the Breakfast Room on the top floor overlooking St. James Park, this room was her favourite repair. Here she surrounded herself with beloved objects, pictures, her writing table, and a gallery of portraits on both sides of the fireplace. When friends were absent she had their portraits for company: General Paoli, Mr. and Mrs. Swinburne, Angelica Church, d' Hancarville, Lady Lyttelton, Anne Damer, Princess Lubomirska, and Trumbull's miniature of Mr. Jefferson were the intimate companions of her solitude.

'Mr. Morris, how good of you not to forget us. Mr. Cosway will regret missing you this evening. He is out, I fear.' She held her hand out from her couch drawn close to the translucent orange of the hot coal fire. 'Dear Angelica, pray sit close to me so we can warm each other. You were kind to brave this disagreeable snow and cold to come to see me.'

'My Maria, Mr. Morris insisted that we come, and I longed to see how you were.'

'Yes, Madame, I could not return to London without passing to see one of its most gracious hostesses.'

'I fear that our hospitality is much reduced this year due to my uncertain health. But tell me what is the news from Paris? And from America? Have you letters from Mr. Jefferson?'

'Only business correspondence from America and no news of a personal character. As for Paris, alas, matters are far from a resolution. Many of your friends and acquaintances are already emigrating abroad.'

Angelica added, 'You surely know that the Duke of Orleans has spent the winter here with Madame de Buffon, and I find London is crowded with French arrivals.'

'Yes, my friend Monsieur d'Hancarville wrote me some months ago that Paris was becoming deserted of our acquaintance. The Princess Lubomirska has left her beautiful house, sold her furniture or shipped it to Poland. One of her daughters and her husband barely escaped hanging by a Parisian mob; Monsieur d'Angiviller has fled to Spain; the King's brother, the Count d'Artois, is gone. How soon Paris has changed!'

'Yes, my dear lady,' Mr. Morris said, 'and the trouble is not finished.'

'Mr. Jefferson thought order would be restored before the spring, before his return. I have not heard a word from him since his departure. Last week I sent him a few lines just to recall me to his mind and tell him that I hoped he would think of me in the delightful air of his country, a place I wish I could admire in person as well as I do from a distance. All the Americans I meet make me long to see what land nurtures such natural civility.'

'Ah, Mrs. Cosway, you see only those who have benefited from frequenting drawing rooms such as yours and Mrs. Church's, where we have had our rough colonial manners gently polished by ladies accomplished in the fine arts. So, tell me what have you been painting? Shall we be seeing your pictures at the Academy this year?'

'I fear not. Poor health has not permitted much painting. I have laid aside my brushes for other concerns. But our family has a new and talented representative of the arts, my brother George. The Academy has voted to give him an annual pension of £100 a year for three years in Rome to study architecture.'

'Maria, that is splendid news. I did not know of this honour,' Angelica generously commented.

'Yes, we are all extremely proud. It was partly the doing of Miss Moser, who suggested at an Academy meeting that George should spend some time in Italy to improve his study of architecture. This proposal carried the day and she voted with the majority of the Academicians to award him the travelling studentship. Wasn't that kind of her? 'Tis unfortunate there are no more than two ladies who are members. Since Miss Moser and Angelica Kauffman, not a single feminine talent has been added to the Academy since its founding over twenty years ago.'

'Mrs. Cosway would be a most worthy candidate for admission.'

'Oh, Mr. Morris, I did not wish to suggest such an idea, I assure you. It would be immodest of me to do so, but the absence of other feminine members is *generally curious. There is the talented Mrs. Damer, for example. She was asked to do a statue of His Majesty.'*

'Indeed, there is Mrs. Damer, a lady of merit who deserves more attention.'

'Are you proposing to fulfil this need?' Angelica asked.

'If I had time for gallantry, I should be pleased to do so. You know the press of business allows me no moments for such agreeable pastimes.'

Morris called weekly in April, amusing Maria with a tale about having his good right leg modelled in order to have a left leg made in copper. He swore he would never wear it, as he was quite used to his plain stick. This impediment in no way affected his popularity in society. Toward the end of the month he was invited to the Churches' elegant ball, graced by the Prince of Wales, his brothers, Mrs. Fitzherbert, and the Duke of Orleans, but Maria was too close to the day of her child's birth to venture out.

The first week of May, a benevolent sun finally streamed through the window panes of Maria's bedchamber. On 4th May 1790, the morning broke in fine clear weather, and she

The Honble Mrs Damer

gave birth to a lovely little girl. The child was named 'Louisa' after her godmother, Louise de Stolberg, the Countess of Albany, 'Paolina' after her godfather, General Paoli, and 'Angelica' after Mrs. Church. The General was in Paris on his way to Corsica and had called on the Countess with a letter, asking if she would honour the Cosways by being their child's godmother. She graciously assented, sending Mr. Cosway a proxy, for neither she nor General Paoli could leave Paris to attend Louisa's christening. Although weakened by the continual illnesses of confinement and the suffering of lying-in, Maria passed the first month with her little daughter in the normal way – the first week lying in bed, the second week sitting up, the third week, moving about in the bedchamber, and the fourth downstairs. At the end of May she was well enough to receive callers. Among the first were Angelica, Anne Damer, Lady Jersey, and Morris. During her recovery she had been designing an emblem to be painted on the ceiling of a garden temple at Down Place. It was composed of a large A for Angelica, being adorned with flowers by the Three Graces. A feminine figure signifying Friendship sat under the A, and Love, a young cherubim, surmounted all

54. Louise de Stolberg, Countess of Albany. *The wife of the Last Pretender Charles Edward Stuart.*

holding the head and tail of a serpent, which encircled the emblem symbolising eternity.

Morris, who had a gift for spontaneous verses, was inspired by her design to give her this one:

> *Here Friendship adorn'd by the Graces we see*
> *Maria, design'd by thy Art.*
> *Yet the Emblem was sure not invented by thee*
> *But found in Angelica's Heart.*

This happy afternoon was the last time Maria ever saw Morris. Shortly thereafter, on her first venture outside the house, she went out to attend mass on a cold, windy day. She fell ill again with a pleurisy and perhaps a serious case of post-partum depression. At any rate she could not recover her strength. It had become fashionable for ladies of all ranks to suckle their babies. She could have begun, but soon was forced to call in a wet nurse to feed Louisa. According to Maria's later account, which may have been exaggerated, the doctors feared for her life. Although Cosway and Loutherbourg were interested in healing, they could do nothing for her. Any maternal joy she may have felt was of brief duration. In a black mood, she could well have felt abandoned. Jefferson waited until late June to write to her from America, leaving it to others to tell her that he would not be returning to Europe as promised. He had accepted an appointment as Secretary of State to President Washington. She had always known that all was working against their friendship, but his promise to return in several months kept at bay the secret fear that she would never see him again. Affection is a gauge on the future. One cannot imagine the future without its object. The mind, in the face of all contrary evidence, which one *well* recognises, continues like an unfortunate slave to gaming to wager day after day until the game is definitively ended. The only way it can be stopped is by some brutal event. The beloved completely withdraws, shuts the door firmly, leaving no chink of hope through which the illusion of eternal love can creep through to new life. The imaginary world Jefferson and Maria had constructed, dreaming of her voyage to America or his to Italy, had melted away, leaving only an ineffable understanding between them, secretly carried within. She may have felt this invisible bond, but in her depressed state of mind could only dwell on the terrible reality that she would never hear this particularly loved voice again.

When her condition did not improve, the family thought a change of air might be healing. Maria's brother George was planning to set out for Rome to take up his studies. It was finally decided that she should accompany him to seek a healthier climate. They would have further security by travelling with another friend, Lady Catherine Wright, who was journeying to Italy to nurse her son, who had fallen ill there. Richard and Maria knew Lady Wright from their common interest in the teaching of Dr. de Mainaduc. She was a fellow student of that original thinker. They also shared a long acquaintance with Italy where Sir James Wright, her husband, had been British resident in Venice some twenty years earlier. Cosway was kind enough to purchase a new carriage for the journey. So it was with regret that Maria left her baby daughter in the hands of her husband, her mother, sister Charlotte, a wet nurse and a governess. Unable to care for her baby, she was desperate to recover her health. On the day of her departure she had to be carried out to the carriage by George and her faithful maid Elizabeth Madison, who were to be her travel companions. Although it was July, they kept the windows of the carriage tightly closed to ward off cold drafts of air. Mostly resting, eyes closed, she was unable to enjoy the voyage as she once would have, but the thought of their direction, always south towards her beloved Italy, warmed her somnolence with gentle intuitions of hope.

The news from France was full of recitals of violence – people pulled from carriages decorated with coats of arms, massacres of the well-dressed, hangings, burned chateaux, street-fighting in Lyon. They must have avoided this sad country, passing through the Low Countries, the German states, and Switzerland before arriving in Venice. George left their party for Rome after they passed the Alps. It was a morning in late August when Maria saw the shimmering towers of Venice, emerging from a marine haze.

Rumours abounded that Maria ran away to Italy with Luigi Marchesi, leaving her husband and child. Her version of the reasons for going to Italy can be taken at face value, for there is certainly truth in them. Her departure was no doubt agreed by members of her family. But she must have been seen in Italy with Marchesi, and was often in the same cities as he, which gave rise to the worst interpretation. As a pious school mistress in later life, she destroyed traces of this turbulent period. It is likely that there was an attraction between Maria and Marchesi, but she soon decided against pursuing it. Regardless of whether there was fire in Italy, the smoke of scandal lingered on in London. Hester Thrale Piozzi judged Maria severely in her journal:

29 March 1794 When Mrs. Cosway ran madding all over Europe after a Castrato, leaving her husband & new-born Baby at home here: She was praying at the foot of every Altar & fasting most rigorously all the time – a hypocritical Hussey!... Her Faith is not influenced by her Actions I suppose; She was well persuaded of heavenly Truths, altho' a Prey to almost infernal Passions: or Appetites strangely depraved.

Many years later, when Maria was an old lady in Italy, a published account in the *Library of the Fine Arts* repeated the generally accepted story:

> … the lady one day took it into her head to make a tour on the Continent, without her lord; and not choosing to trust herself alone, she placed herself under the wing of Signor Marchesi, the celebrated vocal performer, leaving her spouse her keys, and the entire control of household affairs…

There is little doubt that Maria and Marchesi saw each other in Venice, where they both spent the winter of 1790 – 1791. Marchesi sang at the opera from October 1790 to March 1791. The Venetian papers were full of the operatic 'combat' between Marchesi at the Teatro San Bennedetto and Madame Todi, another popular singer, at the Teatro San Samuele. All Venice was divided into 'Todi partisans' and defenders of Marchesi. Maria needed a *cavalière servente* to see the city for strict Venetian custom prevented a lady from being seen in public without a gentleman. The couple would have been able to move about freely and discreetly in the usual mode of dress – men in a black mask, three-cornered hat, and white taffeta cloak and women all in black with a hood.

Maria called on another friend to accompany her on excursions, Vivant Denon, the French engraver. Denon was living in Venice, where his mistress, Isabella Teotochi Marini, presided over one of the city's most delightful salons, frequented by artists, intellectuals, and the aristocrats who governed the city. Soon Denon introduced Maria to this circle and she became a friend of Isabella Marini. It was most likely Denon who joined Maria to view the collections of the Galleria dell'Accademia and the Scuola di San Rocco where she copied pictures of Titian and Tintoretto. Indirect evidence that there was someone else in Maria's life is found in a letter from Denon to Isabella Marini:

> Madame Cosway asks me to send her warmest regards. She has been very inconvenienced by a cold but this has in no way put her off the climate in Venice nor the star who tempers the humidity.

Being in Venice that winter was certainly a tonic for Maria's soul. In spite of the fact that French *émigrés* were arriving daily – the Polignac family, the Comte d'Artois and his suite in January – the Revolution did not disturb the social peace and gaiety of the Venetians. The general custom of masking from October to Lent meant that nobles and middle class were dressed in public alike without ostentatious dress. There was almost no resentment against the nobles because they were never recognised. Furthermore, the Inquisition was still active, keeping the authorities well-informed of potential unrest. She could fall into the rhythm of the Venetian day with ease. Mornings for painting or copying pictures, dinner, a long siesta of two or three hours, drinking coffee at one of the cafes on the Piazza San Marco before the theatre or a visit to Signora Marini and her brilliant circle. Often 'Bettina', as Marini's friends called her, would lead them to the Caffe alle Rive at midnight for a hour of conversation and coffee. Maria saw very few foreigners or English people because of the strict separation enforced between Venetians and foreigners, even diplomats. If a foreign diplomat came into a *caffe*, the Venetian nobles were obliged to leave. Maria preferred to stay with the Venetians, which created a compartmentalised social life.

The one exception to this preference was her friendship for Lady Vincent, wife of the English Envoy, Sir Francis Vincent. The couple were kind to Maria, which made Lady Vincent's return to England in January a great loss to her. Lady Vincent carried a letter to Cosway, from whom Maria had received no news. She relied on her mother's letters to have news of her child Louisa and hastened to thank her husband for his care of the child:

> I am happy to hear the child has two teeth without pain & still more glad that you are so fond of her. My mother tells me you are very good to her & was very kind when she was so ill. I thank you much for it.

The main purpose of her letter to Richard was to ask his aid in healing for a lady of her acquaintance who was so ill that she begged Maria to ask for his help or that of Mr. de Loutherbourg.

> She has great faith in our science and has heard a great deal of

the great things which have been done in England particularly Loutherbourg. She first wanted me to treat which I have refused, I will have nothing to do in this country for every reason, but she has so much beg'd I would write to you to get some information about her…

Although not mentioned by name, the sick friend was probably Giustiniana Wynne, Countess Rosenberg, an important member of Isabella Marini's circle and former lover of Andrea Memmo. Giustiniana was ill from late 1790 until her death in August 1791. There is no record of Cosway's response to this request. Maria took advantage of this letter to express her desire that Richard come to Italy himself and closed with 'I kiss Louisa a thousand times.'

After the opera season was over, Maria turned her thoughts toward her childhood home. In early April she set out for Tuscany, so anxious to arrive that she never stopped, sleeping only by fits and starts in the carriage. As she approached Florence, her heart beat with a pleasure she had never before experienced. The countryside took on a special beauty. The flowered houses, kitchen gardens, the meadows and fields, and then the ochre walls, glowing in the April sun, filled her with delight. She saw her home again after twelve years. Only as she entered the Porta San Gallo did she realise how uninhabited the city was, for the two precious beings who had given her most were no longer there. The absence of her father and Signora Cerruoti, who had been more than a mother to her, made the teeming crowds seem like a desert of solitude. Like an ordinary traveller she spent the first few days running hither and yon to see all, visiting the Galleria and finding it just as splendid as she had remembered it. Renewing her friendship with Hannah Gore, Lady Cowper, now a young widow, she was pleased to join her for a voyage to Rome, which they arranged hastily in order to arrive during Holy Week. After only five days in Florence, she was on the road again, reminding her companion that it was her mother, Mrs. Gore, who had taken her to Rome on her first journey so many years before.

Being in Rome was like a perpetual reunion with friends. Besides her brother, she saw Angelica Kauffman. Madame Lebrun was also in Rome, which led the English to say that the three most famous paintresses were in the city at the same time. It was flattering to be named as one of their coterie, but there was a great difference. The other two ladies were able to live by their talents comfortably, and Maria had never done so. She found Mr. Swinburne and d'Hancarville also in residence. The antiquarian had fled Paris with little but his clothes. The poor man always seemed to lurch from one financial embarrassment to the next, living by charm and erudition. Despite a reputation for unreliability, Maria found him to be a sympathetic and loyal friend. In the midst of his own distress, he listened kindly as she confided in him something of her personal difficulties. Shortly after their meeting he wrote comfortingly:

> …my very sincere attachment for you would be increased, if it could, by what you said in Rome of the situation of your domestic affairs and of your health. Often, since your departure I have thought with the bitterness that must cause to a true friend these two unhappy circumstances which I hope will be improved.

Towards the end of May, Maria and Lady Cowper returned to Florence where they were pleased to find the Misses Agnes and Mary Berry. These two intellectual sisters were intimate friends of Anne Damer and Sir Horace Walpole. At first Mary Berry welcomed Maria into her company. They were even staying together. As Horace Walpole wrote,

> I am glad Mrs. Cosway is with you; she is pleasing, but surely it is odd to drop a child and her husband and country all in a breath!

The Berry sisters may have been pleased to benefit from the Florentine's long acquaintance with the Galleria and other little-known delights of the city, but as the sultry summer wore on, subtle changes in Mary Berry's attitude must have become evident. Unknown to Maria, Miss Berry was being influenced by various correspondents in London, who let her know that Mrs. Cosway was not well considered there. It is not clear when Maria must have become aware that her reputation in England was in danger, not just in the press, but among her own acquaintance. Her erstwhile friends not only reproached her for the rumoured friendship with Marchesi, but for the appearance of a broken marriage. Being seen in the opera star's company in Venice was not as scandalous as her apparent independence and insubordination to her husband's wishes. She was beginning to commit the unforgivable indiscretion. By staying away from her husband and child for more than a year, she had made their separation visible, and society never forgave open violation of its conventions. What these critics did not know was that Richard hardly ever wrote to his wife. When he did, he made vague promises about coming to join her. Then after a year's time, he suggested that she should be thinking of returning. The very thought of taking up her former life as a gilded insect, pinned down for display in fashionable Pall Mall, filled her with horror. Surprised by the strength of her revulsion, she dramatised it as a question of survival. The rigours of the London climate had almost been fatal. She had endured them as long as she enjoyed the affectionate care of her husband. His fondness now dissolved by time, there was nothing in England which could attract. It seems odd that she could abandon her young child, but a difficult pregnancy, marital unhappiness and postnatal illness had prevented a bond from establishing itself between her and Louisa.

Maria may have considered returning to London with the Berry sisters, but it is evident from Anne Damer's letters to Mary Berry that this avenue was closed.

In July 1791, Mrs. Damer began to warn her friend in Florence about associating with a lady whom she calls the 'Marchesa', whose reputation had been damaged in London. The context of these letters leads to Maria Cosway as the subject of their disapproval. On 11th July Anne Damer in London wrote:

> Tell me of your Principessa and your Marchesa. The latter is certainly acting a very foolish part, to say the least.

The *Principessa* is most likely Lady Cowper, mockingly referred to as the 'Princess' because her late husband, Earl Cowper, was inordinately proud of his Austrian princely title, granted by the Grand Duke of Tuscany. This was a subject of derision by the English, especially Horace Walpole who scorned Cowper's pride over 'a pinchbeck principality and a paltry Order from Wirtemberg'. The sobriquet *Marchesa* obviously refers to Marchesi.

Damer's later letters of August give more explicit details and the insincerity of her friendship:

> …the <u>Marchesa</u> is best away but they now have <u>talked</u> here & they will not <u>untalk</u> – tho' they will go to the <u>Marchesa's</u> concerts, when ever she returns if they are but <u>well-crowded</u> – I never thought her understanding 'superior' her talents, when I was first acquainted with her seemed to me in an <u>eggstate</u>, but I begin to think that they never will <u>hatch</u>, her house was then, pleasant – if I found any body there in the evening, it was an artist or two, & she used herself constantly to sing & play – this I preferred to concerts, & the locust-like foreigners that since filled her house.
>
> I have also been writing to the <u>Marchesa</u> – I used to write to her & have, and would not neglect now, till the <u>cloud</u> thickens over her head, or is dispersed – her husband, too, begged that I would, he is extremely uneasy at her long absence, tho' not jealous – a queer little mortal, of whom I know no real harm.

In October, as the Berrys prepared to return to England, Anne Damer warns again:

> …that I may not again omit what I have to say of the <u>Marchesa</u>, which I did in my last, thinking little it could in any way affect you. I must tell you that on no account must you come to England with her in company – her conduct is now much talked of much & justly censured – she has written the most absurd letters to her husband – in the last (Jer. told me) she absolutely refuses to return, she says, 'if he uses the authority of a husband he will drag back a corpse, if he withholds his remittances she will try to live by her talents,' *maigre chere,* I fear & if that fails, take refuge in a convent, *qui lui tend les bras.* I suspect that she is grown frightened at her own situation & means now to return – all this is indeed strangely 'misterious' & there appears a duplicity in telling you that her husband did not send her 'the means' of returning, at the moment…that she was protesting these fantastical absurdities.

If Maria did consider returning to England at this time, she may have been snubbed by the Berry sisters and frightened to face the situation awaiting her, or her husband may have cut her off. Damer's warnings continue until the Berrys are on the road:

> ...I perfectly understand why, even without what you, by this time will have known of the <u>Marchesa</u>, you should not choose to let her come to England with you, for reasons unnecessary to enumerate – for heaven's sake! ... I really never knew anything so odd, or so mysterious as her conduct. What you tell me & what I have heard here involves her in ten thousand clouds without a miracle she never can come out clear enough to be <u>visible</u>.

The autumn of 1791 was a turning point and certainly a moment of emotional turbulence for Maria Cosway. She must have begun to realise that it would not be easy to return to London. She was not certain that her husband wished her return and she certainly had heard echoes of scandal. Her sentiments toward Marchesi are not exactly known. At the least he was a loyal friend and at this moment of vulnerability he was an arm upon which to lean, extended with loving concern for her welfare. Luigi Marchesi had not the fine manners of Richard Cosway nor the intellect of General Paoli or Thomas Jefferson, but he was warm and kind. Marchesi took her in when she may have had no place else to go.

During the opera season of 1792-93 Marchesi sang often at La Scala. He kept a large apartment in the Via Santo Spirito and a country house in Inzago. This quiet village east of the city was reached by canal along which many Milanese nobles had built summer villas. There Marchesi had purchased an imposing sand-coloured house, whose U-shaped form enclosed a cool, green garden shaded by cypress and palm. This was no doubt Maria's refuge for almost a year. It is known that she was in Milan during 1792 as General Paoli wrote her in September of that year:

> After your departure from Florence, I had no more news of you, and the letters that you say were written from Milan did not reach me.

One clear indicator that Maria wished to hide her activities between the autumn of 1791 and September 1792 is that there is a total black out of correspondence or sightings of her during this period. One can follow her travels through Italy except for the period of this one year when she drops out of sight. Many years later one of her journal entries does establish that she was in Inzago at this time. For the date 2nd September, she notes:

> This is the day I went from Inzago to Casalpusterlengo for the festival of the Madonna.... . This was my first meeting with P.O. [frate Onorato, Luigi Nina da Pavia, an austere Capucine monk] who was later so helpful to me. I was strengthened in my resolution to distance myself and am sure that this devotion gave me persevering courage. I had to separate myself from a person and live in danger of need.

The year of this meeting was surely 1792, for it was in September of that year she decided to leave Milan and seek entrance to a convent. The friar's counsels gave her the strength to do what she knew she must do – to leave Marchesi's hospitality and risk poverty. She soon put this resolution into action. She went to Genoa with the firm determination finally to put her life back on the road she had wished to take at eighteen and retire to monastic life.

Although Italy had been sheltered from the violence in France, the first rumblings of upheavals to come could be heard. The year of 1792 not only marked a great turning point in Maria's life, but on a grander scale it was a decisive time for France and all of Europe. In the spring war was declared between France and the Austrian-Prussian alliance. The news became more terrifying. In August the Tuileries Palace, where the Royal Family was guarded, was attacked. Swiss Guards and servants were found massacred in heaps in the gardens, in the corridors and anti-chambers. The King was deposed. France had no monarchy. A month later war fever caused the revolutionary government to begin expeditious justice. During three days assassins were sent into prisons and convents to slaughter prisoners, aristocrats, and priests by the hundreds. The first battles were engaged along France's Eastern frontier at Valmy and in the Savoy. Mercifully these horrors were only faint echoes heard in the beauty and peace of the port of Genoa, stair-stepped up the green Ligurian hills. When Maria arrived in the autumn of that year, she was able to see some of the 'first' people of the city through her long friendship with the Genoan ambassador in London, Franceso d'Ageno. It is not clear why she chose Genoa; perhaps because she was not known there. However, if she had not been well introduced by a Genoan, her plans to retire to a convent would have failed. As it was, even the intercession of the Archbishop failed to overcome the reluctance of the nuns in one of the best convents to accept an Englishwoman married to a Protestant. Finally a very prominent and zealous lady introduced her to the Convent of Santa Brigida, where she was accepted. During these months she had written several times to her husband, begging his forgiveness for displeasing him. He never answered her letters. However, he sent word that he would agree to an annual pension of sixty pounds once she had entered the convent. At that time she sent Madison, her loyal maid, back to England with a letter for Mr. Cosway.

> Sir,
> You will receive this by Madison who will give you an exact account of me from the first moment I left England as she has been a constant witness having never been from me one moment, to the time she sees me enter into the convent. May you receive those informations that may please you & some satisfaction about me. Whatever I may have done to displease I again ask your forgiveness as I have done before in one of my letters to which I have had no answer; I shall say no more & trust only to God who hears & sees all, who receives all, & has mercy for all.

> You have never sent me that leave which I ask'd you for, wrote in a manner in your <u>own</u> hand that I might show, which is necessary on this occasion. They now trust to my word, but it has been very difficult. I have not wrote for some time because there have been so many troubles & differences about the convents that it has taken all this time. The first difficulty has been for being married to a protestant being a stranger & married. The nuns are so exceedingly ignorant & prejudiced that it is impossible to make them understand common reason.

After telling him about her Genoan friends and their assistance she tried to assure him of her irreproachable activities.

> Now we have very good preachers in many of the churches every morning, but particularly one which I go every day is really the finest I have ever heard in my life. I have never heard such force, such arguments, such power, such explanations of the word of God, such eloquence.... Several things I have ask'd which are of importance to me you have not deigned to answer me. I have had but one letter from you since I have been here. However displeased you may be with me there are things which you might have given me an answer to.... Being a stranger they have made many difficulties not knowing from whence I received my money & indeed many disagreeable things have been said about it...one report has circulated that you may not continue my remittance after I am in the convent & a thousand such disagreeable things...if it is God's will we are to meet again he will contrive the means, if not I am perfectly happy with my fate & wish for nothing else on this earth. The child is my only wish & thought, & my fears only for her religion, from her first impressions depend her sentiments of the true faith. Let me repeat [to] you to take care they are of the pure catholic...I hope the child is well may God protect her, believe me Your dutiful wife, M. Cosway

> Genoa 1 of March

On 4th May 1793, Maria entered the convent of Santa Brigida not as a nun but as a retired lady. She had attained in some measure her youthful ambition. This separation from the brilliant world she had known in London and Paris was not painful in the least. It corresponded to her innermost desires. It was also the best course at the time, for her marriage was in tatters. Cosway almost never communicated with her and did not appear to wish her return. Although she may have resented this abandonment, she savoured her freedom. Friends sent their affection through letters, and she spent many contented hours with her correspondence. Now that she was in a respectable situation, she wrote to those who had not heard from her during the past year such as Signora Isabella Marini to whom she recounted the peace of a simple existence in a superbly situated convent, overlooking the entire port of Genoa. She wrote that she no longer enjoyed music for want of an instrument, no longer painted, only sketched a little, but never had an empty moment. It was not possible to be happier or more contented. How precious was this tranquillity, this peace that the world could not know!

So life went on gently for over a year until the next summer of 1794. Then letters from Isabella Hadfield, sister Charlotte, and brother George told Maria that Richard now wished her to come home and was willing to pay George to come to fetch her. Finally a letter from her husband confirmed his desire, and she replied,

> I thought it proper to wait for your letters because I knew how
> *we were*…my Mother's letters nor my Brother's were sufficient
> for me to precipitate at their intimation…

She continued that the war with the French meant that no roads were practicable, that she could perhaps travel with other Englishmen returning from Milan or an Italian clergyman who wished to see England. Further negotiations ensued by letter before it was agreed that Cosway would pay the clergyman 130 guineas to accompany her. The story of Maria Cosway could well have ended in Genoa, but in October of 1794 a new page turned as she set out upon another of many journeys across Europe, this time forced to avoid the unexpected movements of whole armies, never knowing if one of the posts on her route could become a scene of battle. Conflicting sentiments also debated in her heart: eagerness to know her child, anxiety to face a distant husband, embarrassment to confront the fickle and unforgiving scandalmongers of fashionable society.

LOUISA PAOLINA ANGELICA COSWAY Ætatis 5.

15

Louisa Paolina

It was a gloomy November day when Maria's carriage passed through the gated entrance of Stratford Place, flanked by two stone lions on brick piers. The horses halted before No. 20, the third house on the left of a *cul-de-sac*. Richard Cosway had moved house during his wife's absence – from

Schomberg House to a newer town house just off Oxford Street. The new house was handsomely built with its ground floor faced in stone around pleasing arched windows. A stone balustrade finished off the cornice over the second floor. Although elegant, this house was less imposing than Cosway's first choice on the corner of Oxford Street. He had only lived a few months in the larger house before public ridicule drove him out. A malicious wit (thought to be John Wolcot, Opie's friend) had tacked the following verse to his door:

> When a man to a fair for a show brings a lion,
> 'Tis usual a monkey the sign-pole to tie on!
> But here the old custom reversed is seen,
> For the lion's without and the monkey's within.

Cosway was more sensible to insults than he let on if he had gone to the trouble of changing his address because of a prank.

When Maria entered the hall of her new home – before she could take off her bonnet – she heard light steps running down the staircase. A charming little girl in a white dress with light blue sash and blond hair flowing over her shoulders, ran into her arms. Maria had seen portraits of her daughter, but confronted with the original was unprepared for a thousand sentiments of affection which swept over her. Louisa's first words to her mother were:

'Maman is crying! Oh why crying? Why are you sad?'

'*Carissima Luigina*, oh Louisa, Maman is not at all sad. I am so happy to see my little girl, my innocent little girl, who does not yet know that there are tears of joy which are not tears of pain. They are not the same. These are tears of joy, *Luigina*, tears of joy to hold you in my arms after such a long time, too long a time. Now we are to be together every day. I shan't ever leave you again.'

After embracing Isabella Hadfield and Charlotte, her sister, with perhaps a perfunctory greeting to Richard, Maria was led away by the elfin figure of her daughter into the sombre cave of an antiquarian's house. The little girl led her up the stairs past Old Masters and classical heads on pedestals to show her mother each room of their home. Cosway had held an enormous sale of his pictures before leaving Schomberg House, but seemed to have as many as before. Among the profusion of *objets d'art*, Maria recognised familiar pieces of furniture: the magnificent Savonnerie carpet, given to them by the King of France, was in the front drawing room as was her piano. Curtains and chairs in green damask served as an elegant setting for the marble mantelpiece, sculpted by their friend Thomas Banks. Displayed on a table was her husband's collection of classical figures by Giambologna. Luisa was eager to be her guide, hastening to remind her mother that her father had Abelard's skull, a lock of Heloise's hair, a real Egyptian mummy, a feather from a phoenix, and a piece of Noah's Ark! Cosway's connoisseurship was still in evidence. Beside his exotic curiosities, which so fascinated their child, the front and back drawing rooms were overcrowded with treasures – ebony and mother-of-pearl *escritoires*; enamelled caskets set with precious rubies or emeralds to hold collections of antique gems; mosaic tables set with lapis-lazuli or malachite; japanned screens; clocks of ormolu & tortoise-shell. Tables were covered with old porcelain – Sevres, Chinese blue and white, German – which glistened against a background of damasked chairs, English tapestries, and Persian carpets. When Maria arrived in her study on the second floor she found her harp, the familiar japanned furniture, and her writing table, covered with old letters. Her mother and Charlotte had carefully arranged many letters which had not been forwarded to her in Italy. Among them she found one dated 23rd June 1790, so long ago, yet awaiting her as a welcoming gift. It was Jefferson's last, which had arrived after Maria's departure for Italy. Despite the time elapsed, its sentiments seemed fresh and living. She had long accepted his absence in America so this old news had no effect. She had only to learn how he felt about this situation. It was strange to read of feelings four years cold, when he had said that the affections of his heart were now divided by a wide sea. Yet his words in French *je vous aimerai au toujours* seemed fresh to her and she hastily penned an immediate response.

> I am come home to England, & have the great pleasure to find I am not forgotten by Mr. Jefferson & is impossible to express my happiness, the less I say the better, & am sure what I should say will be added by a heart who can conceive & interpret sentiments of a feeling & grateful heart. My Angelica has been the greatest

joy on my return. She has flattered me more by telling me my name was mentioned in most of the letters which come from America. Mr. Trumbull tells me the same & offers to send a letter; now I have not time to make one, till now I did not know how to send one, but hope that I shall in another find more to convince you how much I am your most affectionate.

London 13 Novr. 1794   Maria Cosway

Later at her leisure she wrote a proper letter to be entrusted to Angelica, who was sailing to America.

Now this will come accompanied by one from the most charming of women, my Angelica. I love her so much that I think & am persuaded she must be beloved by every one who know her...I will think she has some attachment for me & I value it much. My great fear is that soon I shall lose her. I even thought I should not find her in England, but have been fortunate to meet this pleasure on my arrival & certainly she was a great consolation to me... you know this country & believe you have heard my sentiments on it.

My long stay in Italy & particularly the fine climate & most beautiful situation of Genova has not altered them but increased a surmountable antipathy I feel, though the pleasure of the good society & amiable friends make in great measure a recompense. I often think of America, & everything I hear of it pleases me & makes me wish to come. Why can I not come?...

I have found a pretty little girl. I hope she will make some comfort. She shows natural talent & a good, soft disposition – painting & music for the present are forgotten by me, the long neglect has made me now give them up & find no loss, better occupations will fill up my hours now.... May you have in every circumstance of your life that happiness you so much deserve.... Mr. Cosway desires his compliments & joins with me in all I have said. He might have wrote better English, but my wishes I will not give up to anybody. Remember me ever as one of your most affte. friends.

London 24 Novr. 1794   Maria Cosway

Again the expectancy of a renewed correspondence with the dearest of friends would meet with disappointment. Another year would go by before she would hear from him, but then he had waited four years.

But now she had discovered a gift to fill all voids, Louisa – or 'Luigina' – as she would always be to her mother. As Maria had pledged to her husband in letters, she devoted most of her time and thought to Louisa, whom she came to love intensely. She gave up as many social obligations as possible, only returning the most necessary calls in respect of the laws of civility. She never took over any of her nurse's duties, which many mothers do, for she thought it important that her child should not be aware of how much she was doing for her. By modern standards Maria had austere views on child-rearing. She thought nothing was so damaging to children as to have parents who became their slaves. When she first returned home Maria persuaded her husband never to express disagreement with her on matters of upbringing in front of their daughter or to engage in a dispute on any matter whatsoever before her. Above all she took charge of Louisa's studies, becoming her teacher, and curiously telling her daughter that she did not yet merit real teachers, who had to be paid great sums of money. Maria's motive was to instil in Louisa the value of learning and give her eagerness to profit from it.

Luigina was up at seven every morning in winter, earlier in summer. Nurse would wash her with cold water, summer and winter alike, give her breakfast in her room, and then bring her clean and freshly dressed to greet her mother. Whatever the weather, rainy or cold fog, the child would be taken out for a walk in the park. Upon her return she would say Good Morning to her father and then be brought to Maria's room for her lessons. Luigina was very good at reading. Her father expressed himself with elegance and had never tolerated any mistakes or baby-talk. It was considered essential that she had a nurse who spoke correctly and had a good pronunciation. The Cosways only gave their daughter good books, not excessively serious, but never tales of good fairies or other extravagant and extraordinary stories that filled children's minds with false notions. Luigina liked the stories in Fleury's catechism and in the sacred scriptures and would recite them to her father. Maria gave her prints for her large collection and from them she learned many historical facts. Sometimes Maria took her little girl to a picture gallery, where she often attracted a crowd of people, who marvelled at her ability to identify the subjects of the paintings. After a writing lesson, she would take up sewing, hemming handkerchiefs or other simple work. When all these studies were finished, the reward the Cosways' daughter most enjoyed, fittingly, was to be given pencils and drawing paper. Her scrawled compositions represented the historical events she had read about during the day. The figures were rather distorted, but there was evidence of some artistic talent.

Through this routine Luigina was to receive the rudiments of a serious education, but to her mother's mind the most important lessons concerned her moral upbringing. Upon Maria's return she soon realised that her family, who adored her child – how could they not, she was so irresistibly lovable and extremely good-natured – had let her charm overshadow a number of minor character defects. She could be stubborn and quite wilful. Sometimes she would stop in the middle of reciting her lesson and it was impossible to make her go on. Maria was driven to employ a punishment Charlotte had used: wetting a corner of a handkerchief, she raised the child's skirts and spanked her with it. Naturally there were floods of tears, and the whole family was up in arms, especially Richard. Later when the child was asleep he berated his wife.

'Maria, whatever possessed you to punish Louisa in that way? I won't have it.'

'Mr. Cosway, you might think I had actually killed her. I did her no serious harm. She must learn not to balk during her lessons. And you must remember that you have agreed to leave her education to me.'

'You shall pay the price for this. Your child is going to finish by hating you.'

'I would rather suffer her hatred than to tolerate a defect as distasteful as obstinacy. I am truly sorry to distress you and the rest *of the family, but I cannot be swayed if I believe that I am acting for the good of my child!' Maria was not to be deterred by the views of her mother, sister, or husband. She considered her methods were for the good of the little one, whom God had entrusted into her care.*

A few days after the punishment, she tested her methods to see if, indeed, she was now disliked by her child. When the family was all together one evening, Maria addressed her daughter:

'Luigina, would you like to accompany me for a few days in the country or would you prefer to stay here with Aunt Charlotte or Grandmother or Papa?'

'I would like to be with both you and Aunt Charlotte.'

'I am sorry, my dear, but that is not possible,' Maria replied and left the room.

In a few minutes she returned and her daughter ran to embrace her. Richard explained: 'She does not want to be without you, she knows too well how much you love her and does not wish to be separated from you for even a minute.'

Another fault in Luigina's comportment disturbed her mother. It was the custom in England for children to join their parents at the dinner table when the pudding was served. One day Luigina had been served a large portion of pudding when one of their guests asked to taste a bit. The child pulled her plate away defensively and started to cry. This evidence of a covetous and greedy nature greatly chagrined Maria. She reflected on the way to correct this failing. Seeing that her daughter was struggling between her fear that such an offer would be accepted and her desire to please her mother, Maria would casually place a double portion on the child's plate until she began to share with increasing unconcern. Soon her daughter began to take pleasure in giving away what was dearest to her heart.

In still other ways Maria encouraged Luigina to think of others. The child loved to play with dolls, which was quite normal for little girls of her age. Yet her mother took a severer view of this innocent pastime. Wishing her daughter to develop a keen mind, Maria thought childish toys should be abandoned as soon as possible. One day she took a favourite doll from her child's arms and commented on its dress.

'Luigina, my darling, 'tis a pity that this beautiful cloth has been used to dress an object made of wood. If it was a little larger size I could have given it to a child in need.'

With these words a dark cloud came over the child's face; tears pooled in her eyes. Seeing this reaction, Maria changed her approach:

'How would you like to accompany me to the draper's? We could buy a piece of cloth and together we could sew up a shirtwaist for a poor child?'

She jumped to embrace me. 'When are we going? Can we go soon? What must I do to deserve this?'

'Run and fetch your purse and tell me if you have enough for this purchase. If not, I shall add whatever is needed.' Maria wished to teach the value of money in terms of the good it allows one to do. That day was a joyful one for both.

Later, when they began to sew, Maria continued her lesson on charity.

'Luigina, dear, do you know how many poor children die of hunger for want of a piece of bread? And you leave all that food on your plate which could save their lives!'

'Let them have everything I leave! I shall even give up some of the food I like so that they should have it!'

Upon hearing this, Maria embraced and kissed her, and all that day showed her how much she loved her. Luigina gradually lost interest in her dolls.

In Maria's view young girls were too susceptible to vanity and frivolity. In her absence from London her family had innocently encouraged these faults by taking Luigina out to watch ladies going to St James Palace so that she could admire their beautiful attire. Maria did not approve of this pastime and made a point of showing her indifference in matters of dress. She provided Luigina with everything she needed or that she desired without giving it much importance. She had hats, ribbons, dresses – everything that other little girls had, so that she would not envy others or feel deprived. Yet Maria never made much of what she or her child were wearing. Often she would let Luigina wear her finest dress when they simply went for a walk; on other occasions, when they went to visit someone, Maria would

55. The Promenade in St. James Park, *1793*.

have her wear a very simple dress. She stressed that good taste and politeness were the greatest attributes of good breeding. Gradually Luigina showed less interest in dressing up. She would often tell Nurse that she no longer cared for the frills that she used to like so much because Mama didn't care for them and 'Papa says that Mama is always right'.

Maria took care to dress simply as an example. This was made easier by the fashions of the day. The revolutionary ideas in France had begun to affect dress everywhere in Europe. Instead of stiff embroidered silks, ladies wore light, simple cottons, often white. Ample muslin handkerchiefs covered the shoulders in daytime. Although fitted waists were still in fashion when Maria returned from Italy, soon high-waisted garments imitating neo-classical Greek and Roman models were seen. William Pitt, needing revenues for the war with France, had taxed hair powder. Yet it remained in use for several years. Nevertheless, the elaborate *coiffures* of a decade earlier were simplified. Some ladies even began to cut their hair in close-cropped styles or cover the hair with simple turbans. Naturally the ladies going to court were still extravagantly dressed in fine embroideries, wide skirts, ostrich plumes towering over their heads, and dazzling jewels, but the

Cosways no longer frequented those circles nor saw the Prince of Wales.

A few months after Maria's return, the Prince was married 'officially' for the first time to the Princess Caroline of Brunswick. The seductive and subtle Lady Jersey, whose portrait Maria had exhibited at the Royal Academy, was behind this surprising decision. She conceived a plan to secure her position as the Prince's mistress by persuading him to abandon poor Maria Fitzherbert, his true wife and a quieting influence, for a German princess, who – as the intriguing Lady Jersey hoped – was repellent to the

THEIR ROYAL HIGHNESSES
the Prince and Princess of Wales

Prince from the moment he laid eyes on her. He reportedly asked for a brandy on seeing his bride and was so drunk during and after the marriage that he spent his wedding night collapsed on the floor of the bridal chamber. The couple were only together a few months in the spring of 1795, just long enough for the conception of one Royal child. Although the new Princess of Wales and her daughter, little Princess Charlotte, were painted by both Richard and Maria, the Cosways no longer gave the frequent assemblies and concerts which would have attracted the Prince. His dissipated habits did not suit their quieter life, centred around their daughter's education and the Royal Academy. When the Princess sat for Cosway, he was impressed with her beauty and manners. The Princess had said to him that the Prince did not know her. Joseph Farington and other Academicians repeated gossip that the Princess was treated abominably by the Prince and Lady Jersey, who often drove Caroline to tears with their mockery. They thought it amusing to put brandy into the Princess's wine and then laugh when she became drunk. The Prince spoke disrespectfully of his spouse, saying her person was unclean. The whole Royal family treated the foreign princess with neglect, driving her to request to be sent home and to live separately from the Prince.

Despite the fact that the Cosways no longer received the *bon ton* as they had at Schomberg House, Richard had not lost Royal favour for his work. Knowing that Cosway refused to paint outside his house, the Prince used a ruse to obtain a miniature of his mother Queen Charlotte. Cosway was invited to spend several days at Windsor. After three or four days the Prince took the artist to the Queen's apartment and employing all his affable charm induced Cosway to paint the Queen. Unfortunately this miniature was added to the long list of unpaid bills on the Prince's accounts. Cosway was one of the Prince's oldest creditors, a position he could ill afford. After the royal marriage Cosway decided to present his bill for outstanding work which already totalled more than £1,500. This sum covered over a dozen miniatures and portraits of the Prince, almost the same number of small portraits of the Queen and the Royal Princesses, numerous other portraits and even various services such as decorations for Mrs. Fitzherbert's house in Pall Mall and purchases of pictures bought by Cosway for the Prince's account. Some of these works had been done over ten years before when sitters flocked to the door. Now Cosway was at the height of his artistic powers, but he had less custom. Times were harder with the war. Although they still lived comfortably, attention must be paid to economies. The Cosways had long enjoyed the luxury of a coach and four, one of their greatest expenses, taking into account the horses, extra footman, and the coach tax. As the war wore on, they eventually had to give up the carriage.

Another consequence of the war with France affected Maria's brother, George Hadfield. There was no money for public buildings. As a result it was one of the worst possible times for young architects to get started. After his return from Rome, George was working for one of the established architects, James Wyatt, a rather disreputable, hard-drinking man. The day after New Year's Day in 1795, George received a blow that changed his life forever. Henry Holland, another leading architect of the day, had proposed Hadfield as a member of the Architects' Club, and Wyatt had seconded the proposal. The balloting of 2nd January revealed one blackball had been cast. Wyatt was mortified. He had spoken very highly of George's manners and promising abilities and told the members that he would blackball any candidate thereafter, because a recommended person had been rejected without any reason given. Wyatt later said that he was certain that either Matthew Brettingham or John Soane had blackballed George.

It was at this low moment that John Trumbull came to George's aid. Trumbull had received a letter from America requesting him to find a qualified architect to superintend the building of the new Capitol in Washington. Trumbull consulted Benjamin West, President of the Royal Academy, and Wyatt, before proposing the post to George. In this moment of bitterness, Hadfield accepted the opportunity with alacrity and was only too pleased to put the London scene of professional jealousy behind him. By October he was in Washington to take up his new post as Superintendent of the Capitol. Tragically, this talented, polite young man was to cross swords with the same petty rivalry in America that he had sought to escape by crossing the ocean. Arriving in Washington, the classically trained architect realised immediately that the plans drawn up for the Capitol were wholly inadequate, being the work of a doctor turned amateur architect, a Dr. William Thornton. Unfortunately President Washington had appointed Dr. Thornton to the Federal Commission which oversaw all public building work. No sooner had George assumed his post than he became locked in controversy with his superiors over the proper method to build the Capitol. Hadfield was possessed of perfect taste and fine professional training, but his youth and inexperience coupled with hypersensitivity meant that his three years as Architect of the Capitol were an unhappy struggle, ending with an unjust dismissal by the Commission. His appeals to the President went unheard as he sank into a very precarious situation.

That January the family could not foresee these troubles and held out great hopes for George in America. The same month Maria's sister Charlotte surprised everyone with an important decision. That month's weather was the severest ever experienced in England. Even with fires, the temperatures inside the house were below freezing. During this intense cold Maria received a letter from Charlotte, who was spending the month in the country. She announced to their astonishment that she intended to marry William Combe, a fifty-three year-old friend of Cosway's, and this she did on 28th January 1795, the day after the Cosways received her letter. This was the first they even knew of an attachment between the two. Combe had known Cosway for many years. Indeed Richard had been a witness at Combe's first marriage to a cast-off mistress of Lord Beauchamp. That unhappy union was conceived as a financial transaction; Beauchamp was to compensate the groom for services rendered, a contract never honoured.

The poor woman was rumoured to have been shut up in an asylum. No one was certain if this unfortunate woman was alive or dead at the time of Charlotte's marriage.

The Cosways were a bit shocked at Charlotte's eccentric choice. William Combe started life with a good education at Eton and Oxford, even a Grand Tour. After inheriting a comfortable fortune from an uncle, he set up house in London as a young gentleman of fashion, dedicated to the required pleasures of drinking, gaming, and women. Unfortunately his fortune was not as large as his ambition. He was soon so destitute that he spent years as a soldier and even a tavern waiter. Determined to maintain his standing as a gentlemen, he discovered that he could lead a precarious, but respectable, existence as a man of letters. Although none of his works was considered fine literature, he had been complimented by the King as a clever man after he and Joseph Farington produced an illustrated *History of the Thames*. Charlotte, now twenty-eight, must have wished much for her own home. Having no prospects for a good marriage, she found William Combe, tall and not bad-looking, to be a stimulating conversationalist, a good musician as was she, and a man of parts, friendly with artists, writers, and members of Parliament. She could not see that he would never have the means to give her the home she deserved. After only four years of married life, first in Knightsbridge, then in a small house near Harrow, they were separated by Combe's incarceration in King's Bench Prison for debt. He was able to continue his literary career, often visiting London by day and sleeping in prison at night. In 1810 he had an enormous success with the repeated publication of *Dr. Syntax*, a satire of a travelling schoolmaster looking for the 'picturesque', but Charlotte and her husband were never re-united despite a mutual affection and respect. Poor Charlotte spent the rest of her life as a governess or dependent on the generosity of family and friends.

Despite these family surprises Maria's easy assumption of the new role of motherhood was a source of quiet happiness. Her time was divided between her daughter's education and the renewal of old friendships with Lady Lyttelton, Lady Townshend, and Angelica Church. She even resumed painting occasionally and sent one picture to the R.A. Exhibition of 1796. Entitled *An Hebrew Woman Carrying her Purification Offering to the Temple*, the painting must have provoked unflattering jests among the London wags. It may have appeared that Maria was endeavouring to purify her own life by devoting it to her child as compensation for the apparent neglect of four years' absence. She would continue to exhibit a renewed religious zeal in her choice of subjects for public exhibition.

In December 1795 Maria was able to pick up her old friendship with General Paoli, returned from Corsica just before Christmas and looking fit for his seventy-three years. He weighed much less, having gone through a hard four years with no results. He especially needed friends at this moment. His second attempt to liberate his country had failed through factionalism and then betrayal by the British in whom he had placed so much trust. He and his followers had become the enemies of the Bonaparte clan. The young General Bonaparte had always idolised Paoli, an esteem never returned by the older man. The General was also saddened by the absence of the faithful Boswell, who had finally succumbed to his excesses earlier in the year.

Another old friend gave news. Jefferson replied to Maria's two letters of a year ago. He was now retired to Monticello and wrote to say that he was happy to be away from public life, which, he said, he had always hated. (This was the proper gentleman's attitude. Obvious ambition was considered unseemly.) He seemed content with his life.

> I am eating the peaches, grapes and figs of my own garden & I only wish I could eat them in your native country, gathered on the spot & in your good company.

> I think you, Mrs. Church, & myself must take a trip together to Italy, not forgetting Madme. de Corny.... Having revisited Italy I wonder you could leave it again for the smoke and rains of London. However, you have the power of making fair weather wherever you go.

Then he described an imaginary itinerary through the south of France followed by a description of his life as a farmer and how much it was to be preferred to that in an office. He closed with those expressions which expressed a persistent longing:

> ...whenever I think of you, I am hurried off on the wings of

imagination into regions where fancy submits all things to our will.

I had but to therefore set you soberly before a coal fire, walk out into the sun myself, tell him he does not shine on a being whose happiness I wish more than yours, pray him devoutly to bind his beams together with ten fold force, to penetrate if possible the mass of smoke and fog under which you are buried and to gild with his rays the room you inhabit and the road you travel, then tell you I have a most cordial friendship for you, that I regret the distance which separates us and will not permit myself to believe we are no more to meet till you meet me where time and distance are nothing.

Maria's reply was instant, a spontaneous outpouring of what was closest to her heart. She confided:

At last I have the long wished pleasure of receiving a letter from you! I cannot tell how much it has made me happy for I would not suspect you could forget me.... How glad am I to hear your detachment from the bustling world. What is this world? ...When we ask for the Omnipresent or Omnipotent who sees everything how can we wish, or be disturb'd at the momentary circumstances which pass like lightning to leave everything in ashes.

You will soon have the pleasure of seeing the charming Angelica. I love her.... She is the woman I love most & feel most happy with in this country...

I wanted much to send a letter to you by my brother George Hadfield but the resolution of his going away without waiting have prevented my knowing of his departure till he was gone. However I know you will be kind to all & need not say anything particular for him. I hope he will meet with encouragement; he has talents & an amiable character, tho he is my brother I must be just.

You mention Genova in your letter with satisfaction. Many thanks for I love it very much as well as admire it. How happy I was there in those enchanting walls of the most beautiful situation… . My duties however are here. Here I make my…happiness in the will of God, a will which must be done. Let us follow it with love.

I will not attempt to enter into political news or insignificant things. Theaters, masquerades, assemblies, concerts, & cards, shops & shows make all the occupation of these good people. My little girl, my pencil, my home make mine, & endeavour to make my time very short by making it useful.

What would I give to surprise you on your Monticello! I have your picture by Trumbull on the side of my chimney always before me & always regret that perhaps never can I see the original…at least if I could have often your letters t'would be some compensation, but to be deprived of both is too much.

Maria was to be deprived of his letters and consoling words when she needed them most. She had waxed religious and philosophic when writing to him of the 'momentary circumstances which pass like lightning to leave everything in ashes'. She could not know that in six months time her words would prove prophetic.

It was the end of July, unseasonably cool. Luigina went for her daily walk in the park. Complaining of a sore throat upon her return, she went to bed and became feverish. She would not let her mother leave her bedside for a minute, so a vigil began, day and night. Her parents did not think the child was too ill, which made the shock even crueller when the little girl was lost. One day she was there in her little bed whimpering for her mother, and the next day she was gone. It all happened in a week. Friday, 29th July became the darkest day of Maria's life. Cosway drew the sweet, peaceful face as she lay still in her bed, a lace cap hiding her blond curls, little hands clasping a cross. Maria spent days shut up in her room, overcome with grief and then a painful swelling of her face. General Paoli, Luigina's godfather, tried to comfort her, but there was nothing for it. After a fortnight the collector, Robert Udny, and his wife invited the Cosways to their country house in Teddington, but even there Maria remained aloof from others and kept to her room. She believed in accepting God's will, but could taking a child be His will? She must have thought she was being punished for her errant ways in Italy or other undiscovered sins. The biting remorse for those years away from her child added to the grief gnawing away in her mind. She had only had eighteen months of motherhood. Every day of their happiness together was relived. Maria had been taught resignation, humility, but this was too much to ask. She missed her daughter painfully.

Richard also suffered deeply over the loss of his adored child, but he masked it behind constant chatter, busying himself with Academy affairs, presenting to the world his usual glib jauntiness. Some thought he was unmoved. Horace Walpole wrote to Mary Berry:

> …she [Maria] so affected for her only little girl, that she shut herself up in her chamber and would not be seen – the man Cosway does not seem to think that much of the loss belonged to him: he romanced with his usual vivacity.

This appearance was only that. Richard refused to allow his daughter's body to be taken out of the house, first burying her in the cellar, then asking his friend Thomas Banks to sculpt a sarcophagus. When Luigina was placed in it, this funerary work in the classical style took its place among the other objects displayed throughout the house – the most precious and most macabre of their rich collection.

After the first shock Maria came back into the world, filling her days with a passionate devotion to good works and painting to fill the void in her heart. Her first thought was to continue the tutoring she had begun with Luigina by starting a school for Catholic girls. She wrote to wealthy Catholics such as Charles Townley and the Duke of Norfolk, requesting subscriptions to support the scheme. The summer after her child's death she was busy with this worthy endeavour when a friend came to London who recalled to mind her last stay in Paris. It was the young Pole, Julien Niemcewicz, travelling as companion and nurse to General Kosciuszko, the Polish patriot who had accompanied Lafayette to America and had then failed in his attempt to lead the Poles to independence. Suffering from severe wounds – the General had been partially paralysed by a cannon shot passing too close to him – he spent his days on a couch, sketching landscapes, attended by the faithful Niemcewicz, who was as devoted as ever to his 'chère soeur' as he still addressed her. Cosway drew a portrait of the hero while Maria tried to amuse him despite her own gloom. At the end of the summer the two exiles sailed for America with letters for Jefferson, brother George, and the Churches. Angelica had left earlier in the year to be with her ailing father and reported that Jefferson had made earnest inquiries after Maria, which he could well have directed to London. Maria's circle of intimate friends was shrinking. Lady Lyttelton had died after a long life, several months before Luigina's death. Anne, Lady Townshend, was still loyal although quite occupied with the marriage of her daughter. Anne Damer had recently inherited Strawberry Hill from her friend Sir Horace Walpole, who died early in 1797. Sister Charlotte was living with her husband in Harrow so Maria was left more and more to her own devices.

As often happens in moments of inner pain, feelings are transferred from a person to a cause, which one fancies is worth promoting and, in defence of which, grief may render one somewhat reckless. At this difficult period, Maria took a greater interest in the affairs of the Royal Academy, an interest which antagonised many of her husband's colleagues. She thought it time that Henry Tresham, her friend of over twenty years, should become an R.A. This companion of her girlhood in Italy was an Associate of the Academy, but not a full Member. She called on Fuseli, one of the former band of young artists in Rome, and pressed him to vote for Tresham in the next election. Her pleadings were to no purpose, for he cast his vote for Sawrey Gilpin. Indeed, her efforts had been countered by the skilful manoeuvres of an Academician, who, although holding no office, managed to control much of the Academy's business through his knowledge of finances and his quiet influence. Joseph Farington, a clergyman's son, was a landscape painter of average talent, who had a greater gift for administration and a taste for the exercise of power. After Maria's first defeat at his hands, she complained privately of his influence in Academy affairs. Towards the end of 1797 she resolved that the wisest course was to be friendlier with Mr. Farington rather than to be his adversary. She invited him to call to see the painting upon which she had been labouring. Having gone back to painting after her daughter's death, she felt frustrated over her loss of skill after several years of neglect. Perhaps she thought Farington — author with her brother-in-law Combe, of *The History of the Thames* — would have a natural interest in her new picture, 'The Birth of the Thames'.

The picture was an allegory, symbolising the river's birth by several water nymphs holding the infant 'Thames' among the reeds. It was one of the last of Maria's works to have success. Prints of it were widely sold in London and Paris. The day she showed it to Farington, however, she was still struggling with her painting and hoping for a sympathetic ear, which he

56. The Birth of the Thames *by Maria Cosway, engraving by P. W. Tomkins, 1803. The original picture was exhibited at the Royal Academy in 1800.*

seemed to give. When they were together in the painting room on the ground floor, she observed a tall, distinguished person, who bore himself as a relation of the Walpoles should. This was a man worthy of her confidence.

'Mr. Farington, 'tis kind of you to spend this time looking at my pictures.... . Oh, my, almost two hours have passed. I should have proposed tea to you long ago. Before we go up to the drawing room, I must express my gratitude for your indulgence. Mr. Cosway does not encourage me in painting. I do need encouragement for I begin many pictures and then grow tired. Since I have no obligation to finish them, I do not. I need a stimulus to oblige me to finish. If Mr. Cosway had allowed me to sell my works, finishing would have become a habit. You know he felt that ladies should not stoop to trade, that drawing for me

should remain an 'accomplishment' and so it has. He never wished me to paint professionally, so little by little I lost the skill I had acquired in Italy. Now I am endeavouring to compensate for many wasted years. But I must be tedious with my complaints. Forgive me for being tiresome. Pray, shall we go upstairs and take some tea.'

'I thank you, but I fear I have outstayed the duration of a proper visit. I must take leave of you now. Before I do, Mrs. Cosway, let me reassure you that you have finished many pictures, which have been exhibited at the Academy and I am certain that your newfound resolution will enable more to come to completion. Of course I shall be delighted to see your drawing room again very soon as it is one of the most original in London. A connoisseur could spend hours learning about art from the study of the objects in your house.'

'Mr. Cosway is the connoisseur. It is he who has collected and disposed what you see. I learn from it as you. 'Tis true that we are continually inspired in our work by our surroundings, but I must add, as mistress of the house, that I am ashamed of the collection of dust which this abundance of treasures attracts.' She paused to dust one of the busts in the hall with her handkerchief. 'I do wish your further acquaintance, Mr. Farington, and hope that we shall see you again very soon at Stratford Place.'

'You shall, to be sure. Good afternoon, Mrs. Cosway.'

Farington kept his promise and more. In the ensuing two weeks his influence may well have acted on the Cosways' behalf. The Academy soon came to the conclusion that it had been many years since Mr. Cosway had served on the Council, that it was time he should serve again. No sooner suggested than it was done at the December meeting. The next day the Cosways held a small celebratory dinner, inviting Benjamin West, the Academy President, John Inigo Richards, the Secretary, Paul Sandby, and of course, Farington. They also invited two members of the Society of Antiquaries: Caleb Whiteforde, the diplomat, and George Hardinge, a Member of Parliament. They dined at a quarter past five in the French manner. The cloth was not removed. Maria went up at seven and the gentlemen followed at half past with no lingering over the port. After coffee, Mrs. Cosway played the harp until time for tea. James Northcote came in and all enjoyed conversation until about eleven. There was talk about the characters of various Academy members which Maria did not encourage.

Trying to turn the conversation toward happier issues, she remarked that art and artists were on a more respectable footing in England than in any other country.

With Cosway's election to the Council and Tresham's failure to become an R.A., Maria's efforts on behalf of her friend's election became more intense. She and Farington exchanged visits during that winter. He very kindly gave his counsel to Cosway on the manner of saving rate payments. The Parliament had voted to exempt Academy members from higher rates demanded by the War if the artists had no more than one male servant. This meant the Cosways would have to give up their coach and the extra servants it required, but the saving of over four hundred pounds convinced Richard to do it. From this time General Paoli often put his carriage at their disposition. Shortly after his assistance in this matter, Maria's acquaintance with Farington was broken off by his artful and secret way of directing the Academy's business. It all came to light in the election of February 1798.

In the days leading up to the election Maria had several conversations with Farington about Tresham's candidacy. She wrote him a letter asking for his vote and finally, in the face of his reluctance to give an answer, she called on him the morning of the election with an earnest plea. He received her graciously. When she was shown into his drawing room, she went right to the matter.

'Mr. Farington, forgive my intrusion this morning. I have conveyed to you how displeasing it is that William Beechy was spreading round the false rumour that I had taken Mr. Tresham to see you. I have tried not to interfere in such a way as you know. I have only written to Mr. Dance and to Mrs. Lloyd. You know that all depends on you. There are two or three votes waiting to see what you will do. If Mr. Tresham is elected it will be owing to you.'

'Madame, I have indeed made up my mind for whom I shall vote, but I have not taken an active part. Last year Tresham and Beechy accused me of giving dinners to serve Gilpin, but that was entirely false. If Tresham's voters are true, it will be a near run, but if either Tresham or Beechy gain, it would cause no uneasiness to me. I have not said a word to Dance or any others on this subject.'

'I trust then that you have a mind open and will reflect upon my request.'

'Indeed, I shall, do not fear.'

Later, Maria felt ill-used for this man had been entirely false to her. He later told Northcote that her request *obliged* him to vote against Tresham. The election went to Beechy easily. Many who had promised their vote to Tresham stayed away expressly after consulting with Farington and his friends. In a fit of pique, which she later regretted, Maria sent a message through Northcote expressing her displeasure, which Farington considered 'impertinent'. From that time they never had further relations except for perfunctory greetings at large gatherings. Farington held a longstanding grudge against her from this moment. In the following years, especially before elections, he often recalled to Academy members Mrs. Cosway's improper 'interference' and even prepared a *memoire* for Benjamin West on her behaviour.

A year later Henry Tresham attained the rank of R.A. without assistance. As two places were vacant, the Cosways' friend, Joseph Bonomi, was hoping for a happy issue to his long struggle to become an Academician. Sir Joshua Reynolds had resigned from the Presidency over his failure to have Bonomi elected in 1790. The native of Rome, known for his vast architectural knowledge, had been employed by the Adams brothers and had later designed several important country houses. Mindful that she must not appear to interfere, Maria refrained from soliciting votes for Bonomi although she did take him in General Paoli's coach to see Loutherbourg, Bartolozzi, and Banks, where he pleaded his own cause. This slight kindness brought down much criticism from all sides until Richard urged her not to meddle. It became evident that even the smallest gesture on her part was enough to compromise a candidate's prospects. Bonomi lost out narrowly to Thomas Daniell. Sadly he never achieved the membership he deserved.

Although Maria never thereafter took part in Academy business, accusations continued to fly. Matters were aggravated by a schism opened by Tresham as soon as he became a member. Those who had been for him, which included Cosway, largely agreed that the Academy's Instrument of Institution had not been followed. Instead of the prescribed rotation of office of the Council, with newly elected members having first place, open elections had been held. This practice deprived Tresham of a place on the Council right after his election. There were now two parties: Tresham's supporters and the Farington-West 'cabal'. Since the Cosways were identified with the former, West took Maria's charitable calls during his illness as part of a 'plot' to discredit him with the King. Maria had no desire to injure West but she did speak frankly and openly to him. She told him during one call that her husband had not accompanied her because he did not wish to meet Beechy, Smirke or Farington. Cosway was now disgusted with the Academy. Maria also boldly told West that the Gentlemen (Cosway, Tresham and their friends) were determined to break the combination which influenced the Academy.

After these commotions Maria turned away from controversy and withdrew into painting. With the approach of the new century she worked harder than ever, exhibiting seven pictures at the Academy exhibition of 1800: *The Birth of the Thames* and four portraits. One of them, a likeness of Angelica Church, was inspired by Samuel Rogers' verses 'How oft inscribed with Friendship's votive rhyme, The bark now silver'd by the touch of time!'. That year was the most productive of her artistic life. Richard could not discourage this febrile activity by his lack of enthusiasm. They had steadily grown apart since the death of Luigina. Maria now pursued two interests, religion and painting.

A great stimulus to her art was the co-operation and encouragement she found from a print publisher in London, Rudolph Ackermann. German by birth, this enterprising man had a large shop in the Strand in the building where Richard had studied drawing with William Shipley. This shop was a centre for the decorative arts. Mr. Ackermann's watercolours and lead pencils were considered of the finest quality. The first major work Maria undertook for publication by Ackermann was a series of thirty-six soft ground etchings of Richard's drawings. Etching in this manner permitted her to draw with a pencil, instead of an etching needle, pressing into the paper covering the waxy ground laid down on a copper printing plate. When the paper was lifted, it took away the ground under the pencil marks and left lines where the acid could eat into the copper plate. In February, the first edition of six etchings came out on heavy pale blue paper, called *Imitations in Chalk*, etched by Mrs. Cosway, from Original Drawings by R. Cosway, Esq., R.A. Almost every month a new edition was published until the end of the summer. Also published that year was a work of Maria's own conception, engraved by Anthony Cardon after her drawings. The two companion volumes, entitled *A Progress of Female Virtue* and *A Progress of Female Dissipation*, were inspired by her deep attachment to the moral education of young girls. The sepia aquatints taught the happiness of maternal duties opposed to the folly of feminine vanity, when the accomplishments of music and dancing become vehicles for showing off one's beauty, and leisure was devoted to tea-drinking and cards. These were not great history paintings, only simple portrayals of women engaged in noble or frivolous pursuits by which she hoped art would have an instructive aim.

That same year she used her pencil for a charitable purpose. She agreed to illustrate a poem by Mary Robinson, the actress. Once a stunning beauty, she was now a crippled invalid in distressed circumstances. Mrs. Robinson had become a poet and rather successful novelist after leaving the theatre. She depended on an annuity from the Prince of Wales to get by. This stipend had been obtained by blackmailing the Prince with passionate letters addressed to her, his 'Perdita', and signed 'Florizel' from the characters in *A Winter's Tale*, the play which had begun Mrs. Robinson's brilliant career. The former actress had recently evicted her lover, Colonel Tarleton, because of his advances toward her daughter, thus further reducing her income. Now in the last year of her life, she wrote a morality tale in verse entitled, *The Winter Day*. The twelve drawings alternated, as did her verses, between scenes of poverty, illness, or death and the rich gaiety of balls, gaming parties, banquets and other amusements of the *bon ton*. Maria liked nothing better than a morality project. In one of the drawings the allegorical peacock Pride presides over the death of Merit and Hope. To Mrs. Robinson this sombre note reflected her bitterness at the end of a glittering life. The first drawing for the book, portraying a lady reclining in her boudoir by the fire, was not gloomy, for Maria endeavoured to picture her own interior. The lady is considered to be a self-portrait, but the general classicism of her profile is hardly like Maria's.

Another more difficult commission came her way in 1800. She was asked to paint a mother with her little blonde daughter of four years old, the age of Luigina when Maria returned from Italy. Caroline, the Princess of Wales, and Princess Charlotte could not be refused. Maria worked very hard on the portrait, but never got the heads quite right. Her perturbed soul must have spoiled the picture. The Princess felt it necessary to ask Thomas Lawrence to improve the likenesses.

The Cosways had other royal visitors to Stratford Place that year by way of America. The three little sons of the Duc d'Orléans, painted by Mr. Cosway in Paris during the summer of 1786, were now exiled by the Revolution, wandering back and forth across the ocean. When they came from New York to settle at Twickenham, their secretary, the Count de Montjoye, called on the Cosways with letters from Angelica and Niemcewicz. After consulting her friend Miss Wilkes on the proper form of invitation, Maria sent a note to the Count inviting the young princes to call.

57. Queen Caroline and Princess Charlotte *by Maria Cosway, 1800.*

They may not have called socially, but eventually Cosway was asked by the two elder brothers, the Duc de Chartres and the Duc de Montpensier, to paint their portraits in miniature, as he had done almost twenty-five years before.

By far the most scandalous sitter of Mr. Cosway's that year was the now renowned Lady Hamilton, who had arrived in London after a great progress across Europe with her husband Sir William and Admiral Nelson both in attendance. The humiliation of the cultivated Sir William by the open exhibition of his wife's adultery was cruel to see. It was said that the King had snubbed both of them during a *levée* at St. James Palace, conversing with an unknown military officer for half an hour with his back directly in front of his former Minister to Naples and Lord Nelson. Scandal was never reason to discourage Richard from accepting a famous person's custom. His drawing of the lady was kind, disguising her great girth with Grecian draperies, as she posed in one of her 'attitudes'. Although Lady Hamilton's bold and uninhibited charm could be thought amusing, her company was no longer the kind Maria sought. The truth was that Lady Hamilton had a beautiful face, but had grown fat, drank freely and spoke vulgarly. A great naval hero was completely mesmerised by her, but this consorting with the latest figures of notoriety held no attraction for Maria. Her faith had become the centre of her life. All the pictures she sent to the Academy in 1801 were of religious subjects: *The Guardian Angel, The Call of Samuel, and The Exultation of the Virgin Mary.* There was nothing else and no one else to whom she could turn for succour. Her husband had become a stranger. His changed behaviour was somewhat evident before she went to Italy, but every passing year saw them growing farther apart. Upon her return to London he had made peace, but they never rekindled the warmth and affection of the early days. After Luigina's death, they tried to continue on as before, but the life had gone out of their home. They easily disputed over small differences and greater ones such as her painting or her interest in Academy business. The marriage was undermined by deeper problems than incompatibility.

58. Mary Moser, *later Mrs. Lloyd, by George Romney.*

Maria overlooked those of Richard's acquaintances of whom she disapproved until one day she made a discovery which could not be ignored. While sorting through the portfolios of drawings in their back parlour, a red morocco leather sketchbook fell into her lap. She opened it to find sketches and notes Richard had apparently made during a trip in the country. It was not the sketches that filled her with horror but some of the notes which formed a travel journal. She took the obscene little book into

Cosway's library where she could often find him hunched over one of his esoteric tomes, dressed in a velvet dressing gown and a tasselled silk cap. For the first time she may have had the unkind thought that he was indeed a little simian in fancy dress.

'Mr. Cosway! I have made an interesting discovery while sorting our prints. I found a journal which seems to be written in your hand, but I cannot imagine a gentleman expressing himself in such terms. Could you enlighten me on its origin?' She flounced down on one of his massive high-backed Genoa velvet chairs.

'What journal? Of what are you speaking, my dear wife?'

'Your dear wife indeed! Your dear wife that you leave to go gadding across the country with Mrs. Lloyd. Not content to betray me, you must further write about your disgraceful conduct in the most lewd of narratives, humiliating your 'dear wife' by comparisons with Mrs. Lloyd on the most intimate subjects!'

'Might I remind you Mrs. Cosway, that my sketchbooks are private. If you go prying about, you are liable to disappointment. I should also recall to your mind that at the time of that journey Mrs. Lloyd was still Miss Moser and you, my fair Maria, were not above reproach, being absent from your husband and child for four years. Good taste requires me to refrain from repeating the gossip going around this town on your company at the time.'

'You know that scandal was much talk about nothing. I was obliged to accept the hospitality of friends for you would neither come to Italy nor would you send me enough remittances.'

'That story might well be convincing to your friends, Maria, but the truth demands a better account. You did not wish to return home, did you?'

'Why should I wish to? My husband's attentions were always elsewhere. This gloomy, filthy weather was slowly killing me. Despite the fact that there was nothing joyous left here, I dutifully returned home and cared for our daughter as well as any father could have wished.'

'Yes I credit you with that. As for my jaunt with Mary Moser, that was years ago. That short-sighted, middle-aged lady – now the respectable Mrs. Lloyd – cannot now provoke your jealousy. Can you not put the past out of your mind?'

'If it were only a matter of the past perhaps. Alas, Mrs. Lloyd has a successor. Did you not think I was ignorant of your turning around Martha Udny as a wasp over honey?'

59. Mrs. Martha Udny, wife of the collector Robert Udny, *engraved by Anthony Cardon after Richard Cosway.*

'*Indeed Mrs. Udny is eminently sweet. You hit the mark there, Maria, a young, fair woman with a very old husband, who needs cheerful company from time to time. I am flattered to oblige her.*'

'*You admit your perfidy gaily, doing injustice to a man who has been kind and hospitable to us both. 'Tis too much to bear, and I shall bear it no longer. Without Luigina this house is nothing more than her tomb. I shall seek an occasion to leave this place at the earliest possible date if you will agree to it.*'

'*As you wish, Mrs. Cosway, as you wish. Now will you let me get on with my studies. When you have matured your scheme for a journey, I beg you to inform me.*'

'*Your coldness is intolerable, insufferably intolerable. I shall soon tell you of my plan, I assure you.*'

'You, my lady, could be the subject of a treatise on coldness with your daily Roman masses, always on your knees in prayers.'

'We shall not quarrel again over my religion.'

'No, we shan't. Now, good day, Mrs. Cosway.'

'Sir!'

A rupture in the Cosways' marriage occurred in July 1801. Once again Maria found solace in writing to her old friend in Monticello. After six years of silence on his part, she felt that he would have a reservoir of sympathy in which she could slake her thirst for comfort. If he did not respond, she would find peace in the act of writing, letting her mind speak to him across the ocean. Now she was not only speaking to the soft-spoken gentleman who had been the most affectionate of friends, but to the President of the United States.

I must not look back to the date of our last correspondence. T'would alarm & discourage me from taking the pen up this moment. Your kindness to me has been of all times & your friendship & mine took its date from its beginning. Circumstances, not your will I am sure has deprived me of the pleasure. I used to value so much of receiving your letters. Many, many times my thoughts turned towards you, with a wish to write Would you not receive the congratulations of an old friend, qui *vous êtes sincerement devoué*…. . Could you permit a thought that time or distance has at all lessened my interest in what attends you? This is enough. Words cannot express all. I should say on the subject & you have so much of that sympathising sentiment to enable you to conceive more than I can write & what the occasion would require. May God continue to be your guide, as you have been His choice for the welfare of your country & the happiness of your friends…

Maria sent the letter through her brother George, who needed the new President's favour to find building commissions in Washington. She told the President that her brother looks up to you for protection & trusts in your justice.... Send me few words to assure me I live in your esteem & friendship & you will revive the happiness of ever your aft. Maria Cosway

20 July 1801

South View of THE OLD and NEW LOUVRE

16

Bonaparte's Museum

1801-1803

The opportunity for Maria to escape the warfare in her home came with the first glimmers of peace in the war with France. Lord Cornwallis was in Amiens negotiating with the French. Nothing was signed, but the English, and it was said, Bonaparte, the First Consul, were fatigued with war. Along with the general hunger for peace, there was mounting curiosity in London to see the most famous man in Europe and the amassed treasures of statues and pictures looted from Italy. A month after writing her wistful letter to Jefferson, Maria was on the road alone to Paris. Richard agreed to the journey and to her scheme to engrave drawings of the great pictures in the new *Musée Central* in the Louvre. With a feeling of relief, that Cosway must have shared, Maria confronted the difficulties of living on her own while endeavouring to become the artist she had always wished to be, ultimately independent of her husband's subsidies.

Not having seen Paris since the days of the *ancien régime*, Maria was eager to see the changes wrought by the Revolution and the new First Consul. At each scene some memory would rise to the surface of thought, buoyed by its sweetness. She wrote to Jefferson after arriving:

> I am now in this place which brings me to Mind every day our first interview, the pleasing days we pass'd together.... Have we hopes of ever seeing you in Paris? Would it not be a rest for you after your laborious situation? I often see the only friend remaining of our set, Madame de Corny. The same in her own amiable qualities but very different in her situation, but she supports it very well.

> I am come to this place in the best time for the profusion of fine things is beyond description & not possible to conceive. It is so changed in every respect, that you would not think it the same country or people...

The Paris of the 1780s had been a city where piles of golden cut stones waited to be formed into ambitious projects such as the Church of St. Geneviève (now the Panthéon) or the toll houses marking the barriers of the city or the Duke of Orleans' Palais Royal. A decade of turmoil had stopped this activity and left the buildings dirtier or – like the Tuileries Palace – marred by the scars of firearms. The words *Fraternité, Liberté, Egalité and Proprieté d'état* were painted on all the public edifices. Many churches were now used as stables or warehouses. The general aspect of the city was still handsome although greatly spoiled by shabby black sheds on the Seine, where washerwomen beat their linen against stones. The atmosphere, the look of the people in general and especially the want of taste and manners were evidence that society was no longer the same. Where before one saw many magnificent coaches with coats of arms on the doors and richly-liveried footmen, there were now plain *fiacres* and *cabriolets* for hire. Although there were beggars everywhere in the villages between Calais and Paris, they were better dressed. The masses of people in the capital also appeared to be more prosperous, of middle ranks, but there was everywhere a general lack of modesty in ladies' dress. The antique fashion was followed with exaggerated shows of naked arms, bosoms, and backs, draped with such diaphanous fabrics that undergarments had become a sort of clinging stocking. Ladies went out even in winter with no hats, only a flimsy chiffon on the head or an Indian shawl. The hair was dressed with long curls framing the face and chignons behind after the Roman model and the cheeks heavily rouged. This was the appearance of one society, that of the wives of the newly rich bankers, merchants, and generals. If one was received into the older society of the *émigrés* who had discreetly returned, one found them often living in reduced circumstances, upholding the simplicity and naturalness of good manners and modestly attired. The general laxness of morals had changed the Palais Royal, which Maria had enjoyed seeing with Jefferson. Now it was so filled with gaming houses and women of *petite vertu*, that fewer ladies ventured there, even in the morning.

Above all, Paris was dominated by the presence of soldiers everywhere. It was they who kept order in the streets, in the churches, and guarded in great numbers the balconies and terraces of the Tuileries Palace. Paris was a military city governed by a general whose image was omnipresent. Bonaparte's sober head adorned ladies' 'reticules', was modelled into plaster of Paris busts and etched on morsels of barley sugar. Indeed, his person was one of the great attractions of the city. Foreigners, especially the English, had an insatiable curiosity to see him at one of the monthly military reviews in the courtyard of the Tuileries or to be received by him at one of his *levées* for the ambassadors. At the time of Maria's arrival, he rarely appeared in public, realising that if he were too easily approached he would lose the fear and respect of the people. He withdrew often to Malmaison or

St. Cloud, refusing to receive foreigners who had not been received at the courts of their own rulers.

None of these obvious changes touched Maria as much as the absence of the charming and gentle society she had known some fifteen years before. The Trudaine brothers and André Chénier, whom she knew as Monsieur Saint-André, had been unjustly executed. Worse, they had been betrayed by those from whom they should have most hoped for mercy. Chénier could have been saved by his own brother, the ambitious Marie-Joseph. For a year an unknown lady sent him a note every day with only these words: 'Cain, where is your brother?' The painter David, when a powerful member of the Committee for Public Safety during the Terror, had refused indifferently, even angrily, the poignant requests of his former benefactors, the Trudaines, to intercede for them. He turned his back on innocent people and let them be guillotined. The Marquis de Bièvre had at least died a natural death. Monsieur d'Angiviller was alone in Kiel, refusing ever to set foot in France. D'Hancarville was living impoverished in Italy. Madame de Corny was also living in dignified poverty in Paris. Maria's Polish friends were scattered in Poland and America. Niemcewicz had married an American lady. Of Maria's old circle the two who had not only survived but thrived were David and Monsieur de Non, now prudently known as Denon to hide his noble origins. Another artist who had successfully avoided the Terror was Madame Vigée Lebrun, long exiled, but now as wealthy and popular as ever, despite her former association with Marie-Antoinette.

Amidst the lingering aura of absent friends and the unattractiveness of their newly-rich replacements, Maria had no time for musing over the past. She had not come to Paris as a tourist to see sights or visit salons, but to work as an artist with an ambitious plan to copy and engrave all the pictures hanging in the Grand Gallery of the Louvre. She took every opportunity to send friends a prospectus of her work, even Jefferson, far away in America.

> I send you the prospectus of a work which is the most interesting
> ever published as everybody will have in their possession the exact
> distribution of this wonderful Gallery. The history of every
> picture will also be very curious as we have collected in one spot
> the finest works of art which were spread all over Italy. I hope

you will make it known among your friends who may like to know of such a work. This will keep me here two years at least & everybody seems very much delighted with this enterprise.

At the time of this letter she had great hopes for success. A London paper reported that she had the patronage of Bonaparte himself for her enterprise, which was not precisely true. What she did have was his precious signature in a red leather album of delicately coloured miniatures, used to present her plan to prospective subscribers. By signing he agreed to subscribe as had his wife Josephine, his brother Lucien, his mother, *Madame Mère*, his uncle, Joseph Fesch, and other Bonapartes as well. Beside their names she had also obtained such distinguished signatures as that of her old friend Francesco Melzi d'Eril, now Vice-President of the Cisalpine Republic, the Italian collector Sommariva, and Madame Recamier. In London, her subscribers included the Prince of Wales, the Duke of Cumberland, her friend the Marchioness Townshend, Sir Thomas Erskine, Earl Cowper, Lord Egremont, Dr. Charles Burney, Sir Francis Burdett, John Soane, and Mrs. Anne Damer, who voiced her scepticism in a letter to Richard: 'I do not rejoice at the immense work Mrs. Cosway has undertaken.'

It was an immensely ambitious plan. Maria intended to copy in miniature all the pictures hanging in each of the fifty-seven compartments of the Grand Gallery. Then she would etch a copper plate of this design and sell a coloured or sepia engraving at the rate of two such engravings a month. Thus a subscriber with all the plates could reconstruct a panorama of the entire Gallery in his home. If she had maintained the planned frequency of publication, which soon proved impossible, it would have been completed in two and half years.

She must have obtained the Bonapartes' interest in her scheme through her connection with General Paoli, who introduced Joseph Fesch, Bonaparte's uncle, to the Cosways in London. A few days after the *coup d'état* which vaulted General Bonaparte to the post of First Consul, a 'Priest uncle to Buonoparte' was seen at the Cosways' house by the sculptor Nollekens. Although Paoli had broken with the Bonapartes, whom he never admired, there were still deep ties, profoundly Corsican, between them, going back to the days of their united struggle against the French thirty years before. Upon arriving in Paris, Maria renewed her acquaintance with Fesch, who soon presented her to his half-sister, Madame Laetizia Bonaparte, mother of the First Consul, with whom Fesch lived in a magnificent hotel on the rue de Mont Blanc. Fesch had been a priest until it became wiser politically to forget his vows. He then made a great fortune by following Bonaparte's army to Italy, where he, as well as other family members, richly profited by supplying the army and participating in the spoils of war. During the Consulate Fesch was a young man of fashion about thirty-eight years of age, of medium height with a large round forehead over widely spaced dark eyes and a straight strong nose. Although not handsome he was always elegantly dressed in well-tailored wool redingotes, impeccable white linen and white silk stockings. He adored going to the theatre and spending his fortune on his wardrobe, his carriage, and his passion for buying pictures. His growing collection, started with certain 'acquisitions' in Italy, was one of the most important in private hands. Living in the shadow of a younger and immensely powerful nephew, he was viewed by many as mediocre, although he had been a brilliant student in seminary. Theological questions were no longer the centre of his interests; he was eager to enjoy the new wealth and prestige which his family relished.

It was Fesch's love of art which must have drawn him to Maria's company.

During her first year in Paris they grew to be more than acquaintances. They were constant companions. His frequent calls were more than social. He confided his most intimate thoughts on his career and his relation with the First Consul. It was through him that she obtained subscriptions from the Bonapartes for her work on the Louvre. In late June of 1802 she was ready to present them with the first numbers of her plates, which she carefully retouched and placed in morocco leather portfolios: one for the First Consul, one for Madame Laetizia Bonaparte, and one for Fesch. The next time Fesch called at her apartment in the Hotel de Marigny, Rue de St. Thomas du Louvre, she took her courage in both hands and asked if she could do what she had been anxiously wishing:

'Do you consider it possible for me to deliver my prints to Malmaison in person?'
'No, that will not be necessary. I shall be pleased to carry them for

you.' As ever, those near power jealously guard their proximity to the great.

'Of course. When you go, would you be kind enough to inquire if the First Consul would be willing to receive me so that I might better explain the work to him. I imagine that I should invite Mr. Griffiths to accompany me, but that is an unpleasant prospect in view of his attitude.'

'However did you manage to become entangled with Mr. Griffiths?'

'Now I wonder indeed. One day at the Gallery, I was presented to him, who was described to me as an enterprising young Englishman. This he proved to be, for no sooner had I described my grand scheme of etching all the pictures in the Grand Gallery, than he persuaded me of his enthusiasm for my idea and especially of his great capacity for business, proposing to help me with the practical aspects of the work. I felt encouraged and supported. We became partners and now I am tormented by this association. He is so absorbed with his mistress that he does nothing, is impossible to find, and if I do see him he never listens to a word I say, regards me with disdain, dispensing haughty looks. I have written to break with him, but have not sent the letter. If only your family would show greater interest in this important work, I could overcome my vexations with this unpleasant man.'

'I shall be more than pleased to present your portfolios together with my warm advocacy of your request for an audience.'

'I would be most grateful. Do you know I have been wishing to be received by the First Consul for some time. I thought it might be possible when he came to the Tuileries yesterday.'

'I fear he had other engagements. He took advantage of his passage in Paris to invite his lady, 'la Balla', the singer from the Opera, to come to see him yesterday, which occasioned scenes of jealousy, and other uproars. He was much occupied as you can see.'

'Well I think it curious and rather extraordinary that he has time for a singer and no time to receive me!'

'Madame Cosway, for a lady of experience with society you sometimes express the innocent sentiments of a young girl.'

'Perhaps, yet the first gentleman of the country has a certain dignity to maintain, do you not think so?'

'Most assuredly, but it is he who holds the power to decide how best his dignity will be maintained and does not have the benefit of knowing whether he has been successful, for those with whom he converses would never express opinions contrary to his.'

'Surely his family are free to express their opinions.'

'Some, perhaps. Lucien often, my sister always.'

'And you?'

'Yes, I will, but the question must well deserve the certain irritation I must endure.'

'I am content to hear that, Monsieur Fesch.'

As Maria waited impatiently to have news from Malmaison, she occupied her days with intense labour, either in the Gallery making sketches or at home etching them. She also embarked upon an important picture that she wished to exhibit at the next Salon in the Louvre, held every autumn. In this work she had wonderful instruction from her old friend, David. Her disinterest in politics may have spared her hearing all that he had been and done in the Revolution. Having abandoned all political activities, he seemed satisfied with his position as the pre-eminent painter of France. It was a short walk from the Rue du Saint Thomas du Louvre to David's apartment high in the angle of the Louvre, overlooking the Seine and the Church of St. Germain l'Auxerrois. In the summer, Maria often went to call early in the morning. One day in June she surprised him smoking in his small garden between the palace and the river.

'Ah, Madame Cosway, how is the most industrious artist in Paris this fresh and clear morning?'

'Very well, Sir. Very well, though anxious for the success of my endeavours. However, I did not come to complain or talk of business, but of art. I am thinking of doing a picture for the Salon. I was hoping that you would advise me. Would it be possible with all your labours, students, and other cares?'

'Of course, I shall always be disposed to encourage you, always. You may depend upon me as your friend. Now what subject have you conceived for this new work?'

'One I have attempted before and have meditated upon. It is from

Hesiod's Theogony, *when he describes the birth of Eros, the most beautiful of all the gods, who emerges from Chaos and the Earth.'*

'Eros, always a beautiful subject, yes, Mrs. Cosway, a beautiful subject, but is it the subject for a lady?'

'You mistake, Monsieur David, my intention. This is the Eros born **before** *Aphrodite and the division of the sexes. This is the Eros who represents the generating power anterior to the opposition of contrary forces. It is the primordial Eros, the energy of renewal, the god whom Hesiod says, "is the most beautiful of the immortal gods, …who tames, at the bottom of hearts, the spirit and the wise will." Here I shall show you a sketch of my idea.' Reaching into her portfolio, she searched for her sketches but did not find them.*

'Oh dear, I do not have the drawing I wished to show you. I must return home to fetch it. I shan't be a moment.' This delay in their consultation was unfortunate, for upon her return she found David still in the garden, but conversing intently with one of his students.

'Ah, Mrs. Cosway, listen to a story which shows how serious my students are about their art and what methods one must use.'

The young man continued his narrative. 'Well, sir, I had need of a large dog to copy for a picture. I found a man who agreed to sell me a dead one, but then he reminded me that the dog would be too stiff to arrange in the positions I wished, that it would be better to bring a live one and kill it before me, so that while still warm I could arrange the beast as I wished. This idea pleased me, except that I asked him not to kill the dog in my room, but in the attic of my house. After he took the animal to the attic, I heard cries for help. The man had half strangled the dog, which only enraged him to attack the man viciously.' As the young man recounted his hideous tale, Maria noticed that David often looked at her face to read her sentiments.

'You see, Madame, you see what measures we must take to learn our art,' David said eagerly with a look of joy rather than pain on his face.

'Sir, I am horrified.'

'I have done many things of this sort to learn anatomy. When I was only thirteen I sent for the arm of a dead man to study it.'

He then told Maria many things she did not wish to hear. She saw into a fierce soul behind his deformed visage. Nevertheless, David's kindness towards her rendered forgiveness of his darker side easier. True to his promise, he called the next day and spent over two hours working with Maria on her picture. He placed the figure on a canvas with chalk. She could see already a great mind at work. She praised each mark that he made. This pleased him and he said that it was her genius that made her see this. Many artists are persuaded of their own genius. Maria was further persuaded, after seeing the poor work of one of David's highly praised lady students. She still harboured the excuse that had she the advantage of more serious and regular study and the possibility to paint professionally, she would have shown genius.

As she often walked in the gardens of the Tuileries those last days of June, awaiting news from the First Consul concerning her work, she felt frustration and a terrible loneliness. Sometimes she thought that she did not wish to live and often had morbid desires of death. Yet she ended up thinking she must follow the will of God.

At last Fesch came to give news of his visit to Malmaison.

'Madame, I am pleased to tell you that I have presented your work to the First Consul,' he announced.

'And, was he pleased?'

'He was too occupied to examine it, but I did convey to him your desire to be received by him?'

'Yes, yes.'

'He replied, "Willingly, she only has to apply, according to protocol, to the Prefect of the palace to request the day." So you see it will not be difficult to have your wish.'

'I cannot be wholly confident until he has seen the prints. Then I shall apply to the Prefect.'

'Yes, I suppose that would be prudent.'

A few days later on July 1st Maria noted in her journal: 'During this month the most important things of my life have occurred — either of pleasure or pain the xxxxxxx...which caused me to come here...all my voyages...the death of my little girl.' (Unfortunately the name of the event or person which provoked her to come to Paris was blacked out.) July proved decisive again when Fesch came to call the next day. He had come from the First Consul. When he entered Maria's drawing room, his face was unreadable, calm.

'Do you have news for me?' She went immediately to the matter of concern.

'Yes I do. There is no way to say it sweetly. Your work was the subject of much mockery at Malmaison. The First Consul disapproved it.'

'Why, oh why ever for?'

'He said that he expected something larger, that the pictures were too small and not finished enough.'

''Tis true that they could be more finished. Yet it pains me that he does not understand the intention of the scheme, of which I only sent him a small sample. It is not possible because of the quantity of pictures to quickly give a finished work and idea of the Gallery at the same time.'

After this disappointing conversation with Fesch she wrote to him the next day:

> I am still confident that he will be happier when he understands what I intend. There is no need for him to judge by the first appearance or size. The elephant is large, but should not be our model for form or good taste. Alexander was small and Bonaparte is not tall, yet it is said they are two great men.

Along with the weakening support of the Bonapartes her vexation with Griffiths continued throughout the summer. His infatuation for a certain lady absorbed all his thoughts while their work needed his entire dedication. David was also distracted in the same manner. It was said that he was in love with a lady and that his wife was very jealous of her.

Maria's only distractions were the many English visitors flooding into Paris after the peace of Amiens. She became a sort of female *cicerone*, guiding eminent visitors such as Lord Egremont and Lord and Lady Holland around the Gallery or to the apartments of different artists: David, Gerard, Guerin,

Girodet. She often led English visitors to see Fesch's collection or that of
Lucien Bonaparte or the choice pictures of a Mr. Collot, who had begun
his collecting in the same manner as Fesch and with the same means as a
supplier to the Army of Italy. Maria witnessed great public events like the
military review of 14th July. The place of the Carrousel before the Tuileries
was cleaned; all the houses were washed and appeared to be decors of paper.
The cavalry was standing at one side, the infantry at another place. Although
it was cold and rainy, the First Consul presented the flags to the regiments
but did not speak. Later he appeared several times on the terrace and was
acclaimed. The mass of people were not joyful. They appeared calm and
very indifferent to him. It was already said that he was going to be declared
Consul for Life. Maria was invited to Madame Laetizia Bonaparte's
reception after the parade, but later noted that 'it was nothing extraordinary',
neither were the fireworks in the evening. She had seen better on Saint
John's Feast Day in Florence.

The First Consul's disdain for the Louvre project did not diminish
Maria's determination to push on. Although disappointed, she knew that
this family of *parvenus* were hardly *connoisseurs* and could be expected to
misunderstand an artistic intention. She had invested too much time, and
the funds sent to her by Cosway, to abandon such an important work at its
inception, especially after acquiring subscriptions from so many of the first
rank, both English and French. She still had the strong friendship of Fesch
and the support of France's leading painter. David continued giving her
practical instruction throughout the summer. This must have been a more
precious encouragement than that of a young general.

One day David came to suggest that she study little wax models of the
figure Eros by candlelight, sketching them in different attitudes and
shadows. The next morning when she went to show him what she had done,
he exclaimed,

> 'Madame Cosway, Come in, come in, I expected to see you this
> morning. I told my wife last evening that I was certain you would be
> working on the models and that I would see you today. So let me see
> what you have done.'
>
> 'Yes, I received no one yesterday evening and worked until eleven
> on these.'

'You have worked well. I am happy with these sketches. They are good, very good.'

'You have such an admirable manner to encourage me. Truly it is agreeable to work with you as an adviser. Our discussions about art are equally valuable. I had another question concerning models. A model came this morning who seemed to have a better head than the others. Do you think the ancient artists used different models according to the part of the figure they wished to portray?'

'No, no, I do not.'

'I beg to disagree. It does not seem to me that they could find all the desired characteristics in the same model.'

She and David often had differences of opinion which he tolerated well, never manifesting anger or vanity. That day he gaily changed the subject, but before the conversation was over she had ventured to criticize one of his highly praised works, *Brutus*, telling him that Brutus' upraised arm and hand seemed dead to her. Perhaps he used another dead arm to model it! She also disapproved of putting the picture's principal figure, Brutus, off centre in a dark corner of the picture, a liberty that her classical training never permitted.

Towards the end of July 1802 Maria received another serious blow to her ambitions, although what she perceived as sad eventually changed her life for the better. Joseph Fesch was named Archbishop of Lyon by consular decree. The Consuls had signed a Concordat with Rome in which they retained the power to name bishops and control the hierarchy in exchange for the reinstatement of the Catholic Church in France. The day after the decree Fesch came to speak with Maria at length about his new situation. He was not content.

'I am too young for such a charge,' he moaned, 'but the Consul wishes it. I do not wish to end up as an ecclesiastic or a priest.'

'This is surely a great honour for you,' Maria consoled him.

'Not an honour for me! I have not said mass in years! I knew religion, but I do not wish to return to it now. Whatever would I do in such a position, who have not been living the life of a priest for so long? Such posts carry a great weight of responsibility. I am not fit. I

am not ready. The obligations are tremendous and the bishopric frightens me.'

'Have you conveyed your feelings to the First Consul?'

'Of course I have. He argues that the clergy wants me, for they think no one better could reason with the Consul, could represent to him the needs of the Church and see that they receive their due. That as usual one must sacrifice oneself for essential things. I have resisted him for a long time, but he persecutes me, he will not let me refuse him. Each time we are alone he asks for the conclusion of this affair. He says I would be especially useful as Ambassador to Rome, but that to represent him I need to be in the Church. I am too young and merry for this rank at the present time! What am I to do?'

'I am so interested in your situation, but I cannot advise you. All appears out of your hands. I am truly sorry to see your distress.'

'You are always understanding of others when you have much uneasiness of your own. I am so overcome with my unhappiness I have forgotten to give you news from the legal counsellor I recommended to you, Monsieur Guieu. He says that Griffiths holds firm and refuses to respond to his requests for a meeting.'

'I know, they have come here. I have seen them both together. Monsieur Guieu had advised me that I should write a letter and try to get ownership of my work. When Mr. Griffiths entered, he had a very black look of a bad humour. I told him that it displeased me to use these methods, but I wished to have title to my work. He gave me no satisfaction of course. Monsieur Guieu says that I must be patient, that the contract was made by Griffiths and naturally is all in his favour.'

'I hope this lawyer will be useful to you.'

'As do I, but it is such an imbroglio. *Mr. Griffiths works so slowly it is prejudicial to the work. If I do not push his indolence, we shall never finish!'*

Only four days after this interview Fesch's fate was sealed. He had promised to go and see some pictures with Maria. He entered her apartment with the news.

'I shall be seeing pictures for the last time. The First Consul summoned me to come to his office in haste. When I arrived,

> Talleyrand was there. My nephew announced that I must prepare to
> leave for Lyon. I turned and looked at Talleyrand, who was gazing at
> me intensely. This persuaded me. I said, "I accept." So it is over. I
> am Archbishop of Lyon.'
>
> 'Oh no, it pains me to see you leave. You are so young to give
> yourself to such a life.'
>
> 'That may be, but there is nothing for it.'

Maria felt a great sadness in hearing of Fesch's appointment, for she knew their friendship would never be the same. There was great precipitation in the changes wrought by this ambitious family. There were rumours that Bonaparte wanted to be King or Emperor. Two days after Fesch's acceptance of his charge, the First Consul became Consul for Life, which showed these rumours close to reality. During the short time remaining before the new Archbishop's departure, Maria called more often to see him and his sister, Madame Bonaparte. Maria thought her an admirable woman with an innate wisdom and judgment that many of the family lacked. She was a small woman of about fifty with a dignified carriage. Her large dark eyes and black ringlets around the face were still testimony to her former reputation as the most beautiful woman of Corsica. There was something in the straightness of her strong nose and piercing look that suggested quiet strength, a Roman simplicity. Maria became fond of this unpretentious, serious woman, and her affinity seemed to be reciprocated as the two conversed in each woman's eccentric version of Italian. Laetizia could neither speak nor write French well and was criticised for the deficiency of her education. She was not an accomplished woman by society's measure. Maria valued her friendship for other reasons. Married at fourteen, widowed at thirty-four with eight children, Laetizia Bonaparte was a remarkable mother, a woman of inner strength and masculine courage. General Paoli must have recounted the story of her presence on the battlefield in Corsica, following her husband, climbing through savage mountain terrain, living in caves while pregnant with Napoleon. No one had more endurance, more spirit than this General's mother. A simple demeanour belied the hidden fire which sometimes kindled in her eyes and set her small mouth into a determined line. Each time Maria called at the impressive house in the Rue du Mont Blanc, she was received graciously in

Madame Bonaparte's sitting room, surrounded by Italian pictures and lavish furnishings of purple-striped satin and gold-coloured fringe. The entire house was a magnificent picture gallery for Fesch's collection. The spacious entrance hall and noble staircase were dominated by a colossal bust of Bonaparte in a helmet. The largest *salon* was fitted up with crimson velvet chairs and curtains, priceless carpets, and fine bronze candelabra of modern style. The original dining room had an airy cupola, painted as if incrusted with porphyry and other marbles.

One evening after Madame Bonaparte had served a beautiful collation of meat, fruit and coffee to Maria and a few friends, the hostess began to speak about religion. This was prompted by compliments on the very good supper.

'My dear Madame Cosway. I am pleased that you appreciate our little meal. I do not fear hell and do not think it necessary to fast or to go to mass for that matter. That is the stuff for priests. Now my brother does not wish to eat meat, well then I cannot furnish his cuisine, for I cannot bear such a regimen for too many days. Furthermore,' she warmed to her subject, 'in my opinion all are saved; I have not done wrong in any case. When I was a young girl I amused myself. I took pleasure in being beautiful and I do not think this is a good reason to be sent to Hell.'

'In any case, Madame, I assure you that no one less deserves punishment than you.' Withdrawing cautiously from this conversational terrain, Maria saw that Madame Bonaparte had not received the same education as she had. At this moment they were interrupted by the arrival of Mrs. Palmer, an English lady who had been wishing to be presented to Madame Bonaparte. The new guest was rather mad on the subject of Bonaparte, whom she considered a modern hero. Mrs. Palmer was so overcome at being presented to the mother of her idol, much like an audience with the Virgin Mother, that she began to weep.

'My dear lady, please do not be distressed. What is it?' Madame Bonaparte gently inquired.

' Pray pardon my emotion, Madame. It is my adoration for your son which overwhelms me. He is the saviour of this country, a model *for Europe. I am one of his most ardent admirers as you can judge and am most honoured to see at last his esteemed mother.'*

The banality of Mrs. Palmer's compliments in no way diminished the obvious maternal glow in Madame's face. This Englishwoman amused her more than any other guest and assured the success of the hostess's evening.

Fesch was consecrated Archbishop of Lyon in a great ceremony in Notre Dame on 15th August, also a public day of celebration of the First Consul's birthday. Maria stayed home, not wishing to go to an

60. Joseph, Cardinal Fesch, Napoleon's uncle and Maria Cosway's protector in France.

occasion too painful to watch. In the evening she did watch the fireworks from David's terrace, but they were not impressive. There was an immense and eerily silent crowd of people in the Tuileries. There were no outbursts of joy. No one spoke the name of Bonaparte. Faces expressed discontent rather than approval. The next day the Archbishop appeared at her door in the Hotel de Marigny. He had a new air of importance, rather than devotion, and was one of the most elegant priests she had ever seen. Dressed in an ecclesiastical black coat and knee breeches, he had recently cut and powdered his hair, now rolled into a curl behind as an *abbé*. A white silk handkerchief round the neck partially hid a gold crucifix. Stockings of bright purple, knee and shoe buckles of gold gave dazzling *éclat* to the fashionable cleric. Upon entering, he announced that Maria was the first person he had seen after his consecration.

'I am honoured, Your Excellency?'

'You needn't address me thus. I am too young for this charge and have neither the talent nor the capacity for it.'

'Perhaps you are now required to rely on Our Lord.'

'I have no experience for that. If I think of my past it is with fear or regret. You know that I swore an oath to the Constitutional government in '91? How shall I make peace with all the clergy who refused the oath? Yet I must have confidence in the future or I cannot face it.'

'That is certain. And you shall have all the worldly power of the government behind you.'

'The government! From my prospect, this is not an assurance. The First Consul is badly advised. He advances too rapidly in all, as he did with me. It was evident yesterday that the fête was not marked by joy for him.'

Fesch's consecration soon bolstered his confidence. A few days later they continued their conversation about his plans for Lyon. He came with a hopeful announcement:

'I have been reflecting on your situation. In my new position I should be able to give you the means to establish a school.' Seeing Maria's surprise, he continued, 'Why are you astonished? Has not that been another of your ambitions?'

'Yes, we have talked of that, but after my failure in London I no longer considered that possible?'

'Now you must consider it possible. Reflect on my suggestion. I have plans for Lyon. I may even re-establish the Jesuits. It was after their abolition that the decadence of religion began. Voltaire and the King of Prussia knew well that they were the corner stone, so they attacked them. Of course, there were abuses and great ones, but they also produced great men and an excellent method of education. If I am able to bring back the Jesuits, I can certainly give you a school.'

The new Archbishop's suggestion stirred many deep memories of Luigina, of a buried desire to teach other little girls as she had her daughter. All this had been given up. Would it be possible to succeed in education? She seemed to be failing in art.

The last days of August and early September brought blistering heat. The temperature approached ninety-two degrees, bringing to mind the fine warm days of September spent with Jefferson. Maria's days were now passed with less pleasant visitors from England. Many members of the Royal Academy, attracted by the Salon, descended upon her hotel. Farington and Fuseli arrived together. Mr. and Mrs. Flaxman and Thomas Daniell were also her neighbours. Benjamin West, the Royal Academy President, arrived in late August. When Maria informed David of his arrival, she was immediately asked to carry a dinner invitation to West. This task made her witness to a pathetic scene; she confided to her journal that she never saw anyone more stupid or weak than the Academy President. Debating the great question of the etiquette to follow between artists, he spouted a quantity of foolishness painful to hear. His vanity had elevated the dinner invitation to a question of state, in which the interest and honour of the English nation were at stake. Having learned to curb the vivacity of her exchanges with Academy members, she kept her opinions to herself. She endeavoured to be of service to them and re-establish courtesy on all sides. With this aim she conducted West and the Opies to see the collections of Lucien Bonaparte, Collot, and Fesch. By chance this enabled the English artists to witness a great event in the Archbishop's life. He greeted them at the top of a magnificent staircase with a paper in hand. Taking Maria aside, he let her read the contents of the letter which informed him that he was soon to be a Cardinal. His reaction was to laugh, whether with satisfaction or merriment no one was certain. He was certainly pleased with the honour of it and seemed to be adjusting well to his new life. Later that day Maria returned to find him with the Archbishop of Meaux. They were comparing their rings like children with new playthings. The Archbishop had a splendid emerald presented to him by the First Consul and the Cardinal a sapphire, the gift of Joseph Bonaparte.

About this time Fesch began to speak more often of General Paoli. He and his sister still had traces of affection for *il babbo*, the fond name for the General on the lips of all Corsicans. This was a strong and intimate title for a national leader. It did not mean 'father' but 'daddy', the word of a small child. The tragic rupture between Paoli and the Bonapartes was caused by their conflicting views on France. The Paolists were horrified by Robespierre and the illiberal Terror while Laetizia was convinced that her children's future lay with France, no matter what follies were committed in Paris. The new Archbishop once suggested that Maria could have served as an intermediary between Paoli and the Bonapartes in 1793.

> *'If we had known in Corsica that you were in Genoa nearby and that you were the friend of Paoli, we would have called you to soften his heart in those hard moments.'*
>
> *'I don't know if I would have succeeded, but I would have certainly tried to prevent what happened.'*

This idea of reconciliation germinated for a month. Late in August Fesch came to tell Maria that Bonaparte had also been speaking of the General.

> *'Today when I was with the First Consul I thought perhaps you could be the instrument of his return. You could write to him in a way that could reach him. Would you be willing to do that?'*
>
> *'Oh yes, what a pleasure that would be for me if I could reconcile him with your family and his people! I shall take up my pen at once.'*

The next day Fesch approved what Maria had written, but she had doubts about what the General would do. It seemed to her that the offer of French citizenship struck a false note. General Paoli must have agreed with her for his immediate reply was a polite restatement of his position that:

> the French government of '93 continues and will never cease to inspire me with horror...my dear *comare*, let's leave this subject...which reminds me of scenes I would forget. I should only think of the other world and become a citizen of heaven...

The Archbishop was not pleased when he returned Paoli's letter to Maria.

> *'I have come from reading this to the First Consul.' He waved the note at her. 'He agrees with me that the old man was foolish to refuse our offer.'*
>
> *'It seems to me that he is true to his principles. He says that he*

could have accepted the aid of the Bourbon princes and been named King, but he refused.'

'Running to the English! That was hardly better.'

'He thought their constitutional government closer to his ideals. Then the English betrayed him by neglect.'

'And Corsica was re-united to France where she belongs and where is Paoli? Again a poor exile depending on the English for charity. The First Consul says he must have fallen into infancy.'

'You are unjust, sir! I think he shows character, pride and a noble and honourable resistance. I shall always cherish the friendship of such a man.'

'Of course, well I also bring news of a personal nature: the lawyer Guieu told me that Griffiths resists all your demands.'

'I met Sir Thomas Erskine in the Gallery this morning. He said – what I have learned from bitter experience – that the greatest necessity is to know well the character of persons with whom one enters into business affairs. Lord Erskine is a fine advocate. He advises not to sue Mr. Griffiths. Is it possible that I have such misfortune! Now I hear on all sides of the bad character of my associate.'

To this expression of despair, the Cardinal's only response was a pensive glance at the huge sapphire on his hand.

Maria's affairs did not improve in the autumn. Indeed, they worsened. She saw less of Fesch and more of the English artists. New friends also appeared on the scene to distract her: the Princess Holstein from Berlin, who wished to know her, and Lord and Lady Oxford from London were frequent companions. Lady Oxford was much like the French: she had very flattering manners, was always praising Maria effusively. She said that Lord Erskine spoke with great eloquence of Maria and lifted her to the stars because of her talents. All this talk was not helpful, for the English weren't buying her works. She had begun a smaller series of prints of Gallery pictures at a low price, but no one wanted them. Her picture Eros was praised, but not purchased by the Bonapartes as she had hoped. Fesch, her protector, had become more distant. As soon as he was elevated, the Archbishop had the same manners as the great – aloof. She had asked him several things and he didn't accord her a single one.

Madame Mère remained gracious although her household had more servants, more luxury, more etiquette. This formality diminished the pleasure of seeing her.

The Archbishop now called about once a month to have news. In October the only serious conversation they had was in his carriage on the way to Lady Oxford. He took her by the hand and asked how were her affairs with Griffiths.

'*Everyone advises me to abandon my work. Erskine took me aside the other evening at Miss Williams' conversation and counselled me to give it up. This made my blood cold, to think of abandoning a year's work so callously. It is like abandoning my child. Law and lawyers serve for nothing. I also had a long conversation with Mr. Farington before his departure for London. He gave me further proofs of the unsuitability of Griffiths. He told me that he was the son of a hop merchant, a speculator, a man of abilities but irregular. This I could have well confirmed without his advice. He promised me a third of all profits and after twelve months of work, I have yet to see one shilling! Oh, all my plans, voyages, and hopes to do many things have evaporated. My great fear is that my husband will ask me to return and in this case I shall be obliged to go. Perhaps I could apply for a post in* Madame Mère's *household. I shall do anything to avoid returning to London.*'

'*It is my opinion that you should stay in France and the best course is to give your talents to education. In this I shall aid you as best I can.*'

'*If that should be the means for fixing my residence here, so be it, but I am not yet prepared to give up my work on the Gallery.*'

Maria's wariness of Fesch's protection persuaded her that she must persevere as an artist. At times she felt that he witnessed all her difficulties and did nothing, not the smallest thing. There was much talk, but nothing else. He was immersed in the greatness of being a Cardinal and going to Rome. The eve of his departure for Lyon, he came to bid her goodbye.

'*Remember me,*' *he said,* '*as your best friend.*'

'*I shall and you must be assured of my friendship and esteem.*'

'I promise to write to you and let you know what the situation is in Lyon for the project of your school. I shall do everything possible for its success. In the meantime you should go ahead with your work here.'

'Yes, which of these things will succeed I don't know, but God will have me do his will.'

Maria was not leaving all to God's will. Still desperate to have her work on the Louvre gain the recognition it deserved, she placed her hope in Vivant Denon, a friend of more than fifteen years – first in the Trudaines' salon in Paris and then in the circle of Signora Marini (now the Contessa d'Albrizzi) in Venice. When Denon came one November evening to say that he had been named Director General of all that concerned the arts in Paris, it seemed a stroke of good fortune for both of them. Only a week passed before he disabused her of that notion, for he explained that he could only encourage works undertaken under the protection of the government. She appreciated his sincerity, which was more valuable than the beautiful promises and adulation she received elsewhere. Apparently she did not realise that he was the government's representative and could probably have done more than he did. By early December – at a point of total discouragement – she made a visit to the Sisters of Charity, the only religious order that had survived the Revolution without interruption.

As she climbed the smooth stone stairs and looked through the open door of the Refectory she saw that the tables were laid. All was serenity, perfect order. Suddenly she began to cry. She continued weeping in the Mother Superior's room for some time. These strong feelings puzzled her. It was not that she wished to be in a convent. She felt no vocation, but had just reached a very lonely and low point.

A last desperate idea to save her work came to her just before Christmas. She had not seen Madame Bonaparte for three weeks when she went to call one Sunday morning. Laetizia welcomed her very kindly. Maria thought it wise to make oneself scarce to receive such gracious reproaches for absence. She asked Madame Bonaparte if she could arrange for Lucien Bonaparte to receive her. On a cold Christmas Day Maria received word that she could call on Lucien any day at two o'clock, which she did on the 26th. Lucien Bonaparte had purchased the elegant house of one of Louis XVI's ministers, the Hotel de Brienne on the rue Saint Dominique. There he had assembled a small but choice collection of pictures. The works of Ruysdael, Veronese, Correggio, Titian, Claude and Guido turned an otherwise unremarkable set of ground floor apartments into a rich picture gallery. Mixed in with the masterpieces were many bad pictures too. He and his Uncle Fesch had been cheated by unscrupulous dealers. On several occasions Maria had shown the collection to English visitors but had no time to gaze on this day. She left Mrs. Hunter, a wealthy English friend who accompanied her, to look at the pictures while Maria was ushered to Lucien's study.

He rose from behind a massive writing table and came forward to greet her with a preoccupied look, not quite meeting her eye.

'Good day, Madame, my mother tells me you have urgently wished to see me.' He motioned toward two modern armchairs by the fire. As they sat down he placed his hands firmly on his chair's gilded sphinx heads which glowed in the firelight. Maria felt six pair of eyes staring at her.

'Yes, sir, I needed much courage to come and trouble you because I was persuaded that I was not in your good graces. You may remember that you had placed your signature in the subscription book for my work on the Louvre. 'Tis true that the first plates were done rapidly and did not give a faithful impression of the finished work. As I intend to show all the pictures in the Grand Gallery and their placement, anyone possessing the complete series would have a priceless record of the finest collection in Europe. I have taken into account the just criticisms of the work. For this reason I was exceedingly displeased that you withdrew your name from the subscription list at the moment that I had arranged to improve it. I come to beg you to reconsider your decision. I need not remind you that the patronage of a collector such as yourself is indispensable to the success of my endeavour.'

Maria paused to take in air after expelling this rapid speech. Before she could continue with further arguments, her host replied, 'Madame Cosway, I shall not waste your time. As you have come directly to the heart of your matter, so shall I. I saw the examples of your work, and I thought it so bad that frankly, Madame, I did not wish to admit it into my library. I do not know what else I can say.'

The appalling frankness, if not rudeness, of Monsieur Bonaparte provoked a physical shock in Maria. She could only sputter,

'Oh, I see. Please forgive me, sir, for this intrusion. I feel confused that I have importuned you. I beg you to pardon my boldness. I see that we can have no more business so I shall take my leave.' She rose to go.

'I regret to give you this news.' He rose as well, adding with a slight point of remorse, 'Perhaps it would have been better to have continued my subscription.'

'I should not wish to impose anything you deemed unworthy, sir. I bid you goodbye.' Curtseying hurriedly, she left the room and descended the stairs in a torrent of feeling. She found Mrs. Hunter fulminating with disappointment at not seeing the First Consul's brother, but Maria was in no mood to console her.

The final touch to this black day was Maria's unhappy comparison of her life with that of Madame Vigée Lebrun, when the famous artist came to fetch Maria in her carriage for a planned dinner with the Princess Holstein. Maria gave in to envy of the beautiful house, studios, riches, and pretensions of this artist whom the Princess treated with greater respect, although no etiquette required it. As for artistic merit, Madame Lebrun's graciousness toward Maria forbade her saying what she thought of her friend's art. Maria thought Lebrun's portrait of the little Prince Lubomirski was weak, poor, common, badly drawn, not inventive. She ruminated that if only she had a studio she could paint a picture superior to all Madame Lebrun had ever done.

The year 1802 closed with this entry in Maria's journal:

This year has been monotonous without many opportunities because provoked by Griffiths. Therefore if last year the danger was to have loved too much, in this it was the danger of hatred. The first however is more dangerous for me than the second…I need something extraordinary to make me hate.

It is not known whom Maria loved too much or whether this love was linked to her absence from London. Whoever it was, on 1st January 1803

Maria dined at home alone. She could not help thinking that knowing so many, no one invited her to dinner or showed her the least attention. The next day she went to see Dutertre's drawings of Egypt and then to the top of the Panthéon to see the view of Paris. The cap of liberty had been placed at the top of the cupola. While surveying all the modern buildings spread out below, she thought how we are small! Nothing is comparable to what the Egyptians did. And the cap of liberty? It should be replaced by the statue of Fame. All that was done by the Revolution and by Bonaparte was done for her, not for liberty! Below are the tombs of great men, but where there should be kings, they had Voltaire and Rousseau.

Many of the English visitors in Paris spoke of the brilliant winter season, meaning receptions, balls, dinners. Maria's winter was bleak. Feeling abandoned by the ruling family and faced with failure as an artist, she was at her lowest. Then small miracles began to happen. The first was a letter from Fesch, received a week after the New Year. He wrote that hospitals and schools were being created in Lyon, that the only lack was a school for the daughters of the rich, that

> you are going to direct it. In the present week I am going to visit
> an old convent. The city is going to rent it…it is well situated,
> spacious, needs right away 10,000 in repairs…. At your arrival
> you will find 40 young girls ready to keep you company.

Maria's joy was inexpressible and she was not a little surprised that Fesch had so quickly fulfilled his promise after breaking many others. She found it extraordinary that during the days of Epiphany she had this calling.

The second miracle occurred on the feast day of St. François de Sales. She received a letter from Richard giving his entire approval for her educational enterprise. She hastened to write the news to Fesch:

> Monseigneur,
>
> It seems to me that the will of God has been pronounced in a
> positive way…. Yesterday, the day of St. François de Sales, I
> received the letter from my husband who approves, permits, and
> encourages me in my enterprise, but asks however, that he be

given certain information more precise, what are the conditions and the place, that I must be prudent and without precipitation. But that he is not opposed to a work done for the glory of God for the benefit of the people and on a stable footing. That seems to me a miracle that he agrees with the idea to make a house of education. It surprises me and animates so much that I feel a lion.

For the present it remains for me to break with Griffiths…he doesn't wish to continue, but he doesn't wish to let go. If he tries to force me or to sue me, I don't know how I will get out. My husband told me to do nothing for others, but only what pleases me and could please him and he will pay all my expenses…

If God permits me to reach what I have always desired, I will take that like good fortune and am happier to have become a bad painter and worse engraver…

Please continue to give me your blessings. M.C.

I rely on your more than ever. It must really be God's will. Look at the conduct of my husband. It took a miracle he was so opposed to our religion…. . My friend, General Paoli, writes me no more. I have thus lost him for the first time, after having kept him in all circumstances.

General Paoli did disapprove of her desire to remain in France. He later admonished her:

What demon, my dear *comare*, persuaded you to go to Lyon to direct a school for young girls. You will lose patience. Return to your husband in London. The humours of a husband are always easier to bear and better rewarded that those of young girls shut up against their will.

Events unfolded rapidly. At the end of February, the now Cardinal Fesch returned to Paris and came to announce that her nomination to Lyon was definite. She was so happy that night that she did not sleep. In March the difficulties with Griffiths came to a head. She had continued to work on the plates and after delivering a series, received a note from her partner couched in pretty words, asking her to do as many she could. Inflamed by his manipulations, she wrote a resentful note, saying that she no longer wished to work for nothing. He chose to interpret this as a refusal. The next day she received a letter from his lawyer suing her for £30,000 for stopping the work. A little frightened, she went to see Fesch who indifferently replied that he couldn't do anything, that she should see Mr. Guieu, the legal counsellor. Fesch's coldness saddened her. When she did see Guieu, as a true lawyer, he gave himself all the importance of his perfidious profession. They made an appointment with Griffiths for the next day. When they were all together, Maria began to speak. She acknowledged that she had written in a moment of vivacity without reflecting on the weight of each word. Her legal counsellor said that it appeared to him that this quarrel could never arrive at an accord of the parties and it would be better to dissolve the obligation. Griffiths said that he would not have difficulty with that. Maria suggested that she would be happy if a new agreement could be written in a few words. They both signed and had their liberty. This seemed to her the last miracle of grace. She didn't think it possible without Griffiths insisting on reparations. She lost all her work of a year and a half with all her expenses, and had nothing but travail and vexation, but she felt so happy to have finished with the man that she could only feel consolation and ate little at dinner, revelling in her satisfaction.

Maria's break with Griffiths coincided almost exactly with a much more important rupture. During a reception for foreign ministers at Malmaison, Bonaparte threatened the English Ambassador, Lord Whitworth, questioning him about British engagements over Malta. Before all the assembly, he snarled, saying that the English lacked good faith, that after fifteen years of war, they wanted fifteen more. That they would have them. Misfortune to him who broke friendship; the vengeance of God and men would fall on him who was the cause of death of thousands of persons! The ambassador was taken by surprise by this attack, but conducted himself with dignity and presence of mind. He could not reply without instructions from the Cabinet. Those who were near Bonaparte told Maria that his face had an indescribable expression of disdain, anger, scorn. This news was the subject of conversations all over the city. Usually these matters were discussed in cabinets, but Bonaparte broke with all the rules, wishing to attack the English publicly before the face of all Europe. Now talk of war was heard everywhere.

During the month of April the English began to leave or make their preparations for departure. Maria continued to finish sketches in the Gallery while beginning her own packing. The Cardinal charged her with helping him select and pack all the pictures that he wished to take with him to Lyon. She spent days in his large storehouse or in the rue Mont Blanc discussing art with him and taking the full measure of his deep passion for pictures. Early in the month she had received and answered a formal invitation from the three mayors of Lyon, each governing a separate district of the city, to direct a school for young girls. There was now no doubt that she was going to pursue an activity as close to her heart as painting. The hope of succeeding in education where she had miserably failed in art revived her joy. The Cardinal had assigned one of his vicars-general, Abbé Jauffret, to assist her. Much to her surprise, she discovered that the Abbé's plan for girls' education corresponded almost exactly to her ideas, which boded well for their harmonious co-operation.

The first days of May the war fever mounted. Everyone was in suspense and great wagers were made for and against its outbreak. In spite of this possibility, Maria calmly continued her preparations and began to bid goodbye to her friends. Monsieur Denon called and said that he was very happy with her institution. He kindly parted with one of the treasures he had brought back from Egypt – a pair of small figures carved with hieroglyphs – which gave her immense pleasure. The last time she went to the Gallery to finish colouring Raphael's *Transfiguration*, she met him again. Seeing that she was feeling truly sad, he took her hand and said, 'Poor child!' He understood what her fiasco with Griffiths had cost. She was happier with this man than almost all the others she was leaving.

When Maria went to take leave of Madame de Corny, she was warned that there would be nuns in Lyon who would see her with envy. Maria could not believe that Fesch was not esteemed by all and found these misgivings unwarranted. Of all her acquaintance it pained her most to leave Madame de Corny and another Frenchwoman, Madame de

Rocquefeuille, whose kindness and good manners set her apart from all those of the new system.

To mark her friendship for Madame Bonaparte, Maria prepared a little farewell gift. The day she brought it, Fesch took her aside for a long conversation about his new pictures and about politics. He often repeated what Bonaparte had said to him: that the French were an ungrateful people, just waiting for him to bring back the Bourbons, which he would never do, that the English were proud, but at least they had character. Bonaparte heaped the most scorn on his allies, who smiled and became friends out of fear, but were ready to betray at any moment, the vipers! Maria was relieved when the Cardinal changed the subject to one where she could be useful. He consulted her on the gift that he wished to take to the Pope. After only a few months as Archbishop of Lyon, fewer still as Cardinal, the First Consul had now decided that Fesch was to be Ambassador to the Papal Court. As often happens with newly elevated persons, his resistance to this latest honour was not – as in previous months – based on his feelings of inadequacy, but on his concern that the post was not of sufficient rank!

LAETITIA BONAPARTE.

Fesch now thought that the Ambassadorship to Rome was beneath him, but as always he bowed to his nephew's will. Faced with the choice of a diplomatic gift for the Pope he asked Maria's opinion.

'What do you think of taking two pictures from the French School?'
'Your Eminence, I would be opposed to this choice. Imagine the

Italians' feelings! Giving them French pictures would touch a wound still most sensitive. All their capital *pictures have been carried away by the French! They must be thinking how to replace them. I would not give them the least memory of this as they would compare these inferior pictures with those lost.'*

'Oh, well, yes, that could be their sentiment. Well, what then?'

'There is a fine cup decorated with cameos and precious work coming up for sale, also a bas relief of the Apotheosis of Homer, or some engravings of Italian palaces – but these last may have been sold. The gift must be well adapted and well chosen. That is more important than the value. I think the best choice would be something from the French manufacture of porcelain or tapestry.'

'Perhaps, yes, I shall investigate that possibility.'

'And now pray may I be excused? I have a gift of my own to present to your sister.' Maria went up to Madame's apartments where she found her standing. This gave her the occasion to present her gift as she wished. It was a little belt that she had had made of steel, then the fashion. As she put it around Madame Bonaparte, Maria said, *'I wish to show you my desire to be attached to you for life.'*

'My dear, dear Madame Cosway, what trouble you have taken. I am amazed at your kindness. I am delighted. What can I do for you? Please tell me, what can I do for you?'

'Nothing, Madame. I wanted to show you my devotion before leaving.'

'My dear, you had no need to use this method. I shall always be attached to you. Please tell me what I can do for you.'

'You are too gracious, Madame. Your grace is more precious because so rare. I wished you to know how sensible I am of your qualities.'

'I cannot express how happy your little gift makes me, Madame. I shall always remember you.'

The great and gracious mean well and can be most sincere, but the little steel chains proved fragile in the coming years.

The day after Maria's last interview with Madame Bonaparte, a courier arrived half-dead from London after making the journey in twenty-five hours. He arrived with news of war. Lord Whitworth, the Ambassador left two days later. Before his departure Maria proposed to him the purchase of her picture of Eros, but received a polite written refusal. Within a week, 14th May precisely, Abbé Jauffret and his servant, Maria and her maid, set out by post chaise for Lyon. She had never left a place with less displeasure. Her future now lay in an unknown provincial city in a country at war with her own.

VUE DE LA VILLE DE LYON

17

Lyon

1803-1811

'... Here I have been two years & my establishment goes on extremely well and have the consolation of being mother of 60 children. Nothing is more interesting than rendering oneself useful to our fellow creatures & what better way than that of making their education! Lyons, 10th of October 1805.'

Maria Cosway to Thomas Jefferson

'Madame Cosway, Madame Cosway,' the maid spoke softly, 'you have a visitor, the mother of one of your girls. Please forgive my disturbing you, but she is most insistent.'

'At seven o'clock in the morning? Whatever has possessed her? It must be of an urgent nature to call at this hour. Give me a few minutes…please show her to my study.'

'Yes, Madame.'

On a warm July morning in 1806 strong rays of sun threw blocks of light onto the bedroom floor as the young servant opened the shutters. This early call did not disturb Maria; she was used to continual interruptions, consequent to the direction of an establishment harbouring forty to sixty young girls from five to twelve years old. Throwing a dressing gown of grey watered silk around her shoulders, she could have entertained the thought that it was far too elegant for her present station. So was most of her wardrobe, which for reasons of economy she now attempted to render plain. Frocks she would have embellished were now reduced to the simplicity befitting the example of a schoolmistress.

A haggard young woman with red-rimmed eyes waited in Madame Cosway's study. Rebel wisps of hair escaped from the hairpins of her tight chignon.

'Oh, Madame Cosway, please forgive my intrusion, but I could not wait another hour. I have not slept this night and have been weeping over the news.'

'My dear Madame de Feynoul, please sit down.' Maria took the young woman's hands: 'What has caused this upset?'

'Madame, the news has gone about Lyon that the City no longer wants your establishment, that the Mayor no longer wishes to pay for your school. I know what you have given to Suzanne and the other girls. Where will we go for such an education as you provide? There is nothing comparable in Lyon, nothing outside of Paris! Suzanne must not lose you, Please tell me that this rumour is false!'

'I shall tell you at once that I know nothing of this. Please be calm and don't distress yourself further. I shall find out the truth of the report. Now you must go home, be comforted, and rest. Don't be agitated over gossip.'

It was easy to calm her fears, but less so Maria's own anxiety. As soon as the young woman was comforted enough to return home, Maria prepared to make a morning call. It was to one of her staunchest defenders, other than Cardinal Fesch, Etienne Mayeuvre de Champvieux. Monsieur Mayeuvre, of an old and noble family, was one of the few connoisseurs of the region, a man of taste and enlightenment. He promoted the arts with sincere enthusiasm, having directed the School of Flower Drawing, whose graduates enriched the local silk industry. A family fortune, built on commerce, had been used to form one of the few choice collections of paintings in Lyon. Maria's heart held a special place of gratitude for him. A friend of Madame de Corny, he had welcomed her kindly and had been the first of the Lyonnais to invite her to his country house at St. Germain au Mont d'Or. From the beginning, Monsieur Mayeuvre, whom the Prefect had named to a supervisory board for education, had seen the value of her educational system. He was also a member of the Municipal Council and could easily put her fears to rest.

It was a short walk across the Place des Terreaux from the ancient Benedictine abbey, St. Pierre, which housed Madame Cosway's school, to the elegant hotel of Mayeuvre de Champvieux. She could see the steep hill of Fourvière, dominating the terracotta roofs of the old city, nestled below on the banks of the Saône. She had been prepared to love this city. Its southern architecture in dusty pastels spoke to her of Italy. Its silk weavers had learned their craft from Venetians and Genoans after years of trade across the Alps. Its climate was warmer and air purer than the gloomy cities to the North. But the Lyonnais! What to make of them? Although quite a few had befriended her, she never overcame their general prejudice against the *anglaise*. Of course, the country was at war with England and orders had been given to hold Englishmen hostage in Paris. But Maria had trusted in the influence of the Cardinal to overcome provincial resistance. Another ally was the Prefect, Jean-François Bureaux de Pusy. When Madame Cosway's school opened in November 1803, the Prefect's daughter and the child of one of his domestics were her first two pupils. The City government had also supported her. Until the last few months the city had been governed by three mayors, one for each of three districts, West, East, and South. The Mayor of the North, Jean-Marie Parent, had been frank and sincere from the first, giving the new headmistress concise and gossipy portraits of the local gentry. The other two, Sain-Rousset and Bernard-Charpieux, professed much enthusiasm for her school, but were less helpful, the latter working against her behind her back. But now there was only one mayor, Nicolas Fay, Comte de Sathonay. A member of the closed circle of wealthy merchants who had ruled Lyon for centuries, Sathonay came from the class who should have appreciated the value of feminine education. But from the moment of his nomination he manifested hostility to Maria's enterprise. Unmarried and said to be the richest man in Lyon, he was concerned only with finances, budgets, economies. The previous March she had given the city a detailed financial report, which showed a slight surplus in her accounts. The municipal council reproached her for not having more charity pupils. She explained that it was the tuition of boarders that enabled the school to balance its accounts, and she had no more room for boarding students until the City found a suitable permanent location for the school. When the fees were lowered to attract more children or non-paying pupils were accepted, the City Council balked at reimbursing the deficits and then criticised her plan for not respecting the principle of equality. Why could these merchants not see the value of the educational system being offered to them? At least Monsieur Mayeuvre was sympathetic to her cause.

Mounting the staircase of his handsome house in the rue Puits-Gaillot, Maria was relieved that it had been cleaned. So many of the entries in this city reminded her of the filthy ones in Rome, although they were not quite so foul. Peeling plaster, scuffs and scratches, years of encrusted dust were found in the best homes. The servants were careless because of the indifference and indolence of their masters. The same servant would one moment be a coachman and the next serve at table dressed as a peasant with no stockings. The drawing room of Monsieur Mayeuvre was an exception to the general disorder. When she entered, he rose to greet her.

'Madame, it is always a pleasure to see you, but I fear that the object of your visit is not a happy one. Has news of the City Council's deliberations reached you?'

'Sir, I am not certain if the news I have originates with them. Early this morning one of the mothers of my children came to me in tears, having heard that the City no longer accepted me. Is this true?

You are now the only friend I have on the Council; the others being new.'

'It is painful to tell you but the Mayor's report shamefully recommended that the City had no legal obligation towards you, that it would be too costly to renovate the convent of the Bleus Celestes *for you, and that you must leave St. Pierre, which is destined for other uses. Despite the Prefect's request that another building be found and that the City fulfil its promises to you, the Mayor prevailed.'*

'Then it is worse than I thought.' She slumped back in her chair. 'I knew that they wished me to leave the Abbey, but could not imagine that after inviting me to Lyon with the promise of providing all the means for a school, I would be so rudely treated.'

'Madame, I earnestly tried to make them hear reason, but the general attitude was one of coldness, indifference. I proposed that they read the favourable reports made earlier. This was rejected. Then I asked that they look at how the money was used for your establishment. Again rejected. Totally alone, I pleaded with zeal your case, but they scarcely listened and when I spoke of the patronage of His Eminence, Cardinal Fesch, they laughed. Then I became so indignant that I couldn't speak.'

'You are good, sir, but the Mayor does not like priests or nuns and his head I cannot change.'

'Yes, but he should be a gentleman. When he observed that your apartment at St. Pierre was needed, I said that at least they should give you time to find another and that they could not put you in the street like a...well, you know. It was unworthy of them all.'

'What a disgraceful manner! My first reaction is to leave a country where the authorities are so decided against me.'

'I can well understand your feelings, but what shame for us to lose you and the benefits you bring to our children.'

'I shall go to the Prefect and ask his advice and of course write to His Eminence at once. It seems impossible to me that the Mayor doesn't see the utility and the beauty of my plan.'

'Yes, it is a mystery. I am truly sorry, dear Madame Cosway, that I could do nothing more, but I was alone to defend you. Do go to see the Prefect.'

'I shall do so immediately. All my gratitude, dear sir, for your faithful support. Please forgive this call so early in the day. I shall let you know what can be done and leave the rest to Providence. Good day, Sir.'

Maria crossed the street and went at once to the office of Monsieur Bureaux de Pusy. The Prefect received her as cordially as ever, but could only advise that she wait for the decision from the Minister of the Interior on the petition to recognise her school officially as an institution for daughters of members of the Legion of Honour. The Prefect was a good man, but wished to please everyone and therefore did not strongly defend any cause. A liberal aristocrat and military man, he had spent five years in an Austrian prison with General de Lafayette and then emigrated to America. After finding favour with Napoleon, he had been named Prefect of the Rhone Department where he was happy to lead a quieter life. When Maria arrived in Lyon the Prefect and his wife welcomed her into their society. They had taken her to visit the factories of the great silk merchants to see how superb satins and velvets were made. As a parent the Prefect seemed satisfied with the education his daughter received, but did not fully appreciate its quality. Nor did most of the citizens.

Lyon was a test of humility. After her first lonely week there, three years earlier, Maria noted in her diary:

> Mayor told me that in society all who had seen me were very happy and that it was said that I was just the teacher that they needed.... Truly it is curious that after having passed my life in the greatest society I come here to pass an examination! It's not important...it is enough that it finishes well.

The seeds of the problems with the City Council lay in an incompatibility with the citizenry that Maria came to see after bitter experience. As she later wrote to the Cardinal,

> ...in this country they don't need an elevated education which is necessary for a certain rank of lady destined for the *'grand monde'*

as France is now becoming. These merchants, rich as they are, are limited in their principles of domestic education, wishing wives or daughters who are useful in commerce, in their correspondence or in the supervision of children, without seeing the need to advance one step beyond their ancestors…'

Although she wished to furnish a free education to the daughters of the poor and train domestics, as well as future ladies of fashion, Maria knew that her system was better for the higher ranks than for the poor. To accommodate the various stations of her charges, she devised a plan offering three sorts of education. All three included religious instruction, reading, writing, French grammar, and arithmetic, but the First Class at the higher tuition of 1,200 francs also furnished an education approaching that of young men, including English, Italian, geography, ancient and modern history, physics, natural history, botany, astronomy, drawing and painting. To round out the young ladies' accomplishments Maria also taught vocal music, piano, harp, embroidery, sewing, flower and lace-making. The Second Class was destined for girls of the middle to lower orders who wished to become schoolmistresses or wives of shopkeepers. From these ranks she tried to identify those girls with talents that could be nurtured, giving them a better education and better profession than their circumstances would predict. Finally, the Third Class was for poor children destined to become domestic servants. To the basic course of study was added weights and measures, sewing, laundry and ironing, and general housekeeping. The city fathers may have been wealthy traders and lawyers, but some had liberal principles in the name of which they attacked her system of three classes. Even the Cardinal interpreted the desire to give a complete education to girls as frivolous worldliness. From Rome he dispensed a fearful scolding by letter on this point:

I don't understand how you can think of raising ladies of the Court and not mothers…you should animate [them] with simple Christian virtues, not instruct them in the sublime and always unhappy principles of grandeur and worldliness.… . The grandest ladies are those of whom one never speaks, that live unknown by the world.… . No instruction is better than that of a mother…

29t

MAISON D'EDUCATION

POUR LES JEUNES DEMOISELLES,

Etablie par la Commune de Lyon, et dirigée par Madame COSWAY, *dans les Bâtimens du Conservatoire des Arts (ci-devant St-Pierre).*

LES Magistrats de Lyon, désirant que toutes les classes de citoyens trouvassent dans cet Etablissement les moyens de donner à leurs filles le genre d'instruction qui peut leur convenir, ont, d'accord avec madame Cosway, divisé les élèves en deux classes, dont l'enseignement est organisé ainsi qu'il suit :

PREMIÈRE CLASSE.

L'Instruction religieuse, la Lecture, l'Ecriture ; les Langues Française, Anglaise et Italienne ; l'Arithmétique, la Géographie, l'Histoire ancienne et moderne ; les élémens de Physique, d'Histoire naturelle, de Botanique, d'Astronomie ; le Dessin, la Peinture, la Musique vocale, le Piano, la Harpe.

Le travail des divers ouvrages à l'aiguille, de la broderie, de la couture ; la fabrication des fleurs artificielles, le raccommodage de la dentelle, et généralement tous les ouvrages qui peuvent être utiles aux femmes dans leur application à l'économie domestique.

Le prix de la Pension pour la première classe, est de 1,200 fr.

O o 2

61. Description of Maria Cosway's House of Education for Young Ladies from the Almanach de Lyon *of 1805.*

Maria did not disagree with the Cardinal that the object of feminine education was to produce good mothers, but she still intended to give them every attribute of mind and grace of spirit that an intelligent and cultivated woman should have.

Madame Cosway's system was worthy of comparison with other well-known educators of women. She had no intimate knowledge of the celebrated St. Cyr, founded by Madame de Maintenon, but had studied at first hand the methods of Madame Campan — who educated Hortense de Beauharnais and won the Emperor's favour — and Madame de Genlis, Governess of the Duke of Orleans. Before leaving Paris Maria spent several evenings with Madame de Genlis, withdrawn in quiet retirement in the Arsenal. The former tutor of the Orleans children graciously recounted her original methods of forming the young princes into honest republicans. Although lip service was given to religion by readings in the New Testament, her favourite themes were taken from ancient history. Medals of the Roman Emperors with names and dates were displayed around her room. The children read Cincinnatus, Epictetus, Marcus Aurelius and then viewed scenes of ancient history by means of an ingenious magic lantern, commissioned by their governess. Following the modern ideas of Rousseau, the princes did manual work, learned carpentry, carried wood and water, ate frugally and slept on tables with thin mattresses.

While Maria admired Madame de Genlis's originality, she followed the tradition of Madame de Maintenon and Madame Campan, the former Lady of the Bedchamber of Marie-Antoinette. When she visited the latter lady's school in St. Germain-en-Laye, her first impression, unrelated to the quality of its education, was the air of nostalgic luxury in the small reception room, decorated with relics of Europe's grandest palaces. Maria had rarely seen such a profusion of beautiful things – drawings, porcelains, a charming gold coffee pot. She was greeted by one of the mistresses, Madame La Grange, who paid her many compliments, saying that by Maria's reputation she had thought her an old lady and was amazed to see a young person. When taken round the school, Maria observed that certain of the young girls had not been taught proper comportment, but she was in complete sympathy with the philosophy of the directress, that religion was the basis of the girls' education, that their learning should be adapted to their future position in life, which must be that of good mothers.

Madame Cosway had no intention of blindly following the models of other educators. Searching for the newest and most effective methods of teaching was a constant occupation and her main interest. She introduced many concepts from Charles Rollin's brilliant plan of studies, emphasising the importance of drawing high moral lessons from Sacred History as well as Greek, Roman, and French history. Since all young ladies should be accomplished letter-writers, she gave her pupils a thorough course in correspondence with some forty different models of letters that they might be called upon to use. She further innovated by following the methods of one of the most eminent modern educators, Abbé Louis Gaultier, who invented many games for teaching geography, reading, grammar, history, and languages. A few months before the unfortunate decision of the City Council, Maria had the privilege of receiving Abbé Gaultier in the school during a period of five weeks during which he taught classes and worked with her to explain his methods, which she thereafter applied with success. After his visit the Abbé sent words of encouragement along with a pessimistic assessment of the city fathers:

If reason directed men, and above all the Lyonnais, no doubt the result would be favourable, but at the bottom of my heart I have little faith in your gentlemen. I believe them in large part false, invidious, and not very intelligent. Your school offers so many advantages and so much evidence that they should be forced to favour and support it.

Despite the strong representations of Cardinal Fesch on her behalf, the city did not feel forced to favour her. She could not complain of lack of support from the Cardinal. The problem was his absence. During the years 1803-1806 he passed through his diocese on only four or five brief visits, the longest being about two weeks. When he did come a fortnight after her arrival, the first day at eight in the morning he received her for a two hour talk, putting all the numerous vicars, priests, and canons in the anti-chamber. They visited the disaffected Convent of the Carmelites, so that she could show him the location she had picked out from the other confiscated monasteries. She was happy that day, for she saw that she could make that house and garden into a paradise.

But then the Carmelites became unavailable because of a lawsuit and Maria was forced to accept temporary quarters at St. Pierre. After a year Fesch urged the City to give her a permanent location writing to them,

...it is already a year that Madame Cosway is in Lyon, and nevertheless, you have not yet been able to find her a suitable location. If this state of affairs should continue for some time, it is to be feared that such slowness will finally disgust this esteemed schoolmistress, and I do not hide from you that I would regard her departure as a very great loss for my diocese and for Lyon.

By this time Maria's character had become well-formed. She was now a determined woman with a mission, easily impatient if obstacles were not instantly vanquished. In Fesch's absence his Vicars-General, Jauffret and Courbon, were forced to absorb the shocks. The Cardinal had to calm them. To Jauffret he counselled:

Madame Cosway is a lady who has been soured by the slowness

of those who called her and by the vivacity of her character... .
It is necessary, therefore, that you bear her, she will be useful and
of a very great weight for us...

Fesch also re-affirmed his support of Maria to Courbon:

> Madame Cosway is a woman little accustomed to strong
> contradictions. However, I believe her very apt to promote good
> taste, drawing, and the arts which Lyon needs so much. I believe
> her useful and necessary; she has much intelligence... . Above
> all she has much experience of society and much tact, and I believe
> that [she] must always remain mistress of the battlefield, indeed
> a joke! Poor Mister Jauffret!

When the City then asked Maria to leave St. Pierre without giving her
another building, the Cardinal stepped into the breach and promised –
swearing her to confidentiality – to furnish funds for the purchase of the
Capucines' convent. Other events intervened before such a purchase became
necessary. A month after the City fathers decided to abandon Maria's school,
the Cardinal wrote to the Emperor on her behalf, requesting that she be
allowed to merge her institution with an order of Visitandine nuns, that
they be given a building, and that the school be recognised officially as one
of those welcoming daughters of holders of the Legion of Honour. He
enclosed letters of recommendation from the three previous mayors. Maria
also received an official letter from Madame Laetizia Bonaparte's Secretary
with this endorsement:

> Her Imperial and Royal Highness being informed of the success
> of the establishment that you have formed in Lyon for the
> education of young ladies charges me to tell you of her
> satisfaction with the zeal and the charitable sentiments that animate
> you. When benevolence directs the usage of a distinguished talent,
> one acquires, like you Madame, double rights to public esteem
> and gratitude. Her Imperial and Royal Highness always eager to
> favour all that is useful, to encourage all good deeds authorises

me to give you a special assurance of her benevolence and the desire that she has to encourage with all her power your success.

Fine words, but Maria wondered if the Emperor would remember his visit to St. Pierre on his way to Italy in 1805. The *Bulletin de Lyon* had reported the visit of Napoleon and the Empress Josephine.

> Their Majesties entered the *Salle des Peintures* where they were awaited by a group of young pupils of the establishment directed by Madame Cosway for the education of young ladies. One of the children complimented the Emperor in the Italian language and presented him with a branch of bay leaves. The daughter of the Mayor of the Northern Division offered the Empress a bouquet of roses... . This naïve homage was received with kindness... . The two young people, Mlle. Parent and Mlle. Martin, who had recited with all the graces of their age their compliments to Their Majesties...received each the next day from Her Majesty the Empress a superb ring of brilliants.

A few days later another honour followed when Pope Pius VII visited her school. He, too, was on the road south after the strain of his visit to Paris, where he was a somewhat humiliated witness to the Emperor's self-anointed coronation.

The fate of the school and some seventy-seven children depended upon the Imperial will. Months went by without a decision. The delay was partly occasioned by the delicate choice of religious orders to be recognised and by the long absence of the Emperor. Shortly after Cardinal Fesch made the formal request that Maria's school be chosen for daughters of Legion of Honour members, the Emperor left for a long campaign in the East, pushing the Russians back to the Niemen and fighting battles at Iena, Eylau, and Friedland. She could not know that he was thinking of Madame Campan as the directress of such a school. For nearly a year Maria laboured in limbo, still in the Abbey St. Pierre without a definitive location or statute for her thriving school. During this period she reflected on the lowliness of her position in society, in sharp relief with better days. As she confided in her journal:

How I thank God to give me so many occasions to know men and the weaknesses of the world and to be humbled. … How much I was poisoned with pride and looked down on certain persons who were not in the Court of St. James in London. If curiosity attracted me to a fete I didn't fail to add my own ridicule or look for my name on the list of persons honoured with an invitation. And what did I do then? I enjoyed my position by all possible means, indifferent to adulation but welcoming the greatness which habit rendered familiar. I come to Lyon pushed by zeal and an extraordinary fanaticism, work like a slave, am treated like an intruder and an adventuress. My right to be publicly recognised is contested;…I am humiliated by the Prefect and the Mayor who come often to this palace but not to see me nor are they interested in my establishment. … But probably I give too much importance to what my heart imagines and God wishes my humility and not my presumption.

Having been abandoned by the City, she seriously considered entering a religious order. That seemed the best solution to organisational difficulties. The Cardinal had always advised against her various schemes for associating the school with a religious society, using nuns as personnel, but keeping the direction herself. At the very beginning he wrote to her, '…speaking of the order of Visitation. This is enough to bring down the work, and to have it perceived as an institution without unity or method.' When Maria persisted, he relented and let her have a few nuns and now he had requested that the Emperor recognise the Visitandines and let Madame Cosway become associated with them under a special convention. But after the day-to-day inconvenience of working beside these ladies, Maria raised the subject of taking the habit:

…The more I think about the plan to associate myself with nuns the more I see the difficulty…they will always see me as secular…. The habit alone would smooth out many difficulties and spare me much work. Since I have always desired it…why can't I ask my husband for permission to take it now representing to him the need to more perfectly fulfil my charge.

During most of the year 1806 this step seemed the answer to her struggles, but it was not to be. There was the problem of being a Protestant's wife and the reluctance of the government to permit religious orders to grow. So she continued to seek original organisational solutions.

Cardinal Fesch's long visit to his diocese in the first half of 1807 was a great solace for it was the only period when her protector was present in Lyon for any length of time. Yet, even he, the Emperor's uncle, could not save them both from further humiliation at the hands of the Mayor. This provincial noble did not understand that her visits to the Archbishop's Palace were for the sake of friendship and the good of her school. Just before the Cardinal's departure for Paris in early June, an Imperial Decree was published concerning the Palace of St. Pierre and its designation as a house consecrated to the fine arts. As the city offered no other building, Maria's first reaction was to leave Lyon, but the Cardinal took that as an affront to him so she moderated her pique. She would take another house and wait three months. The Carmelites now being available, the Cardinal agreed to pay the rent. The evening before they closed the transaction, Maria received a terrible letter from the Mayor. It had been a year since Fay-Sathonay had begun his campaign against her school and now the conflict came to a head. She hurried to the Archbishop's Palace of Saint Jean, overlooking the strong currents of the Saône. Their rushing energy was reflected in the windowpanes of the palace, echoed by the briskness of her steps, and the confusion of her thoughts.

Upon entering his study, she could not contain her indignation.

'Your Eminence, please excuse this precipitation, but I have just received a letter from the Mayor full of insults directed more towards you than me. I thought you should see it at once.'

After reading the missive tranquilly, Fesch only said, 'Well, well, I shall give you an answer,' and he dismissed her. He must not have taken in the full import of the letter, for as soon as she arrived home, a message came to return to the Archbishop's House. This time she found a very agitated prelate.

'In re-reading this letter I saw the affront to me. You must not stay in this country. I shall let you choose to go to Rome, Milan, or Paris, whichever you like.'

'I should like to go to Milan to be near my sister I think.'

'Very well. I shall tell you how to reply to the Mayor tomorrow.'

'Yes, but what pain to leave my girls and abandon them.' This realisation brought quick tears, which she held back.

'You can begin on a better foundation elsewhere.'

This was a Friday evening. On Saturday Madame Cosway gathered the school mistresses in her room and announced her departure, but urged them not to tell the girls or parents. Then on Sunday, the Cardinal had a change of heart and summoned her again.

In a composed voice he said, *'After having confessed and examined myself, I find that I have been too heated over this business. If you wish to stay, I shall not oppose it. I believed your work was good for my diocese, but as I cannot seem to do anything more for your institution, I would encourage you to leave.'*

Not knowing what to do, Maria spent the rest of Sunday besieged by the parents who had heard rumours of her departure. They wished to go to the Cardinal, but she forbade them. They were so insistent that she returned Monday morning to tell him of the mothers' request.

'Well, let them come and let them speak. I'll do what I can.'

After he had received a delegation of fifteen mothers in carriages, they came to Maria's rooms in St. Pierre.

'Well, did your audience go well?' she asked.

Madame Cornelle-Chalandon threw her arms around her neck saying, *'Madame Cosway, now all depends only on you. The Cardinal said that you had created this establishment under his protection and that we must persuade you to stay, that he gives his consent. Please say that you'll stay.'*

At the moment emotion overwhelmed her. She realised that – apart from the hostility of the officials – there were those in Lyon who valued her life's work. The mothers, most directly concerned by her efforts, appreciated all she had done for their children. Her feelings were so strong that she momentarily fainted, causing a rush of mothers and girls around her that was suffocating. But all was well. Before leaving for Paris the Cardinal told her that the Mayor had called on him to apologise for the letter, telling him it was the fault of his secretaries.

These tumultuous days marked a change in Cardinal Fesch's attitude. He still remained a friend, earnestly seeking to find a permanent situation for Maria, but was now convinced that Lyon was not her place and therefore her educational plan had less importance for his diocese. Some of the suggestions in the Mayor's attack had embarrassed the Cardinal's dignity. As he wrote her a few days later from Paris,

> Since the Mayor's letter, I've told you more than once that the good I could do for your house was to protect it, but never to give funds, buy or lease the house.... I must refuse to guarantee the rent. That would be unsuitable of me.... Despite my desire to obtain a good education for the young ladies of Lyon, I cannot become involved in a transitory affair at the time that I must think of the solidity of the founding of seminaries and so many other works which concern the clergy. If I neglected them to think of the education of girls I would be guilty before God and before men.

The Mayor's misunderstanding of the Cardinal's protection for her school had set Fesch looking for another city to welcome her institution. She had scarcely settled into the Convent of the Carmelites on 25th June 1807 when he wrote of a new opportunity:

> The King of Naples [Joseph Bonaparte] is going to found a house of education for young ladies whose parents have been killed in service...this house will be under the special protection of the Queen.... The Directress must be attached to the reigning dynasty.... The Queen approves of you, she has agreed with me that as soon as I have your reply she will propose you to the King.... You will be dealing with a Queen who is the best woman in the world. For a long time I perceived the difficulties of establishing in Lyon your institution. I shall not say more.

Without hesitation she wrote her agreement, but a month later word came from Fesch:

The King of Naples did not agree to the request of the Queen. You can imagine the reason, it is that you are married to an Englishman. There we are fixed in Lyon, as long as it pleases Providence.... The Queen is sorry for this deliberation of the King, but she won't make him reconsider.

So Maria turned to the task of re-organising her work in a new house with new ladies. The Carmelites' former convent was an elegant ensemble, built in the eighteenth century on the side of a steep rise north of the city. Endowed with a magnificent entrance and staircase, the convent was both imposing and graceful. One had the choice of withdrawing into the peace of its interior cloister or expanding thought on walks in the surrounding gardens with their prospect over the city. In the evening Maria liked to take her worries out to the garden and look over the tile roofs spreading to the south towards the confluence of the Saône and the Rhône. This was the home she had desired during the last four years and now it was hers. The housing for her girls was now assured for the present, but the difficulty of finding permanent teachers persisted. All the Cardinal's warnings about the impracticality of combining the school with various religious orders proved prescient indeed. As Maria wrote to him soon after his departure,

> All goes well except the nuns.... These ladies cannot conceive of my plan nor of Your Eminence's intention for a public good.... They hold on to their old customs, believing it more important to miss doing good than to deviate, even with the authority of the Archbishop, from their rules that are full of a thousand pettinesses and prejudices.... The principal base of my plan is religious. It is known that my sentiments have never varied and that all that I have suffered from the city is much less than what I have had to bear from the nuns.

She suffered, but she could not do without the nuns, for she remained convinced that she needed to imbed her school in a religious society to assure its survival, that it should not depend on one person. The frailty of such a system had now been proved and was reinforced by a bout of ill health, which commenced with the news of her rejection by the King of

Naples and continued until the end of the year. Her sleep was perturbed for months. She had troubling dreams. Once she awakened anxious and perspiring after dreaming that she pursued Fesch, the new Pope, through the palace of the Vatican, asking him why he refused to give her communion. His answer was to take a coal from the fire and try to put it on her head. This seems an obvious reflection of her anxiety over losing Fesch's protection. He still assured her of his support, but always advised against staying in Lyon. Nevertheless, he asked Madame Chartres of the Visitandines to join the school. She took over the accounts and Madame Stanislaus, a former Clair, the supervision of the dormitories. The *Bulletin of Lyon* duly announced on 7th October 1807 the move of Madame Cosway's establishment to its new location.

A period of relative tranquillity followed the school's installation at the Carmelites. It was perhaps about this time that Maria managed to paint one of her last pictures, a portrait of two pupils, Annette Prodon, who was about twelve and little Suzette de Feynoul, aged five. Entitled *Innocence*, this charming picture of the little girls embracing each other was kept by Maria until she bequeathed it to Annette in her will. To Maria's great joy Annette eventually became one of her teachers and filled the empty place in her heart as a second daughter.

1809

Paris, 14 January 1809

...I am sorry you have been ill, but don't give into temptations questioning God.... Don't be shocked if priests are unjust, they aren't perfect...be happy to be away from the world and heresy...

This year of disillusion opened with an admonition from Cardinal Fesch to accept with patience the imperfections of those clergy with whom she sought an alliance. The previous year she had formed a society with two parish curates, Monsieur Goulard of Notre Dame de St. Louis and Monsieur Borelly of St. Polycarpe, to supervise education. Under the steady hand of Bochard, one of the Cardinal's Vicars-General, they spent months trying to draw up a convention for an association. It was finally Bochard who

34. *Plate from Maria Cosway's* Galerie du Louvre. *Conceived as a project to show all the pictures of the Louvre's Grande Galerie in their actual places, each number was to include four engravings.*

THE HOURS.

35. The Hours *by Maria Cosway, engraving of picture exhibited at the Royal Academy in 1783 and in Thomas Macklin's Poets Gallery c. 1788.*

36. Young Bacchus *by Maria Cosway, engraving of picture exhibited at the Royal Academy in 1787. A portrait of George Lamb, thought to be the son of Lady Melbourne and the Prince of Wales.*

37. Lodona *by Maria Cosway, engraving of picture exhibited in Macklin's Poets Gallery c. 1788. Based on a passage of Pope's 'Windsor Forest', Lodona, a woodland nymph symbolising the river Loddon, dissolves in tears into a stream.*

38. The Death of Miss Gardner *by Maria Cosway, exhibited at the Royal Academy in 1789. The artist portrayed the experience of her friend Anne, Lady Townshend, and her niece, who said she saw one of her deceased parents at the time of her passing.*

39. Anne, Marchioness Townshend, *portrait miniature by Richard Cosway.*

40. William Combe, *portrait miniature by Richard Cosway.*

41. *(right)* Mary 'Perdita' Robinson, *engraving after Richard Cosway.*

42. *(below)* Portrait of Maria Cosway *by Maria and Richard Cosway. One of the illustrations for Mary Robinson's* The Winter Day, *this drawing is considered to be a portrait of Maria in her boudoir in Stratford Place.*

43. (left) Richard Morton Paye's Self-portrait *shows the artist engraving, using a mirror to reverse the subject as he etches it.*

44. (below) Maria Cosway's engraving of Richard Cosway's drawing, Winged woman and Lion.

45. *(right) Maria Cosway's engraving of Richard Cosway's drawing,* Two Prisoners.

46. *(below) Hubert Robert,* La Grande Galerie du Louvre entre 1801 et 1805.

47. *(right) Maria Cosway,* Giulia Beccaria. *This portrait of Maria's friend was probably painted in Paris in 1802-1803, when both were living there.*

48. *(below) Gabriele Rottini,* Baroness Maria Hadfield Cosway listening to Vittoria Manzoni, *c. 1835. Seated among her teachers and pupils, Maria listens to the granddaughter of her friend Giulia Beccaria. The nuns are members of the Order of English Ladies.*

brought them together for two days until they agreed. The effect of this accord was to hand over the school to a larger society. Maria was to be responsible for the teaching of orphans and the boarding school for young ladies, but the new institution would also be a retreat for women, and a home for ladies who wished to live in retirement under religious supervision. The house would be governed by a council composed of the religious superior, Maria, and two others. In case of disagreement the two founding curates and the Vicar-General would decide. Maria would be paid a salary of 1,000 francs and any fees from drawing lessons; she would receive interest on the capital represented by her furniture. She was not otherwise reimbursed for a school which had annual revenues of some 25,000 francs. Maria's intuition urged her to seek assurances on possible indemnities should she leave or be forced to leave, but requests for advice on this point went unanswered. Unwisely she turned her lease and all her accounts over to the curates in April. Almost immediately Madame Chartres, the nun who handled the finances, began to have deficits where there had always been surpluses.

Graver still was the immediate deterioration of her relations with the sisters and Monsieur Goulard. From the outset the nuns seemed determined to oust Maria from all decisions, even those concerning instruction, and told the pupils that Madame Cosway was no longer anything in the school. One could say that she should have foreseen such a lack of consideration once she had given up the direction of the school to become a simple schoolmistress. She had willingly sacrificed pride for the good and longevity of an educational plan, but now the plan itself was sacrificed to the nuns' desire to see their religious order survive. For them education was only a pretext to gain recognition from the Emperor. Most of the trouble lay at the feet of Madame Chartres, a veritable dragon, who led the nuns in their rebellion and insulted the girls until they cried. There was also a Madame PetitJean, who had the title of Informer, that is of all the abuses of the community. Under a demure exterior she upset everything, reporting the most petty affairs and repeating incessantly that Madame Cosway was no longer to be obeyed. This unseemly behaviour destroyed Maria's girlish ambition to join the ranks of the religious. As she wrote to the Cardinal: 'If at other times I had the sincere vocation to become a nun, the experiences of these years have made it vanish.' As soon as she entered this infernal situation, the Cardinal secretly informed her that he might have to give up the Archdiocese of Lyon because he could no longer keep the two posts of Paris and Lyon. In that event Maria felt no obligation to remain in a city which had come to treat her as a foreign adventuress. Relations with the two nuns and Goulard deteriorated throughout the summer. The Vicar-General, Bochard, came to recognise too late the incapacity of Goulard. As Maria warned the Cardinal, 'The good curate is not made to direct this institution, he listens to all the gossip…is frightened by the state of the finances without taking the time to reflect a moment.'

Goulard seemed obsessed with worries about money. Fearing that Maria would leave, he threatened her with the financial consequences, claiming that she would be liable for the rent and the mythical advances he claimed to have given her, all to be guaranteed by her furniture. Exhausted by the day-to-day pettiness and injustice of the situation, she sought advice from Bochard. With his usual lucidity, he outlined three choices: She could retake the school or continue to live in the society or separate. As for the first she had no desire to retake a work built after much reflection and now spoiled by so many changes. Continuing seemed impossible. Separation was the only recourse. A long hesitation to take such a drastic step exposed her to public scenes during the late summer. Goulard wrote a letter saying they must separate, then convoked her to a public meeting with the teachers and pupils before which he asked Maria if she wished to take back the school or relinquish it. The final harassment was the day in September when he entered her bedroom and asked why she had not left. The former headmistress was literally put out of the Carmelites without her furniture and forced to find temporary lodgings near the Church of St. Polycarpe. Her intention was now to leave Lyon. Again the parents beseeched her to stay, even offering help in the search for a new house. Her humiliation continued, hidden behind the brief announcement of 23rd September 1809 in the *Bulletin de Lyon*:

> Madame Cosway, before located in the Carmelites, occupies since September 20, the first floor of Billion House, Grand Cour des Feuillans, by the Main Staircase. She gives drawing lessons to young ladies, both day students and boarders.

This solution only lasted a few weeks. By the end of the year, she found a pretty wing of an old convent of the Visitandines, Sainte Marie du Bellecour, all newly fitted up and papered. Her room between cloister and garden looked out over the gardener's hut where St. François de Sales had died. This peaceful view was one of the small comforts of life, for Goulard pursued her still. Since ordering her out of the Carmelites in September he had not ceased to harass her with claims of monies owed him for boarders' fees that she had supposedly spent and drawing lessons for which she had wrongly pocketed the receipts. As a final insult he held her furniture as a gage. All his demands were entirely unjustified. The fees had been collected and administered by Madame Chartres without Maria's interference. It had been agreed in their convention that Maria would keep the receipts for drawing lessons in addition to a salary of 1,000 francs. In all justice – instead of owing Monsieur Goulard 4,000 francs – it was he who owed indemnities for taking a flourishing establishment with over 20,000 francs of annual revenues, destroying it in three days, and then refusing to indemnify its founder for an abrupt and unreasonable dismissal. It is not an exaggeration to say that Maria was furious, venting her indignation on poor Bochard, to whom she wrote an apology:

> I was wrong to let myself be transported by my vivacity with you, but I couldn't contain my indignation…. If seven years of irreproachable conduct and labour and devotion and zeal for good don't justify me Providence will do with me what She wishes, but it's a painful reflection for a daughter and wife of Protestants to find herself in such a situation with Catholic ecclesiastics. It would be better to finish amicably.

At last Maria undertook a law suit to recover her property as she reported to the Cardinal:

> I had to put in the hands of a lawyer the affair of my furniture. Don't know what to do, persons present me as a foreign adventuress driven out of the Carmelites. Luckily I have remained here because if I had left it would be without my reputation. The thing is too contemptible to speak of…. The curate of St.

François de Sales posed many questions before confessing me. I satisfied him but was mortified to see that after seven years of work there are still so many prejudices in this country.

During the month of November there was a heated exchange of notes between Goulard and Maria. She claimed he made false declarations, which she refuted point by point. Bochard kept Fesch regularly informed of the controversy. In his letters, it seemed at first minor: 'M. Goulard worries Mme. Cosway with affairs of money.' Then the next week more aggravated: 'The affairs of Mme. Cosway with M. Goulard take a more furious turn,' and a few days later, 'I hope that this time again she will settle without a lawsuit.' At last they were able to settle the dispute out of court thanks to the tactful intercession of Bochard, who reported, 'Finally the affairs of Mme. Cosway are over. They almost had a very big lawsuit. The opposing party was hot and excited…but I was happy to make peace where war was almost inevitable.'

Now Maria was free to re-open her school on a reduced scale in St. Marie de Bellecour. The months of 1810 passed calmly for the obscure schoolmistress that she now was, listed in the Almanach of Lyon as Madame Maria Cosway, Teacher, rue Sala. What a difference from the two full pages in the Almanach of 1805 dedicated to the flourishing 'House of Education for Young Ladies established by the City of Lyon and directed by Madame Cosway in the buildings of the Conservatory of Arts (formerly St-Pierre).' With some twenty young boarders and a few nuns she persevered. Although still corresponding with Fesch in Paris, where his duties as Grand Aumonier and Archbishop of Paris kept him occupied, she was no longer his protégée in a practical sense. He was swept up in the great event of the year, the Emperor's marriage with the Archduchess Marie-Louise, having been asked to officiate at the wedding ceremony in the Salon Carré of the Louvre. Had the influence of the Cardinal been exercised as vigorously as before on Maria's behalf, it would soon have come to naught, for he was to be disgraced himself over his handling of the delicate arbitration between his nephew and Pope Pius VII. The Emperor reproached him for results too favourable to the Vatican. By the end of the year Fesch was replaced as Archbishop of Paris and was ultimately exiled from the Court. Without a powerful protector it seemed impossible to build the institution that she still dreamed of, a religious society devoted to her educational plan. A series of Imperial decrees had now established the framework for feminine education. There were two schools for daughters of the Legion of Honneur at St. Denis and Ecouen, furnishing expensive instruction similar to hers. Since Maria's school had not been chosen for this honour, there was little room for her. The Emperor had instead recognised existing religious orders to educate young girls, instructing his prefects to give them disaffected convents.

It was now clear that her stay at Lyon was drawing to a close. She began to fear a growing isolation. In the summer of 1810 she received word of the death of her mother in London. To Richard's credit he cared for her until the last. Maria did not feel deep grief. She felt her mother had always afflicted her. The notations in Maria's journal reflect a certain cold-heartedness, harking back to religious differences:

> …Oh, how is tremendous the justice of God! She didn't wish to let me become a nun to have me with her: little has she enjoyed my company and died without the consolation of any of her children nearby.

Not wishing to end her days alone in Lyon, Maria decided there was no recourse but to return to her husband. No one could travel to England without an Imperial passport; the Emperor himself had to approve every request for such a voyage. To gain support for her petition Maria wrote to an old acquaintance, the Comtesse Anne de Brignole, now lady in waiting to the Empress.

> I am trying to obtain a passport to return to my husband and a country where being a foreigner would do me no prejudice and is not a sin, and where I would know friends… . My husband could die and leave me without resources… . My brother and sister are no longer the same…

Although resigned to returning to London, she did not envisage giving up an educational vocation. She began to elaborate a new plan for a school in Chelsea, conducted by nuns of the Visitation who would not live by rules of their order but would follow the statutes of her new association. The Comtesse de Brignole did intercede on her behalf with the Minister of the Interior, the Duc de Rovigo, and claimed to have obtained his accord, but there was no news of a passport. In such cases the Minister of Police required a local police investigation, which took some time. The final report sent to Paris by the Commissaire Général of Police of Lyon is a tissue of inaccuracies, but one passage, which tells of locally observed events, may well explain the rapid disaffection of the Mayor for Madame Cosway's school:

> His Excellency when he was only Archbishop of Lyon had Madame Cosway come to this city. He protected her and had established in the Abbey St. Pierre (now the Conservatory of Arts) a secondary school for young ladies. Madame Cosway directed this school and with the help and protection of the Archbishop, the Prefect, and other authorities, the institution was soon lifted to the highest point of prosperity. Unfortunately its lustre was of short duration; an accident occurred which tarnished it and troubled all the families. Several young boys gained access to the house, a pupil became a mother. To hush up this event Madame Cosway moved her institution to another location. She transferred it to the Carmelites. It seems that she lost favour with the authorities and that gradually the institution was reduced. She is now in a private lodging under the simple title of house of education.

While waiting for the Imperial passport in the summer of 1811, Maria undertook a short voyage to Italy to visit her sister Bettina, whom she had not seen in some thirteen years. Two years before, she had contemplated such a visit, but was frightened by the stories of violence and brigandage on the roads. It was relatively easy to have a passport for Italy so Maria set off in July and discovered her little sister as the wife of a prosperous farmer, Vincenzo Mola, and the mother of a large brood of children. The Molas' farm with its imposing house and courtyard was outside the village of Maleo in the rich Lombardian plain. Although Maria needed rest that summer after the years of struggle in Lyon she could not resist satisfying her professional curiosity about Italian schools. She visited several, which only confirmed the impression given by her nieces and nephews – the education of Italian children was in a poor state. In spite of her intention to return to London, the attraction of her true country of origin was still vibrant. She wrote to Fesch from Maleo:

> …nothing gives me more pleasure than to speak of my love for Italy where my heart is… . It is still possible with my weak means to be useful for the need is much greater in Italy than France. Here is my position: I have no more courage to begin again and above all to be exposed to suffer new woes and to fight against intrigues and jealousy.

These lines reflected her fatigue, but the renewal of an old friendship was soon to give her the needed courage.

Francesco Melzi d'Eril, a young man noble in heart as well as birth, had frequented her house in London, when her receptions burned with the brilliance of expensive wax tapers and the *éclat* of distinguished guests. Introduced by a letter from the slightly unreliable d'Hancarville, the young Count Melzi was the most reliable of men. His voyage to Paris and London was the only indulgence in a life devoted to the service of his native Lombardy. Accompanying the Marchesa Paola Castiglione – it was said as her *cicisbeo* – the young Milanais impressed immediately by his learning, a serious demeanour, and an idealism imbibed with the virtues of the Enlightenment. Over the years Maria had lost touch with the Count Melzi, but cherished her memories of him. Since their first acquaintance he had risen to eminence. He embraced the arrival of Bonaparte in Italy with enthusiasm, seeing the French as representatives of revolutionary values, who liberated Lombardy from the despotic Austrians. After the Battle of Lodi, Melzi was among the first Milanais to welcome the young General Bonaparte. When the Italian Republic was created with Napoleon as its President, it was Melzi he chose to be Vice-President or effective ruler of northern Italy. Somehow the mutual confidence of Napoleon and Melzi had survived the mutation from republic to empire. Recalling their first meeting, the Emperor had named his loyal servant, one of the few who dared speak frankly, *Duc de Lodi*. Under the Empire, Maria's friend was now Chancellor and Minister of Justice of the Kingdom of Italy, but more importantly was the moral guarantor of the integrity of Italy, the most esteemed public servant of Lombardy or perhaps Italy.

Maria had the privilege throughout her life to know such men as Paoli, Jefferson, and Melzi, to count them among her closest friends. She maintained a long correspondence with each of them. The fact that these men with great public charges valued her friendship and these leaders of their fellows enjoyed Maria Cosway's company is testimony to her intellect and charm.

When she renewed a correspondence with this old friend, Maria did not know if he had retained his former simplicity of manners. The contact came about through the intervention of Guiliana Beccaria, who had seen him in Milan. Then Bettina Mola had seen him. In the summer of 1810 Maria discovered through letters that he was still the same. Soon she was pouring out the story of her unhappy efforts in Lyon. '...Oh how many times I said to myself if I had gone to Melzi, would've succeeded better, he would have not abandoned me.' Her complaints did not go unheard. One day in August, while she was still at Bettina's farm, a missive arrived from Bellagio on Lake Como. What a balm to read Melzi's words, '...you must be assured of my great desire to see you and to speak of the devotion you've always had for Italy, where it is possible, given a good opportunity, to reconcile an institution of education with your genius.' Having heard of the terrible fire which had just devastated the Mola's family farm, Melzi proposed to change the sombre scenes of destruction before her eyes for the romantic gardens of his new villa on the shores of Lake Como. Accepting his invitation as manna from heaven, Maria was slightly disingenuous in her next letter to the Cardinal. To explain a delayed return she blamed the fire: 'I hoped to leave as I had planned, but [there was] a horrible fire in my brother in law's house, which fortunately was in the day, otherwise we would all have burned, but I must stay a bit to keep them company on this sad occasion.'

Those two days in Bellagio were another of the turns in a road which led through many changes of residence in three countries. Cosseted by Melzi's hospitality and lulled to sleep by the gentle lapping of the lake, Maria felt at last that Providence was a favourable force on her behalf. In the long summer evenings during easy conversation with Melzi, the idea of a school in Italy began to germinate. Nothing was decided upon before her departure, but the encouragement of such a serious and eminent friend had helped to stiffen her resolve to leave Lyon. Without knowing whether she would ultimately be moving North or South, she took immediate steps to settle affairs in France, even going to Paris to push her request for an Imperial passport. She kept her real intentions – to go to Italy if Melzi succeeded in finding a situation for her – from Fesch. One day in Paris he presented Maria to the Queen of Naples (not the wife of Joseph Bonaparte, but now Caroline Murat, the Emperor's sister), and left them alone to talk of the new Queen's desire that Madame Cosway direct her school in Naples, the Casa Carolina, but Maria did not like her way of speaking about the proposition and hesitated, wary of the instability of their kingdom at that time. Whether it was Naples, Milan, or even Bologna, which had also been mentioned, Maria cared not. Her only desire was to leave Lyon. Her method of deciding was, as she wrote to Melzi, '…I shall leave Lyon immediately and once in Italy Providence will make me see clearly.'

In November she made arrangements to cede her school to a new director, sold her furniture, and kept in constant touch with Melzi. Having begun to look for a house for her establishment, he had now agreed to send funds for the voyage to Milan. In mid-December she wrote to the Commissaire Général of Police of Lyon to ask for passports for herself and two young schoolmistresses accompanying her.

> I have the honour to announce, that being called by My Lord, the Duke of Lodi in Milan to found an establishment for the education of young ladies, I have decided to go with two mistresses to assist me, Mademoiselle Prodon and Mademoiselle Lambreaux; although I had requested a passport for England; not having received any reply since then and after the great sacrifices that I made leaving my establishment in Lyon and not being able to make the expense of a voyage to England, I have accepted the propositions that My Lord the Duke of Lodi made to me while waiting until I have a reply from my husband for the funds that are necessary for the voyage which my special interests do not permit me to renounce. I beg you therefore, Sir, to accord me the passport for Milan that I request.

Without regrets she wrote to the Cardinal to tell him of her decision.

> …Thank God that the moment to leave this country has come after so many troubles. No other city was more favoured. Your Excellence has put all his zeal, they didn't wish the school, don't deserve another…'

Fesch understood her situation perfectly. His lack of resentment enabled their friendship to continue as before. Indeed, after she was well settled in Italy he wrote to reassure her:

> …you should congratulate yourself to have the resolution to abandon Lyon. I begin to know this city and every day I have reason to be convinced that we could not establish a good and beautiful education for girls and it would never be directed by a foreigner. All is done here by coteries, even charitable works! This spirit is dominant in all classes…

Through innocence and zeal she had attempted the impossible – to direct a religious society of education without being a nun, in a provincial city without being a native, in a country at war with her own. The only woman who had succeeded with a similar organisation was Madame de Maintenon, who did it with the ideal patron – Louis XIV, an absolute ruler. Yet Maria's time in Lyon was hardly wasted. All the foundations of her methods and their ultimate success were laid during these years of trial. She left Lyon with a precious resource – eight years of experience in forming young ladies of learning and accomplishment.

62. G. Manefredini, Detail of bust of Maria Cosway.

18

Lombardy

1828

On the terrace of her country house Signora Cosway often looked through rustling chestnut trees to watch the hypnotic waves, dancing over Lake Como. It was a pastime of pure tranquillity. Yet if she lifted her eyes to the opposite shore she saw – floating in the evening light – a part of turbulent

England. It was the palace of the late Queen Caroline, once painted by Maria. Across the lake, in an elegant waterside house, the wretched queen took the first steps towards her disgrace. One of the servants, Pergami, wormed his way into her confidence and then her bed. Stooping to consort with a major domo gave the King the evidence he wanted. He almost succeeded in getting rid of her by trial in the House of Lords. The masses supported the unfortunate queen, pitying her as the victim of a cruel husband. Her popularity was so great that the politicians didn't dare to find her guilty of adultery. Maria was in London at the time, caring for Richard after his health failed. Her letters to Annette Prodon, now one of her schoolmistresses, were full of the *cause célèbre*:

> We have a terrible example in the Queen; one cannot find her criminal and the King would give, I believe, half of his empire for a divorce; and yet here she is! In what a state! Upsetting all the Nation, herself plunged in an abyss…all by an imprudent conduct. Ah! my dear, inculcate in the children religion, morality, common sense, a healthy judgement…

The poor queen was unlucky or unwise on the shores of Como, but Maria found the key to the rest of her life in this lacustral paradise. In Bellagio, a few miles to the north, Melzi had introduced her to the magical region on her journey back to Lyon. And it was here that the plan for a school in Italy was born, later supported by Melzi with deeds as well as words. His confidence in Maria's methods took concrete expression with the purchase of a disaffected convent in the town of Lodi, some twenty miles south of Milan. With a patron like Melzi all went swiftly. Five months after visiting him, the Convent di Santa Maria delle Grazie was hers and three months later on 1st April 1812, Signora Cosway opened a school with one pupil, Giuseppina Menrisi, and two French mistresses, Annette Prodon and Josephine Lambreaux. By the end of the year there were some forty young girls in her charge and now over thirteen years later more than fifty. After Richard's death in 1821, an inheritance permitted her to enlarge and embellish the original convent by purchasing three houses to the east. A charming garden and the fine views over a rich countryside from almost every window made Maria feel mistress of a little world where order and

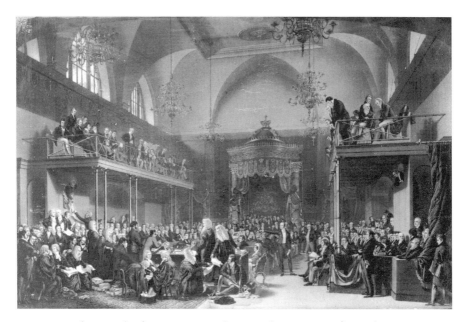

63. The Trial of Queen Caroline in the House of Lords, *1820*.

simplicity reigned, good was done for the young girls, and there were even some English comforts. After the Napoleonic wars, the Austrians – seen everywhere in white uniforms and yellow moustaches – were back in Lombardy. The Emperor Franz and Empress Maria Karolina had visited Maria's school, not only to see the instruction, but the remnants of Richard Cosway's works. The college was cited in the Guide to Lodi for its collection of paintings, which were often visited by travellers.

It took years of struggle to create Maria's haven and now she could rest. With the fruits of the last sale of Cosway's works in London, she bought her charming *casino* overlooking the port of Blevio. She found it when visiting her friend Maddalena Sannazzari, whose villa was the scene of her niece Enrichetta's first meeting with her future husband. The young man, Allesandro Manzoni, was the son of another of Maria's long-time friends, Giulia Beccaria, whose portrait she painted in Paris. So the threads of destiny continued their strange weaving. When Maria sat by the lake late in the day, all the scenes of London, Paris, and Milan faded in memory beside the exuberant beauty of oak and chestnut trees spilling down steep hillsides to water's edge. A picturesque little barque, with fringed canopy and swaying crimson curtains, tugged gently at its lines, ready to transport Maria in

Byzantine style to visit friends on the lakeshore. She could at last enjoy the satisfaction of a life's work, which partially compensated for the loss of her daughter. As she wrote to Melzi of her joy in opening a school in Lodi:

> I would never have believed one could do so much with this location. I cannot say how happy I am…. This "House" is my firstborn daughter and you have done for me what no one else has done. My sensitive heart promises you eternal gratitude.

Melzi's fidelity assured the early success of her project. The policy of the Italian government was much more welcoming of private schools than that of Lyon, especially for girls. The Italians welcomed initiatives which relieved pressure on public money.

Melzi's death in early 1816 meant that her troubles were not completely over. Maria had many ups and downs with the new Duc di Lodi, Melzi's young nephew, who first promised the same patronage as his uncle, then wavered, believing every shred of gossip circulated by the pupils or the local townspeople. This was one of the reasons Maria was never able to completely institute the three classes of education she had advertised in the new school's manifesto. Poor children couldn't be subsidised adequately by the fees for the girls of better families, who flocked to her house. The course of study she had perfected was best adapted to young ladies of a certain rank. It included Italian and French languages, calligraphy, arithmetic, sacred and profane history, geography, the rules of good manners, the principles of religion and its morality, some practical feminine works such as embroidery. She had been criticised in Lyon for teaching young ladies the accomplishments of music, drawing, and dance. In Lodi she proposed them as optional lessons, but still defended these graces. Describing a fête given in Melzi's honour, she wrote to him:

> …I hope the Bishop won't be scandalised by the dancing of the girls, but if he saw how it was done, he could not have difficulty permitting it. I maintain it is good exercise and teaches not to abuse this amusement and have good manners in presenting oneself is necessary for a good education.

Maria was happy in those early years, supervising the masons and plasterers, always improving the convent with its delightful open terrace overlooking the countryside beyond the city wall. She was proud when the opening was announced in printed brochures:

> Opening in Lodi in the location of Madonna delle Grazie, formerly the Little Fathers, a college of education for young girls under the direction of Sig. Maria Cosway, which has the approval of the Director General of Public Instruction. Will accept young girls from the age of six to twelve years. They must be of sound constitution and have been vaccinated or have had smallpox.

Always perfecting the work begun in Lyon, the headmistress wrote a course in Roman history from the foundation of Rome to the end of the Empire, subdivided by epochs and persons. Each emperor was pictured with a medallion and biographical details. She also developed further the course in French history through Napoleon and the histories of England, Spain, Germany and Italy and wrote a course of the history of science, describing scientific instruments and physical phenomena. Since the most important skill for a lady was mastery of language in writing and speaking, Mrs. Cosway always emphasised to the girls the supreme importance of a well-written letter. She gave them forty examples of letters such as those appropriate for parents, superiors, brothers or sisters, friends, well-known persons or those typical of letters of congratulations, condolences, etc. They could not write, however, without a thorough grounding in analytical grammar and for this Maria still employed the wonderful manuals of the Abbé Gaultier. Emperor Franz I and his wife, Maria Karolina Augusta, were so impressed with the girls' skill in analysing parts of speech that the Empress wished to introduce Gaultier's method in her country. The Collegio delle Grazie was viewed with favour in Vienna since the Emperor's first visit in 1816, when he heard recitations in all the classes, liberally praising the pupils with 'Marvellous' or 'Good'. He seemed pleased and amused when Maria reminded him that at age thirteen she had copied his portrait from Zoffany's portrait of all his family. With a smile, he asked, 'Well, did you recognise me now?' They had both been raised in Florence, the Emperor in the Pitti Palace as a son of the Grand Duke of Tuscany and

Maria a few streets away as an innkeeper's daughter. She had observed his family throughout her childhood and tried to paint them. Now her life was again dependent on the goodwill of the Habsburgs.

The Emperor's brother, Archduke Rainier, was now Viceroy of Lombardy; he and his wife also observed Maria's classes and spoke favourably of them in the highest levels of Milan society. The Inspectors of Public Instruction generally gave the school a good report, with one exception. The teaching of Italian was not perfect, suffering from the Directress's years spent in other cultures.

Still, the best houses in Lombardy had a flattering impression of her. When Melzi reported that the Milanais thought that she must have been the daughter of a prince or an Italian or both to judge by her manners, she let him know this was not necessarily a compliment.

> …you thought certainly to pay me a compliment telling me what was said of me at this brilliant and distinguished dinner of 40 persons. Yes I should be flattered, but my manner of thinking is different; I was not born the daughter of a prince nor an Italian as my manners (not to repeat the fine things that were said of me) would have one believe. And it would be a compliment compromising the truth about my mother. No, this humiliates and mortifies me. Because an honest man who knows the value and the price of a good education, who makes sacrifices, who speaks to his children should he not succeed and be distinguished from the vulgar? Perhaps are these things only given to the nobility? … If I acquired something it is the merit of my parents, but not my illustrious birth…to take away the truth of my birth would be injurious. I am not then offended in England because little attention is paid to this, but if the Father is grand, the children participate with impunity in this honour without thinking of the poor mother.

The Milanais of Melzi's circle may not have thought that taste, politeness, and a cultivated mind could be disassociated from birth, but Maria knew how much her father's sacrifices for her education had done for her. This personal experience animated her desire to give her girls the same advantages. In this latter half of life what happiness she had came from this work and her dear Annette Prodon, now one of her school mistresses.

Another source of milder satisfaction was the healing of the Cosways' broken marriage. Richard's failing health prompted his wife to undertake two arduous journeys across Europe to care for him – the first in 1815, and a second in 1817, which kept her in London until her husband's death in 1821. Although Maria would have preferred to direct her college in Lodi, she seemed pleased to be reconciled with Richard during his last years. That she was able to care for him properly and put order in his affairs was a benediction for them both. It was something of a miracle given his neglect of her over many years. This neglect had created a gnawing fear inside Maria of the possible shame, should she be labelled a 'divorced woman'. How else did others interpret the fact that she had no means of support other than her teaching? Such rumours did circulate in Lyon, and she lived in constant uneasiness that they would resurface in Italy. She had been content in her new life except for the nagging uncertainty of an unravelled marriage. After the school at Lodi was well-established, Maria had the opportunity to begin reweaving the strands of her marital relationship. She was helped by correspondents such as her former lady's maid, Madison, and Miss Charlotte Jones, one of Cosway's former pupils, who kept her informed of his health and other pertinent news. In the spring of 1815 she received several reports of her husband's illness. She wished to return immediately to London, but each day there were also alarming bulletins on the coming battles between Napoleon's old forces and the other European powers. When Madison wrote that Cosway had the intention of writing to his wife, Maria preceded him.

> …I am in such fears of seeing again all communication stop'd that I write to you…. Your apparent indifference for me grieves me very much. Perhaps you think I deserve it, if this makes you happy I can regret it the less. … Remember my good Mr. Cos. how many years we were happy. My wishes were to second and follow yours; your indulgence towards me was boundless, and nothing ever made me forget it… . Until you began to divide your thoughts, first with occupations in Bedford Square…a miss P engrossed them. Afterwards with Hammersmith and the L. in

this I found you immersed on my return from Italy, but they did not disunite you from your wife, lastly with the Udnys and this ended our happiness. — You changed more and more daily. No more regard, affection or consideration. You must remembr our conversations were always <u>disputes</u>. I confess my weakness in not being able to bear it, my temper itself was alterd, and fell often even on poor Madison. Time and distance has brought reflection on me and as they all bind me to you, I may feel sorry for the past, but you are still bound from me,

All through the month of April 1815, Maria was tormented with indecision, torn between the need to be at her husband's side in his illness and frightened of travelling in wartime. At the beginning of the month the Austrian commander of the military garrison in Lodi came into her garden and told her that Napoleon and all of France were going to be destroyed, that the Corsican had troops, but lacked munitions, provisions, horses, and money. War was in the air, but at the end of April Maria received a letter from Miss Jones which hardened her resolve to leave. She learned that her husband was still in a poor state and that Mrs. Udny had total power in his house. That was enough! Jealousy spurred her to action. She sent a warning shot, writing to Martha Udny, in direct but diplomatic language:

Dear Madam,

You will be perhaps surprised to receive a letter from me, but if you dont forget the kindness which you had a long time for me, I should be ungrateful to forget it...

Several persons come from England have given me a melancholy account of Mr. C. as I heard also, some time ago, that a Lady was very kind to him, this gave me infinite pleasure, and immediately guessed it was <u>you</u> and convinced that gratitude you deserve, and only waited for the moment I could make my acknowledgments in person. It has been my intension every since I have been abroad to return to England, at one time could not get Eng. passport...however, now nothing of this kind retains me… . All I have to beg of you is to prepare Mr. C. as you think proper and more to if you think it possible could you not induce him to make a journey and return with me? The change of air, the amusement he would have in seeing these fine things in Italy, would I think do him good, and what could prevent you of being of the party?… The kindness everybody has for me, the confidence of the many parents, the attachment of the children, the establishment, the noble conduct of the duke, deserve from me every proper return and regard. At the same I feel (and everybody must feel with me) that my husband is my first duty, and has ever been my thought tho unable to prove it… . Receive dear Madam my acknowledgements and entreaties in favour of your ever most obliged Maria Cosway.

Three weeks later, despite the lowering clouds of war, Mrs. Cosway was on the road to London, travelling alone from Como, across the lake, then up the Mera River into the Alps. In Chiavenna she had to bargain with a group of peasants to carry her over the mountains. They opened the bargaining with a price of nine louis, saying it would take six men to carry this 'colossus of a lady'. Fortunately she wasn't offended by their insult. When she balked at the price, the innkeeper proposed a little horse, more the size of a sheep. She protested that she didn't know how to ride, so he persuaded his brother to lead the horse and that is how the portly Mrs. Cosway crossed the mountains on horseback. To avoid France she passed through the German states, took an ugly boat, full of men smoking, down the Rhine. Despite the dirty atmosphere of the boat the avid lady traveller drank in the beauty of the shore – country houses, castles, vineyards on the hillsides – as they slowly descended a river as wide as Lake Como. Although the German cities were bursting with soldiers of all nations – in Heidelberg the inns were so full of them she couldn't find a place and in Mainz the city's population was trebled – she never had such a pleasant journey. She was enchanted with the cleanliness and beauty of the cities; Darmstadt was the prettiest, built in the Italian style. Utrecht impressed her as well by the picturesque turning of the Rhine around fortified bastions and beautiful gardens. She was enchanted with her arrival in Rotterdam on a pretty road between two canals. On either side green-shuttered houses were reached by little drawbridges. The gardens were charmingly varied; some had statues, but all full of every sort of flower, often in great baskets. She took many ideas for her garden in Lodi from this immaculately clean Dutch city. Helveitzloos, where she waited for a ship to England, was a different story. The stagnant canals gave off a bad odour, but the shops were handsome so she took advantage of the wait to do a bit of shopping. She went to buy a silk shawl when she heard that woollen shawls were not worn in London in summer. Unlike the youthful Maria, the older schoolmistress now wished to be unremarkable. When the lady in the shop showed her beautiful shawls from Lyon, she thought of Annette. She rejected a large-bordered shawl, considering it too beautiful and gay and chose a more modest one.

The sea voyage was calm and then rough, but without illness. She wrote to Annette of the difference between the luxurious inn in Harwich and those in Italy. The former innkeeper's daughter still appreciated a good inn, noting each detail: the sumptuous dinner of two fat chickens, peas, cauliflower and potatoes served in silver covered dishes; porcelain and crystal on the table; a clean bed with white-fringed curtains. The next day the English coach literally flew to London, seventy-two miles in a day, but as they approached the city she was depressed by the familiar smell of coal, the deafening noise of many carriages, the little brick houses. She was back in the sombre atmosphere of London after fourteen years.

Richard Cosway was much changed, but in better health than she had been led to expect. He expressed all sorts of attentions towards her and wanted to spend all his time showing her his works. Madison, her maid, and Miss Cosway, a cousin, almost fainted with joy at seeing Maria. All this was very satisfying, but she still missed Annette and Lodi terribly. Almost her first act in London was to write to her real home:

> My dear child, How could I tell you how much I love you? Oh, my good Annette! Believe me that I don't find expressions, that I miss you everywhere. I have you always present and nothing will fill the emptiness I have not to see you. Well, here I am! in this place that I so much desired. Perfectly well-received. The demonstrations of joy well beyond what I could have imagined. Am I happier! No, my good friend. All is sad for me I cannot

accustom myself to the climate, the noise, the confusion, the odour of smoke…. My heart is heavy, I don't know why, I don't find myself. But change the subject. How are you? Apart from the pain of not seeing me, are you happy?

The six weeks spent with her husband in the summer of 1815 passed pleasantly enough and improved their relations. It was also a great comfort to see friends of forty years as James Northcote and Prince Hoare. As she could not be away from Lodi longer, Richard made her promise to return the next year. She put off this second journey repeatedly. First Annette was called to Lyon on family business and then her husband refused to send funds for the journey. The marriage was still not healed. A friend who looked in on Cosway, a Mrs. Chambers, did her best to bring them together. She wrote to Maria that Richard now had certain conditions that he wished fulfilled if his wife returned to him – she should love him as if nothing had been done, that he wanted to know that she preferred no mortal to him, for he had <u>never</u> been unfaithful to her. Maria's reply to these demands gave a full account of her view of the marriage.

> Am I not to love a man who took me without fortune? who bestowed on me every kindness, generosity, seconded <u>all</u> my wishes? in <u>every</u> respect? who took such care of my poor Mother to her last moments. Oh! this is ever before me, kind to my brothers and sisters. —— You well observe Love does not grow old. … does he wish for <u>proofs</u>? … But is it not necessary to mention how the change happened to the appearance of the reverse? ——The moment he gave himself to <u>Hammersmith</u> by one to lead him from me and from his home. No one but God himself can know all I suffered when with child My journey to Italy restored my health…. On my return my dear child engrossed all my attention. His were from home Hammersmith was drop'd for another acquaintance which kept him farther from me. Peevish, cross, we were not happy. I thought my journey to Paris would do away and calm by distance that friendlessness difficult to mend. … When I was invited to Lyons for the establishment I did not promise until I <u>had his permissions.</u> …

Much did I wish to return to him, but when he gave me leave to remain surely t'was no proof he wishd for me. War was declared, no more <u>correspondence</u> nor <u>remittance</u>. Some smiled, some pitied me, some murmured, some invented malicious things thru jealousy for being so highly favoured and protected, even to say I was divorced, evidently abandoned by my husband…he never took any notice of me, how I lived, or what I had, or where I was for 14 years, my good Mrs. Chambers, what could I think! Can a husband who loves his wife neglect her so? I knew he was well and I was constantly told of his attachment to Mrs. U. let it be pure and without a fault. The appearance could not please me. Is this <u>love</u> or <u>indifference</u>?

It was finally the summer of 1817 before Maria could arrange her affairs well enough to depart. She had wished to leave the college in Annette's hands, but her 'child' was still in Lyon. Annette's mother, an unstable and possessive woman, wished to keep her daughter there, a natural feeling. Maria maintained – probably reliving her experiences with her own mother – that Madame Prodon exerted her influence against the interest of a sensitive child, urging her to marry against her inclinations or at the least, become a better paid school mistress in Lyon than she was in Lodi. Now the girl's mother wished Maria to make a settlement on Annette as the price of her return. Maria felt that she, unlike Annette's mother, only wished the girl's happiness, even if it meant their separation. But conveniently Maria was sincerely convinced that staying in Lyon was not in Annette's best interest. She dared to scold the girl's mother in the strongest terms:

Well, Madame, keep your child. Enjoy seeing her unhappy. Expose her to grief, to the danger of being ill, & then buy her happiness, her health, even life with your money. It is not with me that you should bargain. I fulfilled my task & my duty. I rendered your child clever, and I always made her happy.; If she had not been, would she have stayed so long with me? … I always told you that I considered her like my child and she is convinced of my feelings for her. But you are a cruel mother, without heart and without gratitude… . You tell me a thousand times that if one asked you your life for the good of your child you would give it and now she begs you herself to let her come to me and you resist!

It is impossible to know which of the two adults – Mrs. Cosway or Madame Prodon – truly knew what was best for Annette, but there is no doubt that Maria's emotions were now totally engaged with the young girl who had come to replace Luigina. She seems to have fallen in love with Annette in Lyon, when she saw that the little girl was an exceptionally good child. She went so far as to caution the schoolmistresses to treat her with gentleness not rigour. In Maria's eyes the child had the character of an angel, a natural sweetness that should not be embittered. As Annette grew into a young woman her virtues only confirmed Maria's earliest opinion. When in London Maria wrote to her protégé that the young girl's demeanour was an example for her headmistress.

> You must begin by conquering your own repugnance and conquer the children with a persevering <u>sweetness</u>, gradually they will bend more easily…I am more sharp than you, perhaps more intolerant of their faults. … I remember more than once to have been touched by your way, your sweetness with the little ones…. Well, do the same with the others. I confess that I was also severe and experience has shown me that I gained nothing by it and I assure you that at my return I shall behave differently.

Annette's character stood out in bold relief compared with the disappointing behaviour of Maria's nieces and nephews. One of the reasons their aunt came to Italy was to remedy the deficiencies in their education. The Mola girls did come to her college, mostly to sow seeds of disorder and discord. Angelina Mola was the worst, gossiping about the college all over Lodi whilst Maria was in London. When informed of this, she appreciated Annette all the more writing to her:

> Alas! it is so rare to find true friendship in this world, that when we find this treasure it is enough for an inappreciable and complete happiness…. As for my nieces I am sorry that they afflicted you,

but the harm must be more sensible for me…they tried to make it seem that they were the objects of jealousy, especially Angelina, the most ambitious, laziest, meanest!…did she have to abandon me and harm the college! … None of that family will ever enter in my house. I've had enough! It was for them that I left Lyon. I thought it was a praiseworthy reason; I am pained…

Annette had become Maria's family. After the girl's departure for Lyon in 1817, Maria wrote her of the pain of their parting:

> You saw that I couldn't cry…having so much suffered when my child died…the touching manner that you asked my blessing had an effect on me that I cannot explain and I needed to cry which relieved me and left me ill all day and not sleeping the night…[it's] difficult not to see you. I cannot be accustomed to it…
> Your affectionate second mother

Madame Prodon finally relented, but not before Maria's journey to London. The college was left to the direction of Josephine Menrisi, her first pupil in Lodi, now a young lady capable of teaching and directing the establishment. Maria's written instructions to Josephine stressed an abiding concern for <u>order</u> as much in the accounts as in the studies.

> …Demand that they work hard. Rigorous surveillance during the recreation… . Give fifteen days of holiday to the girls, beginning from 15 September to 15 October and reasonable holidays to those remaining in school… . Give them prizes as usual each month, I recommend to give them for <u>order</u>, punctuality, kindness, politeness, silence, good conduct. … In a particular emergency consult Don Carlo Mancini, whom I leave as my proxy in Lodi, and my brother-in-law Vincenzo Mola, ask them for advice. If other extraordinary needs arise, inform His Excellency the Duke of Lodi and Cavalière Gaetano Giudici who will help you, being a true friend of the school.

The next five years in London were dedicated to duty. Maria's choice would have been to stay with her girls and tend to a flourishing enterprise. The new world she had created in Italy suited her. In spite of the affection of family and friends in London, Maria confided to Annette in a letter: 'I am loved perhaps more here than there, but their ice and my fire do not blend together.' After Annette overcame her mother's objections and returned to the college, the person Maria loved best in the world was in Lodi. Their correspondence during Maria's London years was her source of happiness and comfort, but as she advised the young girl: 'the best of lessons, the most essential of a good education, which a lady should exercise, [is] submission to her husband.' Although Maria feared that her absence would destroy a fine establishment, duty required that she care for her husband. This decision elicited much carping from the citizens of Lodi. The headmistress complained to her diary: 'Why must I suffer for devoting myself to a useful work when once I thought only of amusement!'

During her long absence Maria's heart was with Annette and the college. Her commitment to providing a superior education for her young girls was all-absorbing. From afar her thoughts kept turning to improvements in method or discipline. She filled her letters to Annette with instructions about school matters and accounts of her visits to those London schools which impressed her. These investigations were one of her few distractions in Regency London, confined as she was by her husband's care. At a private school for only twelve young girls she was impressed by the pristine green velvet on their work table without holes, cuts, or ink spots and the impeccable order of the little girls, all dressed in white percale finely trimmed with lace, hair cut short. She exclaimed to Annette, '…how they hold themselves! How their shoulders, how their bodies were erect!'

At a public school for poor children she discovered the Lancaster method – 400 boys were standing in a surprising silence in circles of about twenty. In each circle the teacher was another boy who listened to the others read. In another room 340 girls learned by the same method in perfect silence. These poor youngsters, clean, well-behaved and teaching each other, left Maria stupefied.

Most amazing of all was the school for the poor children of military men, founded by the Duke of York. There she saw 900 boys and 400 girls from five to twelve years old in beautiful scarlet and dark blue uniforms, the boys in black straw hats and the girls in yellow straw. When Maria arrived, the boys were marching on the lawn with superb uniformity, not a head out of place. At the sound of drums they marched two by two into the refectory and then drums signalled when they should go to their seat, say the benediction, and then sit down. She could not wait to write to Annette:

> Oh, how my heart was at Lodi! What pleasure for me to see such order, cleanliness, & silence!…the most beautiful institution I ever saw & a great credit to its founder.

Her greatest discovery in London was a remarkable method for teaching music to children. It was so extraordinary that she wished to send English children who knew it to Lodi or have Annette come to London to learn the method. She tried to describe it in a letter.

> I saw them play 4 up to 12 together with surprising force the most difficult sonatas of Corelli, duos of Mozart. They learn composition and accompanying with great facility…it's like the grammar of Gaultier on a board… . They have a machine for placing the hands, to learn the notes, finally in three months they play perfectly several things… . It's a pleasure to see the little ones learn the most boring theory with pleasure… . I am crazy for it… . I have been twice and will return…I know it would succeed in Italy.

From London Mrs. Cosway was able to spread the reputation of her college far and wide by signalling it to English travellers. The most successful result of this was the laudatory mention Lady Morgan gave the college in her popular but controversial book *Italy*. Maria prepared the writer's visit well, informing Annette in advance:

> You will have the visit of Lady Morgan. I beg you to fete her very much, to explain to her the method, to speak of me, how much I am loved and desired. I have reasons for that… . It means

much to me that she be satisfied as well as all the English that I send to you…

Her protégée followed these instructions well, for the lady traveller wrote that Melzi, who commenced a female seminary in Lodi, had asked the advice of:

> one whose name is well known in England, one endowed with every talent, and every feminine accomplishment, the celebrated Maria Cosway…the <u>pensionat</u> in Lodi became, what it still is, one of the most excellent institutions for female education in Italy, perhaps in Europe.

In spite of missing her life in Lodi, Maria had the satisfaction of doing her duty and putting order in Richard's affairs. The first year or so in London was not unpleasant. Cosway was weak, but was able to paint and to go out to dinner. Mrs. Cosway's day began at seven o'clock, going out to hear mass in the Spanish chapel. After returning home, they had tea, coffee, bread and butter, read the gazettes and had conversation until eleven when Richard went into his studio to paint. Maria often watched him before going out to the shops or making visits at one hour after midday. At five she returned home to dress for dinner which they had at six o'clock. After dining Richard often wished to take a walk or a drive. At nine they took tea, biscuits, bread and butter until about eleven. Some evenings they looked at antique prints and drawings and went to bed shortly before midnight. Maria set up her harp and spent hours amusing herself with it as well as reading. Besides the gazettes, she found ample amusement in her husband's library. Always looking for good literature for her pupils, Maria recommended that Annette read Milton's *Paradise Lost* for its sublime descriptions of the greatness of God and the power of Satan. But her one great pleasure was the quiet hour she spent conversing by letter with her dear second daughter. The newspapers were full of events that she recounted in detail, especially the tragic deaths of Princess Charlotte and her baby in childbirth. Richard Croft, the Princess's doctor, blew his brains out, unable to bear the criticism of insufficient care. The papers had forgotten about the Cosways, but it was a rare pleasure for Maria to read the published verses 'Lines on a portrait of Princess Charlotte painted by Maria Cosway' which harked back to a portrait she had painted of Princess Charlotte and her mother, Queen Caroline.

In Maria's first spring in London she arranged two Italian evenings for a few friends, a mere echo of the crowded concerts in Pall Mall, but the guests appreciated an Italian *improvisatore*, who recited two scenes from Alfieri and a bit of Dante. Then an Italian singer, Madame Cittadini, who claimed to be a student of Marchesi, charmed everyone. Maria wrote to ask her sister Elisabetta Mola to write to Marchesi to verify his connection with Cittadini. That year Richard was well enough for them to go to the private view of the Academy exhibition on the day reserved for the Royal Family. They saw the Regent, but no other royals. It was a very good show and the atmosphere much like it was in Maria's youth. All the pretty women went to be seen and the men to look at them, the pictures being second. No matter...the Academy made a lot of money.

Maria's principal worry concerning Richard's health was his lack of reason. He claimed to have conversations with more than one person of the Trinity. He believed that he had visits from Charles I, William Pitt, even Praxiteles and Apelles. Apart from the vagaries of his mind, her husband was fairly well until an attack the winter of 1819, which left his hand and arm partly paralysed. Although he could walk, their life became quieter. To Cosway's credit he remained cheerful and very grateful for all that his wife did for him. She confided the stress of caring for him to a few correspondents, complaining to one:

> ...now I am a nobody; at one time it was enough to be heard by me to succeed, now I have no more music or company.... . The health and age of my husband keeps me sequestered from the world to play the nurse rather than the Elegant. You had no reason to reprove my husband for not writing, he has not the use of his hand, and he was always lazy at writing.

The cares of nursing were not her only responsibility. Her husband's financial affairs were in as great disorder as his books and prints. Both had to be examined and put in order. She started by cataloguing his thousands of books, but soon found she should look at his accounts. Cosway had neglected collecting his credits for over forty years. When Maria had a proper inventory of their possessions and debts in 1820 she found they were owed over £7,680. The Prince Regent alone owed £2,832 and appears never to have paid for Cosway's work, including nearly fifty portrait miniatures of the Prince himself.

In the midst of her cares after Richard's most serious attack, she received more terrible news that winter. Elisabetta Mola, her sister, was taken ill and quickly succumbed. Maria's grief was aggravated by Annette's apparent insensitivity to these misfortunes:

> ...I have been afflicted to lose this good sister who loved me so much...you spoke of balls at the college and I could not imagine that you would have the children dance the day after her death. However this has been the case which gave me much pain.... I wrote the news to my sister in Ireland, although I tried to soften the blow, she fell down in apoplexy. They had to bleed her three times...

> I am surprised that neither you nor Josephine speak about my husband. A month and a half ago I sent you news of his paralysis and it seems I speak continually to you of my worry about this...

Then, a month later Maria was writing to Annette of another loss:

> Here I am in the deepest grief. The best of my friends is dead. It is a great loss for me. The Marchioness Townshend that you know by the portrait. It is one of the drawings of my husband that I had in my study. The most beautiful, the most virtuous, the kindest.... All is of sadness for me here that I feel this loss still.

To whom could she turn, other than her very young second daughter, for an understanding ear? After a hiatus of some fourteen years – no letters exchanged since Lyon – Maria re-opened a correspondence with Jefferson.

In times of need her thoughts often turned to the kind American. She confided in him once again:

> To the length of silence I draw a curtain. Remembrance must be <u>ever</u> green… . Often I have read your name in the papers. Therefore have been acquainted of your proceedings in that honorable way which was expected from you. … Forgotten by the arts, suspended the direction of education (tho it is going on vastly well in my absence) I am exercising the occupations of a nurse… . In your Dialogue your head would tell me, 'that is <u>enough</u>', your heart perhaps will understand, I might wish <u>for more</u>

There was one friend left in London who remained steadfast. Forgotten was the disapproval of Maria's escape to Italy after Louisa's birth. Anne Damer, the sculptress, opened her country place to the Cosways the last summers of Cosway's life. York House in Twickenham had belonged to Queen Anne. Its sweeping green lawn went down to the Thames between ancient trees. Baskets of every variety of flower were scattered on the lawn. Mrs. Damer's company was charming and she gave her guests the freedom to do as they liked. These country visits were wonderful for Cosway's health; he always returned to London refreshed and well, except for his arm. Still, Maria had to cut his meat for him and to write for him. When King George died, she was obliged to accompany her husband to give his condolences as the new King's Principal Painter. Not being able to write, Richard asked her to write a letter on the black-bordered paper placed in the palace, which he signed awkwardly.

With the advice of some of Cosway's friends Maria was able to arrange his affairs so that they remained comfortable, if in more modest circumstances. John Soane, an old friend from the Academy, advised her on the condition and value of their house in Stratford Place, before they gave it up. The lawyer and travel writer, Sir John Carr, advised them to put their possessions in trust. Then he helped with Richard's will and became with Francis Douce, the antiquarian and collector, one of his trustees. All this required a vast amount of time to count, sort, inventory, and decide what to sell. Maria spent the better part of a year preparing for moving house. In the spring of 1821 she settled Richard in his new home, which troubled him not at all. With great satisfaction she reported to Annette:

> My husband has already gone to the other house, he is so happy
> & is very well. I shall be happy there also, it's a very pretty house,
> but I spend all day here. However, here is my address where you
> can direct your letters – No. 31 Edgeware Road, London,

The last days at Stratford Place were spent preparing the sales of some pictures, *objets d'art*, curiosities, armour, books, then the furniture and the house. The first sale was held in mid-May. A superb catalogue announced the variety of treasures:

A CATALOGUE
OF THE VERY CURIOUS AND VALUABLE
Assemblage of Miscellaneous Articles
OF
TASTE AND VIRTU
The Property of that distinguished Artist and Virtuoso
RICHARD COSWAY, ESQ. R.A.
CONSISTING OF
ANCIENT ARMOUR,
BUHL & INDIA CABINETS,
Antiques Bronzes, Marbles, Terra-cottas
CANDELABRA OF RICH ORMOLU,
SPLENDID CARVED TABLES, TRIPODS AND
BRACKETS,
OLD CHINA
An EGYPTIAN MUMMY *and an* IBIS,
AND NUMEROUS OTHER ARTICLES OF TASTE AND
CURIOSITY.

With rare excitement Maria described all to Annette:

> ...this sale makes the greatest sensation. The arrangement is
> magnificent, the effects superb. We sent cards for the <u>private view</u>

during two days. The first nobility came. The King asked for the catalogue. It was even said that he would come. I had a magnificent one bound & sent it to all the Royal Family. It's an enthusiasm, an admiration as has never been seen. ... I am so happy to leave this house, the other is charming. I come here every morning at 9'oclock after mass & return to dine at six with my husband who is there since three weeks.

The excitement caused by the sale did not translate into the material benefits she had hoped for. Another sale on the same dates attracted all the collectors and artists. Mr. Christie auctioned the estate of Sir Joshua Reynolds' niece, the late Marchioness of Thormond, who had inherited the Old Masters, prints, books and many paintings by Sir Joshua himself. Unlike Richard Cosway, the former President of the Academy was still in fashion. His works commanded great prices in the heat of contested bidding. The seven or eight thousand pounds Maria received was much less than expected, and the house was so deteriorated that they realised half of what her husband had spent. It was thought best by Stanley, the auctioneer, to put off the sale of the prints and drawings to a more propitious moment. Nevertheless the Cosways were now on a firmer financial basis. Sadly Richard enjoyed his new home a very short time, a bit more than two months. In July Maria was writing to Jefferson on black-bordered paper:

The appearance of this letter will inform you I have been left a widow. Poor Mr. Cosway was suddenly taken by an apoplectic fit – And being the third proved his last. At the time we had hoped he would enjoy a few years – for he never had been so well & so happy – the change of air was found necessary for his health. I took a very charming house & fitted it up handsome & comfortable with those pictures & things he liked most – ... He had neglected his affairs very much and when I was obliged to take them in my hands was astonished. I took evry means to ameliorate them & had succeeded at least for his comforts. and my consolation was his constantly repeating how well and how happy he was. We had an auction of all his effects & house in

Stratford Place, which lasted two months…the sale did not produce as much as we expected, but enough to make him comfortable & free from embarrassment, as he might have been if I had not acted accordingly – everybody thought he was very rich, & I was astonished when put to the real knowledge of his situation. – He made his will two years ago & left me sole executrice & mistress of everything. After having settled every thing here & provided for three cousins of Mr. C, I shall retire from this bustling & <u>insignificant</u> world to my favourite college at Lodi, as I always intended…I long to hear from you – the remembrance of a person I so highly esteem & venerate affords me the happiest consolation & your <u>patriarcal</u> situation delights me…. I will write again before I leave this country…I shall pass thro' Paris & taulk of you with Madame de Corny. Believe me ever your most affectionate & obliged Maria Cosway

Maria was not desperate with grief after losing her husband. The couple had lived apart so many years that her thoughts were entirely absorbed by her educational project. Her affections were satisfied by the attachment to her darling Annette. In spite of her strong desire to return to Italy, Maria had done everything in her power to prolong the life and happiness of her husband. She could be satisfied that all was done that a wife should do. He passed his last days in comfort and dignity. More importantly his cheerful character persisted, rendering him happy and appreciative. After Richard's death it took his wife a year to dispose of his collections.

64. Richard Westmacott, Memorial Plaque to Richard Cosway, *St. Marylebone Church, 1821.*

To Maria's great joy she was joined in London by her sister Charlotte, who came from Ireland to be with her after so many years of separation. This happiness was tinged with disappointment that Charlotte could not be persuaded to leave her Irish friends and come to live with her closest relative. Maria did not grasp Charlotte's desire to escape the shadow of a celebrated and opinionated sister. This loss was soon compensated by the arrival of Annette, who joined them in the autumn.

Maria was occupied with the delayed sale of drawings and prints which took place in February 1822. John Thomas Smith, Keeper of Prints and Drawings in the British Museum, came every day to advise her on the arrangement of the prints. After taking him into her trust – even serving him tea from Dr. Johnson's teapot, lent to her by a friend so that Smith could draw it – the rude man betrayed her with a wretched portrait of Cosway in his book, *Nollekens and His Times*. Smith had become disgruntled over money. She explained to Francis Douce:

> I received a very extraordinary letter from Mr. Smith which really hurt me very much. He reproaches me the money £1000 I take out of England and my being wanting to him…you know sir that nothing is <u>settled</u> and I don't even know what I have to receive from the sale…I only wish he had not hurt so cruelly my feelings…

Smith had expected compensation for helping with the gargantuan task of arranging thousands of prints and drawings – the sale of 1676 lots lasted eight days. One day's sale was devoted entirely to Cosway's extraordinary collection of over a hundred drawings and many hundreds of prints after his favourite, Rubens. Now the Flemish painter was out of fashion and brought the least of all. Other artists were well represented with multiple examples of the work of Rembrandt, Jordaens, Van Dyck and all the major Italian artists, especially Correggio, Parmigiano, Giulio Romano, Titian, Michelangelo, Raphael, and Mantegna.

After the prints and drawings Maria had to sell most of her pictures and miniatures and the furniture from the Edgware Road house. She spent an inordinate amount of time organising an exhibition of Cosway's works to be offered by private sale. Many who came to view his collections had said they were disappointed not to see more of his works. She thought it would be an honour to show them one last time. Before the exhibition she sent a case of the best works down to Brighton for the King. Sir Thomas Lawrence spent a whole morning helping her select them. She offered to take the snuff boxes and miniatures herself. To her dismay Cosway was as out of fashion as Rubens. She gave an unhappy account to Francis Douce:

> The pictures and drawings are all come home safe from His Majesty with a fine letter thanking me for the sight of them. I have £30 to pay for the expences. I have done my duty to Mr. Cosway…

The exhibit took place for over a month. Maria was there every day, but had to report again to Douce her lack of success.

> Mr. Cosway's exhibition went off very bad, nobody came, and I have an expence. I don't regret because the intention was honourable to his memory. The King returned all I sent. T'was not his fault but those about him.

After all the harassment of selling and moving, Maria and Annette made a tour of Scotland during the month of May 1822, where the people and the countryside pleased them immensely. This favourable impression was reciprocated by one of their hostesses, Mrs. Anne Grant:

> Of all the strangers I have seen of late none please me so much as Maria Cosway, who is going to reside in her native Italy but came down to see Scotland before she takes farewell of Great Britain. She spent the last evening with me…greatly deepen'd the impression her character and manners had made on me before. Her opinions are so sound & independent of the fashions of the world & so superior to those of a mere artist; her dress too & primitive goodness so well preserved with so much intercourse with the world, & all her various talents made subservient to the love of God & her fellow creatures. It does me good to meet such an unsophisticated being.

At last in July Maria and her protégé were ready to leave. As she had promised Jefferson, one of her last tasks in London was to send off a letter to him.

> I have at last finished all the affairs which have kept me after the loss of poor Mr. Cosway and am returning to the tranquillity, good climate & favourite as well as useful occupation of my dear college at Lodi…. In appearance Mr. C. passed for being very rich, but in reality was far from it, little had but which depended on the sale of his valuable & immense collection & that sold for very little, the times are bad here…. However, if what I have is not sufficient for this country where I am going I shall be comfortable and at ease. My activity requires some occupation & what I have chosen is a glorious one…I have lost many valuable old friends and at my age & my sentiments new ones I little care for…. I wish I could see you on your charming Monticello! Could I drop back some of my years I should be happy to pay you a visit. I have visited Scotland and have been delighted, the scenery beautiful & the nation brave;

Jefferson's last letter to Maria was written a few months later. Despite years of separation, he thought of the persistence of their common interests. They both had built educational institutions.

> The sympathies of our earlier days harmonise, it seems in age also. You retire to your College of Lodi…I am laying the foundation of an University in my native state…. We have still one building to erect, which will be on the principle of your Pantheon, a Rotunda like that…I wish indeed you could recall some of your by-past years and seal it with your approbation. You have two friends here, still living, Trumbull & myself to whom such a visit would be real beatitude.

That voyage was the one never taken, the only one she was never able to make. In every letter to her American friend she wished for it. From London she wrote:

'Oh how often have I thought of America! wished to have exerted myself there.'

And later after Richard's death:

'I wish <u>Monticello</u> was not <u>so far</u>! I would pay you a visit if it was ever so much out of my way, but it is impossible…'

After her return to Italy she still dreamed:

I wish I could come & <u>learn</u> from you, was it the furthest part of Europe nothing would prevent me but that immense sea makes it a great distance.

Knowing that she would never see him again, in her last letter to America – which was never answered – she consoled herself with a request:

…I have had my great saloon painted, with the representation of the 4 parts of the world & the most distinguished objects in them. I have at a loss for America, as I found very few small prints – however Washington town is mark'd & I have left a hill barren as I would [like] to place Monticello, & the Seminary, if you favor me with some description that I might have it introduced you would oblige me much.

The hill remained barren with nothing to mark the passage through her life of a friendship which represented the ineffable and unattainable. Jefferson's last illness prevented his replying to her request. He died before he could describe Monticello to her – in 1826 – the same year as Maria's brother, George Hadfield, whose life ended in Washington.

Now in 1828, Maria and Charlotte Combe were the last Hadfields and few of Maria's old friends remained. Jefferson and Denon were gone. She corresponded with John Soane, but often to trouble him with business matters. Most English travellers went straight to Bologna or Florence and never stopped at Lodi, but Mrs. Cosway did have the pleasure of entertaining

Mr. and Mrs. Colnaghi and their daughters, who were brought down from Milan by Ferdinand Artaria, the print merchant. The Artarias sometimes came to stay in Blevio and Maria had other local friends whom she hospitably welcomed to Blevio. Her house was often so full that she had to write to Annette to send up more beds from the college. Richard's cousin, Sir William Cosway, and his young wife spent a day with her on their way to Genoa. She never understood why her husband would never see him. She thought he made a good figure in the world and travelled in high style. Maria impressed her guests as a stimulating hostess. Francesca Colnaghi described her at this time:

> …she was lively and intellectual, in spite of Old Age, whose touches tho' seen and felt, were resisted successfully by activity of mind and body.

Mrs. Cosway's dining room in Lodi remained fixed in the memories of those who saw it. Local artists helped her decorate it. Painted as an arbour with vines climbing up a trellis, the room was like a garden with trees and stonework in the foreground and orchards, vineyards, and mountains in the distance. The fireplace was disguised as a garden grotto. Beside it a painted replica of Richard Cosway's monument in St. Mary-le-bone Church emerged from the verdure. Opposite the fireplace a playing fountain accompanied meals with the music of falling water.

Guests were also impressed by concerts of eight to eleven girls playing several pianos in the grand ballroom. This room, too, was decorated with mural paintings of the four continents. It was there Maria wanted to put Monticello, but never could.

All her visitors, including the Emperor Franz and Empress Karolina Augusta, considered the paintings and drawings of Richard Cosway the great point of interest, worthy of the trouble of coming to quiet little Lodi. They also admired Maria Cosway's last work of art – the life she had created in a monastic paradise, where order and beauty, charity and tranquillity reigned in an aesthetic whole. The deep impression of such a life, etched on her child's mind in Il Conventino, had finally taken form.

65. *Engraving of Richard Cosway's* Woman and child *by Paolo Lasinio,
1823. Maria Cosway commissioned the Florentine engraver to do a series of
her husband's drawings, which she offered as gifts.*

Epilogue

After the purchase of her *casino*, as Maria Cosway called her Blevio country
house, she seemed to enjoy life at some distance from the school she loved,
but maintained at the cost of continuing difficulties with personnel, unruly
pupils, and unappreciative local citizens. There were serious administrative
problems up until 1830, when she appealed to the Imperial family to help

her resolve them. Maria always demonstrated the gifts of a superb courtier, as well as a genuine friendship for her intermediary with the Habsburgs, Countess Sophia Wayna. Many letters from this Austrian noblewoman, a Lady in Waiting to the Archduchess and Vice-Queen of Lombardy, are filled with gratitude on the part of the ruling court in Milan for the many gifts showered on the Countess Wayna, the Vice Queen and the Empress Maria Karolina Augusta in Vienna. The Vice Queen and Empress received engravings of Richard Cosway's drawings. The Countess Wayna was offered prints of Maria Cosway's paintings *The Hours* and *The Birth of the Thames* as well as more precious mementoes such as Maria's own artist's palette, a writing desk, and loans of many English books. The two ladies seemed to share common interests and enjoy a sincere friendship, although there was certainly an element of self-interest in the educator's careful cultivation of the Austrian court. She became a welcome visitor to the Imperial Palace in Monza near Milan and was ultimately able to pass a memorandum, outlining her administrative difficulties, through the Countess Wayna to Archduke Rainier, the Viceroy, and then to the Emperor himself. Their sympathy for her project led to the solution that Mrs. Cosway had sought since her days in Lyon. When the Empress Maria Karolina visited the college in Lodi and learned of the founder's desire to have the work continue as part of a religious society, she immediately thought of the Order of English Ladies, well-established in Austria and close to the Imperial family. Maria Cosway found this suggestion in perfect accord with her plans and hastened to request that two members of the order join her staff.

The denouement rapidly fell into place in 1830. In June of that year she donated the school buildings and £4,000 held by her in the Bank of England to the Imperial Treasury, keeping a life interest in the bank stock. The Empress herself wrote to the Superior of the order, Countess Giulia Mailath, and ordered that two nuns be sent from St. Polten to Lodi. Regina de Starkmann and Maria Mariacher arrived in June 1831 to form the nucleus of what eventually became a school governed by the Order of English Ladies. As Maria Cosway had always wished, she was able to keep the direction of the school during her lifetime and see that her methods were strictly observed. She wrote with satisfaction to John Soane, 'I have therefore the consolation to see my house styled the English Ladies; an English woman was the founder of this useful work and an English woman has brought it into Italy.' The burden of not knowing how to make her work permanent was at last eased. A year after the nuns arrived, the school was formally donated to the Order of English Ladies by a legal instrument.

The final consecration of thirty years of determined struggle to build an institution for the public good arrived in November of 1834 when Emperor Franz I accorded the title of Baroness to Maria Luisa Caterina Cecilia Hadfield Cosway. This ennobling of a woman in her own right attests to the remarkable qualities of intelligence, fortitude, and perseverance that Maria Cosway demonstrated over many years, alone and unaided except for the intermittent confidence of powerful friends, earned in the early days by her charm and later by her merit. The times were not yet those of emancipated women. The dossier prepared before the Emperor's bestowal of her title shows that the Court required a full biography of Richard Cosway and proof of his membership in the Royal Academy before approval of her elevation.

As a local dignitary Maria Cosway's last years were comfortable and secure. She remained in excellent health until her last year, except for dim eyesight, which prevented her writing. Her later letters are in a secretary's hand. She maintained a correspondence with John Soane, Charlotte Jones and her sister Charlotte Combe, although we have only indirect evidence of letters from the women. All her most intimate correspondence was lost or destroyed. Her papers contain no notes or letters from her husband, sisters, mother, Thomas Jefferson or Luigi Marchesi. She saved for posterity only those records which could be classified as business or friendship. In the last decade of her life she experienced both the satisfaction and the aggravation of being memorialised in London publications. She should have been pleased with the romantic depiction of the Cosways' receptions in Alan Cunningham's *Lives of the Most Eminent British Painters, Sculptors, and Architects*, and satisfied that she was a contributor to this result by passing autobiographical details to Cunningham through a letter to Sir William Cosway in 1830. She was surely displeased if she read a review of Cunningham's book in the *Quarterly Review* in which the reviewer, speaking of 'some painters still respectable', adds this footnote:

'We should except Cosway, the fantastic miniature painter, of whom & his musical parties Mr. Cunningham had he known much would probably have thought it right to tell us little. We remember that <u>set</u> well, & wonder how our author should have contrived to converse with no one capable of giving him a hint of the true state of the case, which he now decks out in sentiment & romance.'

We know she was upset by John Thomas Smith's *Life of Nollekens* for its portrait of Richard Cosway. She complained of it to John Soane:

'In London not only I have lost most all my best friends, but have most bitter enemies, whose malicious observations & reports most hurt my feelings. I have heard of the horrible book published by Mr. Smith. He used to come to us as he used to go to poor Nollekens with interested views.'

Smith vexed her with descriptions of Richard as 'one of the dirtiest boys' who became 'ridiculously foppish', was 'a well-made little man…much like a monkey in his face'. She must have been embarrassed that Smith recounted Cosway's interest in the supernatural and the artist's conversations with the departed from Charles I to William Pitt.

No matter what reputation Cosway enjoyed in London or what obscurity he might now have, his widow was eminently respectable. The Baroness Cosway travelled to Rome in the spring of 1835, where she was able to see her old friend Joseph, Cardinal Fesch, almost on an equal footing. In the fall of the same year she was received in Vienna by the Dowager Empress, Maria Karolina Augusta, who remembered the interesting artist and educator from Imperial tours to Milan and Lodi. In these years Maria Cosway had kept old friends such as Giulia Beccaria, who was now in Milan with her daughter and famous son-in-law, Alessandro Manzoni, author of the popular *I Promessi Sposi*. Giulia's granddaughter Vittoria Manzoni was duly enrolled in Maria's school where her grandmother wrote to her in 1832:

'Oh my dear Vittorinetta! you are with a friend I value so highly, Mme Cosway: a happy instinct made you love her as soon as you met her.'

Maria Cosway demonstrated in later life a talent often overshadowed by her artistic sensibility and musical gifts. This was her hard-headed attention to the details of economic life. Her obsession with order led her to draw up several wills and codicils, including a will in England dated 27th July 1829 and seven Italian instruments over the period 1829-1837. Always managing her business affairs with extreme prudence, she prided herself on avoiding debt in a letter to one of her English executors, Sir John Soane:

> '…I never do any thing unless I have the money in hand to pay…
> . Poor Mr. C. gave me the example and the happiness I felt in having no debts to pay for him made me richer than he was in reality.'

Her friend Francis Douce (or one of his secretaries) considered her economy downright meanness, noting on the bottom of one of her letters:

> '…I wouldn't interfere in the business for this mean & troublesome woman who wishes to save herself a little expence.'

The English will provided for legacies of £100 each to be left to Richard Cosway's cousins, Elizabeth and Jane Cosway. £500 was left to both Henry Whiting and his wife Mary. Charlotte Combe, Maria's sister in Ireland, and Annette Prodon each received £1,000 and Miss Charlotte Jones, the friend and former pupil of Mr. Cosway £200. The Cosway sisters and Mrs. Elizabeth Madison, Maria's former maid, were already beneficiaries of a trust set up in 1822 with £2,800 invested in British public funds.

The Italian codicils give a glimpse into the intimacy of Maria Cosway's daily life, reflected by her possessions. She drew up detailed lists, designating specific items – miniatures, snuffboxes, porcelain, and jewellery – to be left to a large group of family and friends. Two of her more precious pieces, a diamond ring and brooch each containing locks of her daughter's hair, were left to her sister Charlotte in Ireland. The Mola nieces and nephews each received special gifts: a set of necklace, ring, earrings and brooch in gold and lapis lazuli to her niece Isabella and a similar set in garnets to her least favourite niece, Angelina, apparently forgiven after having sowed discord in the college and spread rumours in Lodi about its management.

The wayward girl also received a silver bas relief of the interment of Christ to keep her mind on the right path. The three Mola boys were treated somewhat better. Each received 30,000 Austrian pounds and various mementoes which she thought worthy of passing down to the family. Gian Maria, probably the eldest, received a cup made from a tree supposedly planted by Shakespeare in his garden, a box made from Nelson's ship, two rings, one of which 'having been always worn by my Father. I have preserved it as a memorial. Gian Maria will preserve it as having belonged to the Father of his Mother, my sister Bettina.' Bartolomeo received a ring, a silver cup, and a box with General Paoli's cameo, and Vincenzino, who became a priest, was given a portrait of Pope Pius Septimus in cameo, a Japanned writing box, and a ring with the stone in the form of a heart. Although not a legal bequest she thought enough of her executor Sir John Soane to send him a special gift which she described to him in a letter.

> When I was at Paris, my friend Monsieur Denon, whom you must know by reputation, was just returned from Egypt with B. He gave me two small Egyptian figures he found himself. They are in perfect preservation, and tho' small, the work is with much taste & beauty & their hieroglyphs perfect & clear. I even left the Egyptian dust on them. These I put in a small box with a Mercury & a Minerva found here at Lodi Vecchio...

Aside from family and friends she made important bequests to persons of rank, which certainly made the point that she considered herself of their number. There was certainly more than a trace of pride in two precious bequests to the Great Duke of Tuscany: Richard Cosway's portrait of General Paoli and a hard-stone snuffbox given to Paoli by the Elector of Saxony, Frederick Augustus III. She left the Archduchess and Vice-Queen of Lombardy a wooden and ormolu cabinet fitted for writing and drawing and two oil portraits of Rubens and his wife by Richard Cosway.

The person dearest to her in later years, Annette Prodon, was the object of a continual concern. Her closeness to Maria Cosway is reflected in several legal bequests. In addition to the £1,000 sterling left to Annette in an English will, Maria made a special codicil in 1832 specifically for 'my dear Annette Prodon living with me in the said college whom from affection I consider as my adopted Daughter'. This codicil established a trust in Milanese pounds which would give Annette £1,000 pounds in annual revenue. Maria also specified that Annette should continue to occupy her room in the college with furnishings. If the young girl chose later to 'secede' from the Society of English Ladies, the Society should continue to furnish her the same lodgings, board, servants as then provided. She should not be obliged to teach. It was apparently very important to also specify that Annette would have free use of the bath placed 'in the middleways' to place therein her furniture. All Maria's personal effects, not listed in earlier wills, were left to Annette: wardrobe, apparel, laces, silver tea service, china, damask tablecloths, napkins, silver candlesticks, 'my large necklace in gold with a cross, linen and bed furniture, matching window curtains'. The codicil concludes with a statement of her attachment to her adopted daughter: 'my predilection for the said Annetta Prodon arises from the constant affection which she had for me and from her excellent deportment which undoubtedly will continue...' In a handwritten document of 1830, which is the last holograph will of Maria Cosway, her trust and devotion to Annette could not be more strongly expressed. It ends with the following paragraph:

> 'As the Lady Annette Prodon has a knowledge of my effects and can write to London to my executors to send her my casket of jewels, I leave at her disposition all those things which remained and particularly mentioned and bequeathed by me to the various persons. She is to have the keys of all the cabinets and cases so that she may facilitate the said distributions and keep or bestow those objects which are not named as I have commissioned her in a letter addressed to the said Annette Prodon.'

This responsibility was apparently troublesome to the Baroness's executors. When the old lady became bedridden, partially paralysed, unable to write, barely able to speak or to see, her attorney and executor Dr. Carlo Mancini read her several codicils before witnesses in 1837, which she either signed with a mark or acknowledged with a nod of the head. These changes annulled Annette Prodon's power to dispose of any property according to Maria Cosway's wishes in 1830. More significantly they gave to Dr. Mancini control over her entire estate – other than the £4,000 put in trust for the college. A codicil drawn up on 13th May 1837 during Maria's last illness states that Mancini may dispose of all the residue of her estate apart from the trust – '…to make such use of it as will be conformable to the direction by her…without the obligation of giving any account of it to any one so ever.' These later 'oral' codicils reaffirmed the validity of all previous wills and codicils except for the 1830 paragraph concerning Annette Prodon and the disposition of her art collection. Maria Cosway's original wish, expressed in 1830, that her large collection of Richard Cosway's drawings and all his oil paintings – except that of Paoli which went to the Grand Duke of Tuscany – be left to her husband's cousin Sir William Cosway was nullified by the 1837 codicils. Sir William's death four years earlier may have caused her to reconsider a bequest to the Cosway side of the family. Another of her directives from the 1830 document was apparently changed verbally. Carlo Mancini made a sworn statement before a notary on 8th January 1839, a year after her death, that her desire to be buried in Blevio beside her friend Maddalena Sannazzari had been supplanted by a request to obtain clerical approval of a tomb in a chapel of the Santa Maria delle Grazie Church adjoining her college. This was granted. On the 6th November 1838 she was laid to rest near her beloved college after a temporary burial in the public cemetery.

In spite of her regular attention to business matters two choices of professional help proved disastrous. Her lawyer in London, Thomas Gill, was more or less useless and of dubious character. Entrusted with the list of Richard Cosway's debtors, he collected little. He was of no help in the disposition of George Hadfield's estate. Maria had to turn to Prince Hoare instead of her attorney. More alarming was a newspaper report, transmitted by her sister Charlotte, that Gill had been arrested for embezzlement. Although Gill did no serious damage to the Cosway estate, another of her representatives did. In 1834 Prince Hoare, one of her oldest friends and an executor, died. His replacement, apparently approved by the other executor, Soane, was a Newbold Kinton, who did not give the college the £4,000 set aside in trust nor the residue of the estate which was to go to the Italian executors. Annette Prodon and the executors were forced to sue Kinton in London. The suit was resolved in 1841 in the plaintiffs' favour, awarding them the contested sum with interest and a further £2,800 which remained in the estate. The Dickensian accounting recorded in the Master's report for the case seems to indicate that after Mr. Kinton's expenses were deducted the plaintiffs received much less than their due.

Annette Prodon's association in the law suit demonstrates her continued dedication to Maria Cosway's work. Annette spent the rest of her life in Lodi and probably became a member of the Order of English Ladies. It has been suggested that she appears as one of the nuns in the group portrait of Maria and some of her pupils painted around 1835.

66. Memorial to Maria Cosway in the church of Santa Maria delle Grazie, Lodi.

Today a marble plaque in a small chapel of the Church of Santa Maria delle Grazie in Lodi marks the place where Maria Cosway finally rests after many voyages across Europe and many encounters with a good number of those whom history considers the fathers of the modern West. Her name is not remembered. Yet those whose names have been burnished by time deeply admired this gifted woman, treasured her friendship, and were fascinated by a character delicately balanced between charm and strength. Maria Cosway's ephemeral celebrity has vanished, but there remains a lasting admiration from those who turn aside to learn the facts of her life.

Notes

PAGE 1

The attempted murder of Maria Hadfield as an infant has been widely reported in various printed sources. Her own account is to be found in an autobiographical letter from her to her husband's cousin, Sir William Cosway, dated 24th May 1830 in the National Art Reference Library, Victoria and Albert Museum, London, M.S. (Eng.) L.961-1953. An interesting variation of this account is to be found in Stisted, *Letters*, pp.479-482. Mrs. Stisted claims to have heard this version from Charlotte Hadfield Combe, Maria's sister.

Two other farfetched accounts of Maria Cosway's origins circulated in France during her residence there from 1801-1811. Both seem based on a mixture of rumour and legend. The first, an article in a ladies' magazine, may have been inspired by Madame Cosway, the educator, as publicity for her school. This version, with a pronounced religious colouration, has Isabella Hadfield suffering from a difficult pregnancy and promising her nurse to raise the expected child as a Catholic if both survive. Later, the nurse confesses to the murders of previous children on her death bed. (*Le Petit Magasin des Dames*, No. 43, 1806.)

The second, a police report, should have been more accurate, but is certainly both fiction and fact. When Madame Cosway applied for an Imperial passport for England, i.e., a document approved personally by the Emperor, the Ministry of Police required a full report from the Commissioner-General of Police in Lyon. His amazing report of 18th November 1811 first explains its delay by the fact that the Commissioner wished to verify the surprising results of the investigation. He then continues: '… an Italian prince, during a sojourn in London met the mother of the lady Cosway, took her to Leghorn, and there they had several children. Having different religions, the lovers often discussed the children's religion, the father wishing Catholicism and the mother Protestantism. The Catholic nurse, hearing these discussions, thought to do a religious work in strangling the fruits of love of the Italian prince until the birth of the lady Cosway when the mother consented to raise her as a Catholic. The lady Cosway received a fine education and was they say lady-in-waiting in some little court in Italy. She married a painter who died when the French entered Italy.' (Archives Nationales, F7.) It is difficult to know where this story originated, but it is a version which conveniently minimises Maria Cosway's links to England or her very much alive English husband still living in London.

PAGE 2

The christening records of six children of Charles and Isabella Hadfield can be found in the Chapel Register of the Protestant Society at Leghorn. Two Hadfield boys were christened before 1760 – John on 28th January 1755 and Horace Arthur on 9th April 1757. The death of John is also noted on 13th October 1758, but not that of Horace Arthur. The record of the christening of 'Lucy Hadfield' appears to be that of Maria Hadfield, since Louisa was one of her given names and the date corresponds with the presumed year of Maria's birth:

> Lucy Hadfield, Daughter of Charles & Isabella Hadfield was born at Florce the 7 [or 17 or 11?] July 1760 & baptized the 22 Nov following. Godfather Sir Brooke Bridges. Godmother Lady Lucy Boyle and Miss Thulis – by me. Everard Hutcheson.

On 11th June 1803, Maria Cosway noted in her journal that this day, 11th June, was the date of her birth. (Archivio Fondazione Cosway, Lodi – A.F.C.L.) It is possible that the poorly legible number in the Chapel Register of Leghorn, which appears to be a 7 or 17, is an 11. However, the month July is quite clear. Either the Reverend Hutcheson or Maria Cosway was mistaken about the month.

William Thomas Hadfield was baptised on 25th October 1761.

Charlotte D. Hadfield was baptised on 5th May 1766, at three weeks old.

Another Hadfield baby was christened Maria-Ann on 13th November 1769, but the date is impossibly late to be *the* Maria. It could be the younger sister Lisabetta or another child who did not survive.

There is no record of George Hadfield's christening.

Page 3

The marriage of Charles Hadfield and Isabella Pocock is recorded in the Chapel Register of the Protestant Society of Leghorn, Public Record Office, as taking place 5th August 1753. It is difficult to tell if the last digit is a three or a nine. Later clerks transcribing the original register transcribed a 9, but it seemed to me a 3. 1753 seems a likely date, not only because of the numerous children born after this date, but because Lord Bruce, whose chaplain married the Hadfields, was in Siena in 1753 and was in England in 1759. However, given the casual versions of marriage common at that time, anything is possible.

Maria Cosway to Count Francesco Melzi d'Eril, 2nd May 1812, A.F.C.L., Diario D.

Page 5

A handwritten note of F. J. B. Watson in his annotated copy of his Walpole Society article on Thomas Patch suggests that the small portrait of a lady on the same wall as a portrait of Charles Hadfield in the Patch painting 'A Gathering at Sir Horace Mann's' is that of Isabella Hadfield.

Page 6

P.R.O., Chapel Register of the Protestant Society of Leghorn.

Page 7

It is unlikely that James Boswell remembered Maria Hadfield as a child or she him, but they were most likely under the same roof in 1765.

Page 8

Details of the Bembridge portrait of General Paoli are found in W. T.

Whitley's *Artists and their Friends in England, 1700-1799* London: Benjamin Blom, 1928, Reissued 1968, I, pp.187-188.

The style and generosity of Sir Watkin Williams-Wynn is recorded in the Mann-Walpole correspondence and Sir Brinsley Ford's article 'Sir Watkin Williams-Wynn: A Welsh Maecenas', *Apollo*, vol. 99, June 1974.

PAGE 8

Florence's cleanliness compared with other cities is recorded in George Finch, 9th Earl of Winchilsea's letter to his mother, Lady Charlotte Finch of 3rd April 1773. (Leicestershire Record Office, Finch M.S.S.)

The records of the convent of San Francesco di Sales detto Il Conventino in Florence were destroyed by the flood of 1966. This institution had a major influence on the life of Maria Hadfield, creating her lifelong attachment to the Order of the Visitation, where she sought refuge in Genoa and Lyon. Although the modern order has no record of a branch ever having been in Florence, St. François de Sales was a founder of the Visitandines and was ever associated with them. Il Conventino was an institution for the education of young girls from the eighteenth century to the present time. Maria Cosway's correspondence with Il Conventino's Superiora Anna Scopatina in 1828 gives evidence that this institution was the model for her work in Lodi. (A.F.C.L.)

PAGE 11

In short autobiographical notes in A.F.C.L., Maria Cosway records that Violante Cerruoti gave her drawing instruction for four years from ages eight to twelve and that she then was introduced to Johann Zoffany while she worked in the Grand Duke's Gallery. She also records that her three-day encounter with Joseph Wright of Derby in the summer of 1775 was even more significant.

Maria Hadfield's childhood vision is recounted in autobiographical notes made in her own hand. (A.F.C.L., n.d.)

PAGE 13

Maria Hadfield's requests to copy specific pictures are to be found in the Archivio della Galleria degli Uffizi in Florence. (A.G.U.) These requests are mentioned in: Borroni Salvadori, Fabia, 'Artisti e viaggiatori agli Uffizi nel Settecento', *Labyrinthos: Studi e ricerche sulle arti nei seccoli XVIII e XIX*, IV, nos 7-8, 1985 and VI, no 10, 1986.

Page 16

Maria Hadfield's admiration for Sir Joshua Reynolds' self-portrait and its superiority to that of Anton Mengs is expressed in her letter of 2nd December 1775 to Ozias Humphrey. R.A., Humphry Corr. M.S.S., H.U./ 2/36.

Page 17

A.F.C.L., M.C. Autobiographical M.S.

M.C. to O.H., 20th January 1776, R.A., Humphry Corr. M.S.S., H.U.2/ 40/41.

Charles Townley, a wealthy Catholic from Lancashire, assembled one of the outstanding collections of antique sculpture in the eighteenth century, now in the British Museum. On three Grand Tours in Italy he relentlessly pursued his antiquarian passion for the best examples of classical art. His papers, also in the British Museum, reveal that Charles Hadfield assisted him with many transactions and that Townley was a good friend of the artist Richard Cosway with whom he shared certain lascivious tastes.

Page 18

Maria Hadfield's practice of lunching with Ozias Humphrey and other artists in the Grand Duke's Gallery is revealed by a correspondence with the Gallery's direction in which the artists complained of a new policy to close the Gallery between one and three in the afternoon. See Borroni Salvadori, I, p.55.

Page 19

Ozias Humphrey and his unfortunate pursuit of Miss Paine are found in:

> Williamson, G. C., *Ozias Humphrey, R.A*, 1918.
> Smith, John Thomas, *Nollekens, Vol. II*, 1829.

M.C. to O.H., 2nd December 1775, R.A., Humphry Corr. M.S.S., H.U./ 2/36.

PAGES **20-21**

M.C. to O.H., 23rd [December] 1775, R.A., Humphry Corr. M.S.S., H.U./ 2/33.

   M.C. to O.H., 20th January 1776, R.A., Humphry Corr. M.S.S., H.U./ 2/40/41.

PAGES **22-23**

M.C. to O.H., 20th January 1776, R.A., Humphry Corr. M.S.S., H.U./2/ 40/41

   M.C. to O.H., 2nd December 1775, R.A., Humphry Corr. M.S.S., H.U./ 2/36

   On Dean, Edward Edwards, *Anecdotes of Painters...in England*, [1808], p.108.

   The Grand Duchess, Maria Luisa de Bourbon of Spain, hardly ever danced as she was with child every year. Arriving in Florence the year of their marriage in 1765, the Imperial Couple expected their ninth child shortly after the carnival of 1776. They were a handsome couple, but the Grand Duchess took an immense amount of snuff, which had disfigured her face.

   The pathetic state of Charles Edward Stuart, the Last Pretender, was widely reported in Sir Horace Mann's correspondence with his superiors in London. (Public Record Office, Kew – P.R.O., State Papers [S.P.] 105.)

   See also Moloney, Brian, *Florence and England*, p.68, and Wraxall, *Memoirs*, 1815.

   The suggestion of a connection between the Pretender and Charles Hadfield was alleged by Clotilda Stisted to have been told her by her governess Charlotte Hadfield Combe in Mrs. Stisted's *Letters*, pp.479-482. In any case Mann's remonstrances with Charles Hadfield about the wisdom of receiving Charles Edward in 1770 are authentic. See Sieveking, *The Memoir of Sir Horace Mann*, pp.250-251. The British envoy to Turin, Sir William Lynch, commented on the incident to his colleague Mann with an unflattering reference to Charles Hadfield: ...if I recollect his intellect right no one will ever suspect him of a plot.' P.R.O., S.P. 105/320, f.213.

PAGE **24**

M.C. to O.H., 20th January 1776, R.A., Humphry Corr., H.U./2/40/41

   M.C. to O.H., 24th February 1776, R.A., Humphry Corr., H.U./2/42

Chapter Two   Grand Tour

Page 27

Maria Cosway quotes her father's last words to her in a letter of 29th May 1816 (A.F.C.L.)

Page 28

The birth and christening of George Augustus, Lord Fordwich, are recounted in Sir Horace Mann's letters to his superiors in London. P.R.O./SP 105.

In Maria Cosway's autobiographical letter of 24th May 1830, she tells of going to Rome with Mrs. Gore: 'He [Charles Hadfield] meant to go to England with all his family as he wished I should see Rome, Mrs. Gore the mother of Lady Cowper took me with her. There I had an opportunity of knowing all the first living Artists intimately; Batoni, Mengs, Maron, and many English Artists, Fusely with his extraordinary visions struck my fancy. I made no regular study, but for one Year & half only went to see all that was high in painting & sculpture, made sketches, Etc. – I lost my father in this time & my Mother recalled me to Florence to go with her to England. My inclination from a child had been to be a Nun, I wished therefore to return to my Convent but my Mother was miserable about it & I was persuaded to accompany her…' (Victoria and Albert Museum, National Art Library, London – V.A., M.S. [Eng.] L, 961 – 1953.)

Information on the Gore family can be found in Ingamells, D*ictionary of British Travellers*, pp.410-411. Since the dates of Lord Fordwich's christening and Maria Hadfield's probable departure for Rome with Mrs. Gore were close together I presumed the linkage of the two events.

There is a record of Maria Hadfield's presence in Florence, which gives some evidence of the dates of her two Roman stays. The local parish records of the Church of San Fredegno, the *Stato di Animi,* show that she took Easter communion there in the years 1774, 1775, 1776, and 1778. Thus, she was in Rome in early 1777 and again in 1779. The only other Hadfield noted is her brother William, who was listed in 1775 and 1777.

Page 30

There is no evidence that Maria Hadfield met either James Byres or Thomas Jenkins in Rome, but it is probable. For her excursions she certainly relied on the guidebook by Guiseppe Vasi, *Itinerario Istruttivo diviso in otto Giornate per ritrovare con facilita tutte le Antiche e Moderne Magnificenze di Roma*…3rd ed., Roma, 1777 inscribed in her hand: 'Maria H. 1777 Roma' still found in her library in Lodi.

PAGE 32

The following notice appeared in the *Gazzetta Toscana* , No. 48, 1776 (30th November):

> 'Despite the death the previous day of Sig. Carlo Halfhid Innkeeper in the Fondacci di S. Spirito, the heirs have the intention to keep open for the accommodation of foreigners this dignified inn; and to satisfy the requirements of justice, the widow Sig. Elisabetta Halfhid notifies the public that whoever may be a creditor of the deceased for any reason should present the debt's justification to the house of this inn, which will be satisfied.'

On 10th December 1776, Sir Horace Mann wrote to Sir John Dick, English envoy at Leghorn: 'I wrote a few lines to you by the Milan courier on Saturday night to inform you of the death of Mr. Hatfield who appointed you & me Executors of his will, but as his widow is tutrix to his children with ample power to do what she pleases our office becomes useless, nevertheless as things may turn out differently. I have thought it proper as to myself to declare that I renounced that office though I have assured Mrs. Hatfield that I shall always be ready to do her any service that may be in my power, with which assurance she seems perfectly satisfied.' Dick M.S. Correspondence (Brinsley Ford Archive)

Despite Hadfield's testamentary wish to be buried in the Protestant Cemetery, Leghorn, no record of such a burial in the register of the English Chapel nor headstone in the cemetery was found by the author.

Charles Hadfield's will of 11th April 1774 is found in the *Archivio di Stato*, Florence.

PAGE 33

Louis Dutens described the details of Cardinal Albani's villa in his travel journal first published in Paris in 1775.

There is no record of Maria Hadfield's visits to the Villa Albani and Villa Borghese although it is probable, given Ozias Humphrey's introduction to these collections.

Pages 34-35

Maria Hadfield may not have been included regularly in the circle of English artists in Humphrey's 'academy', but she was certainly exposed to the unique art of Henry Fuseli, whose style influenced her later works, much to the Swiss painter's irritation. Hazlitt, *Conversations with James Northcote*, 1894.

Page 36

William Parsons' proposal of marriage to Maria Hadfield and Isabella Hadfield's advice to her daughter is documented in two letters: W. Parsons to Isabella Hadfield, 4th February 1777 and Isabella Hadfield to Maria Hadfield, 8th March 1777, both in the Royal Academy –R.A., H.U./2/55. Interestingly enough they are both in Ozias Humphry's correspondence, proving that they ended up in his possession despite Mrs. Hadfield's admonition not to show them to anyone.

There is no proof that Maria Hadfield visited the Palazzo Rospigliosi, but it is highly likely. Critics have seen the influence of Guido Reni's Apollo and Aurora on her painting of the Hours, exhibited at the Royal Academy in 1783.

Pages 37-38

The scene of Ozias Humphry's proposal is imagined, but there is evidence that Maria's s sentimental life became complicated in the years 1777-1779. She no doubt attracted the attention of young men easily, but none of them seemed inclined to enter into a permanent attachment except William Parsons whom she disliked and perhaps Humphry.

The evidence for Humphry's proposal is slim and may be the reflection of a rumour rather than reality. It is found in a letter from Elizabeth Banks to Humphrey cited in the text. Elizabeth Banks to O. Humphry, n.d. [1778], Royal Academy, H.U./2/68.)

Page 40

Prince Hoare to William Hadfield, 7th July 1777, Beinecke Library, Osborn Coll.

Giovanni Bastianelli to Prince Hoare, 17th January 1780, Beinecke Library, Osborn Coll.

PAGE 41

The evidence for the attentions of Prince Hoare and her attraction to him is found in the correspondence of Elizabeth Banks, Giovanni Bastianelli, and Hoare himself. In January 1781 at the time of Maria Hadfield's marriage to Richard Cosway, Hoare wrote to James Northcote to profess amusement at the visit of Thomas Banks, sent to break the news of the approaching marriage gently. Hoare claims that he had come out of the affair unwounded and that he had no regrets, except for Miss Hadfield, who could have done much better. (W. T. Whitley, *Artists in England, 1700-1799*, Vol. 2, pp.312-313.)

Thomas Banks to O. Humphry, 13th December 1777. (Beinecke Library, Osborn Coll.)

Elizabeth Banks to O. Humphry, n.d. [1778], R.A, H.U./2/68.

The archives of the Accademia del Disegno list the admission of 'Signora Maria Hadfeild Pittrice Inglese' on 27th September 1778. (Archivio di Stato, Firenze.)

Notice of her admission is also given in the *Gazzetta Toscana*, No. 41, 10th October 1778.

Although it is thought that Maria Hadfield received a silver medal from the Accademia del Disegno no record of this prize was found.

PAGES 42-44

Various mentions of Maria Hadfield, including her departure for Rome, are recorded in Joseph Mercer's *Diary of a Tour in France and Italy*. (National Library of Scotland, Acc.7952.) On Sunday, 15th [November 1778] he notes '...opera – Pretender asleep whole time...sat by Miss Hatfield.' On Saturday, 21st: 'After dinner we took an agreeable walk with Miss Hatfield to Country House of Grand Duke – mile from Porto Romano.' Monday, 30th: 'Signora Hatfield sang charmingly.' His mention of her frock of pea green satin was noted on Tuesday the 8th [December].

James Northcote noted Maria Hadfield's arrival in Rome, writing to his brother on 26th December 1778: 'We have now in Rome a Miss Hadfield, who studies painting. She plays very finely on the harpsichord, and sings and composes music very finely and will be another Angelica [Kauffman].

She was with us on Christmas Eve.' (W.T. Whitley, *Artists in England, 1770-1799*, Vol. 2, p.312.)

Northcote was in Rome from May 1777 until April 1779 and claimed later that his intimate friends at the time were Prince Hoare, Henry Fuseli, Thomas Banks, and Maria Hadfield. His recollection of her is from Gwynn, *Memorials of James Northcote*, p.149.

Mercer's Diary, 30th January [1779] National Library of Scotland, Edinburgh – N.L.S.

PAGES 45-46

James Northcote later recalled that he was one of the party of English artists that visited Naples in April 1979. 'In the month of April following I went to Naples in company of a party of my friends (artists), amongst whom were Maria Hadfield, Thomas Banks, the sculptor, Prince Hoare, Henry Tresham, Alexander Day, miniature painter and dealer in paintings, Mrs. Banks, and others. After tarrying about a month and seeing whatever was curious in that country, I returned again to Rome.'(Gwynn, *Memorials of James Northcote*, p.164.)

Typical sights on the road to Naples and in the city itself are vividly recorded by Thomas Jones in September 1778 (*Memoirs of Thomas Jones*) and Joseph Mercer's *Diary*.

The meeting with Sir William Hamilton and the first Lady Hamilton is presumed as many English were received by the Hamiltons. The Cosways did know the Hamiltons later when Hamilton's second wife, Emma, was painted by Richard Cosway.

PAGES 47-48

Unfortunately Maria Cosway left little record of her voyage to Naples, but she did note that she visited Vesuvius on the back of an ass. Much later in a letter describing her crossing of the Alps she wrote '...the innkeeper offered a little horse which was a sheep, if only [he] had proposed an ass on which I went to Vesuvius and Tivoli.' M.C. to Annette Prodon, 26th May 1815. Biblioteca Comunale Laudense, Lodi – B.C.L.

Vivid descriptions of Vesuvius in 1770, 1778, and 1779 are given by Charles Burney, Thomas Jones, and Joseph Mercer.

Chapter Three   Journey to London

PAGE 51

The Welsh painter, Thomas Jones, notes the date of Maria Hadfield's departure from Rome on 18th May 1779: 'Banks the Sculptor & his family with Miss Hatfield Set off for England...' ('Memoirs of Thomas Jones', *Walpole Society*, 32, 1951.)

The date of the Hadfields' departure from Florence is recalled in Maria Cosway's journal of 25th June 1802. 'This same day I left Florence for London in the year 1781[sic] against my will and they were obliged to take me out of a convent where I had decided to stay.'(A.F.C.L., Diario A.) In 1781 Maria Cosway was married and living in London. It is certain that she journeyed to England in 1779.

PAGE 52

G.B. to P.H., 11th December 1779, Beinecke Library, Osborn Coll.

Passport records in Florence show that on 14th June [1779] passports were issued to 'Hadfield widow Elizabeth, George, Maria, Charlotte and Elizabeth her children and Elisabetta a maid.' (Archivio di Stato, Firenze.)

The sale of Carlo's inn to John Megit is documented in Sir Brinsley Ford's archives and *A Dictionary of British and Irish Travellers in Italy 1701-1800* ed. Ingamells, pp.652-653.

The Hadfields' voyage to London is imagined, but based on one of the most frequent itineraries described in many contemporary diaries. Some of the travel journals consulted were those already cited of Louis Dutens, Hester Lynch Piozzi, Charles Burney, Ann Flaxman and James Northcote.

PAGE 57

The Hadfields' address in Paris is given in a letter from William Hadfield to Prince Hoare of 11th July 1779: 'Monsieur Northcote can write to my sister Mlle. Mlle. Hadfield chez Monsieur Foucault, Hotel Royal de York, rue Jacob à Paris...But he needs to write immediately.' (Osborn Coll., Beinecke Library.)

One of history's little ironies is the evidence that Maria Hadfield's first nights in Paris were spent in the same hotel that first welcomed Thomas Jefferson in 1784. The Archives of the French Ministry of Foreign Affairs contain a report that 'M. Jefferson, Delegate of the State of Virginia has recently arrived from America and is staying at the Hotel d'York, rue Jacob. This foreigner comes here as Minister Plenipotentiary and deputy to Messrs. Adams and Franklin to negotiate commercial treaties on behalf of the United States.' 20th August 1784. (C.E.53/f.81.)

PAGES 61-62

Maria Hadfield's introductions are recalled in her autobiographical letter of 24th May 1830 to William Cosway: 'I had letters from Lady Rivers for all the first people of fashion. Sir J. Reynolds, Cipriani, Bartolozzi, Angelica Kowffman [sic].'

Impressions of Sir Joshua Reynolds were taken from James Northcote's reminiscences in Gwynne as well as Smith, *Nollekens and His Times,* Vol. II and Wendorf, *Sir Joshua Reynolds,* 1996.

Evidence that Reynolds was shown Maria Hadfield's copy of the Raphael Madonna is a letter from Baroness Lucan to Earl Cowper of 5th January 1780: 'Sir Joshua Reynolds after seeing Miss Hatfield's copy of your Raphael thinks original would be worth 4 to 5,000 pounds…' (Panshanger Papers, D./E.P. F310/7, Hertfordshire Record Office.)

PAGE 65

There is no evidence of Maria Hadfield's reaction to the Gordon Riots of June 1780, but they certainly impressed any English Catholic living in London. Immediately after the riots Isabella Hadfield hastened to insure her furniture and apparel on 17th June 1780. (Royal Exchange Register, Vol. 5, p.107, Guildhall Library.)

PAGE 66

D'Hancarville's misadventures in Florence were reported by Sir Horace Mann to his superiors in London in 1772. After his fishing scheme fell through, the copper plates of several volumes of Sir William Hamilton's work on Tuscan Vases were sequestered by creditors while d'Hancarville hid in a convent. (P.R.O., S.P. 105/296.)

Chapter Four   The Macaroni Painter

PAGE 68

Charles Townley's friendship with Richard Cosway and the likelihood that he was the link between Cosway and Maria Hadfield is seen in correspondence found in the Townley Papers, British Museum. The intimacy and ribaldry of their friendship can be seen in excerpts from a letter of 24th February 1772 from Cosway to Townley.

'*Carissimo Amico,*

> …I must not omit telling you how much you are regretted by everybody here. Dillon swears he'd be after you as soon as the parliament breaks up, as there can be no <u>Life</u> here without you, Wynne is quite envellop'd in <u>c</u>___ – but, alas, tis his Wife's-I believe you don't envy him… .With respect to <u>shagging</u> A is much the same as when you left us (your part omitted,) – but as to myself I stick as close to Radicati's arse as a Bum Bailif to Lord Deloraine's – Italy for ever say I – if the Italian women f___ as well in Italy as they do here, you must be happy indeed – I am such a zealot for them that I'd be damned if ever I f___an English woman again (if I can help it) by the time you return I will almost venture to pronounce you may f___ the first Woman you meet? Let her be who she will – as there are no less than eight divorce's on the tapis in Doctors Commons since you departed – a <u>clergyman</u> has just published openly a treatise on f_____ under the title of the Joys of Hymen – so that upon the whole you see things go on as they shou'd do –… Addio – nothing on earth (f_____Radicati always excepted) can make me so happy as hearing from you, when you have hours relaxation from virtu & f_____ – believe me ever most affectionately yours,
> Rd Cosway'

The combination of art appreciation and erotic pleasure enjoyed by Townley and his friends is well illustrated in a painting by Richard Cosway, *Charles Townley with a group of connoisseurs*, 1771-1775.

Townley's collection of antique sculpture (now in the British Museum) was magnificently displayed in his London home, where it attracted artists and connoisseurs from across Europe. (See Dan Cruickshank, 'Queen Anne's Gate', *The Georgian Group Journal*, 1992, pp.56-67.)

Page 69

Sir Horace Mann described Louise, the Countess of Albany's separation from her husband to his friend Horace Walpole in a letter of 12th December 1780: 'You know undoubtedly the extravagance of his behaviour, which has of late manifested itself in his cruel and indecent treatment of his wife. On St. Andrew's day, which he always celebrated by an extraordinary dose of wine and stronger liquors, he used her extremely ill, and at night committed the most nauseous and filthy indecencies from above and below upon her, tore her hair, and attempted to throttle her.... She made her case privately known to the Great duke and then concerted with a lady of her acquaintance the method of putting her resolution in execution, which was admirably well managed. She invited that lady to breakfast with her on Saturday morning, as she had often done before, in company with the Count, who after proposed to the ladies to go out in the coach, and they conducted him to a sort of a convent where men are permitted with the first door. The Count followed, but they shut it in his face, and on his persisting to have it opened, the lady who has the superintendance[sic] of that place for the Great Duchess and had orders to be there, came to the grate to tell him that the Countess Albanie had put herself under the Great Duke's protection...'(*The Yale Edition of Horace Walpole's Correspondence*, W. S. Lewis, editor, 48 vol., Yale University Press, New Haven, 1937-83.)

Page 70

The economist Jean Fourastie suggested that the present-day values of past currencies can be calculated by comparing average hourly wages between past and present. (Maurice Rheims, *Les Collectionneurs*, ed. Ramsay, Paris 1981) By this method a rough equivalent of £2,800 sterling in 1781 would now be well over a million pounds. Perhaps a more realistic ratio is to multiply former pounds by 50 giving the sum of £140,000 sterling, still an important settlement. This gives a better understanding of the dilemma which must have faced the young Maria Hadfield. Northcote on Cosway marriage in Stephen Gwynne, *James Northcote*, pp.149-150.

PAGE 71

An unfinished letter dated 20th January 1781 from Maria Cosway to Violante Cerruoti is the beginning of a long justification of her marriage, explaining why she was forced to give up her youthful religious vocation. She claims that her mother induced her to come to London with promises that it was only a temporary voyage and she could return to Florence, that she was subject to her mother's 'importuning' and 'real persecution'. She didn't wish to leave her two little sisters in a Protestant country with such a mother. In the fragment she does not speak of her husband or her marriage just the background for her decision. (A.F.C.L.)

In 1830 she summed up her marriage tersely, suggesting it was her mother's choice: 'I became acquainted with Mr. Cosway his offer was accepted, my Mothers wishes gratified & I married tho'under age. – I kept very retired for a twelve-month until I became acquainted with the society I should form, the effect of the exhibition the taste & character of the Nation.' (M. Cosway to Sir William Cosway, 23rd May 1830, V. & A.)

Gwynne, *James Northcote*, pp.149-150.

PAGES 72-74

None of the attire attributed to the bride Maria Hadfield – although of historical exactitude – is known to be hers except the set of pearls and amethysts, which figures in a codicil of her will. (A.F.C.L.)

PAGE 75

St. George's Hanover Square Parish Register for January 1781 (microfilm) records:

> 'No. 30 Richard Cosway Esq. and Maria Cecilia Louisa Hadfield, a Minor, both of this Parish were married in this Church by Licence by and with the consent of Isabella Hadfield the natural and lawfull mother of the said Minor this Eighteenth day of January in the Year of 1781 by me. Rd. Pitt, Curate.'

It is signed by R. Cosway and Maria Hadfield and the witnesses Thomas Banks and Isabella Hadfield. (City of Westminster Archives, Victoria Library.)

The licence obtained from the Archbishop of Canterbury to permit the marriage of a minor was issued on 3rd January 1781. The application for the licence and the bond were both signed by Richard Cosway and Isabella Hadfield. (Lloyd, 'The Accomplished Maria Cosway...', *Journal of Anglo-Italian Studies*, Vol. 2, pp.108-139.)

PAGE 79

The story about Cosway being bitten by his own baboon is reported by Lloyd, who gives a source in the Townley Papers. (*Journal of Anglo-Italian Studies*, Vol. 2, p.117.)

Dr. Lloyd also cites William Blake's satire 'An Island in the Moon' wherein Blake calls the Cosways Mr. and Mrs. Jacko. Blake was inspired by a popular circus act, advertised in London by Astley's Amphitheatre: 'General Jackoo, the celebrated Monkey from Paris, will, for the first time, this season, change the whole of his dress in a surprising manner, and perform his war manoeuvres, dance on the tight rope with fetters on his feet, &c.' (Philip H. Highfill Jr. et al., *A Biographical Dictionary of Actors, Actresses...*, *vol. 8*, p.108.)

The anecdote of the Turk's Head Tavern is recounted in Williamson, 1905, p.32.

Although portraits do not suggest a simian resemblance, John Thomas Smith claimed unkindly in *Nollekens and His Times* that 'Cosway though a well-made little man, was certainly very much like a monkey in his face;'. (II, p.407.)

A study of Maria Cosway in the same costume as that of Susanna Lunden in Rubens' portrait *Le Chapeau de Paille* can be found in the Fondazione Cosway, Lodi.

PAGE 82

Richard Cosway's method of miniature painting is described in G. C. Williamson, *Richard Cosway, R.A.*, 1905.

PAGES **83-84**

It is not certain that the Cosways attended Philip Jacques de Loutherbourg's Eidophusikon, but it is probable.

Chapter Five   Mrs. Cosway

PAGE **85**

M.C. to Sir William Cosway, 24th May 1830, V.A.
    Between 1781 and 1801 Maria Cosway showed forty-two works at the Royal Academy's annual exhibitions, participating every year in the 1780s. (Algernon Graves, *The Royal Academy of Art, Vol. II,* 1905-6.)

PAGE **87-88**

The conversation between Maria Cosway and Prince Hoare is imagined, but he was in London, they did continue their friendship and could very well have crossed paths at the Academy. The paintings cited were those exhibited in 1781.

PAGES **88-89**

The press reviews cited were found in the V. & A. Press Clippings, Vol. 1, pp.201-205.

PAGES **93-95**

The first meeting of Maria Cosway and the Duchess of Devonshire is imagined, but the artist's portrait of the Duchess gave the young artist an immediate celebrity.
    Maria Cosway later described her early success modestly:

'Mr. Cosway's wish was I should occupy myself as hitherto done in the Arts & so I did. The first pictures I exhibited made my reputation. The novelty & my Age Contributed more than the real Merit – The portrait of the Duchess of Devonshire then the Reigning beauty & fashion – in the Caracter of Cynthia from Spencer seemed to strike & other historical subjects from Shakespeare, Virgil & Homer – encouraged but never proud I followed entirely the impulse of my imagination'. (M.C. to Sir William Cosway, 24th May 1830, V.A.)

The press reviews cited were found in V & A Press Cuttings, Vol. I, p.227 and Stephen Lloyd, *Richard & Maria Cosway*, p.45.

The sixth Duke's opinion of Maria Cosway's portrait of his mother, which now hangs at Chatsworth, is cited by the Dowager Duchess of Devonshire in her foreword to Brian Masters' biography *Georgiana*.

PAGE 96

John Wolcot's satiric odes on the Cosways are from *The Works of Peter Pindar*, Vol. I, London 1812.

PAGE 97

'Astrea instructing Arthegal' from Sir Edmund Spenser's *The Faerie Queene*, v. i. 6, 7, 8.

PAGE 99

The flattering press comments comparing Maria Cosway's style to that of Fuseli were found in V&A Press Cuttings, Vol. I, p.194.

Chapter Six   The Goddess of Pall Mall

PAGE 102

Only the façade of Schomberg House has survived. What remained of the eighteenth-century interiors was destroyed in the twentieth century conversion of the building into the offices of an insurance company. The lay-out of Schomberg House in the eighteenth century was pieced together from the Survey of London, Vols. 29, 30, Part I, South of Piccadilly; *A Catalogue of…Pictures of Richard Cosway, 1791;* and Walsh, 'Merchants à la Mode,' *Country Life*, 16th December 1993.

PAGE 103

Dr. James Graham's sex therapy consisted of a night spent in a bed which he advertised as a

> 'Celestial or Magnetico-electrico bed…placed to the right of my orchestra which produces the Celestial fire…this brilliant Celestial Bed is supported by six massive brass pillars with Saxon blue and purple satin, perfumed with Arabian spices.'

The treatment was not cheap, costing fifty guineas a night. (Porter, *The British Journal for Eighteenth Century Studies*, v, 1982, pp.199-206.)

The Cosways had an African servant whose full name was Quobna Ottobah Cugoano also known as John Steuart or Stewart. He is portrayed in an etching of the Cosways in their garden, all dressed in fashionable seventeenth-century costumes, an allusion to Rubens and Van Dyck, whose pictures often featured black servants. (Lloyd, *Richard and Maria Cosway*, pp.46-47.)

The young Andrew Plimer was engaged by Mrs. Cosway as a studio boy to clean, mix colours, and announce callers. After Plimer skilfully copied a miniature, Cosway sent him to learn drawing and may have paid for his lessons. (George C. Williamson, *Andrew & Nathaniel Plimer*, 1903, p.11.)

PAGES 106-107

Tiberus Cavallo to Prince Hoare, 8th February 1788, Beinecke Library, Osborn Coll.

M.C. to Sir William Cosway, 24th May 1830, V.A.

Sir Horace Walpole to Lady Lyttelton, 28th October 1787, *The Yale Edition of Horace Walpole's Correspondence*, W. S. Lewis, (general ed.) XLII, p.200.

PAGE 108

Richard Cosway did many miniatures of the Prince of Wales, his family, friends, and mistresses. Both Cosways painted Maria Fitzherbert. The Duke of Wellington, asked by George IV before his death to stay with his body and let all ornaments then on it be buried with him, discovered Cosway's miniature of Maria Fitzherbert around the King's neck on his funeral bier, after the couple had been long separated. (Munson, *Maria Fitzherbert*, 2001, pp.350-351.)

The revels of the Prince of Wales' fast set are disapprovingly recounted in Lady Mary Coke's M.S. Journal. (Lewis Walpole Library, Farmington, Connecticut – L.W.L.)

PAGE 110

The Chevalier d'Eon, a former French spy, had retired to England. Usually seen dressed as a woman, his sex was in dispute, until a post-mortem examination declared him male.

Sir Horace Walpole wrote about his encounters with Mlle. La Chevalière d'Eon and Earl Cowper at Mrs. Cosway's concerts in letters to friends:

> I received a little Italian note from Mrs. Cosway this morning to tell me that as I had last week met at her house an old acquaintance without knowing her, I might meet her again this evening *en connaissance de cause* as Mlle la chevaliere d'Eon, who, as Mrs. Cosway told me, had taken it ill that I had not reconnoitred her, and said she must be strangely altered – the devil is in it if she is not! – but alack! I have found her altered again! Found her loud, noisy and vulgar – in truth I believe she had dined a little *en dragon*. [Eon had once been a French dragoon] The night was hot, she had no muff or gloves, and her hands and arms seem not to have participated in the change of sexes, but are fitter to carry a chair than a fan. (H.W. to Lady Ossory, 27th January 1786, W. S. Lewis, XXXIII, pp.510-511.)

> I was made easier last night by Lord Cowper.... Well! You find I have seen your principied Earl. Curiosity carried me to a great concert at Mrs. Cosway's t'other night – not to hear Rubinelli, who sung *one* song at the extravagant price of ten guineas, and whom for as many shillings I have heard sing half a dozen at the opera house: no, but I was curious to see an English Earl who had passed thirty years at Florence, and is more proud of a pinchbeck principality and a paltry Order from Wirtemberg, than he was of being a peer of Great Britain when Great Britain was something. (H.W. to Sir Horace Mann, 29th May 1786, XV, p.646.)

Earl Cowper was very proud of having been named a Prince of the Holy Roman Empire.

PAGE 113

A rendezvous between the Prince of Wales and Maria Fitzherbert at the

Cosways is not historical fact, but artists' houses, and specifically that of the Cosways, could well have been the scene of their meetings.

PAGE 114

Fraser's Magazine, 1840, quoted in Whitley Papers, p.377, B.M.P.D.

PAGE 115

Peter Pindar [John Wolcot], Ode VIII, *More Lyric Odes*, 1785.
    John Hoppner attacked the Cosways' pictures in the *Morning Post* editions of 2nd, 5th, and 17th May 1785.

PAGES 116-117

Adams Papers (Massachusetts Historical Society, Boston, Mass – M.H.I.)
    Conversations of James Northcote, R.A. with James Ward on Art and Artists, E. Fletcher (ed.) London, 1901, pp.79-80.

Chapter Seven   Friendship

PAGE 121

Fanny Burney wrote of the favourable impression made by General Paoli after she met him in 1782:

> He is a very pleasing man, tall and genteel in his person, remarkably well bred, and very mild and soft in his manners.... His English is blundering, but not unpretty. Speaking of his first acquaintance with Mr. Boswell— 'He came,' he said, 'to my country…but I was of the belief he might be an impostor, and I supposed…he was an espy;…Oh! He was to the work of writing down all I say! Indeed I was angry. But soon I discover he was no impostor and no espy;…Oh, is a very good man; I love him indeed; so cheerful! So gay! So pleasant! But at the first, oh! I was indeed angry.' (*Diary and Letters of Madame d'Arblay*, Vol. II, Henry Colburn, London 1842, p.155.)

PAGES 122-123

Letter on visit to Johnson, P.P. to M.C. [December 1784], A.F.C.L.

M.C. to Sir William Cosway, 24th May 1830, V.A.

The conversation between General Paoli and Maria Cosway is imagined, but reflects Paoli's views on marriage.

PAGES 124-125

Boswell, *Malahide Papers*, xvi, pp.81-125.

Giusto Tenducci had a great career as a *castrato* in London and had given singing lessons to Mozart.

Boswell candidly records Johnson's and Paoli's unsuccessful efforts to curb his drinking in his Journal. Commenting on Dr. Johnson's admonition to drink water, Boswell noted, 'I in my own mind schemed to enjoy the satisfaction of drinking wine.' (*Malahide Papers*, xiii, p.37.) He also notes that Paoli often scolded him. On 6th May 1781: 'General Paoli gave me a lecture and took my promise that I would drink no more than three glasses.' Later that week Paoli told him that if the King named Boswell as Paoli's secretary to go with him to Corsica that the General would not have him. ' "From his fault, I cannot trust him." ' Boswell chose to avoid his friend when under the weather. He notes: 'Very ill. Ashamed to be seen by General.' or 'Awaked ill. Lay snug till the General went out.' (*Malahide Papers*, xiii, p.218; xiv, pp.301-302.)

PAGE 125

J.B. to M.C., 30th June [1785] Beinecke Library, Osborn Coll.

J.B. to M.C., 28th July [1785] Beinecke Library, Osborn Coll.

Boswell's Journal describes the evening at Astley's. On 28th July [1785] he notes:

> Unfortunately I had engaged myself to go to Astley's with the General and Mrs. Cosway...the General came in his coach and took me up, and then we took up Mrs. Cosway and Miss Charlotte her sister. I was much entertained at Astley's. Lord and Lady Melbourne, Lady Duncannon, and Lord William Gordon sat before us in the same box. ... Cosway himself was with us. He walked both to and from. We passed the evening at Cosway's rather insipidly. (*Malahide Papers*, xvi, p.115.)

Another time he also expresses boredom with the General's friends:

'Monday 19 September.... Dined Cosway's with the General and several foreigners. Was ENNUYE' (*Malahide Papers*, xvi, p.125.)

PAGES 126-127

A view of the Cosways' circle of friends is given in the letters of Francesco d'Ageno, the Ambassador from Genoa, to Angelica Schuyler Church, in which mention is made of Mrs. Anne Damer, Elizabeth, Lady Lyttelton, the Swinburnes, d'Hancarville. The Cosways, Charlotte Hadfield, Francesco d'Ageno were often guests at house parties at Down Place, the Churches' country house.(University of Virginia, Charlottesville – V.I.U., Church Papers.)

Later Maria Cosway wrote to Thomas Jefferson of her esteem and affection for Angelica Church: 'I love her...she is the woman I love most, & feel most happy with in this country.'(M.C. to T.J., 4th December 1795, M.H.I.)

PAGES 127-128

The conversation between Maria Cosway and Angelica Church is imagined, but the anecdote about Lucy Paradise and Mary Moser Lloyd comes from Smith's *Nollekens and his Times*, Vol. I, p.320.

Richard Cosway's drawing of the Duc d'Orléans' children is now in the Musée Condé, Chantilly.

PAGE 130

Tiny Cosmetic (R. Cosway) describes his wife and the Prince of Wales in these terms:

...the Prince not giving Maria entire satisfaction by his performance, what does Maria do, but lay hold of the prince's hair pencil, which he took with infinite good humour;...to be even with my poor Maria for snatching his pencil so rudely *damme*. What does the Prince, but catches hold of my wife's brush! ha, ha, ha! – though it was cover'd with hog's hair...as black as my hat.' (Anthony Pasquin [John Williams], *The Royal Academicians*, 1786.)

Maria Cosway and John Wilkes' conversation is recounted in Wilkes' letter to Mary Wilkes of 4th July 1786, and Wilkes' praise of Maria in a letter to Mary of 18th July 1786, both quoted in *Whitley Papers*, p.364, British Museum Department of Prints and Drawings, London – B.M.D.P.

John Wilkes, highly intelligent and witty, although very unattractive, would probably have shocked Maria Cosway in his youth, when he was an active and enthusiastic member of the debauched Hellfire Club.

The Chevalier d'Eon, when in the secret service of the French, wrote an interesting letter to the Comte de Broglie undated [1773] about Wilkes and Paoli:

> Wilkes costs us a lot to feed, but the English have the Corsican Paoli whom they welcome and they feed also against us… . Let's keep one bomb for another. (Claude Manceron, Vol. I, *'Les Vingt Ans du Roi', 1774-1778*, p.283.)

Chapter Eight   Paris   1786

PAGE 134

The date of the Cosways' departure for Paris and their stop at Brighton is reported in John Wilkes' letter to his daughter Mary of 18th July 1786:

> Mr. and Mrs. Cosway set out on Sunday [16th July] for Brighthelmstone on their way to Paris, but I suspect very much that the Prince will not permit them to embark very soon, and especially as I understand that Mr. Cosway has something in hand to be finished before his departure… (B.M.P.D., *Whitley Papers*, p.364.)

It is known from Thomas Jefferson's note of 5th October 1786, addressed to 'Madame, Madame Cosway, rue Coqheron' that the Cosways were lodged in that street.

The Cosways were probably guests of the Duchess of Kingston at the Hotel Parlement d'Angleterre located in the rue Coqheron. The Duchess and Mrs. Anne Damer took up residence there in the summer of 1786 according to the *Mercure de France* for the former and Archives of the French Ministry of Foreign Affairs for the latter. (C.E.61/f.93.) A thorough search of the Ministry's weekly reports of arriving foreigners, still in pristine condition for the year 1786, yielded no mention of the Cosways. Similar records of the Lieutenant General of Police were burned in the destruction of the Prefecture of Police during the Commune of 1871.

In her memoirs the Baronne d'Oberkirch explains that the Hotel Parlement d'Angleterre, where many English stayed, was no longer a commercial establishment:

> 'She [Duchess of Kingston] enjoyed a fine hotel in the rue Coq-Heron, which was formerly called the *hotel du Parlement d'Angleterre*, which she rented for life, where she received the most brilliant and the most curious society, great lords, artists, and intellectuals of all nations.' (Baronne d'Oberkirch, *Memoires*, vol. 2, p.287.)

PAGES 135-136

The circumstances of the Cosways' visit to the Louvre are imagined. Richard Cosway did, however, have the idea of giving his cartoons to the King's Gallery after visiting the Grand Galerie of the Louvre. (Cosway thought the works were by Raphael and Guilio Romano, but they were later attributed to a minor follower of Guilio Romano and the subjects are not from the *History of Camillus* as thought in 1786, but from the *Fructus Belli* and *History of Scipio* cycle of tapestries. (See Lloyd, 'Richard Cosway, R.A....' *Apollo*, CXXXIII, No. 352, June 1991.)

Baron d'Hancarville, who certainly made himself useful to the Cosways during their Paris visit, was their intermediary, writing to the Comte d'Angiviller with Cosway's letter enclosed to propose the gift of tapestries. (D'Hancarville to d'Angiviller, 29th August 1786, Archives Nationales, France – A.N.F, O1 1919/265.)

Angiviller's prompt reply to Cosway of 5th September 1786 underscores his recognition of the value of the gift:

> I was eager to put this homage before the King's eyes, and I believed the best way to make it interesting was to give him your letter to read. He read it, Monsieur, with the sensibility that it inspires and by accepting the offer that you have made, he has

asked me to express that to you…I hope the time approaches when all the riches reunited and assembled will become a continual pleasure for all those who love and cultivate the fine arts. You will have more rights than any other by your talents, by those of Madame Cosway who cultivates them – all with an equal superiority…(A.N.F., O1 1919/266.)

PAGES 137-138

It is not certain if the first meeting of Maria Cosway and David was in Rome in 1777-79 or later in Paris, but they most certainly did begin a friendship in 1786. ('Deux Letters de David a Maria Cosway,' in Philippe Bordes, *Le Serment du Jeu de Paume de Jacques-Louis David*, pp.132-134.)

If Maria met David in Rome, it was through her friend James Northcote, who later recalled that he and David were admitted to the Vatican to draw and study the sculptures in summer when the Pope was away. (Gwynne, pp.154-155.)

David's studio in the Louvre is described by Trumbull. It is not clear from his autobiography exactly what artists' ateliers he visited with the Cosways, although he may have been with them to visit Vincent, Pajou, Boileau, and Paillet the day he breakfasted with them on 11th August. (Trumbull, p.111.) That the Cosways met and observed the artists working in the Louvre is certain. Baron d'Hancarville, who was a great flatterer, must not have exaggerated too much when he wrote to Maria Cosway 26th February 1787:

> The door of the Academy of Painting has two panels, which will willingly open to give both of you entry; if Robert and Vincent had not offered to propose you, David and Vernet would have the ambition for this pleasure. (B.C.L.)

PAGES 139-140

Joseph-Hyacinthe-François de Paule de Rigaud, Comte de Vaudreuil, (1740-1817) was one of the leading collectors of French painting until bankruptcy forced the sale of his collection in 1787. He was an intimate of the Duchess de Polignac and therefore of the Court, but also enjoyed the company of artists, especially Madame Vigée Lebrun. (Bailey, *Patriotic Taste*, pp.163-206.)

It is not clear whether the Cosways were first introduced to John Trumbull in London or Paris. He suggests in his autobiography that the first meeting was in Paris, writing,

> …Mr. and Mrs. Cosway, of London, were in Paris; he (then the admired miniature painter of the day) had been invited by the Duke of Orleans, to paint the duchess and her children. I became acquainted and intimate with them… (Sizer, p.93.)

The Churches' patronage of the young painter was another link between them. (Sizer, pp.94-95.)

Page 141

Trumbull notes that he visited the Luxembourg Palace with the Cosways on 9th August thanks to the intervention of Madame de Polignac. (Sizer, pp.107-108.)

Richard Cosway's brother-in-law, William Combe, cites the portraits painted in Paris in his biographical notes on the Cosways. (British Library, London – B.L. Add. 71585.)

On 12th August Trumbull records the Cosways' visit to Versailles. (Sizer, pp.111-116.) He writes of the 'apartments' of Angiviller, which implies that they were in the chateau, but the Director of Works usually spent his summers in a pavilion in Versailles. (Silvestre de Sacy, *Le Comte d'Angiviller*, 1953.)

Page 142

Hotel Langeac and its neighbourhood near the *Grille de Chaillot* described in Rice, *Thomas Jefferson's Paris*, pp.51-54.

Page 143

Evidence that the Cosways frequented the circle of the Trudaines is given in Bordes, pp.20-23, and especially in the letters of d'Hancarville of 1787 (B.C.L.) to Maria Cosway. This correspondence gives a clear insight into the acquaintances made in Paris, often citing those of the circle: the Marquis de Bièvre, André Chénier, Vivant de Non, Madame de Bonneuil (mistress of Chénier), Marquis de Cubières.

Pages 144-145

Chénier, *Oeuvres Completes*, pp.112-114.

Thomas Gray, 'Ode on the Spring', *A Collection of Poems by Several Hands*, London, Robert Dodsley, 1748.

According to an undated letter of d'Hancarville, probably written in February 1787, the Trudaines, great dog lovers, had promised to send one to the Cosways:

> M. de Trudaine hasn't forgotten the dog he promised you. It is a present for you and they are taking care that it is well-trained, very clean and very handsome.

The breed is unknown, but the dog in the portrait of Maria Cosway at her breakfast room window, painted in 1787, appears to be a whippet. (B.C.L.)

Chapter Nine   The American Envoy

Page 148

The date of the first meeting of Thomas Jefferson and the Cosways is uncertain. It could have been late August or the first week of September. If one takes his account book as a possible guide, 3rd September is likely. On that day he notes that he paid six francs to see the Gallery of St. Cloud. Then, with one exception, he neglects his accounts until after the accident of his broken wrist [probably 18th September], which distorts his handwriting. On the day of their first meeting, it is known that they visited St. Cloud. The details of that first day are remembered in Jefferson's letter of 12th October 1786 to Maria Cosway:

> *Heart:*... Sir, this acquaintance was not the consequence of my doings...The Halle aux Bleds might have rotted down, before I should have gone to see it...
> *Head:* ...It would have been happy for you if my diagrams... had gotten you to sleep on that day... . While I was occupied

with these objects, you were dilating with your new acquaintances, and contriving how to prevent a separation from them. Every soul of you had an engagement for the day. Yet all these were to be sacrificed, that you might dine together. Lying messengers were to be dispatched into every quarter of the city, with apologies for your breach of engagement. You particularly, had the effrontery to send word to the Duchess Danville [Duchess d'Enville-la Rochefoucauld], that on the moment we were setting out to dine with her, despatches came to hand, which required immediate attention. You wanted me to invent a more ingenious excuse; but I knew you were getting into a scrape, and I would have nothing to do with it. Well; after dinner to St. Cloud, from St. Cloud to Ruggieri's, from Ruggieri's to Krumpoltz [Krumpholtz]; and if the day had been as long as a Lapland summer day, you would still have contrived means among you to have filled it. (Library of Congress, Washington, D.C. – D.L.C. and Boyd, 10, pp.444-445.)

PAGE 151

Although it is known that the Cosways, Jefferson, and, presumably Trumbull, dined together at their first meeting(T.J., 12th October, 1786), the place, the Restaurant Mecanique, is imagined. This first self-service restaurant did exist, however, and its ingenuity would certainly have appealed to Jefferson. (*Tableau du...Palais Royal,* Vol I, 1788, p.29 and *Almanach, 1786.*) 'The feet of the tables are formed of two hollow cylinders, whose prolongation is connected with the kitchen...which is under the room. To have what one desires, it is necessary to pull a ring on each cylinder, this ring is connected to a bell in the kitchen; then a valve opens on the table to receive the order; this valve closes immediately and only opens again to present a dumbwaiter of two levels.'(*Almanach,* 1786, p.139.)

It is also possible that the party travelled by water to St. Cloud and dined at the Hotel Duc du Chartres on the banks of the Seine, which had a fine view. Another tourist, Mrs. Cradock, described the boat, which took about two hours to transport passengers to St. Cloud:

The water bus or [patache] is a sort of immense barque which can carry more than 100 persons: in the middle of which is a long, narrow chamber lighted by windows on each side. In the centre and around are the benches. It is guided by a helmsman and pulled by six horses. (*Cradock*, pp.26-27.)

The conversations of Jefferson and Maria are imagined, although their activities on the day of first meeting – and subsequent days – are known by his letters and account books.

Page 154

The *Journal de Paris* for Sunday, 3rd September 1786 announces the following program of fireworks at Ruggieri (held only on weekends or holidays):

Aujourd. 3, chez le Sr. Ruggieri, Fetes champetres, danses; feu d'artifice; les Forges de Vulcan; le Combat de Mars, & la Salamandre.

This date concurs with Jefferson's notation of a visit to the Gallery of St. Cloud on 3rd September. Other information on the spectacles at Ruggieri is found in Claude Ruggieri, *Précis historique sur les Fêtes and Spectacles...* Paris 1830.

Mrs. Krumpholtz, née Anne-Marie Steckler of Metz, married Johann Baptist Krumpholtz (1742-1790) a Czech harpist and composer. She was a virtuoso, but her husband was the greatest harpist of his time, composed five concertos for harp and helped develop the instrument. They came to Paris in 1777. After her infidelities and departure for London in 1788 he threw himself into the Seine. She was described by a contemporary as very elegant:

She invented the pedals for different keys, which wonderfully improved the effect of the instrument...a most elegant little woman, beautifully formed...taste so exquisite that she was consulted by the nobility about their superior dresses...harp made a proper size for her, she was too small to use a full-sized one. (Papendiek, *Journals*, vol. 2, p.253.)

Mrs. Krumpholtz no doubt played at one of the Cosways' concerts in 1788-89, as evidenced by the following note from Georgiana, Duchess of Devonshire, to Maria Cosway:

> I am extremely sorry that my Mother's illness prevents my going out & coming to you to night – If you have the harp woman (I forget her hard name) I wish you wd tell her that I hope to see her as soon as my Mother is better. (Chatsworth.)

Carlo Antonio Campioni (1720-1793), the Italian composer of chamber music, was the Grand Duke of Tuscany's M*aestro di Capella* in 1770. (Burney, *The Present State of Music*, p.117.)

According to one published source ('Conversations on the Arts', *The Repository of Arts, Literature, Commerce*...No. XI, Vol. VII, April 1812, p.196) about the same year of 1770 Maria Hadfield was something of a child prodigy:

> Her instrumental performance was in the superior mode; what that was, may be readily conjectured, when it is known that at ten years of age she sometimes, at the request and to the acknowledged gratification of the Grand Duke of Tuscany, presided at the harpsichord in the first concert of Florence.

If that is so (examination of journals of record such as the *Gazzetta Toscana* and other sources yielded no verification of the fact), Maria Hadfield surely heard the music of and possibly played with Campioni. Her association with the Italian composer must have impressed Jefferson since it is thought he held a strong preference for this composer.

> He (Jefferson) also listed separately the works of Carlo Antonio Campioni and itemized them more completely than anything else .... These facts, plus a music manuscript fragment in Jefferson's handwriting, indicate that Campioni must have been one of his favourite composers. (Cripe, *Thomas Jefferson and Music*, p.85.)

The only composer for whom he left some record of preference was Carlo Antonio Campioni. (Cripe, *Thomas Jefferson and Music*, p.92.)

Jefferson notes in his account book that he paid three francs to see the King's library and six francs for Madrid on 5th September. A description of the Chateau of Madrid in the 1780s is found in Thiery, I, pp.31-32 and in Henry Swinburne, *Memoirs of the Courts of Europe*, Vol. II, p.43.

> Walked to Madrid, which is in a very ruinous condition, propped up in many places, but still inhabited; the outward ornaments all tile and baked earth of various colours, to imitate porphyry; a strange mixture of Grecian colours and barbarous entablements.

Pages 155-157

The Chateau de Madrid being next to the Bagatelle, it can be presumed that they were visited the same day. The exact day of the visit to the King's garden can only be imagined as some time later. The only clue is Jefferson's mention of it after Madrid and Bagatelle in his letter of 12th October 1786 to Maria Cosway:

> 'Recollect too Madrid, Bagatelle, the King's garden, the Dessert.' (DLC and Boyd, 10, pp.445-446.)

Details of the picturesque gardens of the Chateau de Bagatelle were taken from Thiery, I, pp.25-30.

The popularity of Ossian, the fictional Scottish bard, was an international phenomenon among cultivated readers in the eighteenth century. Jefferson wrote of his poems, supposedly discovered by Macpherson:

> These peices [*sic*] have been, and will I think during my life continue to be to me, the source of daily and exalted pleasure. The tender, and the sublime emotions of the mind were never before so finely wrought up by human hand. I am not ashamed to own that I think this rude bard of the North the greatest Poet

that has ever existed. (Boyd, I, p.96 and Gilbert Chinard, 'Jefferson and Ossian', *Modern Language Notes*, 38, 1923, pp.201-05.)

The Marquis de Chastellux described the intensity of Jefferson's enthusiasm for Ossian during one of their conversations at Monticello:

> I recall with pleasure that, one evening, as we were conversing over a 'bowl of punch,' after Mrs. Jefferson had retired, we happened to speak of the poetry of Ossian. It was a spark of electricity which passed rapidly from one to the other: we recalled the passages of those sublime poems which had particularly struck us ... (Chastellux, *Voyages...*, II, p.36.)

There is no record of such a scene between Jefferson and Maria Cosway, but it is likely that their shared taste for the poet was evoked at some time. There is no doubt that she was equally immersed in the cult of the sublime as evidenced by her choice of subjects from Ossian for two paintings exhibited at the Royal Academy: 'Darthula in defending the body of her vanquished father, discovers herself to Cairbar her lover' in 1782 and 'Althan stood in the wood alone, and saw a ghost in the darkening air, his stride extended from hill to hill' in 1783. (Graves, II, p.174.)

The first verses recited, beginning 'O thou that rollest above...' and 'the moon, cold and pale...' are from the Address to the Sun in 'Carthon', which Jefferson had copied into his commonplace book of philosophers and poets. (*Ossian*, Tauchnitz, p.163.) This was Jefferson's favourite short Ossianic poem. (Degategno, pp.104-105.) The verses from 'Darthula' are found in *Ossian* , Tauchnitz, pp.282-283.

PAGES 158-159

The description of the King's Garden, now the Jardin des Plantes, is based on Thiery, II, pp.25-30. The Duke of Orleans' liaison with the Countess de Buffon is recounted in Lever, pp.267-269.

PAGES 160-162

Jefferson noted the following in his account book for Thursday, 7th September 1786 (M.H.I.):

| Pd. seeing machine of Marly 6f | the Chateau 6f |
| Pd. Petit towards dinner at Marly 12f | pd. at Louveciennes 6f |

PAGES 163-164

Jefferson's account book notes the two excursions to a concert and the theatre in early September (M.H.I.):

Sep.8 pd. at concert spiritual 6f

Sep. 9 pd. at Italians 6f

The *Journal de Paris* of 8th September 1786 gives the programme for the *concert spirituel*.

Beginning at 6:30 p.m. the concert was lengthy; in addition to two Hayden symphonies, Madame Mara sang two arias, a M. Gervais played a violon concerto, Mlle. Rose performed a sonata and air of her composition, and there were two other pieces performed by a Mlle. Vaillant and M. Lays.

The unusual atmosphere of the Tuileries concert hall is described in correspondence between the Director of the *concerts spirituals*, a Monsieur Le Gros and Angiviller. In one letter of 1st May 1786, Le Gros complains that '...one of the inhabitants of this hall has even dared to complain during the last two weeks that he cannot work at his forge during the concerts.... The parquet has been infected several times by great quantities of meat placed there until the moment of rehearsals.... Finally, everyone has keys to this hall except me.' (A.N.F./O.1 1683.)

The attendance of various diplomats from Sardinia, Venice, Malta, Denmark and Genoa was duly noted by the Foreign Minister's informers. (A.A.E./C.E. 61f.124.)

The *Journal de Paris* announced for Saturday, 9th September 1786, this programme for the *Theatre italien* :

60th performance of *Richard Coeur de Lion*, comedy in 3 acts by
M. Sedaine, music by M. Gretry;
13th of *Mariage d'Antonio*, one act

Les Deux Billets, Comedy in one act, in prose by M. de Florian

Jefferson had previously seen *Richard Coeur de Lion* with John Quincy Adams in 1785. This comic opera set in the Middle Ages was very much in vogue. (Rice, pp.46-49.)

Although it is not known if the Cosways had seen *Nina, ou la Folle par Amour* on 30th August 1786, its most recent performance, the immense popularity of this operetta and Madame Louise Dugazon, who played the title role, had made them both subjects of prints and paintings. Maria Cosway's compositions *Songs and Duets* contains an Italian paraphrase of Nina's famous song, '*Mais je regard...helas!...helas!/Le bien-aime ne revient pas!*'

Evidence that Jefferson and Maria Cosway had most likely seen *Les Deux Billets* together on 9th September 1786, is found in his letter to her of 12th October 1786.

Chapter Ten 'Le Désert de Retz'

PAGES 167-173

Jefferson noted in his account book: 'Sep. 16 pd. seeing Desert 6f'.

Evidence that he visited the garden with Maria Cosway is found in his letter to her of 12th October 1786 (Boyd, 10, pp.445-446):

'Recollect too Madrid, Bagatelle, the King's garden, the Dessert. How grand the idea excited by the remains of such a column! The spiral staircase too was beautiful.'

(For the sake of historical accuracy it must be noted that Richard Cosway may have been with the party, although this is not known.)

PAGES 175-176

Jefferson's accounts show that he paid two surgeons twelve francs on 18th

September. (M.H.I.) This seems the most likely date of his accident. This conclusion is consistent with the thorough analysis of this incident found in Butterfield and Rice, 'Jefferson's Earliest Note to Maria Cosway…', *William & Mary Quarterly*, Vol. V (January 1948), pp.26-33. The authors point out that Jefferson most probably had neglected his accounts from 4th September until a date after his accident, when he brought them up to date, writing with his left hand. This is also consistent with his being distracted by an intense program of excursions with the Cosways, which most probably began on 3rd September.

The date and place of the accident are further confirmed by a letter from Franklin's friend, Louis-Guillaume Le Veillard, to William Temple Franklin on 20th September 1786.

> 'Day before yesterday Mr. Jefferson dislocated his right wrist when attempting to jump over a fence in the Petit Cours.' (Boyd, 10, p.432.)

The exact circumstances of Jefferson's accident are not known. He left no account of how and with whom it occurred. He did comment rather mysteriously in a letter to William Stephens Smith of 22nd October 1786:

> 'How the right hand became disabled would be a long story for the left to tell. It was by one of those follies from which good cannot come, but ill may.' (Boyd, 10, p.478.)

Jefferson's daughter Martha wrote many years later that her father broke his wrist while on a 'ramble' with a friend (of the male sex) some miles from home; that he concealed the injury from his companion until near home; then he 'left him to send for the surgeon'. (Randall, *Life of Jefferson*, I, 456.) Butterfield and Rice conjecture that Martha's imperfect memory or genteel sense of propriety may have changed the sex of her father's companion.

As for the locale of the accident, the Petit Cours or Cours de la Reine was a promenade along the Seine near the Champs Elysées. The 'fence' may have been a paved ditch as such a feature did separate the Cours de la Reine from the Champs Elysées. The other circumstances of the excursion with Maria Cosway and her loss of a fan are imagined, although the fan as described still exists.

Page 177

The details of the Cosways' visit to the Duchess of Kingston and then to Jefferson's house are described in Maria Cosway's letter of 20th September 1786 to Jefferson:

> '[I hope] you don't always judge by appearances [or it wo]uld be Much to My disadvantage this day…it has been the day of contradiction, I meant to have had the pleasure of seeing you *Twice*… . This Morning My Husband kill'd My project, I had proposed to him, by burying himself among Pictures and forgetting the hours, though we were Near your House coming to see you, we were obliged to turn back, the time being much past that we were to be at St. Cloud to dine with the Duchess of Kingston; Nothing was to hinder us from Coming in the Evening, but Alas! My good intention prov'd only a disturbance to your Neighbours, and just late enough to break the rest of all your servants and perhaps yourself. (Boyd, 10, pp.393-394.)

Elizabeth Chudleigh, the Duchess of Kingston, was tried and convicted of bigamy, but managed to inherit the Duke's large fortune. Highly original, she travelled across Europe, where she was well received despite her reputation. A sympathetic portrait is given by one of her contemporaries, Baronne d'Oberkirch, in her *Mémoires*, 2, pp.266-284.

Pages 178-180

The Cosways' visit to see Jefferson is imagined, although Maria Cosway did declare her intention to visit him in the letter of 20th September 1786, cited above. The Cosways may not have yet followed a course of study with Dr. John Bonniot De Mainaduc in 1786, but they did do so in the late 1780s and were certainly aware of the various healing methods popular at the time. (See Lloyd, 'The Accomplished Maria Cosway…', p.123.)

The circumstances of Maria Cosway's presentation to the Duchess d'Orléans are not known, but evidence that they met is found in the Baron d'Hancarville's letter of 26th February 1787 to Maria Cosway:

> '…Mad. la duchesse d'Orléans, while speaking of the portraits
> of her children, showed the Marquis de Lusignan some engraved
> prints after the drawings of Mad. Cosway whom she praised and
> assured him that you have promised her to come to Paris this
> summer and to come to see her.' (B.C.L.)

Pages 180-181

The visit of Maria Cosway to Jefferson's home is imagined, although the
tenor of their subsequent correspondence reflects the fact that an intimate
friendship did develop in the relatively short space of a few weeks.

Page 182

It is known from d'Hancarville's correspondence with Maria Cosway that
the Cosways had been introduced to Albaret and shared his passion for
music. After her return to London, Maria sent Albaret a set of musical
scores, probably her own compositions. (D'Hancarville to Maria Cosway,
n.d. [1787].) Later d'Hancarville wrote:

> 'The musical Comte d'Albaret…absolutely wishes me to write you
> and tell you he has written you…' (26th February 1787, B.C.L.)

It is not known but quite possible that the Cosways attended the concert
of the Comte d'Albaret, given on 30th September. Informers to the Ministry
of Foreign Affairs gave the following report:

> 'The 30th the Comte d'Albaret gave a concert this morning where
> were found, the Ambassadors of Sardaigna, Portugal, Venice,
> M. Brantrin [Envoy of Denmark], the Minister of Genoa, M.
> Hailet and several foreigners.' (30th September 1786, C.E./62/
> f.13.)

Pages 183-184

Jefferson's accounts reveal nothing about his last carriage ride with Maria
Cosway, but evidence they were together on 4th October is in his note to

her of 5th October 1786, and her reply, both cited in the text. (Boyd, 10, pp.431-433.)

The deathbed promise of Jefferson to his wife was part of the family's oral history. One version passed from six female slaves (including Betty and Sally Hemings) who were supposedly present. They repeated the story to Jefferson's overseer, Edmund Bacon, who then gave his reminiscences to the Rev. Hamilton Wilcox Pierson, published by him in 1862 and republished in *Jefferson at Monticello*, ed., Bear, p.99-100.

If such a promise was made, it is not known if Jefferson revealed it to Maria Cosway.

Pages 184-185

The last exchange of notes between Jefferson and Maria Cosway on Thursday, 5th October 1786, is found in Boyd, 10, pp.431-433.

Pages 186-187

The Cosways' immense popularity with all they met during their relatively short time in Paris is reported by d'Hancarville in a letter to Charles Townley of 1st February 1787. (Townley Papers, British Museum, London – B.M.)

> '...Mr. Coswai has a character which pleased everyone and I cannot express to you the sensation that was made here by the intelligence, the good manners and the talents of Madame Coswai. Distance, far from diminishing, seems on the contrary to have increased this sensation.'

Jefferson opened his memorable letter of 12th October 1786, to Maria with the paragraph cited.(Boyd, 10, p.443.)

Chapter Eleven 'The Next Year'

Pages 190-191

John Trumbull was charged to be the intermediary between Jefferson and Mrs. Cosway in a letter of 13th October 1786 (T.J. to J.T.):

Not knowing Mrs. Cosway's address, I take the liberty of putting the inclosed under your cover, and of begging you to deliver it personally. Your reward will be the visit it will occasion you. She promised to write to me. Be so good as to take charge of her letters, and to find private conveyances for them, or to put them under cover to Mr. Grand banker rue neuve des Capucines a Paris. Or she will do the last herself. All letters directed to me are read in the post offices both of London and Paris.(Boyd, 10, p.460.)

Was Jefferson disingenuous in pretending not to know Mrs. Cosway's address? A trade card in the Massachusetts Historical Society bears his scrawled question: 'What is Mrs. Cosway's address?' and Trumbull's handwritten reply: 'Mrs. C – Pall Mall, London.' (Boyd, 10, p.460.) Or perhaps he enclosed the card in this cover letter.

The meeting of Trumbull and the Cosways in Antwerp is reported in a letter to Jefferson from Trumbull dated 9th October 1786, Antwerp:

Mr. and Mrs. Cosway arrivd this morning at 3oc having rode all night in the rain, not much I fear to the benefit of his Health.

Enclosed with Trumbull's letter was a note from M.C. to T.J. [in Italian]:

I am adding a couple of lines to ask you how you are. I hope the trip to St. Dennys did not cause you to remember us painfully, – I shall soon receive news of your complete recovery, which will give infinite pleasure to your always obliged and affectionate Friend, Maria Cosway – Mr. Cosway adds his compliments to mine. We arrived here Sunday, three hours past midnight. (Boyd,10, pp.438-441.)

Pages 191-193

Jefferson's 4,000 word letter of 5th-12th October 1786, to Maria Cosway, the dialogue between the Head and the Heart, is testimony to the dazzling impression she made on the reserved ambassador in the short space of a month's acquaintance. The original letter is found in the Library of Congress.

Although it is not known if Jefferson or the Cosways attended a performance of Sacchini's opera *Dardanus,* on Tuesday, 3rd October 1786 (*Journal de Paris*) they obviously were familiar with the air '*Jour heureux*'. The words of this air are translated from a text in Boyd, 10, p.459.

PAGE 194

Letter of M.C. to T.J. [30th October 1786] Boyd, 10, pp.494-495.

PAGE 195

P.P. to J.B., 8th November 1786, Joseph Foladare, *Boswell's Paoli,* p.144.
P.P. to M.C., Bath, 10th November 1786 (A.F.C.L.).
Also in *Pascal Paoli a Maria Cosway,* ed. Beretti, pp.58-59.
M.C. to T.J., [17th November 1786] Boyd, 10, pp.538-539.

PAGES 196-198

M.C. to T.J., [27th November 1786], Boyd, 10, p.552.
J.T. to T.J., 29th November 1786, Boyd, 10, p.556.

I have the pleasure of committing to Colo. Smith's care for you, a letter of Mrs. Cosway, and a book of songs of her composition. [*Songs and Duets Composed by Mrs. Cosway*] She has written twice to you before, since receiving your first and only one thru my hands; and having no answer, is anxious least they should have missd their way tho I addressed them in the manner you directed.

T.J. to M.C., 29th November 1786, Boyd, 10, p.555.
M.C. to T.J., 1st January 1787, Boyd 11, p.3.

PAGE 199

T.J. to M.C., 19th November 1786, Boyd, 10, pp.542-543.
T.J. to M.C., 24th December 1786, Boyd, 10, pp.627-628.

PAGES 200-201

M.C. to T.J., 15th February 1787, Boyd 11, pp.148-150.

PAGE 203

Baron d'Hancarville (Pierre François Hugues) to M.C., 26th February 1787. (B.C.L.)

The d'Hancarville correspondence, consisting of twenty letters from the 'Baron', covers the period 1787-1791.

The Baron d'Hancarville sent a letter of introduction for Melzi to the Cosways:

> I met *chez* [the Countess of Albany] the Count Melzi for whom I shall give you a letter: he recommends himself for he is a man of great sense, a good mind, and much knowledge: it is knowledge which will be very agreeable to General Paoli whom I greet...Melzi is the nephew of Madame Simonetta who married the late Duke of Modena. (2nd April 1787, B.C.L.)

D'Hancarville also introduced the Princess Lubomirska to the Cosways.

> ...this epistle will be delivered by the Princess Lubomirska who desires to know you and who will surely be satisfied with your acquaintance, like all who have seen you, who have the happiness that we envy to see you now.... Recommended by the prodigious fortune which she enjoys, by the grandeur of her birth, by her relation with the King of Poland, the Princess is even more so by the extreme kindness of her heart; she has with her a nephew who has the face of an angel united with a character and mind worthy of a beautiful face. She will propose, I believe, to Mr. Cosway to do his portrait: she saw and admired that of the Prince of Wales, owned by the Duchess de la Vallière.(10th May 1787, B.C.L.)

PAGES 204-205

According to Graves, II, pp.174-175, the pictures exhibited at the Royal Academy by Mrs. Cosway in 1787 were:

1   Young Cybele with two nymphs; portraits (*Lady Charlotte, Lady Anne, and Lady Frances Villiers*)

65 Young Bacchus ; portrait *(Hon. Mr. Lambe)*
80 An Enchantress; portraits of a lady with two of her children. *(Countess of Jersey)*
170 Psyche; portrait. *(Mdlle. Pinto)*
251 Portrait of a lady. *(Mrs. Cosway)*

Nos. 1, 65, and 80 can be seen in miniature in the print of the exhibition by Pietro Antonio Martini after Johan H. Ramberg, *The Exhibition of the Royal Academy at Somerset House 1787.*

Press articles are from *World*, 3rd May 1787 p.365, Vol. IV, Whitley Papers on Villiers' portrait and *St. James Chronicle*, 10th-12th May 1787, p.366, Vol. IV, Whitley Papers.

Other press comments were:

> No. 251 Portrait of a Lady – We are glad to find the fair artist so excellent in portrait. If we are not mistaken, it is intended for herself and like <u>herself</u> it is a very pleasing production. This Lady hath some other pictures in the room that exhibit genius.(V.&A. P.C. Vol. II, p.315.)

> Cosway is not inferior to former times – Mrs. Cosway excels. (V.&A., II, p.337.)

The portrait of Maria Cosway at her breakfast room window was praised in the *Morning Herald*, 15th May 1787:

> No. 53 Mr. Hodges 'View from a room of a gentleman's house in Pall Mall with the portrait of a Lady –This is a pleasing.... From Mr. Cosway's breakfast room. The view is the Park, which is prettily executed. The portrait is Mrs. Cosway, who is drawn with a faithful adherence to the accomplished original and the artist, by whom this was added is Mr. Cosway.'

Richard Cosway's testimony in the trial of the picture dealer Vandergucht is described in William Whitley, *Life of Gainsborough*, pp.276-282.

PAGES 208-209

The sources for Petit's trip to London to fetch Maria (Polly) Jefferson were: T.J. to Abigail Adams of 1st July 1787 (Boyd, 11, pp.514-515) and T.J.'s instructions to Petit [2nd July] in which he orders him to deliver a letter to Madame Cosway.(T.J. to M.C., 2nd July 1787, Boyd, 11, pp.519-520.)

PAGE 210

M.C. to T.J., 9th July 1787. (Boyd, 11, pp.567-569.)

Chapter Twelve   Alone in Paris

PAGE 212

> The Duc d'Orléans, his Duchess, and their highnesses offspring had their portraits taken by Mr. Cosway during his excursion to Paris last year. The sketches were brought by that artist to England, who is now engaged in composing this illustrious family in two pictures – The Duke and Dutchess are introduced in one piece, and their children in the companion picture. (*Morning Herald*, 23rd January 1787 in B.M.D.P., *Whitley Papers*, p.266.)

Maria Cosway travelled with Princess Lubomirska, who arrived in Paris between 25th August and 4th September 1787. (Archiwum Glowne Akt Dawnych, Warsaw – A.G.A.D., Potocki Correspondence.)

Her arrival in Paris and the fact that Jefferson had already attended the Paris Salon is confirmed by a T.J. letter to Trumbull:

> The Salon has been open four or five days. I inclose you a list of its treasures...

> Come then and take your bed here. You will see Mrs. Cosway who arrived two days ago .(30th August 1787, Boyd, 12, p.69.)

PAGES 213-216

The paintings exhibited in Salon du Louvre, 1787, are described in *Mercure de France*, 22nd September 1787.

The scene at the salon is imagined. Maria Cosway surely visited it as well as Jefferson, the Trudaines, David, and Chénier.

The success of *Death of Socrates* was commented on by Jefferson in a letter to Trumbull: 'The best thing is the Death of Socrates by David, and a superb one it is.'(T.J. to J.T., 30th Aug 1787, Boyd, XII, p.69.) It was commissioned by Trudaine de la Sablière. (See Philippe Bordes, pp.21-22.)

Jefferson's account book notes for 30th August 'Pd reading glasses 42F' (M.H.I.)

The verses said to be recited by André Chénier are from a poetic fragment endorsed on the back 'Mrs. Cosway, Pall Mall, London' in Chénier, *Oeuvres Completes*, ed. Walter, p.944.

It may be significant that Jefferson began his regular retirement to the community of hermits outside Paris shortly after Maria Cosway's arrival in Paris. His account book notes payments began on 5th September 'took possession of apartments at Mont Calvaire Paid dinner at Mont Calvaire 6f'. On 14th September and again on 20th September he 'pd. crossing at Suresne', which is on the way to Mont Calvaire. Again on 12th October 'pd. at Mont Calvaire 60 f…'.

In late September Cosway was seen at the *Comédie française*, possibly with an English gentleman, although the record is imprecise. On 1st October Ann Flaxman wrote to her father:

> On Thursday the day of our arrival we went in the evening to the French comedy…we there recognized Mrs. Cosway the famous paintress & an English gentleman who is on his journey to Rome & to whom we had been particularly recommended by some of our London friends. (B.L., Add. M.S.S. 39780 *#162.*)

PAGE 218

Stanislaus Potocki to his wife, 17th September 1787, A.G.A.D., A.P.P., 262/1.

Descriptions of the life and collections of the eccentric Princess Isabella Lubomirska are from Bozenna Majewska-Maszkowska, pp.601-606.

Mesmer's membership in the Freemasons and his introduction into

French society thereby is described in Manceron, *le vent d'Amerique 1778-1783*, pp.327-334.

Lafayette, an investor in Mesmer's Paris enterprise, wrote to General Washington before a visit to America:

> A German doctor, named Mesmer, having made the greatest discovery of animal magnetism, has taught pupils, among whom your humble servant is called one of the most enthusiastic.... . Before leaving, I will obtain permission to give you Mesmer's secret, which, you can believe, is a great philosophical discovery... (Manceron, le *bon plaisir 1782-1785*, p.372.)

Page 219

Mainaduc's teaching expounded in *J. B. Mainaduc, M.D., Member of the Corporation of Surgeons*, London, 1798. (B.L.)

S. Potocki to his wife, 6th November 1787, A.G.A.D., A.P.P. 264/I.

It has been sometimes stated that Richard Cosway's enthusiasm for 'mesmerism' or unorthodox healing practices created a rift between him and his wife. On the contrary, it is quite clear from Stanislaus Potocki's letters that Maria Cosway was a serious follower of some sort of practice which he called 'magnetism'.

Pages 220-221

Maria Cosway's visit to Jefferson's home is imagined, although it appears (by a phrase open to interpretation in one of her letters) that she had visited him more than once and during those visits Jefferson's secretary, William Short, exercised discretion by being absent: ' I hope Mr. Short will not be out as his usual when I have the pleasure to come to you.' (M.C. to T.J., [24th November 1787].)

Sally Hemings was in Paris during Maria's 1787 visit, having arrived with Polly Jefferson the previous July. The young servant's immaturity is confirmed by Abigal Adams' opinion of her in a letter to T.J. of 6th July 1787. (Boyd, 11, p.551.) Writing of Polly Jefferson, Mrs. Adams comments:

> The Girl she has with her wants more care than the child, and is

wholly incapable of looking properly after her, without some superiour to direct her.

What is known of Sally Hemings' appearance comes from a fellow slave, Isaac Jefferson:

> Sally Hemings' mother Betty was a bright mulatto woman, and Sally mighty near white; she was the youngest child. Folks said that these Hemingses was old Mr. Wayles's [Martha Jefferson's father's] children. Sally was very handsome, long straight hair down her back. ('Memoirs of a Monticello Slave as dictated to Charles Campbell by Isaac', *Jefferson at Monticello*, James A. Bear, Jr., ed., p.4.)

If John Wayles, Jefferson's father-in-law, was Sally Hemings' father, then she was Martha Jefferson's half-sister.

The Cosways' servant, Ottobah Cugoano, was born in Ghana. He was enslaved in 1770 at the age of thirteen. Sold to a West Indian plantation in Grenada, he was brought to the U.K. and set free by his master in 1772. Advised to become a Christian to avoid further enslavement, Ottobah went into service with Richard Cosway. It is thought that Cosway sent him to school to learn to read and write. By 1787 Ottobah had become well-known in anti-slavery circles in London and in that year published a well-reasoned attack on all pro-slavery arguments, *Thoughts and Sentiments on the Evil and Wicked Traffic of the Slavery and Commerce of the Human Species, humbly submitted to the Inhabitants of Great Britain*, by Ottobah Cugoano, a Native of Africa, London, 1787.

Trumbull's letter to Jefferson with the message that Maria Cosway's family and friends were complaining about her silence was dated 17th September 1787. (Boyd, 12, pp.192-193 M.H.I.). Jefferson's reply slightly suggests that Maria Cosway, the Comte de Moustier, and Madame de Bréhan could have been at his house at the same time when he shared Trumbull's letter with them.

> I showed to Mrs. Cosway the part of your letter respecting her, and begged her to consider the scold as hanging over her head

till I could get a machine for scolding invented, because it is a business not fit for any human heart, and especially when to be directed on such subjects as her. Madme. De Bréhan also read so much as concerned her, and was pleased to find you still recollected her and your promise to her. She and Count de Moustier set out for America in Tuesday next. (T.J. to J.T., 4th October 1787, Boyd, 12, pp.206-207.)

Moustier had been named Minister to the new American government. Once in New York, the couple's manners were deemed unsuitable, especially the ambiguous status of Madame de Bréhan, Moustier's sister-in-law, whose connection to the Minister was thought to be 'improper'. After two years they discreetly returned to France without an actual recall. (Malone, *Jefferson and the Rights of Man*, pp.197-198.)

PAGES 221-223

Jefferson's Account Book notes 'Oct. 10 pd. hearing musical glasses 3f.' (M.H.I.) He may have attended the performance with Maria Cosway.

The scene at the home of Princess Lubomirska is imagined.

PAGE 223-224

Jefferson paid for his expenses at Mont Calvaire on 12th October. (Account book, M.H.I.)

Jefferson 's Account book records:

Oct. 25 pd. for dinner at Palais Royal 24f   Varieties 3f
Nov. 1 pd. tickets to a concert 6f

There is a good possibility that he attended these events with Maria Cosway. The *Mercure de France* , *3 novembre, 1787,* gives the program of the *concert spiritual* of 1st November.

Details of the transport of the Guilio Romano cartoons are in an undated letter from d'Hancarville to d'Angiviller, which directly quotes a Richard Cosway letter to his wife.(A.N., O1/1916.)

PAGE 224-227

Jefferson organised an important dinner for Maria Cosway and her friends, probably held Sunday, 25th November 1787. She speaks of it in the following note to Jefferson which gives information on the guests:

> Saturday Evening [24th November 1787]
> Why will you Make such a great dinner? I had told the Princess of the pleasure I intended My self tomorrow and she seemd very glad to go with me, but had not thought of any body else; to begin by Mr: d'Hancarville he is very sorry not to be able to wait on you as he has been particularly engaged for some time past. Mr: St: Andre I shall see this Evening. Monr: Nimscevik accepts with pleasure your kind invitation, Count Btorki [Potocki] is not here, but I shall deliver to him also your invitation. ... (Boyd, 12, p.387.)

Jefferson's accounts show that he made important preparations for the dinner in the week of 19-24th November. His kitchen expenses were tripled, the harpsichord was tuned, and he made expensive purchases for his table: two silver wine urns, two silver branched candlesticks, three dozen red china plates, soup plates, compotes, glasses. (Account Book, M.H.I.)

The dinner conversation is imagined.

PAGE 227-229

It is not known if Jefferson and Cosway saw each other in the week between the dinner and her departure. They had made plans to breakfast together the morning of her departure and he had at some time been received by her while her hair was dressed as he suggested in a later letter: 'I remember that when under the hands of your Coiffeuse, you used to amuse yourself with your pencil.' Their last meeting is imagined.

Maria Cosway's undated note the eve of her departure [30th November 1787] is from Boyd, 12, p.403 (although the date given [7th December] is impossible because Niemcewicz's letter and the date of her arrival in London prove that she left the week before).

Evidence that she left with André Chénier is from Julian Niemcewicz to Maria Cosway, 1st December 1787:

...we said that you were Saturday evening at Amiens and Monday morning at Calais. I hope that you had heeded my prayers and did not travel at night, moreover Monsieur St. André would never have permitted it. How fortunate he is to be with you... (A.F.C.L.)

Passport records for 5th December show that Chénier arrived at Calais with a mysterious lady: 'Le Chev. De St. André, La Dame Borde arriving from Paris, passport of the King of 27 and 30 November...' (Archives Ministère des Affaires Etrangères, Paris – A.A.E., C.E. 93/f.26.)

Niemcewicz' long and impassioned letter the day of her departure echoes the distress of Jefferson's famous dialogue a year earlier.

...I ran to the Gate St. Martin thinking to reach you, see you once more and bid you a last adieu; vain effort. ... I saw that the moment so feared of being separated from you had arrived, I felt all the bitterness of it...I am alone at home, everyone is sleeping, there is only I who watches and weeps...if you could see my affliction...shut up alone...it will be hard to renounce the only company whose sweetness was all my happiness. Is it possible that this happiness is enclosed in the short space of three months, is it possible that I shall not see you again?... No, I do not wish to abandon myself to this sad thought...you have carried away happiness and gaiety with you, these rooms where we passed whole days so happy, we cannot stay a moment in them.... What I wouldn't give to be with you only an instant, to see this pretty little sister, and her blond hair, and her eyes and that pretty mouth which pleased with so much grace...(A.F.C.L.)

Chapter Thirteen   'Remember Me and Love Me'

PAGE 232

Maria Cosway seemed to think better of her abrupt departure from Paris after her arrival in London. She expressed her curiosity to know Jefferson's reaction in two letters, M.C. to T.J., 10th December [1787] Boyd, 12, p.415 and M.C. to T.J., 25th December [1787] Boyd, 12 pp.459-460.

PAGE 233

Jefferson was apparently more miffed than he admitted, expressing his disappointment in the entire Parisian visit of Cosway in the only letter of the winter dated by internal evidence as [31st January 1788] Boyd, 12, pp.539-540.

PAGES 234-235

M.C. to T.J., 6th March [1788], Boyd, 12, p.645.

The letter cited from Jacques-Louis David to Maria Cosway is reprinted entirely in Philippe Bordes, *Le Serment du Jeu de Paume de Jacques-Louis David*, pp.132-133. It and a second quoted in Bordes are thought to be dated 1788.

Review of Macklin's Poet's Gallery, V.A., P.C., Vol. II, p.406, V.A.

T.J. to M.C., 27th July 1788, Boyd, 13, pp.423-424.

PAGE 236

Richard Cosway was likened to Pandarus in the *Morning Post* of 16th June 1788, B.M.P.D., Whitley Papers, p.367.

André Chénier's dissatisfaction with his life in London is described in Walter, *André Chénier*, pp.89-105.

Chénier's lines on the *intaglio* engraving of Maria Cosway's portrait are translated from 'Marie Cosway' in Chénier, *Oeuvres completes*, ed, Walter, pp.112-113. The poet was inspired by a ring and several portrait engravings in wax executed by the engraver Jeuffroy in Paris. They were sent to the Cosways and to Chénier in the winter and spring of 1788. (B.C.L., d'Hancarville Correspondence.)

PAGES 237-238

Upon returning from a journey to Amsterdam and the Rhineland in March-April 1788, Jefferson gave Maria a brief account of his voyage in T.J. to M.C., 24th April 1788, Boyd 13, pp.103-104. After a rapid delivery to London, Maria answered immediately on 29th April 1788.

PAGE 239

Maria's enthusiastic appraisal of Luigi Marchesi's singing is from her letter of 29th April 1788 to Jefferson, Boyd 13, pp.114-116.

PAGE 240

A description of Marchesi's stage entrances and vocal technique is from Barbier, *Histoire des Castrats,* 1989 and Heriot, *The Castrati in Opera.* His opening night in London in April 1788 is described in Lord Mount Edgecumbe, *Musical Reminiscences,* pp.66-67.

PAGES 241-243

The *Morning Post* described the scene in Maria's opera box in its edition of 2nd July 1788, V.A., P.C., Vol. II, p.367.

During August 1788, Richard Cosway was taken up in town with the decoration of Carlton House for the Prince of Wales.

> The subject of Mr. Cosway's central painting for the Prince of Wale's grand saloon at Carlton House is Apollo seated in the chariot of the sun & beginning his diurnal career. (B.M.P.D., *Whitley Papers*, p.367.)

Cosway's vanity about this commission was mocked in the *Morning Herald* of 22nd August 1788:

> What if the little painter in Pall Mall has a practice of leaving word with his servant —"Should anybody call you'll say I am gone to breakfast with the Prince!" (B.M.P.D., *Whitley Papers*, p.367.)

PAGE 244

Maria Cosway exhibited two pictures in the Royal Academy exhibition of 1788:

> No. 91 Laura *Vide* Petrarch (Mrs. Fitzherbert).
> No.237 Portrait of a Lady and her Son. (Mrs. Parkins) Graves, p. 175.

Her portrait of Maria Fitzherbert was not well-received. Agreeing with the *Morning Post* another reviewer called it '...a very frail attempt to give the personal charms of that lady: She is in a supine attitude, totally devoid of every grace and attraction.' (V.A., P.C., Vol. II, p.359.)

M.C. to T.J., 23rd June [1788] Boyd, 13, pp.287-288.

PAGES 244- 247

Maria Cosway's visit to Down Place in August 1788 is documented by her letter to Jefferson of 19th August 1788, Boyd, 13, pp.524-525, but her conversation with Angelica Church is imagined.

M.C. to T.J., 15th July 1788, Boyd, 13, pp.360-361.

Thomas Jefferson wrote to both Maria and her friend Angelica Church on 27th July 1788. The letter to Mrs. Church does have some pale echoes of his correspondence to Maria Cosway and illustrates that gentlemen wrote married ladies somewhat exaggerated expressions of their esteem. (Boyd, 13, pp.422-423 and pp.423-424.)

PAGE 248

M.C. to T.J., 19th August 1788, Boyd, 13, pp.524-525
T.J. to M.C., 30th July 1788, Boyd, 13, p.435
T.J. to M.C., 26th September 1788, 13, pp.638-639

PAGES 249-250

The gossip from the *Morning Post* began in January in the editions of 20th and 26th January 1789, which reported that both Cosways were designing costumes for *Ifgenia in Aulide*. The domestic scene between the couple is imagined, but inspired by the *Post's* report of 26th February 1789:

> The enemies of a certain amiable votaress of the *Graphic Art* have insinuated that she was too partial to the enchanting powers of Marchesi. These vile calumnies have been circulated with such malicious industry and effect that they have at length reached the ears of that troublesome animal called a husband, who is generally the last to discover what relates to his own honour. In consequence of this, the charming warbler, it is said, was dismissed from the house of the Knight of the Brush, but a little reflection having convinced the latter that the world is full of malignity, & that the whole story which offended him was a mere fiction, the same harmony prevails which has long subsisted between all parties. (B.M.P.D., *Whitley Papers*, p.368.)

PAGES 251-252

M.C. to T.J., 6th February 1789.

T.J. to M.C., 14th January 1789. Boyd, 14, pp.525-526; pp.445-446.
The World, 14th April 1789, gave a description of the gifts, adding:

> … This present in itself so very valuable is further enhanced by
> a letter of much elegant compliment to Mr. Cosway from the
> King and by the assiduities of Mons. De Montmorin, through
> whose application to the Duke of Dorset & Lord Camarthen the
> whole package was cleared of all port duties free. (B.M.P.D.,
> *Whitley Papers*, p.369.)

The altercation between Cosway and Humphry, was also widely
commented upon in the press.

> The late dissention between H. the painter & his brother of the
> pencil, C. at the Acad. Dinner…tho' Master H. under the
> inspiring influence by Bacchus delivered his sentiments with great
> warmth & freedom, little Dicky very prudently made allowance
> for the situation of his rival & did not exhibit any other than
> pacific emotions – The circumstance which appeared most to
> gall H. on the occasion alluded to was C's taking the President's
> chair – tho' indeed it must be confessed that few among the
> Academicians could have conferred on it more grace, dignity &
> value than the sublime Richard Cosway, Esq. *Morning Post*, 20th
> April 1789. (B.M.P.D., *Whitley Papers*, p.368.)

PAGE 253

Maria Cosway exhibited two pictures in the Royal Academy exhibition of
1789:

> 101 *A dying child, summoned by the spirit of its deceased
> parents: an historical fact. (Miss Gardner and Lady
> Townshend* – Walpole.)
> 112 *Medusa.*
> (Graves, *The Royal Academy Exhibitors* II, p.175.)

The Times' sceptical account of Miss Gardner's vision is recorded in the Whitley Papers, p.369. The painting, destined for Lady Townshend, is now in the Musée de la Révolution Française, Vizille.

PAGE 256

T.J. to M.C., 21st May 1789, Boyd, 15, pp.142-143.
Anne Damer wrote to a friend:

> I saw it burned and so fine a sight! It is far beyond description – from the top of Cosway's house in Pall Mall did I see it. (Anne Damer to Sir Charles Hotham, 18th June [1789].)

PAGES 257-259

T.J. to M.C., 25th July 1789, Boyd, 15, pp.305-306.
Gouverneur Morris called on Maria Cosway with his letter of introduction on 9th August 1789. His dislike of English 'routs', which he considered 'stiff and formal,' was noted after each of his first visits to the Cosways:

> I go to-night to Mrs. Cosway's…she is vastly pleasant, but her ladies are all ranged in battalia on the opposite side of the room. Discuss a little with her the *froideur anglaise,* and while she is in conversation with them, throw the pith of that discussion into these stanzas, which I leave with her, being a kind of address to the ladies.
>
>> By nature' various beauty blest,
>> Ah! why your wealth conceal,
>> And why, in cold indifference drest,
>> Her blessings not reveal? …
>> Your conversation, like your coin,
>> Is gold, but yet 'tis strange
>> How oft, when social circles join,
>> You want a little change.

Morris, *Diary*, ed., Davenport, Vol. 1, p.184; pp.187-188; pp.197-198.

M.C. to T.J., 19th August 1789, Boyd, 15, p.351.

Page 260

M.C. to T.J., 9th October 1789, Boyd, 15, p.513.

T.J. to M.C., 14th October 1789, Boyd, 15, p.521.

1789 was a year when the celebrity of the Cosways probably reached its apogee. The press was full of their activities, beginning with the rumours of Maria's preference for Marchesi, then the much-reported gifts from the French king, Richard's advice to the Prince of Wales for the decoration of Carlton House, and the visits to their house of the Duc d'Orléans. As intense publicity eventually generates negative reports, they were not long in coming:

> That the King of France should have sent a present of carpets to Cosway the painter is rather odd; but if his Grace of Orleans had sent a grateful memorial to the artist for the *convenient accommodation* which his house perhaps afforded while the Duke was in London it would not have been difficult to account for the reason of such a present.

> When there is a difficulty for the friends of gallantry to meet each other without Detection, a painter's house has often been deemed a very useful place & some painters are by no means averse to give a very convenient latitude to their visitors. (*Morning Post,* 16th April 1789, B.M.P.D. *Whitley Papers,* p.369.)

Further evidence that the Cosways' house did not have a perfect reputation is found in the opinions of the American merchant class in London, who resented Angelica Church's friendship with Maria Cosway. Gouverneur Morris records in his journal on 22nd April 1790:

> I take home Mr. and Mrs. Low [American Tories in London]. She tells me that Mrs. Church in her Efforts to get into High Life, neglects her old Friends and particularly Mrs. Phyn, This Lady had made a similar Observation to me, farther said that perhaps Mrs. Church had taken Offence at an Expression of

Regret that she was so intimate with Mrs. Cosway whose House is considered as one of those where, from the very mixed Companies which frequent it, dangerous Connections may be formed. (Morris, *Diary*, ed. Davenport, Vol I, p.490.)

Chapter Fourteen   Flight to Italy

PAGE 261

Lucy Paradise wrote to Thomas Jefferson on 2nd March 1790:

> Mrs. Cosway has desired her best compliments also. This Lady is with child for the first time. She has been extremely ill, but is now perfectly recovered & expects in a few months to ly in. (Boyd, 16, p.198.)

Boswell's farewell dinner for Paoli and the list of guests is noted in Boswell, *Private Papers*, Vol. xviii, pp.29-30.

PAGES 262-263

It is not known exactly when the Cosway marriage began to break down. There is only circumstantial evidence that strains began showing in the years 1789-90: the rumours about Marchesi, her departure for Italy and a letter written much later from Maria to a Mrs. Chambers (A.F.C.L., 29th May 1816.)

It is not known to whom the town Hammersmith refers. The suggestion that it was the Loutherbourgs and their healing practices is disproved by Maria Cosway's positive attitude and even occasional practice of 'healing' which is found in her correspondence and that of her friends. (A.F.C.L., M.C. to R.C., 13th January 1791; A.G.A.D., Potocki correspondence.)

A.F.C.L., M.C. to R.C., 22nd March 1815.

M.C. to T.J., 6th April 1790, Boyd, 16, p.32.

T.J. to M.C., 23rd June 1790, Boyd, 16, pp.550-551.

Jefferson began to suffer from prolonged headaches in the spring of 1790, which recurred during the next decade.

PAGES 264-266

The wall decoration of Maria Cosway's study is described in a letter of Francesco d'Ageno to Angelica Church:

> ...your fine picture in drawing that is fixed in Mrs. Cosway's study...I mean in company with those of Lady Lyttelton, Madame Damer, Princess Lubomirsky, General Paoli, Mr. Swinburne, M. d'Hancarville, and other goddesses, heroes, philosophers, and learned men, who all are hanging at the both sides of the chimney... (V.I.U., Church Papers, 22nd September 1787.)

Gouverneur Morris records three visits to the Cosways in the month of April 1791, the first on 13th April with Angelica Church (Morris, *A Diary of the French Revolution*, vol. 1, p.481). On 24th April he found Lady Townshend there where the conversation turned '...on the Man (or rather Monster) who for several days past has amused himself with cutting and wounding Women in the Streets'. When dining with the Cosways on 26th April he complained to his journal '...the soup and ragouts are mixed with cheese and that none of the newest'. (*Diary*, pp.490-491.)

The World reported on 5th April 1790 that George Hadfield had been awarded a stipend of £100 a year by the Royal Academy to study architecture for three years in Rome. (B.M.P.D., *Whitley Papers*, p.369.) The papers also reported that Mary Moser was the Academy member who proposed study in Rome for the young Hadfield. (V.A. Press Cuttings, II, p.500.)

Gouverneur Morris notes in his Journal on 20th April 1791 the visit to a legmaker to '...have my right Leg taken in Plaister of Paris as a Model by which to make a left Leg of Copper'. (*Diary*, I, p.487.)

Maria Cosway began a journal entry of 4th May 1803: 'It is the day of the birth of my little girl.' (A.F.C.L., Diario A.)

Louise de Stolberg sent her proxy as godmother from Paris in May, 1790.

> I learned, Mister Cosway, with great pleasure that Madame your wife gave birth to a girl. Give her my compliments and assure her that I will hold her with great pleasure on the baptismal font

and will give her the name of Louise which is mine. General Paoli has accepted also. I desire that your little one has all possible happiness, and that she resembles her mother that I beg you to kiss for me and tell her to take care of herself so that I will find her in good health when I go to England which will be shortly I hope. ('The Countess of Albany and Richard Cosway', *Notes and Queries*, 10th January 1948, p.16.)

PAGE 267

Gouverneur Morris records his visit to the Cosways on 28th May 1791, where he meets Lady Jersey, Mrs. Damer, and Angelica Church. He describes Maria's design for the Churches' garden pavilion and the verse he wrote to accompany it. (*Diary*, I, pp.529-530.)

PAGES 268-269

Morris noted 14th June 1791: 'Go from hence to Mrs. Cosway's. She is very ill.' *(Diary, I, p.541.)*

After Maria had been named Directress of a school for girls in Lyon, she wrote the following version of her departure for Italy. The letter was addressed to Monsieur Jauffret, the Vicar-General of Archbishop Fesch of Lyon.

'...a pregnancy of continual illness. Difficulty in delivery.... . The first day that I went out to go to Church, a gust of wind gave me a pleurisy and was reduced to extremity. To escape dying I was advised to change air, and it seemed to me that I had set out for the other world so much did I feel bad. I left in the month of July wrapped up in flannel, in an English carriage, well closed, with my brother and my maid. Accompanied by Lady Wright and her family...' (A.F.C.L., n.d.)

For Sir James and Lady Catherine Wright see Ingamells, *Dictionary of British ...Travellers*, pp.1022-1023.

Lady Wright's participation in the Cosways' circle of healers is reported by George Cumberland, the art critic and collector:

…Dr. Mainaduke had many pupils, among others himself, the Duke of Gloucester, Mrs. Cosway, Lady Wright & Mrs. Bush…they pretend to be able to cure diseases by sympathy, and Mr. C. actually said that he was then curing a man at Dublin whom he never saw, and who never saw him…. . Loutherbourg is at the head of this sect… (Cumberland M.S.S., University of Toronto in G. E. Bentley, *Notes & Queries*, p.296.)

Pages 269-270

Maria Cosway's arrival in Venice was noted by several English travellers:

> Mrs. Cosway's brother is arrived in the pension after two years vacancy… . He left his sister at Venice I am told. (B.L., Add. 36496, 3rd September 1790, Jos. Irvine to Geo. Cumberland.)

> Maria Cosway, the famous paintress, is now at Venice, & is expected daily here, we have already Madame le Brun the famous French paintress, & Signora Angelica as you know lives here always, so that we have the three rival paintresses (B.L., Add. 39780, Rome 17th October 1790, Ann Flaxman to Mr. Kirk.)

Thraliana, ed., Balderston, p.875.

'Recollections of Richard Cosway, Esq. R.A'., *Library of Fine Arts*, 1832.

There is nothing in Maria Cosway's papers to suggest a liaison with Luigi Marchesi, but then it is clear that the bulk of her intimate personal correspondence was lost or purposely destroyed. Although she scrupulously saved her letters from Cardinal Joseph Fesch and General Pasquale Paoli and other important correspondents, her archives have certainly been purged of letters from her husband, mother, sisters, brothers, Jefferson and Marchesi. There is little trace of those intimate communications of family and personal relations that every life contains, other than a handful of letters which present her justification for her actions.

Marchesi's confessor in later life, Don Francesco Zoja, persuaded the operatic star that his life in the theatre and his various liaisons were dissolute; Marchesi repented and authorised Zoja, an executor of his will, to burn '…any books, papers, prints, letters, pictures existing in my houses that offend Religion, modesty or good morals…' (Maccapani, *Luigi Marchesi,* pp.54-55.)

Before this order was given, however, Marchesi executed a codicil to his will that left his good friend Maria Cosway '…all my books, prints, music, drawings and similar things in Milano or my house in Inzago, as well as two pictures of Magiolini, and the pictures of her choice in my house in Inzago and my clock from Paris now in the second salon of Milan.'(6th May 1828, Maccapani, p.48.) Maria's importance in his life is underscored by this bequest.

The Marchesi – Todi rivalry in Maccapani, pp.36-37.

P.P. to M.C., 17th November and 20th December 1792, A.F.C.L. and Beretti, pp.80-83.

Maria's introduction to Isabella Marini's salon, a brilliant gathering of literary aristocrats, put her at the heart of Venetian society. She would also have had entrée through her close friendship with the former Ambassador in London, Count Soderini, who had been elected to the powerful Venetian Council of Ten in 1789.

There are glimpses of Maria's Venetian stay in Isabella Marini's correspondence with her and with Denon. From these letters we know that Maria visited Venice with Denon and painted Marini's portrait.

> Madame Cosway with whom I toured the city this morning, asked me to send her regards. You will no doubt find her here, as well as the portrait which I shall engrave. (Denon to Madame Teotochi Marini [Venice, October 1790] *Lettres à Bettine,* ed. Garavini et.al., p.95.)

Denon to Marini, [Venice, October 1790] *Lettres à Bettine,* p.96.

PAGE 271

Maria Cosway saved a copy of this one letter written to Richard Cosway from Venice, probably as evidence that she was in contact with her husband, that she asked after her child, and that she hoped her husband would come to Italy. (A.F.C.L., M.C. to R.C., Venice, 13th January 1791.)

PAGE 272-273

Maria's brief visit to Florence in mid-April 1791, her impressions of her birthplace, and her continued journey to Rome with Lady Cowper are taken from her letter to Isabella Marini of 15th April 1791. (Biblioteca Nazionale Braidense, Milan – B.N.B., Fonds Teotochi.)

In late April Ann Flaxman saw Maria Cosway and Lady Cowper at one of Georgiana Hare-Naylor's *conversazioni* in Rome, where English artists gathered on Thursdays. (B.L. Add M.S.S. 39792.)

B.C.L., d'Hancarville to M.C., 30th July 1791.

H.W. to M.B., 8th June 1791, W.S. Lewis, *Walpole Correspondence*, Vol. 11, p.285.

PAGES 274-276

During the period October 1790 to October 1791, Mary Berry and Anne Damer were regular correspondents. Damer's letters are found in the Berry papers in the British Library. In several dated from July to October 1791, Damer warns her friend of the dangers of associating with a lady whom she calls the 'Marchesa'. The context of these letters clearly leads to Maria Cosway as the subject of their disapproval.

B.L., Add. M.S.S. 37727, 11th July 1791.

B.L., Add. M.S.S. 37727, 15th August 1791.

B.L., Add. M.S.S. 37727, 25th August 1791.

B.L., Add. M.S.S. 37727, 4th October 1791.

B.L., Add. M.S.S. 37727, 10th October 1791.

Marchesi in Milan, Maccapani, *Luigi Marchesi*, p.96.

P.P. to M.C., 29th September 1792, Beretti, *Pascal Paoli a Maria Cosway*, p.80.

PAGE 277

A.F.C.L., Diario A, 3rd September 1803.

The violence in France became extreme in 1792. Gouverneur Morris described the scenes to Robert Morris in a letter of 24th December 1792:

> '...a man applied to the Convention for damages done to his quarry...The damage done to him was by the number of dead bodies thrown into his pit... . Think of the destruction of

hundreds, who had long been the first people of a country, without form or trial, and their bodies thrown, like dead dogs, into the first hole that offered.' (Sparks, *Life of Gouverneur Morris,* Vol. III, p.42.)

PAGE 278

The letter cited of 1st March [1793] from Maria to her husband (A.F.C.L.) is one of the few copies of her correspondence saved from this period, certainly because it justifies her conduct to her husband, assuring him that her servant Madison, who carried the letter, would testify as to her honourable behaviour. It also recounts the difficulties she had in finding a convent that would accept her. Finally, she was very satisfied to find one – Santa Brigida – that was run by the Order of the Visitation, as was Il Conventino in Florence.

PAGE 279

The date of Maria's entry in Santa Brigida was noted much later in her journal of 4th May 1802. (A.F.C.L.) As soon as Maria had a respectable address, a busy correspondence reappears in her archives, beginning with the summer of 1793. She was then in touch with numerous friends: Isabella Marini, Julian Niemcewicz, and various Italians. Her enthusiastic account of retirement is found in a letter to Marini of 2nd July 1793. (B.N.B., Fonds Teotochi.)

PAGE 280

M.C. to R.C., 18th August 1794, cited in Barnett, p.126.
Details of her return are noted in Joseph Farington's journal:

'Met Mr. Coombes at the Shakespeare Gallery…Coombes told me Mrs. Cosway is certainly returning to England. Cosway is to give a person 130 guineas for bringing her from Genoa. She declares her resolution to live quite private and to the education of Her Child Her sole object.' (Garlick and Macintyre, *The Diary of Joseph Farington,* Vol.1, p.234.)

Chapter Fifteen Louisa Paolina

PAGES 282-283

The lion in the verses on Cosway's door referred to the stone lions at the entrance to Stratford Place. *Nollekens and His Times*, Vol. II, p.407.

Maria Cosway's first view of her child, after four year's absence, and their first words are recounted in *Archivio Storico Lodigiano*, XLV, 1926, pp.36-51.

Cosway's richly displayed collections are described in Smith's *Nollekens*, pp.407-408, in which Smith comments: '…many of the rooms were more like scenes of enchantment, pencilled by a poet's fancy, than any thing, perhaps, before displayed in a domestic habitation.' Descriptions of each room's objects are found in the 1820 inventory (A.F.C.L.) published in Lloyd, 'The Cosway Inventory of 1820', *The Walpole Society, 2003-2004*, Vol. 66, pp.163-217.

PAGE 284

T.J. to M.C., 23rd June 1790. (D.L.C.)
M.C. to T.J., 13th November 1794. (M.H.I.)

PAGE 285

M.C. to T.J., 24th November 1794. (M.H.I.)

PAGES 286-289

M.C. to M.G. (*Archivio Storico Lodigiano*.)

PAGES 290-291

E. A. Smith, *George IV*, pp.72-73.
   Munson, *Maria Fitzherbert*, pp.278-279.
   The Diary of Joseph Farington, II, p.589.

Cosway's stay at Windsor in B.L., Add. 71584.

The Cosway's finances in the 1790s were no doubt affected by war, higher taxes, less custom, and non-paying clients. Farington noted in 1795: 'Cosway has little business at present…Cosway's Bill to the Prince of Wales was about £1500… Coombes does not think Cosway possesses more than the House He lives in and £ 500 bank stock, except He has money out on Bond – He has certainly much money owing to him for business done.' (II, pp.415-416.)

Later in 1798 on Farington's advice, Cosway decided to give up his carriage and one or two servants to save £426 a year. (Farington, III, p.966.)

For George Hadfield's exclusion from the Architects Club, see Farington, II, p.287.

PAGE 292

George Hadfield was known as a man of taste. Nevertheless, his emigration to America was not a success. He soon quarrelled with the author of the U.S. Capitol's plans, the amateur William Thornton, who as a member of the Commission for the Federal District was able to vanquish rival architects except Benjamin Latrobe. Hadfield was eventually let go and never fulfilled his promise, although he built a number of handsome buildings in Washington. Among the few remaining are the Custis-Lee Mansion and the old City Hall. Hadfield's fellow architects and artists admired his abilities and generally defended him while recognising his faults – irritability and sloth.

Latrobe came to Hadfield's aid, gave him work and redeemed his Royal Academy gold medal after the impoverished architect had been forced to pawn it. He noted later with regret that Hadfield was '...too young to possess experience and education. Proficient more in the room of design than in the practical execution of great work he was no match for the rogues then employed in the construction of the public buildings or for the charlatans in architecture who had designed them. All that he proposed, however, proved him a man of correct tastes, of perfect theoretic knowledge, and of bold integrity. He waged a long war against the ignorance and the dishonesty of the commissioners and of the workmen. But the latter prevailed, for General Washington, led by his feelings and possessing no knowledge of the subject, sided against him. Thus has Hatfield lost the most precious period of his life, that of the practical study of his profession in the first works he might have executed. He loiters here, ruined in fortune, in temper, and reputation, nor will his irritable pride and neglected study ever permit him to take the station in the art which his elegant taste and excellent talent ought to have obtained.' (*The Journal of Benjamin Henry Latrobe*, pp.133-134.)

Latrobe defended Hadfield in a letter to Jefferson when he had his own confrontation with Thornton:

'In a contest, similar to that in which I am engaged, first with Mr. Hallet, then with Mr. Hatfield, Doctor Thornton was victorious. Both these men, men of knowledge, talents, integrity and amiable manners were ruined. Hatfield had the best expectations in England, when he was called to this country. The Brother of Maria Cosway, and the protégé of the Queen, and the Lady Chesterfield...could not have failed to making a figure in his profession, had he remained at home. ... He is now starving in Washington...' (28th February 1804, Carter et al., *Latrobe Correspondence*, p.441.)

John Trumbull had great regret for his role in bringing Hadfield to America:

'I received a letter from the commissioners of the public buildings, (of whom Dr. Thornton was one) requesting me to select, contract with, and send out a young architect, qualified to conduct and superintend the work. I consulted my friend, Mr. West, and Mr. Wyatt, (then the principal architect in London,) and they united in recommending George Hatfield, a brother of Mrs. Cosway, who had been a fellow student with me in the Royal Academy, from which he had received all the academical prizes, and who had recently returned from a three years' residence in Italy, where he had completed his architectural studies, under the patronage and at the expense of the Academy. He accepted the proffered terms, and came out; but his services were soon dispensed with, not because his knowledge was not eminent, but because his integrity compelled him to say, that parts of the original plan *could not be executed*. Poor Hatfield languished many years in obscurity at Washington, where however, towards the close of his life, he had the opportunity of erecting a noble monument to himself in the city hall, a beautiful building in which is no waste of space or materials.' (Sizer, ed., *Trumbull Autobiography*, p.177.)

PAGES 292-293

The date of Charlotte Hadfield's marriage to William Combe is noted by Farington:

'Tuesday – Febry 3rd Marchant [Nathaniel, R.A.] called in the evening – He was at Cosways last night They told him Miss Hatfield was married to Coombes on Wednesday last. She wrote them a letter the day before acquainting them with her intention which was the first notice they had of any attachment subsisting between them.' (Farington, II, p.301.)

R.A. Exhibition of 1796 in Graves, p.175.

PAGES 294-296

D.L.C., T.J. to M.C., 8th September 1795.
  M.H.I., M.C. to T.J., 4th December 1795.

PAGE 297

Farington notes details of Luisa's death: ' Sunday, July 31st… Mrs. Hoppner told us that Mrs. Banks had informed her of the death of Cosway's daughter, a little girl of 6 years and a half old, of a putrid fever and sore throat, thought to have been occasioned by the Child being exposed to the air improperly after having taken Jame's powders. Cosway is much affected, but Mrs. Cosway is thought not likely to suffer much.' (Farington, II, p.626.)

H.W. to Mary Berry, 16th August 1796, W. S. Lewis, *Walpole Correspondence*, Vol. 25, p.203.

'Sunday Decr. 4th [1796] Coombe has told Westall that Cosway has buried his Child in the Cellar'. (*Farington*, III, p.170.)

'Thursday Novr. 2nd [1797]…Cosway had his child put in a Sarcophagus made by Banks and it is now in his House.'(*Farington*, III, p.913.)

PAGE 298

For Kosciuszko and Niemcewicz visit: *Farington*, III, p.852 and J.N. to M.C., 24th September 1797. (A.F.C.L.)
  Farington, III, p.713, p.775.

PAGES 299-300

Farington, III, p.928. Farington records his discussion with Maria of her painting and her husband's lack of encouragement. The conversation here is not in the exact words but a faithful reflection of his memory.

PAGES 300-301

Farington, III, p.942, p.945.

PAGES 301-302

Farington, III, pp.976-977; pp.980-981; p.983; IV, p.1136.

PAGE 303

Farington, IV, p.1138.
Graves, *Royal Academy Dictionary*, p.175.

PAGES 305-306

Montjoye to Angelica Schuyler Church [3rd March 1800] V.I.U.
  Mary Wilkes to Maria Cosway [1800] L.W.L.
  Although acquainted, Maria Cosway and Emma Hamilton had little in common. Maria may well have shared Lady Holland's opinion of the second Lady Hamilton and her classical 'attitudes':

> ...Her vulgarity destroyed the illusion when I saw her once. She had worked one's imagination up to a pitch of enthusiasm in her successive imitations of Niobe, Magdalen, and Cleopatra. Just as she was lying down, with her head reclined upon an Etruscan vase to represent a water-nymph, she exclaimed in her provincial dialect: 'Doun't be afeard, Sir Willum, I'll not crack your joug.' (Lady Elizabeth Holland, *Journal (1791-1811)*, pp.242-45.)

Graves, *Royal Academy Dictionary*, p.175.

PAGES **306-309**

The circumstances of the discovery of Richard Cosway's journal and the dispute between the Cosways are imagined, but the journal, although lost today, apparently existed and found its way into Maria Cosway's possession. George Williamson claims to have read the document in Lodi. Williamson reports its contents as follows:

'Mrs. Cosway was away for three years, and Cosway during part of that time was travelling in England, accompanied by the well-known lady Academician, Mary Moser...

'The two artists, each of them over fifty years of age, were nominally travelling on a sketching tour, but Cosway in a rough, disjointed manner records in a sort of diary the incidents of the journey, alternating the entries with sketches of the places they visited. The drawings are delightful, but the journal will not bear repetition, as it is confined almost exclusively to lascivious statements about Miss Moser, and invidious comparisons between her and Mrs. Cosway.... The unfortunate journey lasted about six months, but during the time Mary Moser met Captain Hugh Lloyd and at the end of the year married him.' (Williamson, *Richard Cosway, R.A.*, pp.50-51.)

Mary Moser (1744-1819) was the daughter of George Michael Moser, a Swiss goldsmith who became the first Keeper and a Founding Member of the Royal Academy. Miss Moser, a flower painter whose most well-known work was the decoration of Frogmore House for Queen Charlotte, was one of the two female members of the Academy along with Angelica Kauffman. She reportedly had an unrequited passion for Fuseli and married Captain Hugh Lloyd in 1793 at the age of forty-nine. An interesting bequest in her will was fifty guineas 'for the purchase of a ring' for Mrs. Cosway. (Marianne Zweig, 'Mary Moser', *The Connoisseur Year Book*, 1956.)

Martha Udny (1761-1831) was the attractive widow of Robert Udny, a merchant and art collector. She became sub-governess of Princess Charlotte, daughter of the Prince and Princess of Wales. The Cosways went to stay with the Udnys in Teddington immediately after their daughter's death and it seems Richard became close to Mrs. Udny during Maria's absence in France and Italy.

PAGE 310

M.C. to T.J., 20th July 1801. (Bullock, p.153.)

Chapter Sixteen   Bonaparte's Museum

PAGE 312

M.C. to T.J., 25th February 1802. (Bullock, p.161.)

PAGE 314

The story of Chénier's betrayal by his brother is from A.F.C.L. Diario A, p.86.

PAGE 315

M.C. to T.J., 25th February 1802. (Bullock, p.161.)
   Morning Herald, 8th May 1802 in B.M.P.D., *Whitley Papers*, p.372.
   Presentation album for Louvre project in A.F.L.C.
   Anne Damer to R.C., 8th March 1802, in Noble, *Anne Seymour Damer*, p.179.
   It was no doubt Fesch who was seen at the Cosways in London by the sculptor Nollekens after Bonaparte's coup d'état of the 18th Brumaire (8th November 1799). ' Saturday, Novr. 23rd…Nollekens saw at Cosways last Sunday [17th November] a Priest uncle to Buonoparte who He believes is principally supported by General Paoli.' (*Farington*, IV, p.1308.)

PAGES 316-317

The presentation of Cosway's portfolio to the First Consul and her request for an audience were transmitted through Fesch as described. (A.F.C.L., Diario A, p.7.)
   For relations with Griffiths A.F.C.L., Diario A, p.13.

PAGES 321-323

Maria Cosway's visit to David, his help with her picture of Eros and the incident of the dog as well as David's use of cadavers was recorded by her on 14th-15th June 1802. (A.F.C.L., Diario A, pp.3-4.)

Maria Cosway exhibited the painting of Eros at the Paris Salon of 1802 (Catalogue, An X). About this time she wrote to a friend about the picture, enclosing a sketch:

> I painted a picture which I exhibited here at their Salon, but did it more for England than here.... I wanted to send it to Mr. Cosway but he has no room to hang it.... I cannot say much on my own picture but I am very fond of the subject. 'Tis Eros the love creator dividing Chaos &...from Hesiod.... The size is more than a half length... (Maria Cosway to Mrs. Dalton, n.d., [1803?], The Pierpont Morgan Library, M.A. 2849.)

PAGES 320-321

Maria's request for an audience with Napoleon in A.F.C.L., Diario A, p.8. A.F.C.L., Diario, 1st July, p.11.

Napoleon's reaction to Maria's work, A.F.C.L., Diario A, pp.11-12.

M.C. to J.F., 3rd July 1802, A.F.C.L. Diario A, p.13.

PAGES 322-323

Fesch and Collot's wealth came from their participation in the Italian campaign. Their signatures figure on receipts from the sack of the Mont-de-Piete in Milan. (Latreille, *Napoleon et le Saint Siege*, p.69.)

Maria's impression of the 14th July military review. A.F.C.L., Diario A, p.17.

David's instruction, A.F.C.L., Diario A, p.13.

Conversation with David. A.F.C.L., Diario A.

PAGES 324-325

Fesch's appointment as archbishop and his reaction A.F.C.L., Diario A, 26th July, p.20.

Fesch's interview with Napoleon and Talleyrand A.F.C.L., Diario A, 30th July, p.23.

PAGES 326-327

The description of Fesch's home by Mary Berry, *Voyages de Miss Berry a Paris*, p.80.

Cosway is entertained by Madame Bonaparte, A.F.C.L., Diario A, 8th August, pp.26-27.

Fesch's consecration, A.F.C.L., Diario A, p.29.

Fesch's new appearance described in Earland, *John Opie*, p.188.

PAGES 328-329

Conversation with Fesch A.F.C.L., Diario A, p.29.

Conversation with Fesch A.F.C.L., Diario A, p.30.

Visit of English artists, Cosway's opinion of West, A.F.C.L., Diario A, p.32.

Maria shows English artists Fesch's house in Earland, *John Opie*, pp.188-189.

Fesch and Archbishop of Meaux compare rings A.F.C.L., Diario A, p.34.

PAGES 330-331

Attempted reconciliation of Napoleon and Paoli A.F.C.L., Diario A, p.23, p.33 and p.39.

Problems with Griffiths, A.F.C.L., Diario A, p.39.

Erskine's praise, A.F.C.L., Diario A, p.45.

Failure to sell picture Eros, A.F.C.L., Diario A, p.42.

Change in Fesch, A.F.C.L., Diario A, p.51.

PAGES 332-333

Consultations with Erskine and Farington on Griffiths A.F.C.L., Diario A, pp.43-45 and Farington, *Diary*, V, 1826, 1908-09.

Maria's desire not to return to London, A.F.C.L., Diario A, p.45.

Maria's wariness of Fesch, A.F.C.L., Diario A, p.45.

Fesch's promise and farewell, A.F.C.L., Diario A, p.55.

Denon's appointment and failure to help A.F.C.L., Diario A, 54 and 56.

According to one of Denon's biographers, Pierre Lelièvre, Denon was the artistic advisor to Napoleon, proposing to him the subjects of pictures and sculptures and the artists who would execute them. His judgments on works of art had enormous influence. He surely could have done more to help Cosway than he did. (Boyer, *Le Monde des Arts en Italie et la France*, p.108.)

Visit to Sisters of Charity, A.F.C.L., Diario A, 58-59.

PAGE 342

Lord Whitworth refuses painting of Eros, A.F.C.L., Diario A, p.98.
    Maria departs for Lyon, A.F.C.L., Diario A, pp.103-104.

Chapter Seventeen Lyon

PAGE 343

M.C. to T.J., 10th October 1805, Bullock, *My Head and My Heart*, pp.166-167.

PAGES 345-348

Maria's interviews with Mayeuvre de Champvieux and Bureaux de Pusy are recounted in her letter of 8th July 1806, to Fesch, A.F.C.L., Diario B.
    For Bureaux de Pusy see Latreille, *Napoleon et le Saint Siege*, p.96.
    Mademoiselle de Pusy as first pupil. A.F.C.L., Diario A, 29th October 1803.
    For Nicolas Fay de Sathonay see 'Les Maires de Napoleon 1er', *Cahiers de Rhone*, 89, Lyon, No. 14, 1994.
    Fay de Sathonay was no doubt concerned about the general economic crisis in the local textile industry in 1806, which caused him to look at the public financing of education. (Trenard, *Lyon*, II, p.643.)
    A.F.C.L., Diario B [26th May] 1803. The irony of being praised as an acceptable schoolmistress by provincials, who had no idea of her past associations with eminent personalities in London and Paris, was not lost on Maria.

PAGES 349-350

A.F.C.L., M.C. to J.F., n.d.
    A.F.C.L., Diario C, 1st October [1809].
    The first programme of instruction offered by the new *Maison d'Education pour les Jeunes Demoiselles* was outlined in the *Almanach de Lyon, 1805*, pp.292-293.
    Fesch's criticism of Maria's overly ambitious plan is from A.F.C.L., J.F. to M.C., Rome, 8th August 1804.

PAGES 350-351

As soon as Maria Cosway received word of her nomination to Lyon, with her customary thoroughness she began a systematic series of visits to educators and schools in the Paris area, starting with the most distinguished, Madame de Genlis (A.F.C.L., Diario A, 28th February 1803) and Madame Campan (A.F.C.L., Diario A, 24th March 1803).

Cosway's method of education is documented in her archives where her own notes and extracts from Charles Rollin's *Traité des Études*, as well as rules and models of correspondence, are found. (A.F.C.L.)

Abbé Aloisius Edouard Camille Gaultier (1746-1818) fled to London during the Revolution where he founded a school for the children of French *émigrés*. His methods based on learning through play were disseminated through his manuals and educational games. Maria Cosway apparently used his grammar and a game for teaching parts of speech. (See Jill Shefrin, 'Make it a Pleasure and Not a Task' Educational Games for Children in Georgian England, *Princeton University Library Chronicle*, LX:2, Winter 1999, pp.251-275 and James Guillaume, 'Lecture', *Dictionnaire de pedagogie d'instruction primaire*, Hachette, 1887, II, pp.1534-1551.)

PAGE 352

A.F.C.L., A.G. to M.C., 8th February 1806.

M.C.'s choice of Convent of the Carmelites, A.F.C.L., Diario A, 3rd and 15th June 1803.

Archbishopric of Lyon – A.E.L., J.F. to Conseil Municipal de Lyon, 3rd April 1804.

When Fay-Sathonay was named Mayor, Fesch reminded him that

> The institution for young ladies at whose head is Madame Cosway merits the good will and the protection of all persons who are interested in the progress of good education in the diocese of Lyon... . The talents and good intentions of Mme. Cosway are known and it is what determined me to give favour and protection to the establishment of her institution. I beg you therefore, Monsieur, to do for this lady what depends on you... (A.E.L., J.F. to Mayor of Lyon, 15th September 1805.)

At the same time, the Cardinal reminded the Prefect:

> I have the honour to ask your good offices on behalf of an

institution for young ladies in which I take the strongest interest and has Madame Cosway as Directress... . She renders an important service to your Department and to my diocese and I hope that you will not refuse her your good will. (A.E.L., J.F. to Prefect of Rhone, 12th September 1805.)

PAGE 353

A.E.L., J.F. to J.J., 13th June 1804.

A.E.L., J.F. to J.C., 25th July 1804.

Fesch's promise of financing: A.E.L., J.F. to M.C., 13th January 1806.

Request to Emperor for M.C.: A.E.L., J.F. to Emperor Napoleon, 6th August 1806.

PAGE 354

A.F.C.L., L.B. to M.C. [1806].

Imperial visit of 13th April 1805 in *Bulletin de Lyon*, *Nos. 59, 60*, 15th and 18th April 1805.

Pope Pius VII visited the school on 19th April 1805.

His Excellency [Cardinal Fesch] escorted him [Pius VII] to Saint-Pierre Palace to show him the exhibition of products of Lyonnais industry; next he led him to visit the institution directed by Madame Cosway where was found the Duke di Braschi, nephew of the illustrious Pius VI... . Four children, carrying baskets threw flowers before his steps while others laid at his feet palms and wreaths. One of them recited in Italian the gospel of the Good Shepherd. This elicited the greatest tenderness.(Abbé Lyonnet, *Le cardinal Fesch*, I, p.454.)

PAGE 355

Maria Cosway's insight into her own character is recorded in her journal of 18th October 1806, A.F.C.L., Diario B.

Fesch's resistance to combining Cosway's school with a religious order, A.F.C.L., J.F. to M.C., 15th September 1803.

Cosway raised the subject of becoming a nun in a letter to Fesch of 1st July 1806, A.F.C.L., Diario B.

PAGES 356-357

The turbulent scenes with Fesch of early June 1807 were the culmination of a year of tensions between Cosway and the city fathers. Her journal of 4th June begins 'I had a terrible moment of trial.' She then relates the interviews with Fesch and the support of her pupils' mothers in the face of Fay-Sathonay's apparently insulting letter. Fesch's reaction and his subsequent reluctance to appear to support her suggest that the Mayor implied (or stated) that there was impropriety in the Cardinal's protection of Mrs. Cosway. (A.F.C.L., Diario B, 4th June 1807.)

PAGE 358

A.E.L., J.F. to M.C., 10th June 1807.
   A.F.C.L., J.F. to M.C., 26th June 1807.

PAGE 359

A.E.L., J.F. to M.C., 5th August 1807.
   A.F.C.L., M.C. to J.F., 6th June 1807.

PAGE 360

Maria Cosway's nightmares, probably symptoms of a mild depression, are recorded in her journal of 18th October 1807. (A.F.C.L., Diario B.) This was shortly after her move from St. Pierre to the Carmelites' former convent.
   A.F.C.L., J.F. to M.C., 14th January 1809.

PAGE 361

Details of Cosway's agreement with the two curates are given in a letter from the Vicar-General Bochard to Fesch of 18th March 1809. (A.E.L.) Her need of advice and subsequent difficulties with the clergy and nuns are recounted in A.F.C.L., M.C. to J.F., 29th January, 1809; M.C. to J.F., 12th April 1809; Diario C, 20th August 1809 and Goulard file.

PAGES 362

A.F.C.L., M.C. to J.F., 29th April 1809, and Diario B, 10th June 1809.
   Bochard soon shared Maria Cosway's opinion of Goulard's incompetence as an educator and confided as much in letters to Fesch:

'This institution which should be so large and so fine in the Carmelites is not taking a marvellous direction.... I have always foreseen it...it seems to me that it worked better when Mme. Cosway directed it alone with her associates that Your Eminence gave her last year.' (A.E.L., 6th July 1809.)

'I don't have anything to do with M. Goulard. I foresaw that he would leave the Carmelites and his new school doesn't succeed any better than the first. The two nuns who followed him from the Carmelites have already left him so I was not wrong.' (A.E.L., 22nd February 1810.)

A.F.C.L., Goulard to M.C., Diario B, 24th July 1809.
A.F.C.L., M.C. to J.F., Diario B, 3rd August 1809.
A.F.C.L., Diario B, 19th September 1809.

Page 363

Convent of Visitandines, A.F.C.L., Diario C, M.C. to J.F., 12th November 1809.
    Apology to Bochard, A.F.C.L., Diario C, 22nd October 1809.
    Indignation of M.C., A.F.C.L., M.C. to J.F., Diario C, 12th November, 1809.

Page 364

Maria Cosway's version of her dispute with Goulard is well documented in a long memorandum of Goulard (A.F.C.L.) complete with her annotated point by point rebuttal and the following indignant cover letter probably addressed to Bochard:

I have the honour to enclose the memoire of Mr. Goulard which I find so extraordinarily bad and false that I don't believe it merits a reply. However, when it will be time I shall give to my counsel all the information and witnesses that will be necessary since my birth until today: witnesses in all countries and of the highest distinction in the Church as well as in the State, which will be equal to the respectable character of a pious ecclesiastic such as

Mr. Goulard. I shall believe it necessary to justify myself thus publicly in a country that I love very much and where I am satisfied with friends and in the charge that I profess it is necessary that I not leave any doubts on my account.

A.E.L., Bochard to Fesch, 20th October, 26th October, 10th November, 20th December 1809.

Page 365

A.N.F., Empereur à Ministre des Cultes, 15 juin, 1810.
Maria's relationship with mother, A.F.C.L., Diario A, 11th June 1803 and M.C. to J.F., 24th August 1810.
A.F.C.L., M.C. to Comtesse de Brignole, 6th March 1811.
A.F.C.L., Plan for school in Chelsea.

Page 366

The dossier of Maria Cosway's passport request is still in the Archives Nationales with no notation as to its disposition. She probably chose to go to Italy before any decision was taken on a passport for England. The local police report on her early life is mostly fabulous. It says that Maria's father was an Italian prince, who met her English mother in London. They went to Leghorn, where some children were murdered by a nurse until the mother agreed to raise Maria as a Catholic. Maria met her husband in Italy where he died. She met Fesch in Italy when he was a supplier to Napoleon's army and then came to Lyon. (A.N.F., F7, Commissaire Général, Police de Lyon à Ministère de la Police Générale, 18th November 1811.)

Page 367

A.F.C.L., M.C. to J.F., 6th August 1811.

Page 368

A.F.C.L., M.C. to F.M.E., July 1810.
A.F.C.L., F.M.E. to M.C., 2nd August 1811.
A.F.C.L., M.C. to J.F., 7th August 1811.

Page 369

A.F.C.L., M.C. to F.M.E., 21st October 1811.

A.M.L., M.C. to Commissaire Général, Police de Lyon, 12th December 1811.

Page 370

A.F.C.L., M.C. to J.F., November 1811.

A.F.C.L., J.F. to M.C., 10th February 1813.

Maria Cosway's passport record of 12th June 1811 (Archives Municipales, Lyon) gives the only physical description of record. Unfortunately her height was only recorded as 'average'. Other traits described were:

Hair and eyebrows	—	brown
Forehead	—	average
Nose	—	large
Eyes	—	grey brown
Mouth	—	average
Chin	—	round
Face	—	small oval

Chapter Eighteen   Lombardy

Page 372

B.C.L., M.C. to A.P., 7th April 1820.

Pages 373-374

Giulia Beccaria was the daughter of Cesare Beccaria, a Milanese nobleman and author of the famous treatise against capital punishment, *Of Crimes and Punishment*, admired by Thomas Jefferson among others. After an unhappy marriage to an older noble, Don Pietro Manzoni, which produced one son, the writer Allesandro Manzoni, Giulia went to live in Paris with her lover Carlo Imbonati. There she made the acquaintance of Maria Cosway and had her portrait painted by Maria. Although unfinished, this head has an intriguing quality, which leads one to imagine that Maria could have been a successful portrait painter had she pursued this vocation.

Friendships between Maria, Giulia Beccaria, Maddalena Sannazzari, and Allesandro Manzoni are recounted in Piero Campolunghi, *Giuia Beccaria e di suo Figlio Allesandro Manzoni (Verri)*, p.107, and Natalia Ginzburg, *The Manzoni Family*, 1983.

A.F.C.L., M.C. to F.M.E., 15th March 1812.

A.F.C.L., M.C. to FME, 6th October 1812.

PAGES 375-376

Manifesto, Archivio di Stato, Milano – A.S.M., Studi, p.m., cart. 5 fasc.

Angelo Bianchi, 'Maria Cosway e l'educazione femminile: da Lione a Lodi', *Maria e Richard Cosway*, ed. Tino Gipponi, Torino, 1998, pp.171-219.

A.F.C.L., Ctesse de Lazanzky to M.C., 7th May 1825.

The Emperor Franz I noted his visit to the Collegio di S. Maria delle Grazie in his Journal on 19th February 1816:

'On the first floor there is a large dormitory with very clean white beds. There is an apartment for the directress of two nice little rooms. There is a room where the girls learn piano. There are three rooms with a table and benches. In each room there is a class.... There is a large salon where they have conversation.... There are three teachers who supervise the girls...they learn to read, write, French, history, geography by heart...drawing, cooking, and bread-making. To question them in history and geography, there is a game with a wheel on which are names of cities and rivers. There are boards with compartments for nouns and verbs. They write each word of the [grammatical] construction directly in the corresponding compartment....The girls are dressed in a very clean manner and seem in good health. They receive much fruit and bread at noon.... Every month they can visit their parents. The directress Madame Cosway, an Englishwoman, has been a famous painter.... About 40 girls from the best families are there. Each girl pays 100 scudi a year. Several girls have already married. There is a large church with frescoes. In this church there is an oratory for the girls, which is not very large.' (Austrian National Archives, Vienna – H.H.S.T.A., Hofreisen 23.)

These notes were written in a personal shorthand, mixing Latin and German. Without the invaluable help of a paleograph, Monsieur Ansgar Wildermann, they would have remained indecipherable.

The Emperor also visited Cosway's school with the Empress Maria Karolina on 7th May 1825. (Gipponi, *Maria e Richard Cosway*, p.209.)

The Viceroy Rainier visited the school on 10th October 1816 and December 1818. (A.F.C.L. and B.C.L., M.C. to Annette Prodon, 11th December 1818.) The Vice Queen visited in December 1823. (Bodleian Library – B.O.L., Douce M.S.S., M.C. to Francis Douce, 22nd December, 1823.)

On 4th July 1818, the Director General of Public Instruction, Cavalière Luigi Rossi evaluated Maria Cosway's methods positively:

'The discipline is maternal, but severe when needed… . The method of instruction with many exercises praised enough to incite emulation is noted in monthly progress reports to parents. Each day the merits or demerits are noted in a table, which seems worthy of praise and very opportune for the instruction necessary for young girls. The pupils are trained to recite their lessons by memory in French, history, geography, to declaim erudite or poetic verses, to discuss events.' (A.S.M., Studi, p.m. cart. 35, fasc. A.C. 16.)

Another inspector, Canon Palamede Carpani warmly recommended governmental approval of the college on 7th August 1823:

'…will not have the least difficulty, in view of a directress whose ability in all phases of education is well-tested, and whose institution does honour to the country, and is already recognised by the Imperial Government.' (A.S.M., Studi, p.m., cart. 446, f. 89.)

A.F.C.L., M.C. to F.M.E., 2nd May 1812.

Page 378

M.C. to R.C., 22nd March 1815, A.F.C.L.
   A.F.C.L. 2nd April [1815], Diario 22 marzo 1815 – 27 luglio 1817.

PAGES 378-380

A.F.C.L., M.C. to Martha Udny, 30th April 1815.

Maria Cosway's journey through Switzerland, the German states, and Holland in May, June of 1815 was made in the midst of large troop movements preparing for a confrontation with Bonaparte. She arrived in London four days before the Battle of Waterloo. In spite of her anxiety before leaving, her letters to Annette Prodon form a travel journal, which reflects her pleasure in travelling and her delight in this particular voyage. (B.C.L., M.C. to A.P., 21st May – 14th June 1815.)

PAGE 381

B.C.L., M.C. to A.P., 15th June 1815.

PAGE 382

A.F.C.L., M.C. to Mrs. Chambers, 29th May 1816.

PAGE 383

A.F.C.L., M.C. to Madame Prodon, 15th May 1817.
    B.C.L., M.C. to A.P., 29th January 1818.

PAGE 384

B.C.L., M.C. to A.P., 14th August 1818.
    B.C.L., M.C. to A.P., 22nd February 1817.
    A.F.C.L., *Copia della Memoria lasciata alla Guiseppina Menrisi e ai due Procaturi Sig. Mancini e Sig. Mola*, 9th July 1817.

PAGE 385

B.C.L., M.C. to A.P., 23rd December 1817.
    B.C.L., M.C. to A.P., 4th July 1815.
    A.F.C.L., Diario, 18th February 1817.
    B.C.L., M.C. to A.P., 15th June 1815.
    B.C.L., M.C. to A.P., 4th July 1815.

PAGE 394

B.C.L., M.C. to A.P., n.d.
    B.C.L., M.C. to A.P., 20th November 1818.

B.C.L., M.C. to A.P., 18th September 1818.

PAGES 387-388

Lady Morgan , *Italy*, 1821, p.130.
   B.C.L., M.C. to A.P., 4th July 1815.
   B.C.L., M.C. to A.P., 29th May 1818.
   B.C.L., M.C. to A.P., 19th February 1818.
   B.C.L., M.C. to A.P., 8th January 1818.
   B.C.L., M.C. to A.P., 17th April 1818.
   B.C.L., M.C. to A.P., 5th May 1818.
   B.C.L., M.C. to A.P., 8th January 1818.
   Accounts of Richard Cosway's conversations with the spirits of famous persons are given in Nollekens, Vol. 2, p.412.
   M.C. to Menasi, 2nd December 1820, Maggs 1927, 2357.
Maria Cosway's care for her aging husband was carried out conscientiously with her characteristic sense of duty, but she admits to Annette that her affection for the young girl is the stronger tie and her motives are a mixture of self-interest and conscience:

> I shall not be happy until the moment I can be with you. However I desire to do it in the manner that I can be assured to be <u>independent</u> and [not] to risk losing everything here in going away <u>mal a propos</u>. I repeat to you to fail in my duties *vis a vis* an aged husband in a precarious state…the world would be right to scorn me…and my conscience would not be tranquil for the rest of my life… (B.C.L., M.C. to A.P., 7th March 1818.)

   B.C.L., M.C. to A.P., January 1819.
   Lloyd, *The Inventory of 1820*, p.170.

PAGE 386

B.O.L., Douce M.S.S., M.C. to F.D., 22nd December 1823.
   Sir John Soane Museum – A.S.J.M., M.C. to J.S., 8th November 1823.
   B.C.L., M.C. to A.P., 2nd March 1819.
   B.C.L., M.C. to A.P., 2nd April 1819.

PAGES **390-391**

M.C. to T.J., 7th April 1819, Bullock, *My Head and My Heart*, pp.173-175.
  B.C.L., M.C. to A.P., 14th July 1819.
  B.C.L., M.C. to A.P., 6th September 1820.
  A.S.J.M., M.C. to J.S., 1st May 1821.
  B.C.L., M.C. to A.P., 27th April 1821.

Joseph Farington noted in his diary. 'Sir J. Carr said he frequently called on Richard Cosway, R.A. in Stratford Place, and described him to be paralysed in his right arm, but always cheerful.' (*Farington Diary*, 21st January 1820, XVI, p.5454.)

Sir John Soane purchased thirteen lots from the sale of 1821, including small bronze figures, marble bas reliefs, a pair of marble vases, terracotta sculptures of Charles II and two children. Some of these pieces such as the bronzes *Bull breaking an Egg* and *Triform Diana* can still be seen in the Sir John Soane Museum. (Lloyd, *Richard and Maria Cosway*, 1995.)

PAGE **392-393**

B.C.L., M.C. to A.P., 15th May 1821.
  Reynolds sale in Whitley, *Art in England 1821-1837*, vol. 2, p.13.
  M.H.I., M.C. to T.J., 15th July 1821.

On 4th July 1821, the weather was bright if windy. Richard Cosway was invited to take a carriage ride with Martha Udny's daughter. Gracefully exiting the world, he expired in the carriage. On 12th July the funeral procession to St. Mary-le-bone Church was led by a hearse drawn by six horses, followed by five coaches-and-four, one lent by Sir Thomas Lawrence. (B.M.P.D, Anderdon, p.372.) John Soane, James Ward, and Richard Westmacott were three Royal Academy members known to have attended. (B.M.P.D, Anderdon, p.374.) Maria commissioned Westmacott to sculpt a commemorative plaque to her husband, which was placed in St. Mary-le-bone Church. The text, composed by William Combe is:

In Memory of RICHARD COSWAY, Esquire, R.A.
Principal Painter
To His Royal Highness George, Prince of Wales,
He died July the Fourth, 1821

Aged 80 years,
His Widow, Maria Cosway,
Erects this Memorial.
Art weeps, Taste mourns, and Genius drops the tear,
O'er him so long they lov'd, who slumbers here:
While colours last, and time allows to give
The all-resembling grace, his name shall live

(Smith, Nollekens II, p.414.)

Ironically, this plaque now hangs in an improvised kitchen in the church entry directly opposite a similar one honouring the memory of Martha Udny.

PAGE 394

B.L., Add. M.S.S. 29300E, William Combe to Mrs. Swinney, 20th August 1821.

B.C.L., M.C. to A.P., 31st August 1821.

Smith, *Life of Nollekens*, II, pp.401-414.

B.O.L., Douce M.S.S. 29, fol. 182, M.C. to F.D. [April 1822]

Even if one allows for many careless or mistaken attributions of the drawings in Cosway's collection and only one half or even a quarter were accurate, it was a colossal assemblage of Old Master drawings and is now considered to have been – after those of Sir Thomas Lawrence and Sir Joshua Reynolds – the largest collection of its kind belonging to a British artist of that period. (Lloyd, *The Inventory of 1820*, p.167.)

The Sun of 27th February 1822 reported:

'The drawings, prints, books, etc. collected by the last Richard Cosway, Esq., were sold last week by Mr. Stanley & the amount is £1600.' (B.M.P.D., Anderdon p.374.)

PAGE 395

B.O.L., Douce M.S.S. 29, fol. 172, M.C. to F.D., [1822]

B.O.L., Douce M.S.S. 24, fol. 32,M.C. to F.D., 21st April 1822.

B.M.P.D., Anderdon, p.376 quoted from *Memoirs & Correspondence of Mrs. Grant*, ed. by her son J. P. Grant, 1844.

Page 396

D.L.C., M.C. to T.J., 10th July 1822.
  DLC, T.J. to M.C., 24th October 1822.

Page 397

M.H.I, M.C. to T.J., 7th April 1819.
  M.H.I., M.C. to T.J., 15th July 1821.
  M.H.I., M.C. to T.J., 18th June 1823.
  M.H.I., M.C. to T.J., 24th September 1824.

Maria and her sister Charlotte were shocked to be informed of George's death a year and a half after the event and that by a certain William Elliott. This young man, who claimed to be George's student, came to Ireland and England to lay claim to George's estate, but the sisters refused to sign it over to him, little as it was. (Historical Society of Pennsylvania, Gratz Collection, M.C. to J.T., 26th June 1828.)

George wrote rarely, if at all, to his sister. Maria complained to Jefferson of the lack of news from her brother. She enclosed letters to George in her last missives to the Virginia patriarch, who assured her that Hadfield was

> '…much respected in Washington, and since the death of Latrobe, our first architect, I consider him as standing foremost in the correct principles of that art. I believe he is doing well, but would he push himself more he would do better.'
>
> (D.L.C., T.J. to M.C., 24th October 1822.)

Jefferson was too kind, for George Hadfield never had a success commensurate with his talents and education. Maria put it down to his diffidence, writing to Jefferson: 'I am delighted to hear he goes on well, & know he does not put himself forward, this is a <u>family</u> fault.'

On Sir William Cosway, B.O.L., Douce M.S.S., 24, fol. 202, M.C. to F.D.

Page 398

A pretty description of Maria Cosway's house and garden in Lodi is found in the travel journal of Mrs. Paul Colnaghi, who visited Lodi in 1826 with her husband, family, and Ferdinand Artaria.

'The house like a town…ball-room, eating-room, bed-rooms, painted with fine views, the walls of the ballroom representing the four quarters of the globe… . Where we dined was painted as a large garden, with fine romantic views, trees, vines, etc., and so relieved that you might fancy the leaves gently moving. The fire-place a cavern as if cut out of the rock; nearly opposite a fountain continually playing.' (29th July 1826, Mrs. Paul Colnaghi quoted in Williamson, p.80.)

V.A., Colnaghi Volumes, 1844-1855.

Epilogue

PAGE 400

Maria Cosway's relations with the Viceroy's court in Milan are documented in her correspondence with Countess Sophia Wayna over the period 1826-1831 (A.F.C.L.)

PAGE 401

A.S.J.M., M.C. to J.S., 6th February 1832, Soane Correspondence 37.
    Maria Cosway's dossier for title of Baroness in Austrian State Archives.

PAGE 402

Quarterly Review, January, 1834-1835 in *Whitley Papers*, p.377.
    A.S.J.M., M.C. to J.S., 1st July 1830, Soane Correspondence 31.
    Ginzburg, *The Manzoni Family*, p.126.

PAGE 403

A.S.J.M., M.C. to J.S., 8th November 1823, Soane Correspondence 26.
    B.O.L., M.C. to F.D., 22nd January 1824, Douce M.S.S.

PAGES 403-404

Maria Cosway Last Will and Testament, P.R.O., C38/1792.
    Codicil of 10th June 1829, P.R.O., C38/1792.
    A.S.J.M., M.C. to J.S., 19th February 1831, Soane Correspondence 34.

PAGE 405

P.R.O. C38/1792.

PAGES 406-407

Cosway burial, Gipponi, *Maria e Richard Cosway*, p.163, p.166.
P.R.O., C38/1792.

Select Bibliography

Manuscripts

ARCHBISHOPRIC OF LYON (A.E.L.)
Correspondence of Joseph, Cardinal Fesch

ARCHIVES DÉPARTEMENTALES DU RHONE, LYON
Serie F, Fesch papers, Serie G, Serie H

ARCHIVES MINISTÈRE DES AFFAIRES ÉTRANGÈRES, PARIS
(A.A.E.)
Contrôle des étrangers, Mémoires et Documents, France

ARCHIVES NATIONALES, FRANCE (A.N.F.)
O^1 Maison du Roi, O^2 Maison de l'Empereur, 300 AP I, Archives de la
Maison de France, F7 Police Generale

ARCHIVES VILLE DE LYON (A.V.L.)
I^2 Passeports, Serie R Instruction Publique

ARCHIVIO FONDAZIONE COSWAY, LODI (A.F.C.L.)
Papers and Correspondence of Maria Hadfield Cosway

ARCHIVIO DI STATO, COMO (A.S.C.)
Teresiano Catasto, Catasto Urbano

ARCHIVIO DI STATO, FIRENZE (A.S.F.)
Archivi Notarili

ARCHIVIO DI STATO, MILANO (A.S.M.)
Archivi Notarili, Autografi

ARCHIWUM GLOWNE AKT DAWNYCH, WARSAW (A.G.A.D.)
Stanislaus Potocki Correspondence

AUSTRIAN NATIONAL ARCHIVES, VIENNA (H.H.S.T.A.)
Hofreisen 23,52

BIBLIOTECA COMUNALE LAUDENSE, LODI (B.C.L.)

BIBLIOTECA NAZIONALE BRAIDENSE, MILAN (B.N.B.)
Fonds Teotochi

BODLEIAN LIBRARY, OXFORD (B.O.L.)
Douce M.S.S., Eng. Lett. M.S.S.

BRITISH LIBRARY, LONDON (B.L.)
Berry M.S.S., Combe M.S.S., Cumberland M.S.S., Flaxman M.S.S.

BRITISH MUSEUM, LONDON (B.M.)
Townley M.S.S.

BRITISH MUSEUM DEPARTMENT OF PRINTS AND DRAWINGS,
LONDON (B.M.P.D.)
Anderdon R.A. Catalogues, Whitley Papers
Chatsworth M.S.S., Correspondence of Georgiana, fifth Duchess of
Devonshire

HERTFORDSHIRE RECORD OFFICE, HERTFORD
Panshanger Papers

LEICESTERSHIRE RECORD OFFICE, WIGSTON MAGNA
Finch M.S.S.

LEWIS WALPOLE LIBRARY, FARMINGTON, CONNECTICUT (L.W.L.)
Lady Mary Coke Diary, Berry M.S.S.

LIBRARY OF CONGRESS, WASHINGTON, D.C. (D.L.C.)
Jefferson M.S.S., Trumbull M.S.S., William Thornton Papers

MASSACHUSETTS HISTORICAL SOCIETY, BOSTON, MASS. (M.H.I.)
Adams M.S.S., Jefferson M.S.S.

THE PAUL MELLON CENTRE FOR STUDIES IN BRITISH ART, LONDON
Brinsley Ford Archive

PIERPONT MORGAN LIBRARY, NEW YORK, N.Y. (N.N.P.)
Maria Cosway Autograph letter MA 2849

NATIONAL LIBRARY OF SCOTLAND, EDINBURGH (N.L.S.)
Journal of Joseph Mercer

PUBLIC RECORD OFFICE, KEW (P.R.O.)
Chancery Proceedings C38
Foreign Office Papers 79, 95
General Register Office
State Papers 98, 105

ROYAL ACADEMY OF ARTS, LONDON (R.A.)
Ozias Humphry M.S.S., Lawrence M.S.S.

SIR JOHN SOANE'S MUSEUM, LONDON (A.S.J.M.)
Soane Correspondence

UNIVERSITY OF VIRGINIA, CHARLOTTESVILLE (V.I.U.)
Jefferson Correspondence, Church Correspondence

VICTORIA AND ALBERT MUSEUM, NATIONAL ART LIBRARY, LONDON (V.A.)

Autobiographical letter of Maria Cosway, 24th May 1830, MS (Eng.) L. 961-1953

Autograph letters to James Northcote 86.AA.26

Colnaghi Papers

Press Cuttings, 1686-1835, pp.17.G

VICTORIA LIBRARY, LONDON

City of Westminster Archives

YALE UNIVERSITY, BEINECKE LIBRARY, NEW HAVEN, CONN.

Osborn M.S.S.

Primary Sources

Newspapers and Magazines

Cabinet des Modes
Gazzetta Privilegiata di Milano
Gazzetta Toscana
Gentlemen's Magazine
Journal de Paris
Library of Fine Arts
London Chronicle
Mercure de France
Morning Chronicle
Le Petit Magasin des Dames
Public Advertiser
The Repository of Arts, Literature, Commerce, Manufactures, Fashions, and Politics
St. James Chronicle
World

Printed Primary Sources

_____, *Almanach de Lyon, An XIII*, [1805].

_____, *Almanach de Palais Royal*, 1786.

_____, *The Artist's Assistant in Drawing, Perspective, Etching, Engraving, Mezzotint-Scraping, Painting on Glass, In Crayon, in Water-Colours, and on Silks and Satins*, London, 1788.

_____, *A Catalogue of the Entire Collection of Pictures of Richard Cosway, Esq. R.A. . . .* London, 1791.

_____, *A Catalogue of all the Reserved and Valuable Part of the Capital Collection of Pictures, The Property of Richard Cosway, Esq. R.A., . . . Which will be sold by auction by Mr. Christie*, London, 2-4 March, 1792.

_____, *A Catalogue of Sale by Mr. Stanley at No. 20 Stratford Place, 17 May, 1821 and 2 Following Days*, London, 1821.

_____, *A Catalogue of the very curious, extensive, and valuable Library of Richard Cosway, Esq. R.A . . . , sold by Mr. Stanley, 8 -12 June, 1821*, London, 1821.

_____, *The Cosway Collection. A Catalogue of . . . Drawings and Prints . . . the genuine property of the late Richard Cosway, Esq. R.A. . . . , Stanley's, London 14-22 February, 1822*, London, 1822.

_____, *A Catalogue . . . of Pictures by Ancient Masters . . . the property of the late Richard Cosway, Esq. R.A. . . . also a number of valuable articles of vertu . . . , Stanley's, London, 8-9 March 1822*, London, 1822.

_____, *A Collection of Drawings . . . collection of R. Cosway . . . , Mr. Christie, 15 March, 1828*, London, 1828.

_____, *Catalogue of a Collection of Drawings & Miniatures by Richard Cosway, R.A. from the Succession of his Wife, Maria Cosway, Christie's, London, 1-2 June, 1896*, London, 1896.

_____, 'Conversations on the Arts by Juninus', *The Repository of Arts, Literature, Commerce . . .*, Rudolph Ackermann, ed., No. XI, Vol. VII, April, 1812 and No. XLVII, Vol. VIII, November, 1812.

_____, *Journal of a Party of Pleasure to Paris*, London, 1802.

_____, 'Recollections of Richard Cosway, Esq. R.A.', *Library of Fine Arts*, IV, London, 1832, pp. 184-191.

_____, *Memoire pour les citoyennes Trudaine veuve Micault, Micault veuve*

Trudaine et le citoyen vivant Micault-Courbeton fils, Paris, L'an III, [1795]

———, *Memoirs of J. Q. Adams*, 12 vols. Philadelphia, 1874-1877.

———, *Tableau du Nouveau Palais Royal*, Paris, 1788.

Adams, Charles Francis, (ed.) *The Works of John Adams*, Boston, 1851, Vol. III, (1. Autobiography 2. Diary [1778-1796])

Ailesbury, Thomas Bruce Brudenell, 4th Earl, *Journal [Sept. 1786-March 1789]* H.M.C., 15th Report, App. pt. vii (1898) pp.269-306.

Albrizzi, Isabella Teotochi, *Ritratti*, Palermo, 1992.

Angelo, Henry, *Reminiscences... with Memoirs of his late Father and Friends*, 2 vols., London, 1828-30.

Aspinall, Arthur, ed., *The Correspondence of George, Prince of Wales, 1770-1812*, 8 vols. 1963-71.

Baretti, Giuseppe, *An Account of the Manners and Customs of Italy...*, 2 vols., London, 1768. (2nd ed., 1769).

Barry, James, *Works*, London, 1809.

Bear, James A., ed., *Jefferson at Monticello*, Charlottesville, Virginia, 1967.

Beckford, Peter, *Familiar Letters from Italy to a Friend in England*, 2 vols., Salisbury, 1805.

Beckford, William, *Italy; with sketches of Spain and Portugal*, 2 vols., London, 1834.

Bell, C. F., (ed.), *The Annals of Thomas Banks*, Cambridge, 1902.

Beretti, Francis (ed.), *Pascal Paoli a Maria Cosway, Lettres et documents, 1782-1803*, Oxford, 2003.

Berry, Mary, *Extracts of the Journals and correspondence of Miss Berry from the year 1783 to 1852*, ed. Lady Theresa Lewis, 3 vols., London, 1865.

Berry, Mary, *Voyages de Miss Berry à Paris, 1782-1836*, Paris, 1905.

Bettany, Lewis (ed.), *Edward Jerningham and his Friends*, London, 1919.

Betts, E.M. and James A. Bear, Jr., (eds.), *The Family Letters of Thomas Jefferson*, Columbia, Missouri, 1966.

Bombelles, Marquis de, *Journal, Tome III 1789-1792*, Geneva, 1993.

Boswell, James, *An Account of Corsica , the Journal of a Tour to that Island; and Memoirs of Pascal Paoli*, Glasgow,...London, 1768.

Boswell, James, *Boswell on the Grand Tour. Italy, Corsica, and France 1765-1766*, ed. F. Brady and F.A. Pottle, New York, 1955.

Boswell, James, *London Journal, 1762-63*, ed. F. A. Pottle, London, 1950.

Boswell, James, *Private Papers*, eds. I. S. Lustig and F. A. Pottle, New Haven, 1981.

Boswell, James, *Private Papers from Malahide Castle in the collection of Lt. Colonel Ralph Heyward Isham*, eds. G. Scott and F .A. Pottle, 18 vols., New York, 1934.

Boyd, Julian P. et al. (eds.), *The Papers of Thomas Jefferson*, 30 vols., Princeton, 1950- .

Boyle, John, *Letters from Italy, in the years 1754 and 1755,…* London, 1773.

Brightwell, Cecilia Lucy, (ed.), *Memorials of the Life of Amelia Opie*, Norwich and London, 1854.

Burney, Fanny, *Diary and Letters of Madame d'Arblay*, edited by her niece, 7 vols., 1842-6.

Burney, Fanny, *Journals and Letters of Fanny Burney*, edited by J. Hemlow, 12 vols., 1972-1984.

Carr, Sir John, *The Stranger in France, or, A tour from Devonshire to Paris*, London, 1803.

Carr, Sir John, *Les Anglais en France après la paix d'Amiens*, Paris, 1898.

Carter, Edward C., John C. Van Horne et al., (eds.), *The Correspondence and Miscellaneous Papers of Benjamin Henry Latrobe*, 3 vols. New Haven, 1984-88.

Chastellux, Marquis de, *Voyages dans l'Amerique Septentrionale*, 2 vols., Paris, 1791.

Chénier, André, *Oeuvres Complètes*, Paris, 1958.

Combe, William, *Letters to Marianne*, 1823.

Cosway, Maria, 'Lettera sull'educazione dei piccolo fanciulli dal Quattro anni ai sei, Reposta ad une lettera di M. G. sopra l'Educazione data dalla Baronessa Maria Cosway', *Archivio Storico Lodigiano*, XLV, Lodi, 1926.

Cradock, Mrs., *Journal de Mme. Cradock : Voyages en France, 1783-1786*, Paris, 1896.

Cugoano, Quobna Ottobah, *Thoughts and Sentiments on the Evil of Slavery*, ed., Vincent Caretta, New York, 1999.

Denon, Vivant, *Lettres à Bettine*, ed. Fausta Gavarini et al., Arles, 1999.

De Windt, Caroline Smith, (ed.), *Journal and Correspondence of Miss Adams, Daughter of John Adams*, 2 vols.,1841-1842.

Dutens, Louis, *Journal of Travels made through the Principal Cities of Europe*...London, 1782. (Paris, 1775).

Dutens, Louis, *Memoires d'un voyageur*, 5 vols., Paris, 1782.

[Edgecumbe, Richard, 2nd Earl of Mountcumbe] *Musical reminiscences of an old amateur, for fifty years from 1773 to 1823*, London, 1824.

D' Espinchal, Comte de, *Journal*, ed., Ernest d'Hauterive, London, 1920.

Farington, Joseph, 'Joseph Farington's Anecdotes of Walpole, 1793-1807', in Horace Walpole's *Correspondence*, W. S. Lewis, ed., vol. XV,
London, 1952.

Farington, Joseph, *The Diary of* ..., eds. K. Garlick , A. Macintyre, and K. Cave, 16 vols., New Haven and London, 1978- 1984.

Fletcher, Ernest, (ed.), *Conversations of James Northcote, R.A. with James Ward on Art and Artists*, London, 1901.

Florian, Jean-Pierre Claris de, *Les Deux Billets*, Paris, 1780.

Ford, Paul Leicester, (ed.), *The Writings of Thomas Jefferson*, 9 vols., New York, 1897.

Forster, Lavinia Banks, 'Letter to A. Cunningham, March 1, 1830', *The Builder*, 3rd January 1863, xxi, 5.

Gaussen, A. C. C., *A Later Pepys Correspondence of Sir William W. Welles Pepys, Bart. 1758-1825*, 2 vols., 1904.

Genlis, Madame de, *Nouvelle Methode d'enseignement pour la première enfance*, Besancon, An VIII [1800].

Gibbon's Journey from Geneva to Rome 1764, ed. G. A. Bonnard, Edinburgh, 1961.

Gibbon, Edward, *Memoirs of my Life*, ed. G. A. Bonnard, London, 1966.

Gibbon, Edward, *Miscellaneous Works of...*, ed. John Holroyd, Earl of Sheffield, London, I,1796.

Gibbon, Edward, *The Letters of...*,ed. J. E. Norton, London, 1956, I, pp.171-195.

Gwynn, Stephen, (ed.), *Memorials of an eighteenth century painter James Northcote*, London, 1898.

D'Hauterive, Ernest (ed.), *Journal of the Comte d'Espinchal during the Emigration*, London, 1912.

Hazlitt, William, 'On the Old Age of Artists', *The Plain Speaker: opinions on books, men and things*, 2 vols., London 1826, (Vol XII, in *The Complete*

Works of William Hazlitt,... ed. P. P. Howe after A. R. Waller and Arnold Glover (eds.), 21 vols., London, 1934.)

Hazlitt, William, *Conversations with James Northcote*, ed. Edmund Gosse, London, 1894.

Hogarth, William, *The Analysis of Beauty*, ed., Ronald Paulson, New Haven and London, 1997.

Home J. A. (ed.), *The letters and journals of Lady Mary Coke*, 4 vols., Edinburgh, 1889-1896.

Hunt, Gaillard, (ed.), *The First Forty Years of Washington Society: The Family Letters of Mrs. Samuel Harrison Smith (Margaret Bayard)*, New York, 1906.

Jones, Thomas, *Memoirs of Thomas Jones*, Penkerrig, Radnorshire, 1803 and *The Walpole Society*, vol. 32, London, 1951.

Kelly, Michael, *Reminiscences of...*, ed. T. E. Hook, 2 vols., London, 1826.

Latrobe, Benjamin Henry, *The Journal of Latrobe*, New York, 1905.

Lévis, Duc de, *Souvenirs et Portraits, 1780-1789*, Paris, 1815.

Lipscomb, Andrew A. and Albert Ellery Bergh, (eds.), *The Writings of Thomas Jefferson*, 20 vols, Washington D.C., 1904.

Lloyd, Stephen, ed., *The Cosway Inventory of 1820: Listing Unpaid Commissions and the Contents of 20 Stratford Place, Oxford Street, London*, The Walpole Society, LXVI, 2004.

Louis-Philippe, Duc d'Orléans, *Memoires*, I, Paris, 1973.

McIntyre, Ian, *Joshua Reynolds : The Life and Times of the First President of the Royal Academy*, London, 2003.

Mainaduc, John Bonniot de, *Lectures of J. B. de Mainaduc, M.D., Member of the Corporation of Surgeons*, London, 1798.

Mazzei, Filippo, *Memoirs*, trans. H. R. Marraro, New York, 1942.

Mazzoni, Marcello, *The traveller's guide of Milan, with a sketch of the environs and a description of the lakes*, Milan,1836.

Miller, Anna, *Letters from Italy*, 3 vols., London, 1776.

Mercier, Sebastien, *Tableau de Paris*, 12 vols., Amsterdam, 1782-88.

Moore, John, *A View of Society and Manners in Italy*, London, 1781.

Morellet, Abbé, *Mémoire pour les citoyennes Trudaine...*,Paris, an III [1794]

Morgan, John, *The Journal of Dr. John Morgan of Philadelphia*, Philadelphia, 1907.

Morgan, Sydney, Lady, *Italy*, London, 1821.

Morgan, Sydney, Lady, *Memoirs*, ed. W. H. Dixon, 2 vols., London, 1862.

Morris, Gouverneur, *A Diary of the French Revolution*, ed. B. S. Davenport, 2 vols., Boston, 1939.

Nash, Fred (ill.) and John Scott, *Picturesque Views of the City of Paris & its environs...*, London, 1829.

Oberkirch, Baronne d', *Mémoires*, 2 vols., Paris, 1853.

Papendiek, Charlotte, *Court and Private Life in the Time of Queen Charlotte: Being the Journals of Mrs. Papendiek*, ed. by Mrs. V. D. Broughton, 2 vols., London, 1882.

Pasquin, Anthony, [John Williams], *An Authentic History of the Professors of Painting, Sculpture and Architecture...*London, 1796.

Pasquin, Anthony, *The Royal Academicians: a Farce. As it was performed to the Astonishment of Mankind by his Majesty's Servants, at the Stone House, in Utopia, in the summer of 1786*, London, 1786.

Pelissier, Leon-G., (ed.), *Lettres et écrits divers de la Comtesse d'Albany*, Paris, 1901.

Pelissier, Leon-G., *Le Portefeuille de la Comtesse d'Albany*, Paris, 1902.

Pelissier, Leon-G., *Lettres inedites de la Comtesse d'Albany à ses amis de Sienne*, Paris, 1904.

Phillips, R. (ed.), *Public Characters*, London, 1805.

Pilkington, Rev. M. and Fuseli, Henry, R.A., *A Dictionary of Painters*, London, 1810.

Piozzi, Hester, *Autobiography, letters and literary remains of Mrs. Piozzi*, ed. A. Hayward, 2 vols., London, 1861.

Piozzi, Hester, *Observations and Reflections Made in the Course of a Journey through France, Italy, and Germany*, ed. Herbert Barrows, Ann Arbor, 1967.

Porro, Cleto, *Guida della Regia Citta di Lodi compilata per uso de Forestieri*, Lodi, 1833.

Randolph, Sarah N., ed., *The Domestic Life of Thomas Jefferson*, Charlottesville, Virginia, 1978.

Pratt, Mary, *A List of a few Cures performed by Mr. and Mrs. De Loutherbourg of Hammersmith Terrace without Medicine*, London, 1789.

Redding, Cyrus, *Fifty Years of Recollections*, 3 vols., London, 1857 (2nd ed. 1858).

Reynolds, Sir Joshua, *Discourses*, ed. Pat Rogers, London, 1992.

Robertson, Emily, (ed.), *Letters and Papers of Andrew Robertson, Miniature Painter*, London, [1895].

Robinson, Mary (Darby), *Memoirs of Mary Robinson, Perdita*, edited by her daughter and J. F. Molloy, London, 1894.

Robinson Mrs., *A Wintry Day*, London, 1st March 1803.

Sharp, Samuel, *Letters from Italy…*London, 1766.

Sieveking, Isabel Giberne, *The Memoir of Sir Horace Mann*, London, 1912.

Stisted, Clotilda Elizabeth, *Letters from the Bye-ways of Italy*, London, 1845.

Smith, John Thomas, *A book for a rainy day, or recollections of the events of the years 1766-1833*, ed. Wilfred Whitten, London, 1805.

Smith, John Thomas, *Nollekens and His Times*, 2 vols., London, 1829.

Stendahl [Marie Henri Beyle], *Rome, Naples et Florence en 1817*, Paris, 1817.

Swinburne, Henry, *The Courts of Europe*, ed. Charles White, London, 1841.

Thiéry, Luc-Vincent, *Guide des Amateurs et des Étrangers à Paris*, 2 vols., Paris, 1787.

Thrale, Hester Lynch, *Thraliana: The Diary of Mrs. Hester Lynch Thrale (Later Mrs. Piozzi) 1776-1809*, ed. Katherine C. Balderston, 2 vols., Oxford, 1951.

Tilly, Comte Alexandre de, *Mémoires*, 2 vols., Paris, 1929.

Trumbull, John, *The Autobiography of …, Patriot-Artist, 1756-1843*, ed. Theodore Sizer, New Haven, 1953.

Vigée Lebrun, Elisabeth-Louise, *Souvenirs*, 2 vols., Paris, n.d.

Walpole, Horace, *Anecdotes of Painting in England, 1760-1795*, eds. F. W. Hilles and P. B. Daghlian, 5 vols., New Haven, 1937.

Walpole, Horace, *Correspondence*, ed. W. S. Lewis, New Haven, 1937- .

Walpole, Horace, *Works*, ed. W. S. Lewis, 34 vols., New Haven, 1965.

Walpole, Sir Horace, *Letters to Sir H. Mann, 1760-85*, ed. Richard Bentley, 4 vols., London, 1834-44.

Wraxall, Sir N. W., *Historical Memoirs of My Own Time, 1777-84*, 2 vols., London, 1815.

Wilkes, John, *The Correspondence of the late John Wilkes*, ed. John Almon, London, 1805.

Wilmot, Catherine, *An Irish Peer on the Continent (1801-1803)*, ed. Thomas U. Sadler, London, 1920.

Wright, Joseph, *Letters and Journal written in Rome, Naples and N. Italy in 1773-75* in William Bemrose, *The Life and Works of Joseph Wright, A.R.A.,* London, 1885.

Wolcott, John, *More Lyric Odes to the Royal Academicians,* 5 vols., London, 1785.

Wolcott, John, *Works of Peter Pindar, Esq.,* 4 vols., 1809.

Yorke, Henri Redhead, *Letters from France,* London, 1804.

Zangheri, Luigi, ed., *Gli Accademici del Disegno, Elenco Alfabetico,* Firenze, 2000.

Secondary Sources

_____, ' Imitations in Chalk', *Burlington Magazine,* October, 1986.

_____, 'La Mort de Miss Gardiner', *La Revue du Louvre et des Musées,* December, 1994.

Adams, William Howard, ed., *The Eye of Thomas Jefferson,* exh. cat., Columbia, Missouri and Charlottseville, Virginia, 1976.

Alberts, Robert C., *Benjamin West,* Boston, 1978.

Arrighi, Arrigo, *Histoire de Pascal Paoli, ou la dernière guerre de indépendance (1755-1780,),* 2 vol., Paris, 1843.

Augustin-Thierry, A., *Madame Mère,* Paris, 1939.

Baclawski, Karen, *The Guide to Historic Costume,* London, 1995.

Bailey, Colin B., *Patriotic Taste: Collecting Modern Art in Pre-Revolutionary Paris,* New Haven and London, 2002.

Barbier, Patrick, *Histoire des castrats,* Paris, 1989.

Barnett, Gerald, *Richard and Maria Cosway, A Biography,* Tiverton, Devon, 1995.

Batey, Mavis et al., *Arcadian Thames : The River Landscape from Hampton to Kew,* London, 1994.

Becq de Fouquières, L., *Lettres critiques sur la vie, les oeuvres, les manuscrits d'André Chénier,* Paris, 1881.

Benoit, Jermie, *Philippe-Auguste Henniquin 1762-1838,* Paris, 1949.

Berman, Eleanor Davidson, *Thomas Jefferson among the Arts,* New York, 1947.

Bemrose, William, *The Life and Works of Joseph Wright of Derby, A.R.A.,* 1885.

Beretti, Francis, *Pascal Paoli et l'image de la Corse au 18ème siecle: témoignage des voyageurs britanniques,* Oxford, 1988.

Black, Jeremy, *The Grand Tour in the Eighteenth Century,* New York, 1992.

Black, Jeremy, *Italy and the Grand Tour,* New Haven and London, 2003.

Blaikley, E., 'Richard Cosway, miniaturist, artist, fop and man of fashion', *Apollo,* Vol. 62, August 1955, pp. 53-55.

Biver, Marie-Louise, *Le Paris de Napoléon,* Paris, 1963.

Boase, T. S. R., 'Illustration of Shakespeare's Plays in the 17th and 18th Century', *Journal of Warburg and Courtauld,* X, 1947.

Boase, T. S. R., 'Macklin and Bowyer', *Journal of Warburg and Courtauld,* XXVI, 1963.

Bolton, Arthur T., 'Stratford Place', *Journal of the Royal Institute of British Architects,* 1st April 1916.

Bordes, Philippe, *Le Serment du Jeu de Paume de Jacques-Louis David,* Paris, 1983.

Bordes, Philippe, 'Jacques-Louis David's Anglophilia on the Eve of the French Revolution', *The Burlington Magazine,* CXXXIV, 1992.

Borroni Salvadori, Fabia, 'Artisti e viaggiatori agli Uffizi nel Settecento', *Labyrinthos: studi e ricerci sulle arti nei secol XVIII e XIX* (part I), IV, 1985, and (part 2), VI, 1986.

Boyer, Ferdinand, *Le Monde des Arts en Italie et la France de la Révolution et de l'Empire,* Torino, 1969.

Brewer, John, *The Pleasures of the Imagination : English Culture in the Eighteenth Century,* London, 1997.

Brodie, Fawn M., *Thomas Jefferson, An Intimate History,* New York, 1974.

Bruun-Neegaard, T. C., *Sur la situation des Beaux Arts en France,* Paris, 1801.

Bullock, Helen Duprey, *My Head and My Heart,* New York, 1945.

Butterfield, L. H., and Howard C. Rice, Jr., 'Jefferson's Earliest Note to Maria Cosway with some new facts and conjectures on His Broken Wrist', *The William and Mary Quarterly,* 3rd series, Vol. V, No. 1, January, 1948.

Campolunghi, Piero, *Giulia Beccaria e di Suo Figlio Alessandro Manzoni (Verri),* Milano, 1998.

Carocci, Renata, 'Autour de Marie Cosway et d'André Chénier', *Cahiers Roucher-André Chénier, Etudes sur la poésie du XVIIIe siècle, No. 20,* Paris, 2001.

Cazzulani, Elena and Angelo Stroppa, *Maria Hadfield Cosway*, Orio Litta, 1989.

Cendres, Julien and Chloé Radiguet, *Le Désert de Retz, paysage choisi*, Paris, 1997.

Chabaud, Louis, *Mesdames de Maintenon, de Genlis & Campan : Leur Role dans l'Education Chrétienne de la Femme*, Paris, 1901.

Chatelain, Jean, *Dominique Vivant Denon et le Louvre de Napoleon*, Paris, 1973.

Chiarini, Marco and Alessandro Marabottini, eds., *Firenze e la sua immagine, cinque secoli di vedutismo*, exh. cat., Venezia, 1994.

Chinard, Gilbert, *Les Amitiés américaines de Madame d'Houdetot, d'après sa correspondance inedite avec Benj. Franklin et T. Jefferson*, Paris, 1924.

Clayton, Timothy, *The English Print 1688-1802*, New Haven and London, 1997.

Colombani, Hélène, *Le Cardinal Fesch*, Paris, 1979

Cometti, Elizabeth, 'Maria Cosway's Rediscovered Miniature of Jefferson', *William and Mary Quarterly*, 3rd series, IX, 1952.

Comisson, Giovanni, *Les agents secrets à Venise*, Paris, 1990.

Cripe, Helen, *Thomas Jefferson and Music*,, Charlottesville, 1974.

Crosland, Margaret, *Louise of Stolberg, Countess of Albany*, Edinburgh and London, 1962.

Cruickshank, Dan, 'Queen Anne's Gate', *Georgian Group Journal*, London, 1992.

Cruickshank, Dan and Neil Burton, *Life in the Georgian City*, London, 1990.

Decaux, Alain, *Napoleon's Mother*, London, 1962.

D'Hauterive, Ernest, *Napoléon et Sa Police*, Paris, 1943.

D'Ivray, Jehan, *La Lombardie au Temps de Bonaparte*, Paris, 1919.

Dimoff, P., *La vie et l'oeuvre d'André Chénier jusqu'à la Révolution française*, 2 vols., Paris, 1936.

Donald, Diana, *The Age of Caricature*, London, 1996.

Earland, Ada, *John Opie and His Circle*, London, 1911.

Ellis, Joseph J., *American Sphinx*, New York, 1997.

Favaro, Adriano, *Isabella Teotochi Albrizzi*, Udine, 2003.

Fayolle, Rose-Marie and Renée Davray-Piekolek, *La Mode en France 1715-1815*, Paris, 1990.

Fierro, Alfred, *La Vie des Parisiens sous Napoléon*, Paris, 2003.

Florian, Jean-Pierre Claris de, *Théâtre Italien de M. Florian*, Paris, 1784.

Florian, Jean-Pierre Claris de, *Les Deux Billets, Comédié en un Act et en Prose*, Paris, 1780.

Foladare, Joseph, *Boswell's Paoli*, Hamden, 1979.

Foreman, Amanda, *Georgiana, Duchess of Devonshire*, London, 1998.

Fothergill, Brian, *Sir William Hamilton, Envoy Extraordinary*, New York, 1969.

Franchini, Silvia, *Elites ed educazione femminile nell'Italia dell'Ottocento*, Firenze, 1993.

Fraser, Flora, *The Unruly Queen*, London, 1996.

Gaillardet, Frédéric, *Mémoires sur la Chevalière d'Eon*, Paris, 1866.

Gallet, Michel, *Demeures parisiennes: l'époque de Louis XVI*, 1964.

Gambi, Lucio and Maria Cristina Gozzoli, *La città nella storia d'Italia: Milano*, Roma, 1997.

Geer, Walter, *Napoleon and his Family*, London, 1927.

George, Dorothy, *London Life in the Eighteenth Century*, London, 1925.

Ginzburg, Natalia, *The Manzoni Family*, New York, 1987.

Gipponi, Tino, ed., *Maria e Richard Cosway*, Torino, 1998.

Godechot, Jacques, *La vie quotidienne en France sous le Directoire*, Paris, 1977.

Griffiths, Antony, *Prints and Printmaking*, London, 1996.

Guifferey, J. et Rieset, 'Cartons de Jules Romains…' *Nouvelles Archives de l'Art Français*, VII, Paris, 1879.

Hamilton, Harlan, *Doctor Syntax, A Silhouette of William Combe, Esq.*, Kent, Ohio, 1969.

Hardy, John, 'The Discovery of Cosway's Chair', *Country Life*, March 15, 1973.

Haskell, Francis, The Baron d'Hancarville: An Adventurer and Art Historian in Eighteenth-Century Europe', *Oxford, China and Italy: Writings in Honour of Sir Harold Acton*, eds. E. Chaney and N. Ritchie, Florence, 1984; republished in F. Haskell, *Past and Present in Art and Taste:Selected Essays*, New Haven and London, 1987.

Haskell, Francis, and Nicholas Penny, *Taste and the Antique, The Lure of Classical Sculpture 1500-1900*, New Haven and London, 1981.

Heath, Dudley, 'Cosway and 18th Century Miniaturists', *The Connoisseur*, Vol. 13, 1905.

Heath, Dudley, *Miniatures,* London, 1905.

Herrmann, Frank, *The English as Collectors: A Documentary Sourcebook,* London, 1999.

Hill, Bridget, *Eighteenth Century Women: An Anthology,* London and New York, 1984.

Hibbert, Christopher, *Florence, The biography of a city,* New York and London, 1993.

Hibbert, Christopher, *George III, A Personal History,* London, 1998.

Hibbert, Christopher, *George IV, Prince of Wales,* London, 1972.

Hobhouse, Christopher, *Fox,* London, 1934.

Hodgson, J. E., and Fred. A. Easton, *The Royal Academy and Its Members,* London, 1905.

Hoock, Holger, *The King's Artists,* Oxford, 2003.

Hubert, Gerard, *La sculpture dans l'Italie napoléonienne,* Paris, 1964.

Hunt, Leigh, *Autobiography,* Vol. I, London, 1850.

Hutchinson, Sidney, *The History of the Royal Academy* 1768-1968, New York, 1968.

Ingamells, John, ed, *A Dictionary of British and Irish Travellers in Italy 1701-1800,* compiled from the Brinsley Ford Archive, New Haven and London, 1997.

Jenkins, Ian and Kim Sloan, eds., *Vases & Volcanoes: Sir William Hamilton and His Collection,* exh. cat., London, 1996.

Ketcham, Diana, *Le Désert de Retz,* Cambridge, Massachussets, 1997.

Kleinclausz, A., *Histoire de Lyon,* Lyon, 1939-48.

Langford, Paul, *A Polite and Commercial People, England 1727-1783,* Oxford, 1992.

Larrey, Le Baron, *Madame Mère,* 2 vols., 1892.

Latreille, André, *Napoléon et le Saint-Siege (1801-1808)* Paris, 1934.

Lee, Vernon, *Studies of the Eighteenth Century in Italy,* London, 1907.

Legros, P., 'André Chénier en Angleterre', *The Modern Language Review,* 1924.

Lelièvre, Pierre, *Vivant Denon,* Paris, 1942.

Leribault, Christophe, *Les Anglais à Paris au 19e siecle,* Paris, 1994.

Leslie, Shane, *George the Fourth,* London, 1926.

Lever, Evelyne, *Philippe Egalité,* Paris, 1996.

Lewis, Lesley, *Connoisseurs and Secret Agents in Eighteenth Century Rome,* London, 1961.

Lloyd, Christopher, *The Royal Collection*, Sinclair-Stevenson, 1992.

Lloyd, Stephen, 'The Accomplished Maria Cosway: Anglo-Italian Artist, Musician, Salon Hostess and Educationalist (1759-1838)', *Journal of Anglo-Italian Studies, Vol. 2*, 1992.

Lloyd, Stephen, 'Fashioning the Image of the Prince: Richard Cosway and George IV', *"Squanderous and Lavish Profusion" George IV, his image and patronage of the arts*, Dana Arnold, ed., London, 1995.

Lloyd, Stephen, 'Richard Cosway, R.A., The artist as collector, connoisseur and *virtuoso*', *Apollo*, CXXXIII, No. 352, June, 1991.

Lloyd, Stephen, *Richard Cosway*, London, 2005.

Lloyd, Stephen, (ed.), *Richard & Maria Cosway, Regency Artists of Taste and Fashion*, Edinburgh, 1995.

Long, Basil S., *British Miniatures*, London, 1929.

Long, Basil S., 'On Identifying Miniatures', *Connoisseur*, October 1934.

Low, D. M., *Edward Gibbon 1737-1794*, New York, 1937.

Lumsden, E.S., *The Art of Etching*, New York, 1962.

Micali, Osanna Fantozzi and Piero Roselli, *La Soppressioni dei Conventi a Firenze*, Firenze, 1980.

Michel, Olivier, *Vivre et Peindre à Rome au XVIIIe Siècle*, Rome, 1996.

Maccapani, Achille, *Luigi Marchesi, il sopranista pentito di Inzago (1754-1829)*, Inzago, 1989.

Magne, E., *Le Château de Saint-Cloud d'après des documents inédits*, Paris, 1932.

Malone, Dumas, *Jefferson and the Rights of Man, Vol. 2 of Jefferson and His Time*, Boston, 1951.

Marshall, Arthur Calder, *The Two Duchesses*, London, 1978.

Manceron, Claude, *Les Hommes de la Liberté : le bon plaisir 1782-1785*, Paris, 1976.

Manceron, Claude, *Les Hommes de la Liberté : la révolution qui lève 1785-1787*, Paris, 1979.

Manners, Lady Victoria and G. C. Williamson, *Angelica Kauffman*, London, 1924.

Masters, Brian, *Georgiana*, London, 1997.

Molmenti, Pompeo, *Venice, Its Individual Growth from the Earliest Beginnings to the Fall of the Republic*, Vol. 1, London, 1908.

Moloney, Brian, *Florence and England: Essays on cultural relations in the second half of the eighteenth century*, Firenze, 1969.

Mori, Attilo e Giuseppe Boffito, *Firenze nelle Vedute e Piante,* Firenze, 1926.

Morizet, André, *Du Vieux Paris au Paris Moderne,* Paris, 1932.

Millar, Oliver, *The Later Georgian Pictures in the Collection of Her Majesty the Queen,* 1969.

Millar, Oliver, *The Queen's Pictures: The History of the British Royal Collection,* New York, 1977.

Millar, Oliver, *Zoffany and his Tribuna,* London, 1967.

Milner-Gibson-Cullum, Gery , and Francis C. Macauley, *The Inscriptions in the old British Cemetery of Leghorn,* Leghorn, 1906.

Munson, James, *Maria Fitzherbert: The Secret Wife of George IV,* London, 2001.

Napoléon, Charles, *Bonaparte et Paoli,* Paris, 2000.

Negro, Angela, *Il giardino dipinto del Cardinal Borghese,* Roma, 1996.

Nettement, Alfred, *De la Seconde Education des Filles,* Paris and Lyon, 1876.

Nicolson, Benedict, *Jos. Wright of Derby, Painter of Light,* 2 vols., London & N.Y., 1968.

Noble, Percy, *Anne Seymour Damer,* London, 1908.

Pacini, Piero, *Le Sedi dell'Accademia del Disegno,* Firenze, 2001.

Palewski, Jean-Paul, *Louveciennes,* St Germain en Laye, 1968.

Paston, George, *Social Caricature in the Eighteenth-Century,* New York, 1968.

Peham, Helga, *Leopold II. :Herrscher mit weiser Hand,* Graz, Wien, Köln, 1987.

Pelissier, Leon-G., *Lettres et écrits divers de la Comtesse d'Albany,* Paris, 1901.

Petty, Fred C., *Italian Opera in London, 1760-1800,* Yale, 1971, (unpublished dissertation).

Pine-Coffin, R. S., *Bibliography of British and American Travel in Italy to 1860,* Firenze, 1974.

Pointon, Marcia, *Hanging the Head,* New Haven and London, 1993.

Porro, Cleto, *Guida della Regia Città di Lodi,* Lodi, 1833, 1989.

Porter, Roy, *English Society in the Eighteenth Century,* London, 1982.

Pressly, Nancy L., *The Fuseli Circle in Rome, Early Romantic Art of the 1770s,* exh.cat., New Haven, 1979.

Redgrave, Samuel, *A Dictionary of Artists of the English School: Painters, Sculptors, Architects, Engravers and Ornamentists,* London, 1878.

Rice, Howard C., Jr., 'Jefferson in Europe a Century and a Half Later, *Princeton University Library Chronicle*, Vol. XII (Autumn 1950).

Rice, Howard C., *L'Hotel de Langeac, Jefferson's Paris Residence, 1785-1789*, Paris, 1947.

Rice, Howard C., 'Les Visites de Jefferson au Mont-Valerien', *Bulletin de la Societé Historique de Suresnes,* Tome III, No. 13, 1953-54.

Rice, Howard C., 'Saint-Memin's Portrait of Jefferson', *The Princeton University Library Chronicle*, Vol. XX, No. 4, Summer, 1959.

Rice, Howard C., *Thomas Jefferson's Paris*, Princeton, New Jersey, 1976.

Rochegude, Marquis de et Maurice Dumolin, *Guide Pratique à travers Le Vieux Paris*, Paris, 1923.

Roof, Katherine Metcalf, *Colonel William Smith and Lady*, Boston, 1929.

Rosenberg, Pierre and Marie-Anne Dupuy, eds., *Dominique-Vivant Denon : L'œil de Napoléon*, exh. cat. Paris, 1999.

Rosenblum Robert, *Transformations in Late Eighteenth Century Art*, Princeton, New Jersey, 1967.

Roworth, Wendy Wassyng, *Angelica Kauffman: A Continental Artist in Georgian England*, exh. cat., London, 1992.

Royal Commission for Historical Monuments, *Survey of London, St. James/ Westminster, Part 1, South of Piccadilly*, Vol.29, 30, London, 1994.

Ruggieri, Claude, *Précis historique sur les Fêtes & Spectacles...* Paris, 1830.

Scarfe, Francis, *André Chénier, His Life and Work*, Oxford, 1965.

Shepperson, A. B., *John Paradise and Lucy Ludwell*, Richmond, Virginia, 1942.

Silvestre de Sacy, Jacques, *Le Comte d'Angiviller*, Paris, 1953.

Smith, E. A., *George IV*, New Haven and London, 1999.

Smith, E. A., *A Queen on Trial: The Affair of Queen Caroline*, Stroud, Gloucestershire, 1993.

Solkin, David H., *Painting for Money: The Visual Arts and the Public Sphere in Eighteenth-Century England*, New Haven and London, 1992.

Solkin, David H., ed., *Art on the Line, The Royal Academy Exhibitions at Somerset House 1780-1836*, exh. cat., London, 2001.

Stainton, Lindsay, *British Artists in Rome, 1700-1800*, exh. cat., Kenwood, London, 1974.

Steegmann, John, *The Rule of Taste from George I to George IV*, London, 1936.

Steiner, Giovanna Balzanetti, *Tra Città e Fiume I Lungarni di Firenze*, Firenze, 1989.

Steyert, Andre, *Nouvelle Histoire de Lyon*, i,ii,iii, Lyon, 1899.

Summerson, John, *Georgian London*, London, 1988.

Taillandier, Saint-René, 'La Comtesse d'Albany', *La Revue des Deux Mondes*, 1861.

Sumner, Ann and Greg Smith, eds., *Thomas Jones (1742-1803): An Artist Rediscovered*, New Haven and London, 2003.

Trenard, Louis, *Lyon de L'Encyclopedie au Préromantisme*, Vol. II, Paris, 1958.

Vickery, Amanda, *The Gentleman's Daughter: Women's Lives in Georgian England*, New Haven and London, 1998.

Tulard, Jean, *Napoléon*, Paris, 1977.

Tulard, Jean, and Louis Garros, *Itinéraire de Napoléon au jour le jour 1769-1821*, Paris, 1992.

Walker, John, 'Maria Cosway: An Undervalued Artist', *Apollo*, CXXIII, No. 291, May 1986.

Walsh, Clare, 'Merchants à la Mode', *Country Life*, 16th December 1993.

Walter, Gérard, *André Chénier, son milieu et son temps*, Paris, 1947.

Watson, F.J.B., 'Thomas Patch (1725-1782); notes on his life, together with a catalogue of his known works', *The Walpole Society*, XXVIII, 1939-1940.

Webster, Mary, ed., *Firenze e Inghilterra :Rapporti Artistici e Culturali dal XVI al XX Secolo*, exh. cat., Firenze, 1971.

Webster, Mary, ed., *Johan Zoffany 1733-1810*, exh. cat., London, 1976.

Wescher, Paul, *I Furti d'Arte: Napoleone e la nascita del Louvre*, Turin, 1988.

Wellesley, F. & M., *A Handlist of the miniatures and the portraits in plumbage or pencil belonging to F. and M. Wellesley*. With a foreword by G.C. Williamson, 1914.

Wendorf, Richard, *Sir Joshua Reynolds: The Painter in Society*, London, 1996.

Wheatcroft, Andrew, *The Habsburgs*, London, 1995.

Whitehead, Jane S., 'The noblest collection of curiositys: British visitors to the Uffizi, 1650-1789', *Gli Uffizi quattro secoli di una galleria* (Atti del Convegno Internazionale di Studi, Florence, September 1982), eds. P. Barocchi and G. Ragionieri, Florence, 1983.

Whitley, William T., *Artists and Their Friends in England, 1700-1799*, 2 vols., London, 1928.

Whitley, William T., *Art in England, 1800-1820*, Cambridge, 1928.

Whitley, William T., *Art in England, 1821-1837*, Cambridge, 1930.

Whitley, William T., *Thomas Gainsborough*, London, 1915.

Wildenstein, Daniel and Guy Wildenstein, *Louis David, Recueil de Documents complémentaires au catalogue complet de l'œuvre de l'artiste*, Fondation Wildenstein, 1974.

Williamson, G. C., *Richard Cosway, R.A., and his wife and pupils, Miniaturists of the Eighteenth Century*, London, 1897.

Williamson, G. C., *Andrew & Nathaniel Plimer*, London, 1903.

Williamson, G. C., *Life and Works of Ozias Humphry, R.A.*, London, 1918.

Wilton, Andrew and Ilaria Bignamini, eds., *Grand Tour, The Lure of Italy in the Eighteenth Century*, exh. cat., London, 1996.

Wilson-Smith, Timothy, *Napoleon and His Artists*, London, 1996.

Zaghi, Carlo, *L'Italia di Napoleone dalla Cisalpina al Regno*, Torino, 1997.

Zangheri, Luigi, *Feste e Apparati nella Toscana dei Lorena 1737-1859*, Firenze, 1996.

Zangheri, Luigi, *Ville della provincia di Firenze, La Citta*, Milano, 1989.

Index